Case Studies

Our thought-provoking case studies link theory with practice. These features, included at the end of each chapter, encourage you to think critically and put what you've learned into practice, preparing you for the challenges you will face in today's workplace.

Over the course of the text, case studies will challenge you to reform an overcrowded hospital, restructure a local gardening business, and strategically align school food policies. Other case study topics include globalization and consumerism, conflicting leadership styles, generational identity, and gender in fraternities and sororities. For a list of all the case studies, see pages xii–xiii.

CASE STUDY

Crisis in the Zion Emergency Room

For many years now, the emergency rooms in the United States have been in crisis. Part of the problem is a lack of qualified nurses. Everywhere nurses are in short supply, and those who can work effectively in the emergency environment are even rarer. But there are other reasons for the widespread overcrowding of ERs. A large and growing population of people without medical insurance continues to make use of them for primary care needs. Emergency rooms, staffed primarily to serve the victims of trauma or acute illness, are increasingly overburdened by mothers and infants without adequate prenatal and pediatric care, the chronically ill and disabled, patients with HIV/AIDS, individuals with mental illness or drug or alcohol addiction, and the homeless. The end result is excessive wait times, angry patients, and substandard care. The ER at Zion Hospital is no different.

On any given night, Zion's ER looks like a war zone. The halls of the ER are lined with twenty to twenty-five patients on gurneys, lying in limbo until one of the forty-five regular ER beds opens up. Just walking through the ER can be tricky. The overcrowding of the ER results in a distinct lack of privacy, and more important, it creates confusion about the location and status of patients, which increases the potential for serious errors.

You have recently accepted the position of director of emergency medicine at Zion. Expectations are high that you will be able to do something quickly about the dreadful patient satisfaction ratings that have appeared in recent months. Your initial assessment of the situation, however, is discouraging. For the reasons just described, there appears to be an endless and growing stream of new patients into the ER, and the hospital financial committee looks unfavorably at turning people away. Meanwhile, all of your beds are taken, half of them by people who have already been admitted to Zion but have yet to be assigned a bed upstairs in one of the hospital units. Your staff has to find a way of serving these bored and hungry patients while handling the more critical patients lined up in the hall.

Further investigation reveals that your patients are waiting for beds for a number of reasons: (1) Other units in the hospital, such as the heart center and the pediatric unit, have priority over the ER in getting beds; (2) all of the beds in the hospital are full, and those that are physically empty are locked in units that have been temporarily closed due to the lack of qualified nurses to staff them; and (3) there are long delays from the time a viable bed actually becomes empty to when housekeeping can clean the room for the next patient and floor nurses can accept the new patient to their unit.

The situation is miserable and deteriorating. The nursing shortage is not going to end anytime soon, your current nurses are all threatening to quit, patients are furious, and hospital administrators are urging you to "think outside the box" to find some relief.

ASSIGNMENT

Using what you know about systems theories of organization, answer the following questions:

1. How would you define the problem systemically? How does your choice of definition affect your likely course of action?
2. Using the language of systems theories, which "realities" in this case would be most difficult to change, and which are more malleable?
3. What role does communication play in perpetuating the current situation? How does your understanding of the systems approach help you identify specific communication issues?
4. Using your knowledge of systems, what kinds of communication might you use to address the situation? What obstacles would you expect to encounter, and how would you deal with them? Wouldn't dealing with those obstacles—in whatever way you choose to deal with them—also necessarily create new systemic issues? Given your choice of how to deal with the obstacles, what might these new issues be?
5. What role might communication technology play in developing a systems approach to your solution or solutions?

Organizational
Communication

EIGHTH EDITION

ORGANIZATIONAL COMMUNICATION

Balancing Creativity and Constraint

Eric M. Eisenberg
University of South Florida

Angela Trethewey
Arizona State University

Marianne LeGreco
University of North Carolina at Greensboro

H. L. Goodall Jr.
Late of Arizona State University

bedford/st.martin's
Macmillan Learning
Boston | New York

For Bedford/St. Martin's
Vice President, Editorial, Macmillan Learning Humanities: Edwin Hill
Publisher for Communication: Erika Gutierrez
Development Manager and Editor: Susan McLaughlin
Assistant Editor: Will Stonefield
Editorial Assistant: Daniela Velez
Production Editor: Pamela Lawson
Media Producer: Rand Thomas
Production Supervisor: Robert Cherry
Marketing Manager: Kayti Corfield
Project Management: Jouve
Permissions Manager: Kalina Ingham
Text Permissions Researcher: Tom Wilcox
Text Design: Books By Design, Inc.
Cover Design: John Callahan
Cover Art/Cover Photo: petek arici/Getty Images
Composition: Jouve
Printing and Binding: LSC Communications

Manufactured in the United States of America.

1 0 9 8 7 6
f e d c b a

For information, write: Bedford/St. Martin's, 75 Arlington Street, Boston, MA 02116
  (617-399-4000)

ISBN 978-1-319-05234-8

Acknowledgments
Text acknowledgments and copyrights appear at the back of the book on pages 381–83, which constitute an extension of the copyright page. Art acknowledgments and copyrights appear on the same page as the art selections they cover.

Preface

These are dynamic times for our world and for the study and practice of organizational communication. As we write this, we see faint signs that the global recession of the past decade is beginning to abate, but at the same time real wages are stagnant and few are confident that the root causes that led us into our troubles have been effectively addressed. Advances in sustainable energy technology reflect a growing awareness of limits on human consumption, but these advances are being made against a backdrop of persistent income inequality throughout the world. The question of how we relate to and best preserve our natural resources is intimately connected to how, and how fairly, they are distributed among people and nations. Meanwhile, the global political landscape sharply reflects the tension between traditional structures and beliefs (tribes, nations, religions) and the emergence of a broader global ecology. We are heartened by the knowledge that, at least in some of the more developed nations, the idea of resolving conflict through conventional warfare is fading, replaced by a more humane emphasis on diplomacy and economic development. At the same time, we are mortified by the uptick in high-profile terrorist attacks and by the immigration crisis playing out in Europe and around the world. Sadly, the prospect of civil global dialogue and peaceful coexistence still remains a long way off.

As scholars, we look at these events and circumstances as opportunities to discuss the ways—both personal and global—in which organizing and communicating affect the world. Yet we're often surprised that our students initially fail to see the connection between the world around them and the study of organizational communication. For many students, "org comm" is something that people working for Fortune 500 companies "do." It involves organizational charts, agendas, and coping with difficult supervisors. As teachers, we believe that helping our students think critically about the state of all types of organizations from a communication vantage point—and showing the communicative linkages from the university level to the national and international levels—can generate important conversations inside and outside the classroom and can also serve as an impetus for positive social change. We trust that effective communication is the key requirement for creating and sustaining a democratic society in a decidedly diverse and changing world.

This book, therefore, distills what we have learned about the role and importance of organizational communication within today's rapidly evolving social context, and we proudly share it with you. From its inception to this eighth edition, our text has evolved to meet the demands of the field and the organizational communication classroom. Its overarching model, however, remains the same. We continue to emphasize a balance of creativity and constraint—that is, the ability to simultaneously consider the enabling and constraining aspects of communication. Striking this balance helps people achieve their professional and personal goals. As humans, we struggle to be individualistic and heroic (asserting our creativity) yet still belong to a group (responding to social and institutional constraints). Our model examines this struggle through the lens of everyday communication practices as they play out in the world around us.

☐ Overview of the Book

We have two goals for this textbook: (1) to impart the core theories and skills that organizational communication students need and (2) to share the very best of current scholarship, particularly as it relates to rapidly evolving topics like diversity, economics, and technology. We've organized the text as follows to introduce students to our dynamic field.

Part I, "Approaching Organizational Communication," includes two chapters that provide readers with an overview of the discipline and the concepts they'll need to master the ideas and methods presented in the rest of the text. Chapter 1, "Communication and the Changing World of Work," highlights several important issues facing contemporary organizations. Chapter 2, "Defining Organizational Communication," examines four definitions of the concept and offers the notion of ethical and mindful dialogue as a productive way to think about communication at work.

Part II, "Theories of Organizational Communication," covers six distinct theoretical perspectives on organizational communication that motivate research and practice. Chapter 3, "Three Early Perspectives on Organizations and Communication," reviews scientific management, human relations, and human resources and explores the implications of these foundational organizational theories for communication. Chapter 4, "The Systems Perspective on Organizations and Communication," applies various forms of systems theory and demonstrates how they are useful for thinking about communicating and organizing. The next chapter, "Cultural Studies of Organizations and Communication," uses a metaphor borrowed from anthropology and adopted by many organizations to examine the role of communication in the creation, maintenance, and transformation of organizational reality. Finally, Chapter 6, "Critical Approaches to Organizations and Communication," takes a different approach altogether, starting with the premise that research should be directed at illuminating and correcting inequalities at work. Particular attention is paid to how privilege is distributed unevenly across race, gender, and class differences.

Part III of the text, "Contexts for Organizational Communication," explores the various practical settings in which the theories described above can be applied. It starts with Chapter 7, "Identity and Difference in Organizational Life," which examines scholarship on identity as well as differences that affect our communication, from race to socioeconomic status to sexual orientation. The next chapter, "Teams and Networks: Communication and Collaborative Work," looks at attempts to organize through the use of teams and networks, paying particular attention to the ways in which technology and social media have altered traditional industry models and assumptions.

Chapter 9, "Communicating Leadership," reframes leadership as a communicative activity, reviews relevant research, and presents a summary of practical forms of effective leader communication. The last chapter, "Organizational Alignment: Managing the Total Enterprise," argues that for an organization to be truly effective, good communication must be accompanied by many other changes to an organization's current alignment.

Finally, the Appendix, "A Field Guide to Studying Organizational Communication," provides students and instructors with a helpful step-by-step process for planning, researching, participating in, and writing a qualitative account of an organization's communication practices.

☐ New to This Edition

Perhaps the most notable addition to the eighth edition is a new coauthor. Marianne LeGreco joins us from the University of North Carolina at Greensboro, where she holds a position as an associate professor in their Department of Communication Studies. Marianne is intimately familiar with *Organizational Communication*, having used the text in her own courses and written the Instructor's Manual for the previous three editions. Her expertise in organizational policy, community organizing, and the intersections of health and organizing add an exciting new dimension to the book and we look forward to her continued contributions to this text.

Additionally, our revisions to this edition of *Organizational Communication*, and to all previous editions of the book, were guided by our colleagues' suggestions as well as a desire to provide our readers with the most current and relevant research available. We also care a great deal about finding new and innovative ways to offer students practical applications of organizational communication's theories and concepts, particularly in light of today's pressing ethical, political, economic, technological, and environmental issues. As such, we have made the following improvements to this edition:

- **The introductory chapter** has been refocused to highlight key issues facing today's organizations: the inevitability of change, the impact of technology, and changes in the meaning of work. The chapter has also been revised to reflect significant changes in how society is responding to globalization, as well as the proliferation of cyber threats. Throughout, the chapter focuses on ethical issues, setting students up to consider organizational and communication ethics throughout the book.

- **Chapter 5** has been updated to include new developments in theorizing and practicing organizational culture, particularly in the context of multinational organizations where the intersection of organizational, national, and local cultures can create opportunities for creativity and generate constraints. As the socialization process is tightly coupled with organizational culture, we have also addressed some of the exciting directions in organizational socialization scholarship that address new interpersonal, organizational, and international dynamics.
- **Chapter 6** includes new material on the impact that technology and social media have on power relations in organizational contexts.
- **Chapter 8** has been heavily revised again to consider developing topics in the field, such as employee engagement—that is, fostering employee involvement in and enthusiasm about work. In addition, the chapter's most significant revisions involve a sharper focus on technology and teams, particularly how technological devices and practices are reframing how we collaborate in teams and across networks.
- **Chapter 10** also has been heavily revised and reorganized. The chapter features a much stronger emphasis on the role that technology plays in organizational processes related to basic tracking and monitoring, as well as employee privacy and app culture. Additionally, the chapter now includes a new section on policy as a process that allows organizations to strategically align their efforts.
- **Updated research and examples** throughout the text include coverage of the global economic crisis, generational considerations in communication and policy, identity, employee engagement, and social media. They highlight organizational communication's evolving achievements while keeping the material fresh and relevant for students.
- **New *Everyday Organizational Communication* boxes and *What Would You Do?* boxes** throughout the text introduce contemporary, real-life situations—from innovative approaches to paying employees to social media catastrophes to quality enhancement programs—offering students ample opportunity to consider and apply concepts and theories they learn from the text.

□ Enduring Features of the Text

Despite our considerable updates to reflect the ever-changing context for organizational communication, our goal for the text remains the same: to help students to bridge the gap between what they learn in school and what they experience outside the classroom. Toward this end, we continue to offer several unique features that help students think critically about the world of work, the organizations in their personal lives, and the larger global issues that affect their present and future. As always, we are pleased to offer new examples of each feature in the eighth edition of our text.

- **Case studies** link theory with practice. The case studies in every chapter challenge students to put what they've learned into practice. In Chapter 6, for example, students help a fire department discourage firefighters from taking unnecessary risks; in Chapter 7, they help address communication challenges among team members of different ages. The questions that follow each case study encourage student involvement and lively class discussion.
- *What Would You Do?* **boxes** in every chapter help students appreciate complex ethical decision making, presenting them with a variety of dilemmas they may well face in their lives as students, employees, and citizens.
- *Everyday Organizational Communication* **boxes** in every chapter help students recognize the ways in which organizational theory is already at work in their lives, bridging the gap between academic research and everyday experiences. From scientific management in professional kitchens to creativity and constraint in online networking profiles, students will recognize the relevance of the material to life outside the classroom.

In addition, we continue to offer "A Field Guide to Studying Organizational Communication," which introduces basic observational methods to prepare students to assess real-life organizational problems.

☐ Instructor and Student Resources

Over the past three years, we've noticed an increased demand for flexible book formats, additional instructor support, and online student support to accompany our textbook. This need makes sense given the changes in the organizational communication classroom. Increasingly, we're seeing organizational communication courses taught entirely online. We're also seeing many new instructors step up to teach this exciting course. In response, we offer a robust package to support and complement our text. Please visit our catalog page at macmillanlearning.com to order or download resources.

Teachers and students of organizational communication will benefit from the following:

- **LaunchPad Solo for** *Organizational Communication.* LaunchPad Solo brings together all student media and instructor resources for the text in one convenient location that makes it easy to assign homework, assess student progress, and manage the course. The **Video Assignment Tool** makes it easy to assign and assess video-based activities and projects, and provides a convenient way for students to submit video coursework. The **LaunchPad Gradebook** gives a clear window on performance for the whole class, for individual students, and for individual assignments. **Book-specific instructor resources** include the downloadable Test Bank and Instructor's Resource Manual, pre-built chapter quizzes, and a huge bank of customizable quiz questions. LaunchPad Solo features **easy LMS integration** into your school's learning management system.

- **Online Instructor's Manual.** This highly praised, thoroughly updated manual offers a wealth of support for busy professors, including useful lecture outlines, thought-provoking classroom activities, suggestions for useful and relevant movie and television clips, and thoughts on using the book's pedagogy with students.
- **Computerized Test Bank.** This reliable test bank ensures that instructors have options for assessing their students' understanding of the material, including a variety of multiple-choice, true-false, short-answer, and essay questions.

Acknowledgments

Textbooks are published with the authors' names listed on the cover, but in every way publishing a textbook is a team effort. We are especially grateful for the strong support that this edition of *Organizational Communication* has received from Bedford/St. Martin's. In particular, we want to thank Erika Gutierrez, publisher; Susan McLaughlin, development manager/editor; Will Stonefield, assistant editor; Kayti Corfield, marketing manager; Gillian Daniels, marketing assistant; Pamela Lawson, project editor; and Katrina Ostler, project manager for Jouve North America. All of these fine professionals contributed to this project in ways that have made the eighth edition of this text the best book it could be.

We also want to thank our colleagues and friends at other universities and colleges who reviewed our textbook and offered insightful suggestions for improvement. Reviewers for the eighth edition include:

Philip Bakelaar, Montclair State University
Deborah Dunn, Westmont University
LaKresha Graham, Rockhurst University
Meredith Harrigan, State University of New York at Geneseo
Jacob Jenkins, California State University, Channel Islands
Beatrice Kunka, Robert Morris University
Jae Lee, University of Houston
Alex Lyon, State University of New York at Brockport
Caryn Medved, Baruch College
Michael Pagano, Fairfield University
Joanna Showell, Cookman University
June Smith, Angelo State University
Robert Whitbred, Cleveland State University

Reviewers of previous editions include:
Stacey Connaughton, Purdue University
Caryn Medved, Baruch College, City University of New York
Brittany L. Peterson, Ohio University
Brian Richardson, University of North Texas
Suzy D'Enbeau, University of Kansas
Kathryn Fonner, University of Wisconsin-Milwaukee
Sandra Lyn French, Radford University

Virginia Hamilton, University of California, Davis
Jaesub Lee, University of Houston
Janet Lillie, Michigan State University
Canchu Lin, Bowling Green State University
Lacy G. McNamee, Baylor University
Patty Sotirin, Michigan Technological University
Anthony Spina, Fairleigh Dickinson University
Cheryl Wood, George Washington University
Marie Baker-Ohler, Northern Arizona University
Hsiu-Jung "Mindy" Chang, Western New England College
Gail Fairhurst, University of Cincinnati
Bethany C. Goodier, College of Charleston
James I. Olufowote, Boston College
John Parrish-Sprowl, Indiana University-Purdue University Indianapolis
Suchitra Shenoy, DePaul University
Gary Shulman, Miami University

In addition, we are personally and professionally indebted to a number of colleagues, students, and staff members for their support of this project, specifically Steve Corman, Jess Alberts, Sarah J. Tracy, and Bob McPhee of the Hugh Downs School of Human Communication at Arizona State University; Cliff Scott of the University of North Carolina at Charlotte; Alexandra Murphy of DePaul University; Patricia Riley of the University of Southern California; and Tanya Melendez of Bradley University. Thanks also to Graphic World for their fine work on the revisions to the ancillary material.

Finally, we could not have written this edition without the enthusiastic and loving support of members of our immediate families: Lori Roscoe, Evan and Joel Eisenberg, and Jeff and Anna Brown. We are also grateful for our extended families—especially Karner, Candy, and Allyson Trethewey, Susan Soderstrom, Mary Joy Ewers, and Katie and Nathan LeGreco—and our close friends.

As always, we are grateful to those individuals who, despite the intellectual, social, political, economic, and spiritual turmoil of our time, remain committed to continuing the dialogue.

Eric M. Eisenberg
University of South Florida

Angela Trethewey
Arizona State University, Tempe

Marianne LeGreco
University of North Carolina at Greensboro

H. L. Goodall Jr.
Late of Arizona State University, Tempe

THEORY INTO PRACTICE: CASE STUDIES

These case studies, praised by instructors and students as effective and compelling, make the concepts of organizational communication come to life. Timely and relevant, engaging and entertaining, they bring theory to bear on challenges you will face in today's workplace.

CHAPTER 1: Communication and the Changing World of Work

THE CASE OF THE "ITALIAN" SHOES: Consider the implications when a product is not "made in" the city or country noted on the product label in light of what you have learned about globalization. **29**

CHAPTER 2: Defining Organizational Communication

THE MANY ROBERT SMITHS: Do the various ways in which you are perceived by people you encounter in your workplace add up to a complete and accurate picture of you and your place in that organization? **59**

CHAPTER 3: Three Early Perspectives on Organizations and Communication

RIVERSIDE STATE HOSPITAL: As a government investigator, you are called in to probe the accidental death of a patient at a state psychiatric facility. **93**

CHAPTER 4: The Systems Perspective on Organizations and Communication

CRISIS IN THE ZION EMERGENCY ROOM: Zion Hospital's embattled emergency room is overcrowded, underfunded, and understaffed, resulting in long delays in patient treatment and a decline in the standard of care. Use your knowledge of systems to find creative solutions to this dire situation. **122**

CHAPTER 5: Cultural Studies of Organizations and Communication

STUDYING THE CULTURE OF MEETINGS: Immerse yourself in a familiar culture— your class, college, sorority or fraternity, or place of work—and then analyze and write about it in the form of an ethnography. **155**

CULTURAL CONSTRUCTIONS OF GENDER AND SEXUALITY IN COLLEGE FRATERNITIES AND SORORITIES: Investigate the impact that labels, terms, and stories have on the meanings of gender and sexuality among women and men in fraternities and sororities. **157**

Contents

PART III   CONTEXTS FOR ORGANIZATIONAL COMMUNICATION   195

About the Authors

Eric M. Eisenberg first learned about the field of communication from his father, Abne Eisenberg, a communication professor at Queens College. Abne enlisted Eric's help in grading exams and papers, and over the next fifteen years, despite numerous detours (e.g., microbiology, poetry, and pre-med), Eric kept returning to his first love. He graduated Phi Beta Kappa with a bachelor's degree in communication from Rutgers University, having survived and at times even enjoyed a yearlong simulation of a media marketplace called INTERACT.

When selecting graduate schools, Eisenberg went in search of quality training in communication research methods to complement his fine education in communication theory at Rutgers. Michigan State University (MSU) was purported to be a methodological mecca, so Eisenberg packed up his old yellow Ford Fairlane 500 (with no heater!) and headed west. It was at MSU that he discovered that the research that interested him most had a decidedly practical bent. He received his master's degree in communication working with Dr. Cassandra Book on an experiment evaluating the most effective uses of simulations and games in the classroom. Dr. Book was a superb mentor and a master teacher who encouraged Eisenberg to complete a second master's degree in education in 1980. Book also gave him his first taste of organizational research: They conducted a needs assessment and communication network analysis of the American Dietetic Association. He got rid of the Ford the first winter in Michigan.

Having been raised in a household with no links to corporate America, Eisenberg was intrigued by the possibility of learning about the "real world" of organizational communication. Determined to become fluent in both management and communication, and under the expert guidance of Dr. Peter Monge, he immersed himself in management theory and practice, publishing work on organizational communication networks and superior-subordinate communication. Eisenberg received his doctorate in communication from Michigan State University in 1982. He then owned two suits.

The city boy had learned to love the Midwest, but it was time to head east again. Intrigued by the original and expansive writings of Dr. Art Bochner (who had spent a fortuitous semester at MSU), Eisenberg took his first academic position in the Department of Speech at Temple University in Philadelphia. It was there that he wrote his award-winning paper on the strategic uses of ambiguity in organizations and, with the support of his colleagues at Temple, turned his attention more closely to the uses of language and symbols in organizational life. He stayed connected to business practice by launching and directing the applied communication master's program at Temple and teaching at the downtown campus. During this period, he married Lori Roscoe (whom he had met at Michigan State), and they started building a life together.

In 1984, Eisenberg left Philadelphia to join the communication faculty at the University of Southern California (USC). Over the next decade, he was promoted to associate professor with tenure, published numerous studies of organizational communication and culture, and received recognition as University Scholar and Outstanding Teacher. His paper "Jamming: Transcendence through Organizing" received the National Communication Association research award for the best publication in organizational communication in 1990. At the same time, Eisenberg worked closely with Dr. Patricia Riley on numerous grants and contracts aimed at applying cutting-edge knowledge about communication to organizational practice across a variety of industries (e.g., aerospace, health care, electronics, and manufacturing). Meanwhile, Evan and Joel were born at Good Samaritan Hospital in downtown Los Angeles. Eisenberg published his bittersweet poems from this period in a collection called *Fire and Ice: Fiction as Social Research* (A. and S. Banks, eds.).

USC was a world-class institution, but Los Angeles was a hard place to raise a family. Eisenberg took a position as full professor at the University of South Florida (USF) in 1994, staying true to his lifelong pledge to remain within driving distance of a Disney amusement park. He was attracted to USF for its extraordinary faculty, the energy of a young school with a new doctoral program in communication, and his old friend Art Bochner. Immediately he knew he had found his home—an eccentric but winning department where experience and philosophy were privileged over theory and method. More publications followed, including his first textbook (this one!) and other strange forays into the world of communication and organizational change.

Once in Florida, Eisenberg's consulting work shifted toward the hospitality and health-care industries. In 1996, Eisenberg was elected chair of the Department of Communication at USF. In 2008, he was challenged by the provost to put his knowledge of organizational communication to use as dean of the College of Arts and Sciences, a position he continues to hold today. In addition to this textbook, Eisenberg published a "greatest hits" collection of his writings entitled *Strategic Ambiguities*. Eisenberg and his family love the Tampa Bay area, and he is grateful for the opportunities to teach and learn from exceptional people whenever and wherever he finds them.

As a critical communication scholar, **Angela Trethewey** believes she is the discursive product of several intertwining and sometimes contradictory cultural, institutional, organizational, familial, and relational narratives. Trethewey was born into a long line of strong women in Washington State in 1965, during the early days of the second wave of the feminist movement. Her great-grandmother, an immigrant homesteader, spent her life working the family farm. Her grandmother defied both the conventions of her immigrant parents and the social mores of the day by moving off the farm and into the big city (Seattle), where she eventually supported her three daughters as a jazz pianist. She instilled in her daughters a love of music and books and modeled self-sufficiency in an era that did not encourage women to combine work outside the home and family, let alone "balance" those two worlds. Trethewey's research on women's struggles to negotiate effective and efficacious identities in the workplace is both an homage to and a continuation of her foremothers' trailblazing, but very different, lives.

Trethewey spent her childhood in a small town in Northern California in a family in which education was understood to be life's work—both literally and figuratively. She was raised by two public school teachers who embodied the sheer joy and the practical utility of continuous, lifelong learning. Neither her mother nor her father told her that education was inextricably linked to living a rich, full, interesting and productive life; that message was simply evident in all that they did. Today, Trethewey strives to model that same message for her colleagues and students. Her teaching philosophy was honored when she received the Master Teacher Award from the Western States Communication Association.

Trethewey received her undergraduate and master's degrees from California State University, Chico. She earned her doctoral degree in organizational communication at Purdue University, where she had the good fortune to work with two of the brightest minds in the field—Drs. Linda Putnam and Dennis Mumby. She was first introduced to the field of communication in an undergraduate gender and communication course. She was so intrigued by the subject matter that she changed her major from business administration to communication. It was in that same course that she first encountered her future husband, Jeff Brown. More than twenty-five years later, she continues to delight in exploring the complexities and organization of gendered communication—both in her research and in her decades-long partnership.

Trethewey is a professor and the dean of the College of Communication and Education at her alma mater, California State University, Chico. As a leader and manager, Trethewey routinely draws upon her training in organizational communication, communication theory, and critical research methods to help her analyze problems and opportunities, cultivate a culture of innovation, inclusion, and participation, and foster the leadership potential of faculty and students. As a scholar, she has published three books and over thirty articles and book chapters.

Trethewey can trace the impact of her narrative roots as she continues to craft her current story in her everyday life. Today, her own work/life is often complicated by, but always joyful as a result of, her relationship with her smart and capable daughter, Anna Trethewey Brown, who is just embarking on her own college journey. Each day, Trethewey lives the sometimes energizing, sometimes draining identity of a working mother in contemporary organizational and family life in an era dominated by economic uncertainty and global tensions. She uses those experiences to help her reflect on and ultimately change the ways that our culture, organizations, and even family systems, however unwittingly, constrain women's and men's ability to live their lives to their fullest potential.

At the end of the day and at the end of her career, Trethewey hopes to leave Anna with new versions of the narrative gifts she has inherited from her mother — resiliency, intellectual curiosity, gratitude, laughter, joie de vivre, and, of course, a rich, productive, and empowering communicative repertoire! It is in that same spirit that she embraced the writing of this book.

Marianne LeGreco has carved out a presence in the field of communication that focuses on intersections between food, community, and policy. Much of her professional life connects back to her family. She comes from a band of farmers, teachers, chefs, nutritionists, catering managers, and higher education administrators, meaning that food, education, and communication have always been an integral part of her life.

LeGreco grew up thinking about innovative and alternative ways to organize. Her early years were spent mostly in Galena — a small tourist town in northern Illinois that spent most of the late 1980s and 1990s rebuilding and rebranding its Main Street shopping and restaurant scene. When it came time to start her undergraduate education, LeGreco chose Bradley University in Peoria, Illinois. During that time, she competed for the national champion Bradley Speech Team, where she earned multiple individual awards and a national final in Informative Speaking at the 2000 National Forensics Association. At Bradley, LeGreco also had the chance to develop her skills in public speaking, rhetorical criticism, and the (at the time) emerging field of digital media.

After graduating from Bradley in 2000, Marianne headed west to attend Arizona State University and the Hugh Downs School of Human Communication. Her brother Nathan, sister Katie, and mother Susan followed shortly after. During LeGreco's master's and doctoral work, Nathan worked as a chef and Katie worked as a nutritionist. Watching the work of her siblings inspired LeGreco to begin focusing more of her research on food. This didn't mean that she abandoned her interest in communication; rather, she began to examine intersections between food, organizing, and health policy, particularly as they related to discourse and communication. These interests culminated in a dissertation project on school meal policy under the direction of Dr. Angela Trethewey.

During her time at Arizona State, LeGreco also got the opportunity to attend the Institute for Qualitative Research Methods, which turned out to be a pivotal experience in her graduate training. She began developing a research methodology called discourse tracing, which she published alongside Sarah Tracy in *Qualitative Inquiry* in 2009. Since then, discourse tracing has been used to study everything from school meal policy to Scottish whiskey tourism to airport security lines to urban planning initiatives.

LeGreco's professional journeys next took her east, when she joined the Communication Studies faculty at the University of North Carolina at Greensboro.

She quickly began tracing food discourses across a variety of organizational contexts, including food trucks, farmers markets, local food policies, urban farms, food councils, and community-based food efforts. LeGreco is particularly committed to getting her students involved in service-learning, and community-engaged activities surrounding food in their communities. For her efforts to engage students and partners around important social issues in their communities, she received the Service Engagement Award from the Organizational Communication Division of the National Communication Association in 2013.

At the core of LeGreco's work is the idea that we all have to eat. She explored this idea in two talks for TEDxGreensboro in 2014 and 2015, respectively. True to her organizational communication roots, she sees food as a systems issue involving multiple players and complex processes. At the same time, food is also something we organize our lives around every day, meaning "what to eat" is one of the most common decisions that most of us negotiate on a daily basis. She believes that food connects us together and can serve as a starting point to tackle much larger issues facing our communities, like secure housing and quality education. She traces her story around food, in a way that highlights the creativity and constraint that goes in to what and how we eat.

Harold Lloyd (Bud) Goodall Jr. was both a subject and a student of organizations since his birth in King's Daughters Hospital in Martinsburg, West Virginia, in 1952. Reared in a traditional family; educated in public and private schools and universities; employed by large and small businesses in occupations as diverse as short-order cook, college professor/department chair/graduate director/school director, rhythm guitarist in a rock band, organizational detective, account executive for a broadcasting company, member of a counterterrorism and public diplomacy research group; participant and volunteer in community and political activities; co-owner of a publishing house, partner in a consulting firm, and blogger extraordinaire—all of these experiences shaped his approach to studying, writing about, and living his many and varied organizational lives.

He first became interested in researching and writing about organizational communication while a new faculty member at the University of Alabama in Huntsville. As a resident "communication specialist," he was asked to develop training sessions in "effective communication" for scientific and engineering firms that supported NASA's space shuttle program, the U.S. Army's Redstone Arsenal, and the federal government's "Star Wars" project. Later, as his interest in organizations grew from training to consulting, and his scholarly interests shifted from traditional social science to interpretive forms of inquiry, he applied detective methods to various high-technology firms and government agencies. These interpretive methods included his going undercover in the organizations to experience firsthand the lives that were lived there. The results of those years of study and writing were captured in his first two organizational ethnographies, *Casing a Promised Land: The Autobiography of an Organizational Detective as Cultural*

Ethnographer (1989) and *Living in the Rock n Roll Mystery: Reading Context, Self, and Others as Clues* (1991).

Goodall received his bachelor's degree from Shepherd College in 1973, his master's from the University of North Carolina at Chapel Hill in 1974, and his doctorate in speech communication from Pennsylvania State University in 1980. He taught at the University of Alabama in Huntsville (UAH), the University of Utah, Clemson University, and Arizona State University (ASU), where he directed the Hugh Downs School of Human Communication from 2004 to 2009. In four of his academic positions—UAH, Clemson, UNCG, and ASU—he applied his understanding of organizational and learning theories to lead communication departments and curricula in which vision, mission, values, and coursework are strategically aligned and students are better served. His work in the academic community was honored with the Gerald M. Phillips Award for Distinguished Applied Communication Scholarship by the National Communication Association.

Goodall's primary scholarly mission was to change the way texts about organizations and communication are written in an effort to make them more accessible, more representative of everyday life, and more creatively engaging. His ethnographies received laudatory reviews and awards from both academic and nonacademic sources, and over two hundred colleges and universities worldwide have adopted his textbooks. He was consistently featured in the popular press and media from coast to coast for his trade books. Most recently for the trade market he authored *A Need to Know: The Clandestine History of a CIA Family* (Left Coast Press, 2006), a work that combines personal narrative with Cold War history and an organizational study of secrecy, power, and a family during an "enduring war."

As a founding member of ASU's Consortium on Strategic Communication, he was also actively involved in analyzing and developing message strategies deployed in the current "overseas contingency operation." In that work, with coauthors Steve Corman and Angela Trethewey, he wrote *Weapons of Mass Persuasion: Strategic Communication to Combat Violent Extremism* (Peter Lang, 2008). The consortium's work on counterterrorism and public diplomacy was honored with the 2009 Applied/Public Policy Research Award by the International Communication Association.

Overall, Goodall was the author or coauthor of nineteen textbook, trade, and scholarly volumes and over one hundred journal articles, book chapters, and scholarly presentations. He is listed in *Contemporary Authors*, *Dictionary of American Scholars*, and *Who's Who International*.

"Dr. Bud" was diagnosed with stage IV pancreatic cancer in April 2011. True to form, he blogged his "journey through Cancerland" to offer readers (family, friends, colleagues, fellow cancer patients, and strangers) a personal narrative on the overall highs and lows as well as the individual happy, angry, loving, frightening, peaceful, and chaotic days of the last fourteen months of his life. The blog remains active (www.hlgoodall.com/blog.html) to stand as a testimony of Bud's outlook and to inspire others to take every day as a gift, even in the face of a terminal illness.

PART I

APPROACHING ORGANIZATIONAL COMMUNICATION

CHAPTER 1

Communication and the Changing World of Work

From the moment we are born, we are surrounded by people. As we seek to understand those on whom we rely most, we learn many related things at once: a language, a culture, and, most important, a sense of self. We discover who we are through our communication with others.

We spend our childhood and adult lives as members of numerous social groups: family, religious community, school, business, and country. Our membership in these groups shapes our sense of self while teaching us to interact with others who are often quite different from us. Each of us experiences this discovery process, and no two people come out the same. Small differences in genetics or experience result in marked variations in character and perception. Over time, we each develop habitual ways of seeing the world—called **worldviews** or perceptual sets—that reflect our inclinations and experiences. Male, female, or transgender, rich or poor, Jewish or Buddhist, African or eastern European, only child or one of many siblings, people perceive the world differently in accord with their worldview. Even those close friends and family members we consider "just like us" might have quite different views on how the world works, just as those we perceive as very different might have more in common than we ever imagined.

Because our worldviews inevitably differ, we must learn how to communicate with diverse others to become functioning members of society. In primitive times, humans banded together to hunt, gather, and grow food, as well as to propagate the species. Human survival has always hinged on our ability to work together. Seen this way, the history of human civilization is fundamentally a history of *organizing*.

While collaborating with diverse others is unavoidable, it is by no means easy, though it is easier to organize around some tasks than others. In sports, for example,

3

where there are clearly defined rules, roles, and goals, coordination is relatively straightforward. Simple financial transactions, mail package delivery, and traffic patterns on an interstate are other examples of continuous coordination around clearly defined rules that are not open to much interpretation. In each of these instances, people know what they want and have a well-defined notion of what it will take to get it.

Unfortunately, many organizing challenges are far more complex and ambiguous. For example, how does one build a successful business? What is the best structure for local government? What kind of communication characterizes successful work-life balance? We are on very different ground here: Goals, rules, and roles are negotiable and open to interpretation. Particularly in contemporary societies (as opposed to traditional ones), there are few givens in social life—almost everything is negotiable.

In school, the dreaded group project provides an emotionally charged example of the challenges inherent in organizing. At first, the assignment seems straightforward, as we tend to assume that our fellow group members have ideas and work habits similar to our own. In time, however, it all too often becomes clear that group members have very different goals, values, motivations, and worldviews. For every person who seeks perfection, there is someone who has no problem settling for a grade of C; for every person who likes to get work done in advance, there is someone who prefers finishing the project the night before it is due. In any setting, organizing takes work, and the challenge of organizing is to collaborate in ways that both acknowledge and bridge differing worldviews.

The interaction required to direct a group toward a shared goal is called **organizational communication**. Nothing about this process is easy; certain knowledge and skills are required to succeed. Moreover, as we go about our lives, we enter into one interaction after another, always in the shadow of multiple large organizations, whether a school, corporation, or government agency. In each of these interactions, we are sometimes satisfied but more often frustrated by the lack of coordination and the red tape resulting from ineffective organizational communication. A deeper understanding of communication enables us to better comprehend the factors that contribute to successful organizing. We designed this book to help you develop this deeper understanding.

We begin the introductory chapter of this book with the frank acknowledgment that any wisdom we seek to impart here is fundamentally perishable and that the world of work has become so dynamic and complex that the only true constant is change. Success accrues to those most capable of managing in and through this turbulence. With this caveat in mind, we then seek to identify the three main types of changes that we believe a serious student of organizational communication must understand and appreciate: globalization, communication technology, and changes in the meaning and structure of work itself. Each topic is discussed in detail below and throughout this book.

◪ THE INEVITABILITY OF CHANGE

Students embarking on careers often harbor misconceptions about the world of work. Many expect their first "real" job to be more serious and orderly than it turns out to be. Likewise, they expect competent and fair managers. They are often disappointed. Once on the job, they may expect a relatively stable career with a company, only to be surprised by the steady stream of mergers, acquisitions, and joint ventures that regularly change their job duties and add to their workload. The near universal feeling of continuous change is disturbing to some, and each of us, regardless of industry, is challenged to find ways to adapt.

So, how can we deal with constant change in the world of work? There are no easy answers. Even a seemingly straightforward question like "What is the best way to supervise employees?" or "How can we attract and keep clients, patients, or customers?" doesn't permit a simple response. As a result, the definition of effective communication can vary by company and industry, the particular people involved, and an organization's unique culture.

Put another way, answers to questions about organizational communication have a short shelf life. They are highly situated and perishable. By "situated" we mean that communication that works well for an online T-shirt distributor like Digital Gravel may be inappropriate for a mature film-production company like Paramount Pictures. By "perishable" we mean that patterns of interaction which were effective last year may be outdated today due to changes in customer tastes and technology. Companies that fail to recognize the need for change perish. One example from our experience involves a public water utility in California. The general manager, a Marine Corps veteran, modeled the utility's management systems and structures on those of the traditional military—strict hierarchy and leadership focused on command and control. Neither the managers nor the employees were comfortable with the rigid hierarchy or with the general manager's intimidating management style. Eventually, employee resistance turned into open hostility, and the general manager was ousted by the board of directors and replaced by an outsider with a more inclusive, participative approach that encouraged two-way communication.

There are many other examples. The giant media company News Corp (which owns the Fox television network, among many other companies) acquired Myspace—which, given the clear dominance of Facebook, now seems like a bad idea—but at the same time created Hulu with Disney and NBC in a move that appears thus far to be succeeding as Hulu gains ground on Amazon and Netflix. Even the highly successful Google underestimated the economic importance of social media for its future success and is racing to catch up with its competitors on social platforms. While many experts have commented on the technical superiority of Google+ as a social media platform, Facebook has such a significant head start that many people are reluctant to make a change at this point. Clearly what constitutes a winning strategy for communicating with customers is so perishable that, given the lag between when we are writing this and when it will be published, many of the solutions that we identify as effective may be usurped by new approaches and innovations!

We could go on citing examples of entire industries whose fundamental business models have transformed or collapsed. Consider the widespread changes in the music, book publishing, and video rental industries over the past ten years as traditional brick-and-mortar stores have disappeared in the wake of online access to songs, books, and streaming movies. Ride-hailing services such as Uber, Lyft, and Didi are challenging traditional taxi and limousine services worldwide, and companies like Airbnb and VRBO are disrupting traditional hospitality businesses by providing "unique accommodations with local hosts" across the globe. Perhaps the biggest change of all is taking place in the health-care industry, as governments and consumers are pressuring providers to replace costly specialist-based fee-for-service business models with prevention-centric practices refocused on the primary care physician as care coordinator. The Agency for Health Care Research and Quality has posted online a comprehensive guide for how to set up a patient centered medical home (PCMH) to better coordinate care.

The question confronting individuals in every industry is one of urgency—in other words, how much time do we have until our business model is obsolete and we must be prepared to implement a new one? What is absolutely clear is that—in response to the situated and perishable nature of organizing—we must become increasingly flexible and adaptable in our communication practices. Rapid changes taking place today demand speedy, flexible responses since the nature of organizational communication in the business world of even two years ago no longer applies. For this reason, our focus is on enabling you to *ask good questions* about organizations, the specific answers to which will most certainly change over time. Your actions will be guided by how you see and make sense of such situations, by your ability to keep an open mind to various interpretations, and by your commitment to a lifetime of learning. Flexibility enables you to adapt more readily to a turbulent business environment. You will be able to reinvent yourself and your organization both in response to, and in anticipation of, changing times.

With the theme of change as a backdrop, we next identify three main types of changes that you should understand as a student of organizational communication: globalization, communication technology, and changes in the meaning of work.

◼ THE IMPACT OF GLOBALIZATION ON ORGANIZING

Toward the end of the twentieth century, remarkable changes in global politics—the end of the Cold War, the breakup of the Soviet Union, the destruction of the Berlin Wall in Germany, and the forging of a unified European Community—altered or dissolved divisions that once seemed insurmountable. Many saw in the collapse of old structures the promise of new alliances striving to end poverty and suffering worldwide and the potential to adopt a universal, indeed planetary, code of human rights. This is one version of **globalization**, which has been defined as

> the closer integration of the countries and peoples of the world which has been brought about by the enormous reduction of costs of transportation and communication, and the breaking down of artificial barriers to the flows of goods, services, capital, knowledge and (to a lesser extent) people across borders. (Stiglitz, 2002, p. 9)

Many aspects of globalization—such as intellectual and artistic exchange, increased employment opportunities, and easier access to medical care—are universally welcome. But other aspects have been far more controversial and even detrimental to the global community. In this section, we examine both the beneficial and the questionable effects of globalization, including outsourcing, the rise of the global company, challenges of managing a multicultural workforce, global economic concerns, potential abuses of power in the global marketplace, and the dramatic increase in cybercrime. As you will see, the rise of a truly global economic context for business brings with it both unprecedented opportunity and a host of ethical and practical challenges.

☐ Outsourcing

For most westerners, their first introduction to the idea of globalization was through exposure to **outsourcing**, as when a U.S. company chooses to hire people in other countries to do some of their work. What started as an effective way to cut costs in certain industries (notably the employment of workers in parts of Asia to make clothing) has evolved into a new world labor pool. One of the biggest costs that an organization can accrue is figuring out how to pay people to do their work, so businesses today routinely search the globe for the lowest possible labor costs and move jobs to wherever cheap labor can be found. Although such practices have long been controversial (e.g., Nike has been accused of outsourcing to sweatshops in South Korea and Taiwan, and Apple has been criticized for employee working conditions in China), they were once confined almost exclusively to blue-collar jobs. Today, white-collar jobs in most industries are also affected by this trend. For example, most U.S. software designers employ engineering and call-center staffs in India and the Philippines.

While precise estimates are hard to obtain, outsourcing is at least an $8 trillion business. Chief information officers at companies ranging from General Motors to Applied Materials outsource 50 percent or more of their IT budget dollars. Despite its growth as a business practice, outsourcing has its challenges—political, ethical, and operational. Vendor management organizations who contract with organizations to provide broad oversight of a wide range of basic support services continue to be challenged by staffing shortfalls and inadequate service integration—that is, the work that they do does not align well with the other services and systems provided by the company. Until these problems are addressed more effectively, geography will still make a difference. Not all outsourcing of work leads to the loss of U.S. jobs, however. In some cases, European and Asian companies have set up operations in the United States (a practice known in the United States as "insourcing"). U.S. subsidiaries of companies headquartered abroad employ more than five million Americans. The top five insourcing companies today are from the United Kingdom (BP and Royal Dutch Shell) and Japan (Toyota, Honda, and Nissan). Many of these jobs—like those at the Honda plants in Ohio—pay higher wages than the many jobs that are outsourced to other countries.

The potential consequences of U.S. jobs being moved overseas were at the center of the debate over the North American Free Trade Agreement (NAFTA), an attempt to reduce restrictions on trade among the United States, Canada, and Mexico. On the one hand, an expanded labor pool makes U.S. companies more competitive by allowing them to hold down costs. On the other hand, sending work elsewhere can and has led to the decay of U.S. communities that are unable to withstand plant closings or massive job losses. Furthermore, the low wages paid to workers in less developed countries—sometimes as little as 10 to 15 percent of U.S. wages—raise questions about exploitation, which is discussed later in this chapter.

☐ The Rise of the Global Company

As the world economy has become increasingly interdependent, discussions about outsourcing and insourcing that assume a "home" country have morphed into discussions that instead conceive of companies as first and fundamentally global. Amid current economic struggles, the number of organizations that operate globally has grown exponentially. Over three-quarters of all U.S. companies conduct business internationally, which includes having foreign customers, suppliers, and employees. Participation in the global economy has increased dramatically as a result of tremendous advances in communication technology and e-commerce. For example, while more than half of Xerox's 110,000 employees work overseas, more than half of Sony's employees are not Japanese. The United States enjoys imported entertainment, while American music, films, and television command large markets abroad.

Much of this change has been driven by the speed at which the Internet has provided instantaneous access to consumers worldwide. While one would expect to see large companies developing a global presence as they aim to expand their markets, the effect of e-commerce on the globalization of small businesses has been profound. Today it is possible for any small company in the United States to partner with suppliers and sell to customers outside of the country. In a very short time, global business has gone from an option to explore to an expected part of almost every business plan. And this is true across all industries. Even colleges and universities that traditionally had local or regional missions are now seeking a global presence. Broward College in South Florida (formerly a local community college), for example, now runs highly successful baccalaureate programs around the world—and competes with hundreds of other similar institutions.

It is also interesting to note that as U.S. organizations seek to expand their global reach, many are looking at the same locales and trading partners. Recent economic troubles in Europe have resulted in less emphasis on the European Union and increased interest in the Pacific Rim (China, in particular) and Brazil. While globalization clearly offers U.S. businesses an expanded market for their products and services, it also threatens to erode U.S. business because of increased foreign competition. At one time, U.S. consumers could respond to these challenges by "buying American," but the globalization of business has nearly rendered this slogan meaningless. Many new automobile buyers who wish to remain loyal to American brands have discovered that what they thought were "American" cars are in fact manufactured or assembled in foreign countries. Similarly, it is harder to define precisely what is foreign. Jaguar Cars and Land Rover, once British manufacturers, are now subsidiaries of Tata Motors of India, and Volvo, once a Swedish company, is now owned by Ford. The ubiquity of such global interdependencies was highlighted in 2012 when fashion designer Ralph Lauren was criticized for manufacturing the U.S. Olympic team's uniforms in China.

There are some exceptions to this globalizing trend, and they can be observed in the realm of restaurants and food production and other U.S. industries choosing to shift to more local employment and purchasing practices. Over the past few years, a growing emphasis on local foods and farm-to-table dining has created alternatives to traditional global food distribution networks. The growing popularity of farmers markets, pop-up restaurants, and food trucks that source local ingredients shows the potential for a significant alternative marketplace. Many consumers are being more selective about the sourcing of their food. Time will tell whether this trend will become more affordable for the typical shopper and grow into its potential, or if it will eventually be co-opted by and absorbed into the global food production industry.

Meanwhile, a number of companies in other industries have begun moving jobs that were previously outsourced back to the United States. Consider the following:

- In 2010, footwear designer KEEN opened a 15,000-square-foot facility to manufacture boots in Portland, Oregon—moving production from China to a location just five miles from its corporate headquarters. The company also makes bags in California and socks in North Carolina.
- After watching costs rise in its Chinese factories, Master Lock began bringing production back to Milwaukee—the same place where the company was founded in 1921.
- When a 2011 tornado destroyed the Wrangler jeans distribution plant in Hackleburg, Alabama, the VF Corporation—a global leader in branded lifestyle apparel—worked with the local government and investors to rebuild the plant even though it made more financial sense to consider moving to other locations.

These examples illustrate how some corporations are realizing the benefits of investing in local communities over outsourcing jobs.

☐ Challenges of Managing a Multicultural Workforce

International opportunities for expansion—whether through outsourcing or the development of a truly global company—invariably involve a different type of challenge, one that comes through the development of relationships with individuals and groups from diverse cultural backgrounds. Specifically, **multicultural management** is the ability to adapt one's leadership style to both respond to and make the most of pervasive cultural differences in values and practices among a diverse employee population. Globalization does not eliminate differences in language and culture. When expanding business across cultures, it is essential to introduce a product or service that is an identifiable example of the brand but still reflects local tastes and tolerances. McDonald's, the world's largest chain of hamburger fast-food restaurants, for example, has many locations in India, where cows are sacred. In a great example of flexibility, the company's "Maharaja Macs" are made with chicken instead of beef.

Success across national boundaries requires highly sophisticated, global communication skills (Dalton, Ernst, Deal, & Leslie, 2002; Molinsky, 2013). At a minimum, this means that employees must speak the language of their customers and suppliers and, preferably, understand the subtleties of other cultures. Finland has relied on export markets throughout much of its history, and consequently many Finns speak four or more languages.

An infamous example of botched multicultural management is Disneyland Paris (formerly Euro Disney). After achieving outstanding success in Japan, where its meticulously designed theme park was consistent with the local culture, Disney opened a park in France. In this case, however, the park ignored important aspects of French culture and climate. The American-style hotels built around Disneyland Paris offered rooms that cost $300 a night and were therefore not affordable for the typical French family, who usually take three- to six-week vacations. In addition, when the park first opened it did not serve alcohol which conflicted with the French custom of drinking wine at lunch.

With such global ventures, businesses must acquire and address a culturally diverse workforce. At Sheraton's Vistana Resort, an award-winning hotel in Orlando, Florida, the company's environmental services department meets regularly to address communication issues pertinent to the multiethnic staff, which is mainly Latino, Anglo, and Haitian. At computer hardware supplier Kyocera America located in San Diego, California, a Japanese management team is challenged to communicate effectively with the mostly male African American supervisors and mostly female Filipino employees on the line.

Similarly, organizations must acknowledge and address differences in religion, an increasingly important element of diversity in the international workforce. In the United States, organizations continue to define the line between work and personal beliefs, understanding that people with different worldviews must work side by side physically or virtually. Some institutions only select and promote employees with certain belief systems (Ehrenreich, 2005). In some cases, rules concerning the "right" beliefs are stated overtly, but more often they are subtle and covert. For example, a colleague of ours reports on her difficulties in getting tenure at a university with a particular religious affiliation. While no one ever told her outright that she had to be a practicing member of the religion in order to be promoted, she was frequently asked by administrators about her personal religious beliefs. While there is some emerging research exploring the role of religion at work (Molloy & Heath, 2014; Shenoy-Packer & Buzzanell, 2013), we anticipate that this subject will continue to be a hot topic 12. As these examples show, effective organizational communication today must consider and address a host of multicultural and multinational concerns.

In summary, we share findings from the Center for Creative Leadership, a prominent research and development firm in North Carolina. The organization studied the factors that lead global managers to succeed and identified four pivotal skills: (1) international business knowledge, (2) cultural adaptability, (3) the ability to take the perspective of others, and (4) the ability to play the role of innovator (Dalton et al., 2002). The thread connecting these capabilities is effective communication and the ability to forge relationships with diverse others in an open, informed way.

☐ Global Economic Concerns

As business leaders throughout the world look for outsourcing partners and seek to expand their operations globally, they do so in the context of rules and agreements that have evolved between nations to coordinate national economies and regulate trade. In 1944, following World War II, the World Bank and the International Monetary Fund (IMF) were formed to rebuild a war-torn Europe and to prevent future international economic depressions. The same 1944 agreement called for the formation of a facilitating body that would encourage the free flow of goods through measures such as lowering tariffs. More than fifty years later, the World Trade Organization (WTO) came into being, and its conferences were for a period of time a lightning rod for those protesting the negative economic effects of globalization on the environment and the world's poor. In 2001 and 2002, violent protests accompanying WTO meetings (in Washington, D.C.; Seattle; and Genoa, Italy) shined a media spotlight on public opposition at the time to certain aspects of economic globalization.

Domestic unrest in the United States, beginning with the terrorist attacks of 9/11, has significantly impacted the antiglobalization movement and the size and

Religious Differences in the Classroom

One of the most challenging issues facing organizations today is how to honor and accommodate religious differences among their members. In a meeting of the Hillsborough County School Board in Tampa, Florida, a proposal by Muslim residents to add their religious holidays to the school calendar (as days off) was met with resistance. A committee of the board advanced a counterproposal eliminating all religious holidays, instead granting students "personal days" that they could use however they wished. But this proposal also met with resistance. As our societies, schools, and organizations diversify, to what degree must they adapt to the religious beliefs of their members?

Another example of the rising challenge of religious diversity occurred recently between a communication professor and her student at a state university in the United States. The student refused to purchase the required text for her "Women and Communication" class because she objected to the coarse language in the book title (a feminist critique of characterizations of women, it is called *Bitches, Bimbos and Ballbreakers: The Guerrilla Girls' Illustrated Guide to Female Stereotypes*). She explained, "I am a pastor's daughter. I don't swear, and I don't expose myself to this kind of material. And I won't be seen around town purchasing or carrying a book with that title."

DISCUSSION QUESTIONS

1. To what extent are organizations responsible for creating an environment that supports the religious diversity of their members? Is there a difference between accommodating, tolerating, and encouraging religious differences?
2. Have you experienced a time when your own religious beliefs came into conflict with those of an institution of which you were a member? What, if anything, did you do about it, and why?
3. How should the instructor respond to the pastor's daughter? What are the trade-offs between validating individual belief systems and standing up for the value of a more secular and critical approach to education?
4. How might your response to question 3 be translated into policy and practice in a broader range of noneducational organizations? What problems would you anticipate, and how might you address them?

frequency of public protests. People's attention turned to global conflict and problems with the domestic economy and has mostly stayed there since. Dwyer (2013) points out that "it can be difficult to think of trade policy before one's own employment. In that light, globalization has become something of an abstraction." At the same time, the influence of these transnational institutions has declined compared to private investment, which now spends more than twenty times what the World Bank does in international development.

In all, while many of the challenges of globalization still exist, any kind of unified resistance has fragmented worldwide due to numerous other global challenges.

Prior to the global economic collapse in 2008, there was a growing feeling that the institutions promoting a global economy had made a number of serious missteps. The most critical mistakes involved the pace at which it is possible for a country to make the transition to a market economy where prices and wages are determined mainly by the laws of supply and demand, rather than being regulated by the government. An unreasonably optimistic belief in the self-regulating power of a market economy led the IMF in particular to encourage those nations needing its help to privatize their industries and to open their markets before adequate regulatory frameworks were in place. Such changes produced disastrous results in some countries. For example, in Russia, the poor are in some ways worse off under market capitalism than they were under the prior socialist regime:

> Most Russians are poorer since the fall of the Soviet Union. They despise the rich and powerful for having grabbed the crown jewels of the Soviet economy—factories, oil fields, gold mines. The profound changes have left many Russians disoriented. Their country is no longer a great world power. Their economy has shrunk to the size of Poland's. Doctors have to moonlight as cab drivers (Frontline World, 2003).

A second problem with the approach was the failure to recognize that there are multiple models for a market economy and that some versions—for example, the Japanese, German, and Swedish models, each of which has a different tax structure and approach to providing social services—have advantages that may be more useful and a better fit for developing countries than the U.S. version of free-market capitalism. Those countries that have not relied on self-regulation but instead have recognized the role government can play in the transition to markets (e.g., Thailand, Indonesia) have been more successful (Stiglitz, 2002).

The question of the appropriate role of governments in the operation of the global economy became more urgent during the global economic collapse of 2008. After the terrorist attacks of September 11, 2001, the IMF "went from broken to heroic, brokering rescue packages for Pakistan, Iceland, Hungary, and the Ukraine. . . . Whatever form globalization takes next, it will not be despite governments but because of them" (Malcomson, 2008). Blind faith in market capitalism as a model for organizing has been replaced by a more balanced approach that sees an important role for government and international government agencies.

Another related problem associated with globalization is the sheer interrelatedness of national markets and economies, a fact that has been dramatically brought home in recent years. The effects of a 2011 earthquake and nuclear accident in Japan, and economic crises in Greece—whose government as of 2015 received their third financial bailout from European creditors—have had real and immediate impacts on the lives of people around the globe. An immigration crisis caused by instability and violence in the Middle East (Syria, in particular) has placed tremendous pressure on many countries throughout the European Union as well as on more stable Arab nations such as Jordan. And most recently, a British voters voted for their country to exit the European Union, a move that will assuredly have enormous impact on every organization seeking to succeed in the global economy.

One of the most worrisome aspects of a truly global economy is that the United States is not well poised to compete. At a time when the ambitions of countries like China and India are growing dramatically, we are well behind in competitiveness and specifically in education (Christensen, 2010). In what is becoming a global war for talent, noncitizens who earn advanced degrees in the United States are increasingly returning to their homelands to work. Other countries are making enormous investments in education at all levels that are reflected in the widening achievement gap between the United States and the rest of the world. China has more honors students than the United States has students. If we are not to be left behind, our leaders must act quickly to recognize this serious crisis in human capital.

☐ Potential Abuses of Power in the Global Marketplace

It should be clear from our discussion of globalization in this chapter that there is much at stake for both businesses and individuals. As businesses pursue greater profitability in the global theater it invariably puts pressure on individual wages and working conditions. Many workers in the new global economy do not operate with the safeguards that American organizations often provide, including fair wages, health benefits, and safe working conditions. Immigrants to the United States, both legal and illegal, often work in subpar conditions for considerably less than minimum wage as piece-rate workers in the garment industry or as farm laborers who follow the harvest across the country, all the while living in cramped and inhospitable housing. The American economy today could not function without these underpaid and undervalued workers, who come to this country in search of a better life. In fact, most middle-class Americans don't get through a day without consuming the fruit of the working poor's labor, whether it's vegetables from the grocery store or shoes from the mall (Shipler, 2004).

Given the high degree of global economic inequality, it is unlikely that this problem will go away anytime soon. In 2014, U.S. citizens working in the securities

EVERYDAY ORGANIZATIONAL COMMUNICATION

Globalization and You

The more damaging and controversial effects of globalization on the environment, communities, and employees (both domestic and international) may seem overwhelming. How can we respond to and have an impact on such a massive international challenge? Fortunately, several organizations are running campaigns to involve average citizens, from college students to CEOs to retired grandparents, in the effort to counter the negative effects of globalization.

Oxfam America, an international development and relief agency, has developed a student action group that offers "young people a wide range of opportunities to become better educated and join the fight against global poverty and injustice around the world" (Oxfam America, 2013). Such education is achieved through workshops and training aimed at students and through the publication of campus action guides that offer specific plans—such as fighting for fair-trade coffee on campus—to combat problems associated with globalization. The organization also highlights stories of everyday people who are trying to have a positive impact on the world, including a six-year-old boy who went door to door passing out brochures on world hunger to educate his neighbors, and students at Virginia Tech who hosted a "hunger banquet" with proceeds benefiting a local food pantry and Oxfam America to call attention to important global issues (Oxfam America, 2013). The point behind these strategies and stories remains consistent: You can make a difference by educating yourself about the effects of globalization, sharing this information with friends and colleagues, and committing yourself to small but positive lifestyle changes such as supporting a local, independent grocery store.

Several websites offer additional strategies that individuals can pursue to curb the negative consequences of globalization. Visit a few of the following websites and consider their suggested actions:

- fairtradecampus.wordpress.com
- unionlabel.org
- globalcitizen.org
- howtobuyamerican.com
- globalexchange.org
- oxfamamerica.org

(continued, Globalization and You)

DISCUSSION QUESTIONS

1. Generate a list of strategies recommended by antiglobalization advocates (e.g., participating in Adbusters' Buy Nothing Day campaign, asking for fair-trade coffee at your local coffee shop, buying locally, recycling, and urging your campus decision makers to contract with fair-trade suppliers). Which strategies would you be willing to participate in regularly?
2. Which strategies, if any, do you think have the greatest potential to bring about positive social change? Why?
3. What unintended negative consequences might result from these suggested actions?
4. Do you think that the efforts of individuals or activist groups can make a difference in the way multinational organizations operate? Why or why not?

industry (e.g., investment bankers and stockbrokers) made twice as much in bonuses alone as all U.S. employees earning minimum wage. In 2011, Apple, then the highest valued company in the world, reported numerous workplace violations at Foxconn, one of its major suppliers located in Taiwan. Included in the violation report was evidence of numerous underage workers, falsified records, and dangerous work environments. But this is hardly the case of "one bad Apple"—numerous electronics companies rely on Foxconn and similar firms to produce their products (see *Everyday Organizational Communication* on page 15).

Another troubling trend is the expanding global sex-trafficking industry, particularly in Southeast Asia. **Trafficking** refers to the illegal trade of human beings across borders. The United Nations estimates that more than 2.4 million people are trafficked across five hundred different trade routes each year, and most of these are women and children who are sold into the sex trade (Omelaniuk, 2005). Many vulnerable and poor women and children are lured by traffickers who offer promises of a better life, legitimate work, or an education, while others are sold by family members or acquaintances for a profit. These women and girls often end up working in brothels where the need for money "overpowers basic human rights" (Flamm, 2003, para. 3). Victims of trafficking are physically confined, their travel or identity documents are taken away, their families are threatened if they do not cooperate, and they are made dependent on their traffickers for basic needs such as food and shelter. While the United Nations and other organizations are working to curb the illegal trafficking of women and children, it continues to be a significant problem everywhere in our increasingly interdependent world (Belles, 2015).

◪ COMMUNICATION TECHNOLOGY

Although we will detail the role of communication technology in contemporary organizations later in this text, it is important to say at the outset that the global business community—and the global markets, economy, and joint ventures that we have been describing—is in large part made possible by recent advances in communication technology. By **communication technology** we mean any type of electronic tool or device that may be used to enhance or enable information sharing or person-to-person interaction.

In this section, we'll consider topics of significant importance for organizational communication in the twenty-first century, most notably the ability of technology to transcend space and time, the threat of security issues and cybercrime, the concept of urgent organizations, and the importance of communication networks.

☐ Transcending Space and Time

Globalization requires companies to communicate in ways that transcend space and time, making former obstacles to communication (such as geography and time zones) largely irrelevant. For example, software and hardware manufacturer Texas Instruments has operations in Texas, Ireland, and Indonesia that allow it to conduct business 24/7. Before the workday ends in Indonesia, employees forward their work electronically to employees in Ireland, who are just starting the workday. The employees in Ireland, in turn, transmit their work to their counterparts in Texas before they sign off for the day. Increasingly, companies are relying on cloud computing as they store data and programs on the Internet instead of on local servers, ensuring continuous access for anyone in the company who needs it. In addition, programs like Google Drive, Dropbox, and Salesforce.com allow people in different locations to collaborate in the creation of documents and to share information both asynchronously and simultaneously.

We have also witnessed a surge in social media software programs and cloud-based applications that eliminate the need for bulky information clearinghouses and instead provide easy access to others who have the needed information. The explosion of interest over the last decade in programs and apps like Facebook, Instagram, Twitter, Snapchat, Vine, and similar sites reflects a fundamental shift in how people both visualize and access their social networks. These programs remove many traditional barriers and offer numerous tools to promote unprecedented levels of collaboration and connection. The shift is so significant that many people who didn't grow up during the digital age have trouble appreciating it. At a recent dinner party in Tampa, a prominent business leader and philanthropist was complaining about what he saw as increasing reliance on computers, when a twenty-something medical student quietly commented, "Wikipedia got me through medical school." What these programs offer people is extensive, near-instantaneous access to global networks of individuals facing similar challenges and possessing potentially useful information for addressing them.

☐ Contemplating Security Concerns

Increased connectivity has some risks and drawbacks, in part due to the exponential development of "smart" technology and the "Internet of things," which includes both traditional electronics (refrigerators, home-security systems) and everyday items embedded with sensors connected to the Internet. All of these "openings" to potential hackers create a situation in which security is almost impossible to ensure. Over the past few years, there has been an explosion in **cybercrime** worldwide with more than twenty major security breaches (defined as greater than thirty thousand records stolen) recorded annually in the United States, some of which were actually much larger and affected millions of people both practically and financially (e.g., eBay, Adobe).

Threats to identity and security become even more alarming considering that the future of communication technology is aimed at ever-closer integration between information software and biological processes, sometimes referred to as **wetware**. As scientists exploit the advantages of augmenting our bodies with sensors and intelligent software (which already happens when we implant microchips into pets), this also opens us to greater levels of surveillance, control, and attack from hackers or others who wish to steal from us or disrupt our daily activities. Even without a physical human-machine connection, things like smart clothing, the Apple Watch, and the ubiquity of GPS-equipped smartphones afford unprecedented opportunities for surveillance. Finally, the proliferation of drone technology has governments scrambling to establish workable regulations around the rights and responsibilities for dealing with potential widespread surveillance.

☐ Understanding Urgent Organizations

Despite the risks involved, success in organizations depends significantly on their ability to make productive use of the latest communication technologies. Specifically, these technologies are used in two ways: (1) to bring elements of an organization closer together in the service of increased effectiveness and efficiency, and (2) to bring the organization closer to the customer. Both types of connectivity have the similar effect of increasing engagement and connection, and they also raise expectations about access to products, services, information, and response time. Consequently, we view most businesses today as **urgent organizations**, companies whose main challenge is to shorten the time in which employees can respond to customers and to one another. When a new technology allows a dramatic change in the relationship between businesses and their customers, it can lead to a complete reworking of the business model and is considered "disruptive."

A trend that began with fast food, faxing, and overnight mail continues today with the proliferation of ATMs, virtual libraries, medical clinics, and customer service call centers that are open twenty-four hours a day, seven days a week. The main motivation for convenience and speed is increased competitiveness. Customers now expect to get exactly what they want, when they want it (Gleick, 2000). And in the world of public safety, the increase in volume of 911 calls, for example, has prompted some communities to create 912 numbers for other serious situations, reserving 911 for true emergencies. Moreover, this increase in speed is often accompanied by extreme customization.

Speed conveys a number of advantages to one company over another (Stalk, 1998). Consider three examples. First, companies vie to see how quickly they can bring a new product or service to market. Often, the first company to release a new product has an edge and can sometimes set the standard by which future products are measured. Second, businesses today compete over who can provide the quickest response time to customer inquiries and concerns. In the personal computer industry, Dell has made an enormous investment in next-day, on-site service if needed, but most problems can be resolved over the phone with a customer service representative. Finally, companies today strive to shorten delivery times so that products or services are available to customers as close to the moment of purchase as possible. In the past, it was common for delivery to take six to eight weeks for a simple order; today people expect customized items to be shipped within a few days. Amazon, for example, is experimenting with same-day delivery of products using drones. Amazon states on their website that they are excited about their new service called Prime Air that promises to "safely get packages into customers' hands in 30 minutes or less using small unmanned aerial vehicles."

Pressure on managers and employees to work faster and to be available around the clock has increased as they struggle to keep their customers and, ultimately, their jobs. These expectations dovetail what has become a pervasive addiction of people to smartphones, which are increasingly reducing the ability to pay close attention to other individuals. In light of research into the myth of effective multitasking (Crenshaw, 2008), many leadership teams have been considering whether they should create new rules or restrictions about electronic access while in meetings. While 24/7 access to employees has a clear upside for customers, its downside is the toll it may take on productivity, as well as the health of employees and their personal relationships.

An interesting tension emerges from the twin pressures to provide responsive service, on the one hand, and to remain fast and flexible as a company, on the other. The ability to provide instantaneous, customized responses—or what has been called "just-in-time, just-for-me" service—requires a significant investment in people, training, and technology. As a result, large companies with substantial financial resources have a competitive advantage. Since size is itself an obstacle to flexibility and innovation, these large firms often seek to provide more responsive service by purchasing smaller companies with proven technologies and a loyal customer base. A good example is Google's purchase of Waze, the app that takes traffic conditions into account when providing driving directions.

One consequence of this pattern is that it is nearly impossible to compete in any industry today as a midsize company. Midsize companies have neither the entrepreneurial swiftness of smaller companies nor the mega capital and reputation of the big firms to sustain them. Although this is not necessarily a welcomed change, it seems inevitable that in most industries we will soon have only three or four major players that control the vast majority of the market (Hoffman, 2012). At the same time, it will be interesting to see whether recent trends to establish businesses that are expressly committed to local suppliers and local customers can survive in this intimidating economic landscape.

☐ Relying on Communication Networks

Regardless of their geographic reach, successful businesses today must use new communication technology to connect with networks of employees and other stakeholders. Informal **communication networks**—relationships with trusted coworkers characterized by quick, verbal communication—are the most dynamic source of power in contemporary organizations because of the important role they play in responding to a turbulent business environment. Formal reporting relationships specified by the organizational chart (for those companies that still have organizational charts!) are far too limiting to be effective. Informal relationships allow employees to get things done across functions within companies, across organizations, and among business, government, and other stakeholders. And as we mentioned earlier, new communication technology has made social networking easy and commonplace, connecting people worldwide.

This reliance on informal connections for organizing has strong parallels in what has been called the Arab Spring, which began in 2010. Protesters and rebels across a wide range of Middle Eastern countries overthrew their governments, many of which were long-standing dictatorships. Despite dictators' best efforts to suppress the spread of information about turmoil in their countries, tens of thousands of people posted descriptions and videos directly from the sites of the unrest. Many believe that these modern communication capabilities were the key factor in reaching a tipping point in the history of these nations (Hudson, Iskandar, & Kirk, 2014).

The power of new forms of communication to shape social life at all levels continues everywhere in the world. In one example, the leaders of drug cartels in lawless regions of Mexico have been confronted with tens of thousands of citizens supporting the police through anonymous Web postings. Their response was to execute people and publicly display their bodies, but this did nothing to decrease the online chatter. While it might be easy to intimidate a single politician or journalist, it is nearly impossible to silence a network of outrage. Another example was the Occupy Wall Street movement that started in the United States in 2011 and received little mainstream media attention initially but developed an online presence and spread worldwide. A final example is the tremendous outpouring of sympathy and gun control activism that exploded in social media after the mass killing at the Pulse nightclub in Orlando, Florida. It appears that the latest developments in communication technology can, in some cases, deliver on the promise of letting people's voices be heard and encouraging social equality.

◪ CHANGES IN THE MEANING OF WORK

A twenty-two-year-old college graduate defers her law school entrance for one year to serve in the Peace Corps in Central America. A sixty-year-old hospital executive at the peak of his career retires early to spend time with his wife who has chronic health problems. A thirty-seven-year-old working mom gets laid off but becomes a flexible independent contractor rather than seeking new, full-time employment. These individuals illustrate the rethinking of the meaning of work in our contemporary society.

In this final section of the chapter, we explore three dimensions of this shift, focusing specifically on the development of a new social contract between organizations and employees; ethical abuses by corporations which are causing many to be wary of putting too many eggs in one employment basket; and quality-of-life issues that are causing some to reevaluate the role and purpose of work.

□ The New Social Contract

Over the last hundred years, many people left their homes, farms, and communities to work for large companies in exchange for wages. Many of these employees worked for a single company and were rewarded with a secure job and a decent pension. The old social contract stipulated that acceptable performance and good behavior would be rewarded with lifetime employment. At the close of the twentieth century, however, this relationship between organizations and employees became obsolete, both in the United States and abroad. With global competition came plant closings, downsizing, and cutbacks. As economies adjusted, people were rehired under different terms, as either temporary or short-term contract employees.

The **new social contract** is a different kind of employment relationship in which job security is fleeting and tied expressly to whether one's skills fit an organization's needs at a specific time. Many owners jump at the possibility of selling their firm for a tidy profit and employees are often on the lookout for a better opportunity. Many business schools teach their students to think of themselves as a small business and to see their careers as a series of finite contracts with corporations (Hakim, 1995). In this new environment, employees must engage in continual learning to remain in demand; at the same time, businesses strive to attract and retain the best talent. In this spirit, one of Pfizer's senior human resources managers is now director of "talent management," with the job of continually re-recruiting the best employees, making sure that they are challenged, satisfied, and likely to stay with the firm.

Under the new social contract, the career ladder (an expectation that one's career will follow an orderly progression of increasingly responsible jobs in the hierarchy) has been replaced by the opportunity to work on an expanding set of tasks in order to hone one's skills and apply them through a web of work opportunities and projects. Since careers don't usually follow predictable paths in today's workplace, personal connections and interpersonal relationships have become even more essential for success.

But what does success in the workplace mean today? Some have questioned the very existence of jobs in the future, based on the observation that many people are opting out of working for others altogether, pursuing a livelihood based on freelance activities instead. At a 2014 regional planning summit in the Piedmont Triad region of North Carolina, job forecasters argued that most workers are employed using a traditional W-2 classification (i.e., workers are considered full-time employees as opposed to temporary employees using a 1099 form or other mechanism for independent contracting). However, within the next three decades, they anticipate that the majority of workers in the United States will be employed using that 1099 form—meaning that future workers will, indeed, have to think of themselves more as independent entrepreneurs hired by larger organizations.

☐ Ethical Concerns

Another significant cause of change in the meaning of work stems from the distrust many feel toward organizations that have proven to be irresponsible and unethical. For many new graduates in particular, it's hard to imagine investing effort and time in an organization that knowingly harms the environment, denies particular employee benefits, advocates narrow social issues, or in general seems to prioritize profits over people.

The most infamous of these cases is Enron, now synonymous with grievous ethics violations. In 2001, as the company was clearly moving toward bankruptcy, it paid out $681 million in cash and stock to its 140 most senior managers (averaging nearly $5 million per manager), while most of Enron's former employees received a maximum of only $13,500 in severance pay ("Managing to make money," 2002). The documentary film *Enron: The Smartest Guys in the Room* (Gibney, 2005) chronicles one perspective on the spectacular rise and fall of the Enron Corporation, foreshadowing the trials of Enron's most senior leaders (Kenneth Lay and Jeff Skilling), which resulted in their convictions. Lay died before he could be sentenced; and Skilling was convicted in 2006 of multiple federal felony charges relating to Enron's financial collapse and is currently serving the last year of a fourteen-year prison sentence at the Federal Correctional Institution in Waseca, Minnesota.

Another example of a company that struggled to deal with an unprecedented disaster was BP, formerly known as British Petroleum, in the wake of the 2010 catastrophic Deepwater Horizon explosion and the resultant oil spill. Investigations after the fact revealed lax safety inspections and an ineffective contingency plan, which led to eleven deaths and the largest oil spill in the history of the petro-leum industry. Unfortunately, this was not an isolated incident. The *Multinational Monitor* named BP as one of the ten worst corporations in both 2001 and 2005 based on its environmental and human rights records. A CNN report reveals that while the 2010 disaster was horrific, the company's initial response was also most unfortunate:

> BP was slow to acknowledge the problem initially. It consistently underestimated the magnitude of the spill by confessing to being "out of the loop" about decisions and processes on the rig, as CEO Tony Hayward did before a House panel last week. And the company failed to empathize with the plight of those most immediately affected by the spill—the families of those who lost their lives and those whose livelihoods are threatened. In these ways, senior management unintentionally dug itself a huge credibility hole. And as a consequence, it has attracted an extraordinary amount of outrage. (Kimberly, 2010, para. 4)

The actions of both BP and Enron's chief executives turned out to be the begin-ning, not the end, of significant ethical abuses by corporations. Organizations and employees must remain vigilant about the likelihood of such abuses whenever the reputations and personal wealth of a small number of individuals are at stake. One domestic statistic reflects the extreme concentration of wealth in the United States. According to the advocacy group United for a Fair Economy, the average annual CEO pay at top companies in 2014 was $13.5 million, or 373 times what an average employee makes (AFL-CIO, 2015). Income inequality has become an important subject around the world. The most recent data reveals that as of 2014, Russia is the most unequal country in the world, with the highest share of national wealth (84.8%) being held by those in its top 10 percent. The United States ranked sev-enth, with 74.6 percent of its wealth held by the top 10 percent, and the most equal countries in terms of wealth distribution were Belgium (with 47.2 percent) followed by Japan (48.5 percent) and Australia (51.1 percent). Barbara Ehrenreich's book *Nickel and Dimed: On (Not) Getting By in America* (2001) offers numerous dramatic examples of what this discrepancy looks like in real life, revealing how difficult it is to get by while working a low-paying job (or two or three).

In the wake of the historic economic crash in 2008, some of the wealthy and powerful in America used the mainstream, corporate-owned media to distract the public from the systemic realities underlying their struggle, and to call for even greater deregulation of industry and defunding of government programs, wrapping their appeals in the language of civil liberty, rugged individualism, and a renewed fear of socialism. Moreover, these same individuals advanced their beliefs in ways that produced the most polarized state of political dialogue in memory, wherein differing beliefs are routinely exposed to an "us versus them, good ver-sus bad" litmus test. The governments of many developed nations watched in amazement as some of our most educated and articulate citizens made public arguments reflecting a lack of compassion for those in our society who could not financially stand on their own two feet. The 2016 presidential campaign provides dozens of examples of polarization and demonization of the weak, the different, and the poor.

☐ Quality-of-Life Issues

In the midst of the tumultuous change in the social contract and important ethical considerations, new and hopeful values and priorities about employees' **quality of life**—the overall satisfaction with one's work experience in the context of other life experiences, constraints, and aspirations—have emerged. For example, many if not most workers struggle to succeed at work while also attending to the care of their children and parents (Drago, 2007). American workers, in particular, are altering their definition of life success to include not just a career but also deeper involvement with their communities and personal growth through a variety of life experiences. At the same time, today's workers want to feel valued and involved on the job. Where do these seemingly dueling values and priorities come from, and can individual workers comfortably achieve a high quality of life in today's world of work?

When it comes to balancing work and family, researchers often point to two primary factors that have contributed to this overall shifting of priorities, First, with fewer high-paying, unionized manufacturing jobs available in the United States, two-career families are prevalent. More than 66 percent of the workforce consists of dual-earner couples. Second, because grandparents and other members of extended families rarely live nearby, child care is a major expense and is increasingly in high demand. As a result, family issues have become a big part of the national political agenda.

Some businesses are moving to accommodate employees' needs by providing child care, flexible hours, and parental leave. Much of the current debate is over the management of employee time, as individuals and businesses seek ways to reconcile what can be competing priorities (Negrey, 2012). While flexible work programs have been hailed as a low-cost means of recruiting and retaining employees and enhancing productivity, recent trends reveal a surprising pattern. Organizations are offering fewer flextime schedules today than they were just a few years ago. One study conducted by the Society for Human Resource Management (SHRM) reports that 64 percent of organizations offered flextime in 2002. In 2011, that number dropped to 53 percent (SHRM, 2011). Analysts suggest that the current labor market does not require employers to offer flextime and other work-life programs to attract employees. Moreover, many employees are hesitant to ask for or demand flexible schedules because they believe it may signal a lack of commitment to the organization and put their careers in jeopardy. The SHRM also reports that managers tend to distrust women who request flextime, believing that they are using the time for personal as opposed to professional reasons. As such, they are more likely to award flextime requests to their male employees (SHRM, 2013). Nonetheless, a certain level of flexibility has clearly become an accepted part of most American workplaces.

Work, Wages, and Employee Well-Being

The average American adult spends more time working than on any other activity—even sleeping. Organizational communication often focuses on what we do when we're working, how we manage our work alongside the rest of our lives, and how we're compensated for that work. And a primary ethical concern that many organizations face is what to pay people who do the work.

The founder and CEO of Gravity Payments, a credit card processing company, ignited a firestorm across the business community when he announced in April 2015 that he was raising the *minimum* wage at his company to $70,000 a year. In response to his bold move, CEO Dan Price was quoted in the *New York Times* as saying, "I want to fight for the idea that if someone is intelligent, hard-working and does a good job, then they are entitled to live a middle-class lifestyle" (Cohen, 2015).

Many labor rights advocates praised the move, and Harvard Business School immediately launched a case study. However, less than two weeks after announcing the wage increase, Price's brother and cofounder filed a lawsuit against Gravity. Two of his best employees quit. Within three months of the announcement, several key clients canceled their services, citing concerns that the level of customer service *might* drop as a result of the employee raise.

While the employees who saw a significant bump in their salaries were generally appreciative, other long-term employees (many of whom were already making over $70,000 and saw little or no increase in salary) were less enthused. Moreover, management researchers started critiquing Price's motives and ethics for raising his employees' salaries—claiming that the research simply doesn't support the idea that happier workers are more productive workers.

What's particularly troubling about the Gravity case is that most workers, managers, and strategists seem to have accepted a version of capitalism that suggests workers have to be uncomfortable to do their best and that money is not our only motivator. If organizations attempt to be more equitable to employees, why are their leaders viewed with suspicion?

DISCUSSION QUESTIONS

1. To what extent do organizations tend to manipulate employee salaries as a way to increase employee productivity?
2. How would you feel if you were one of the employees who saw a significant wage increase? Would it change the way you worked? Would you work harder or the same as you had before?

(continued, Work, Wages, and Employee Well-Being)

3. Put yourself in the shoes of a long-term employee who was already making $80,000. How would you feel if you received no increase in salary? Would it change the way you worked? Would you treat your coworkers who did receive raises any differently?

4. If you were the founder and CEO of an organization and you had the opportunity to give your employees a significant raise—even if it wasn't a standard practice among your peer organizations—would you do it? Why or why not?

5. What motivates you to work? What kinds of activities would you engage in, even if no one paid you?

6. To what extent do you agree with the statement that happy workers aren't necessarily more productive? Explain your position.

Inspirational stories of individuals and organizations seeking to improve quality of life abound. For example, we find hope in organized efforts on the part of companies and their employees to conduct coordinated service work in their communities. Some of this support is financial, but even more of it is the donation of time to address critical community needs. It seems to us that this trend toward making an impact on the local community is in large part a reaction to globalization, consolidation of business, and the growing anonymity associated with multinational corporations. Local community service gives organizations and their employees the opportunity to express what they stand for and create a public face for the corporation within the community.

Yet not all rumination about quality of life exists outside of the office. Some of the values being espoused today signal a transformation of the meaning of work, rather than a retreat from it—from drudgery to a source of personal significance and fulfillment. Employees want to feel that the work they do is worthwhile, not just a way to draw a paycheck. For example, while white-collar workers and college students tend to view blue-collar workers as being motivated primarily by money, job security, and benefits, the most important incentives for workers at all levels include positive working conditions, good working relationships, and full appreciation for the work one does—all of which depend on supportive communication (Kovach, 1987). As we consider quality-of-life issues here and throughout this book, we must never forget that for many people, prioritizing work, family, community, and other endeavors is a luxury. "Sure," they say, "I want all those things—more meaningful work, more time for myself, more time with family and friends. But most of all I really need this job to survive!" This is especially true in light of the credit crisis and subsequent recession that began in 2007 and resulted in an unprecedented number of home foreclosures and record unemployment in the United States. The unemployed population includes many new college graduates who find that although American corporations have more money on hand than ever before in history, they are creating few new jobs. At the time of this writing, there is some indication that this trend is reversing and there could be significant job expansion in the coming years. At the same time, however, growth in employee wages has been minimal and continues to create problems for full economic recovery.

As the struggle to make work more meaningful continues, we must also seek to improve the education, living standards, and working conditions of those at the bottom of the economic ladder by setting priorities that include everyone. More specifically, we must recognize that traditionally disadvantaged groups—for example, people of color and women—are disproportionately represented among the working poor. This awareness must lead us to redouble our efforts to fight both racism and sexism on the way to establishing economic parity.

SUMMARY

Defining organizational communication for the twenty-first century requires the identification of important social trends and the repositioning of communication practices in an ever-changing landscape. In the current workplace environment, traditional ways of doing business—and of communicating—are no longer effective. Instead, new principles of effective organizational communication must be developed to reflect the new environment—principles that transcend time and space and that acknowledge the formation of a new social contract between owners and employees. Dissatisfaction with current forms of governance and unprecedented corporate corruption has created conditions for a new activism around the nature of work.

More specific changes that are prompting us to rethink the meaning and nature of work include globalization (and its associated advantages and disadvantages), enormous gains in communication technology (particularly social media), and changing values among the youngest generation regarding the role of work in overall quality of life. Taken together, all these factors are causing employees, leaders, and students of organizational communication to ask very different questions about how best to organize.

As we stated at the outset, the history of humanity is the history of organizing, which is in turn accomplished through communication. In the next chapters, we will consider more specifically the theories and definitions that will guide us toward a better understanding of organizational communication today and will equip us with concepts to influence organizing processes in ethical and responsive ways.

QUESTIONS FOR REVIEW AND DISCUSSION

1. Explain what is meant by the idea that organizing always involves bridging diverse perspectives. How is this idea directly related to the study and practice of communication at work?

2. What is meant by the statement "Answers to questions about organizational communication . . . are highly situated and perishable"? How is the answer to this question directly related to the idea that there are no hard-and-fast rules for effective communication?

3. Why might it be more important to learn how to ask good questions than it is to have set answers about communication in organizations?

4. Describe how the global economy, changing management practices, and information technologies have reshaped the world of work. Then explain how each of these changes has affected the study and practice of communication in organizations.

5. Describe the concept of the urgent organization. Explain how this concept relates to the idea of today's business being done in a "turbulent environment."

6. What is meant by the "new social contract"? What social changes helped create it?

7. How can studying organizational communication prepare you for the world of work, regardless of your future professional plans?

KEY TERMS

Communication network, p. 20
Communication technology, p. 17
Cybercrime, p. 18
Globalization, p. 7
Multicultural management, p. 10
New social contract, p. 21
Organizational communication, p. 4

Outsourcing, p. 7
Quality of life, p. 24
Trafficking, p. 16
Urgent organization, p. 18
Wetware, p. 18
Worldview, p. 3

CASE STUDY

The Case of the "Italian" Shoes

Affluent and aspiring fashionistas worldwide put a premium on owning luxury brands of shoes, handbags, and accessories that have long been designed and manufactured in Paris, Milan, and London. Brands like Prada and Burberry conjure scenes of the European countryside and generations of handcrafted excellence.

However, many of these high-end companies have quietly chosen to manufacture many of their products in Asia. There are many economic incentives for doing so. In addition, however, the European owners (speaking anonymously, of course) draw a striking contrast between work attitudes and capabilities in many Asian countries and in Europe. Specifically, they describe European employees as demanding and inflexible and Asian employees (and organizations) as speedy, responsive, and highly adaptive. Moreover, these business leaders describe the craftsmanship coming from Asian suppliers as increasingly on a par with that of Western European workers.

These high-end companies continue to label their wares as "made in Italy" or "made in Paris" because local laws allow such labeling even when only a small portion of the work (typically the final assembly) is completed in the designated country or city. As this situation comes to light, few people can agree about its meaning and appropriateness.

ASSIGNMENT

1. Do you see a difference between what these companies are doing and the illegal production of counterfeit ("knockoff") products that are fraudulently stamped with a designer label and sold on street corners?
2. What are the communication ethics of labeling a product as made in a country (typically for marketing reasons) when it is only minimally true? Do you think that companies should have to disclose all of the locations where their products are made? Why or why not?
3. What effect will the globalization of the workforce, and in particular the rising capabilities of Asia, likely have on Western countries with more traditional, less flexible workforces and often more complicated labor rules?
4. Do you foresee a future for products that feature a specific location as a selling point? What is your prognosis for expressly "local" production (e.g., food or goods from a particular location) in a global economy?

CHAPTER 2

Defining Organizational Communication

Throughout history, humans have been organizing. Whether it's planning an event, coaching a team, or running a multinational corporation, organizing is always involved, as is the concern for how to do it better.

Professionals with an interest in improving organizational communication do not always use the same definitions and assumptions, however. When engineers speak of the importance of communication, for example, they typically refer to its role in promoting clarity and consensus. In contrast, a group of clergy calling for improved communication would likely focus on the power of discourse to build community and compel moral action.

In this chapter, we will discuss the importance of communication definitions and approaches and describe some common approaches to organizational communication, including models of communication as information transfer, transactional process, strategic control, and a balance of creativity and constraint. We conclude with a description of organizations as dialogues and examine the role of dialogue in working ethically and with integrity.

THE IMPORTANCE OF COMMUNICATION DEFINITIONS AND APPROACHES

You may be wondering why you should learn about the competing definitions and approaches. Your study and understanding of organizations and communication will be enriched by this knowledge because each approach offers a different way of understanding communication and responding to it when working in organizations. This is because definitions are shorthand terms for situations (Burke, 1984). They sum up how you decide what needs to be accomplished and then provide direction for the best way to act. And they offer an additional advantage: They prepare you for success. Understanding key definitions is an important foundation for learning how to talk about communication in business settings.

Consider the following short list of common business terms and definitions:

- *Accounts payable (AP)*. The bills that a business needs to pay. An example of an AP is the invoice a business receives when buying supplies from a manufacturer. These bills are considered liabilities.
- *Accounts receivable (AR)*. The debts owed to a business. If the business sells a product or service to a customer who does not pay at the time of sale, the money owed to the business is considered an AR. These debts are considered assets.
- *Assets*. Property that a business owns. This includes anything that has value such as cash, ARs, inventory, supplies, and equipment.
- *Earnings*. A business's income or profit; its revenues minus its expenses.
- *Equity*. The difference between a business's assets and its liabilities.

Knowledge of these terms and definitions, as well as of the theories that inform them and the case studies that make use of them, is expected of anyone who graduates from college with a degree in communication or business, or has completed a course in organizational communication. The ability to use these terms in everyday conversation is part of what it means to work effectively and add value in any organization. Without this knowledge of basic terms and definitions, you would be less valuable to your employer because you would lack the foundational language of business to inform your choices and actions.

APPROACHES TO ORGANIZATIONAL COMMUNICATION

Having established the importance of the definitions and approaches of organizational communication, we introduce you to the four approaches that have attracted the greatest number of adherents: (1) communication as information transfer, (2) communication as transactional process, (3) communication as strategic control, and (4) communication as a balance of creativity and constraint.

Communication as Information Transfer

The **information-transfer approach** views communication as a pipeline through which information flows from one person to another. Managers communicate well when they transfer their knowledge to subordinates and others with minimal spillage. According to Steven Axley (1984), this version of communication has four assumptions:

1. Language allows us to transfer thoughts and feelings from one person to another.
2. Speakers and writers put thoughts and feelings into words.
3. Words contain those thoughts and feelings.
4. Listeners or readers extract those thoughts and feelings from the words.

The information-transfer approach, popularized in the 1950s, compared human communication to the flow of information over a telegraph or telephone wire. Clear one-way communication was emphasized as a means of impressing and influencing others. Viewed this way, communication is defined as "the exchange of information and the transmission of meaning" (Dessler, 1982, p. 94), and the process of transmission is not seen as problematic—that is, "If I say it and you can hear it, you ought to understand it" (Feldman & March, 1981). An analogy can be made to the classroom teacher who relies completely on lectures, never stopping to engage with students. The underlying belief is that since the professor said it, students should get it.

According to this perspective, *miscommunication* occurs when no message is received or when the message that is received is not what the sender intended. Typical communication problems include information overload, distortion, and ambiguity.

- *Information overload* occurs when the receiver becomes overwhelmed by the information that must be processed. Three factors can contribute to information overload: (1) amount, or the quantity of information to be processed; (2) rate, or the speed at which the information is presented; and (3) complexity, or the amount of work it takes to process the information (Farace, Monge, & Russell, 1977). For example, a government worker in an understaffed bureaucracy may have to deal with mountains of simple, steady work; an ER nurse may face varying amounts of complex information at a relentless pace; a community member may have to consult several different city and county offices in order to process a single urgent request.
- *Distortion* refers to the effects of noise on the receiver's ability to process the message. Noise can be semantic (the message has different meanings for the sender and the receiver), physical (like when you have a poor connection and only hear every other word on a cell phone call), or contextual (the sender and the receiver have different perspectives that contribute to the miscommunication). An example would be trying to communicate with a coworker who is experiencing a personal crisis. Although you may be saying potentially helpful things, the coworker's internal emotional "noise" may prevent him or her from hearing your message.
- *Ambiguity* occurs when multiple interpretations of a message cloud the sender's intended meaning. Abstract language and differing connotations are common sources of ambiguity. When a manager asks two different employees to

work a little harder, for instance, one might put in an extra half hour a day, and the other might work all night.

The information-transfer approach is summarized in the linear model of communication. In it, communication occurs when a sender shares a message through a specific channel to a receiver. The sender encodes an intended meaning into words, and the receiver decodes the message when it is received, though noise (both internal and external distractions) can alter the intended meaning. The linear model is depicted in Figure 2.1 below.

The information-transfer model remains a useful way to explain certain communication situations in organizations, such as the giving and receiving of technical instructions, or general announcements among employees. It is especially helpful in considering broadcast messages in which it is key to reach large numbers of people at once (e.g., safety alerts). This model also highlights beliefs about communication that are still practiced by many managers and supervisors who often assume that when they send a message, workers automatically get it.

The information-transfer approach reveals one way of thinking about communication and evaluating its effectiveness that is based on receivers understanding what meaning senders intend and doing what senders tell them to do. In some situations—for example, giving instructions to a child about the care and feeding of a family pet—it's fine. Once you understand the definition of *information transfer* as well as the strengths and limitations of that approach, you are better able to select it as a communication strategy when it best fits the situation and make it work for you.

Critics of the information-transfer approach argue that it is simplistic and incomplete, as it paints a picture of communication as a sequential, linear, and almost automatic process (i.e., "I throw you a message, then you throw one back"). It assumes that the receiver remains passive and is uninvolved in constructing the meaning of the message. Despite these objections, the information-transfer

FIGURE 2.1

The Linear Model

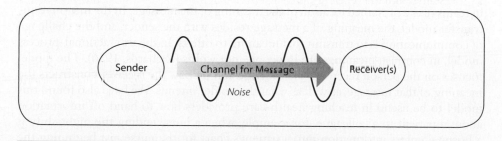

approach persists in many people's understanding of organizational communica-tion. For example, the general manager of a large aerospace company hired several Air Force pilots to fly over his manufacturing plant and drop hundreds of flyers with the message: "Satisfy your customer with first-time quality." When one of us met with this manager a month later, he was dumbfounded to learn that employee attitudes and behaviors had not changed to comply with the message—they were continuing to produce work that did not meet customer expectations. His exact words were "I told them what to do, so why aren't they doing it?"

□ Communication as Transactional Process

Dissatisfaction with the limitations of the information-transfer approach to com-munication led to the development of the **transactional-process model**. This approach asserts that in human communication, clear distinctions are not made between senders and receivers. Rather, people play both roles simultaneously. "All persons are engaged in sending and encoding as well as receiving and decoding messages simultaneously. Each person is constantly sharing in the processes, and each person is affecting the other" (Wenberg & Wilmot, 1973, p. 5).

The transactional-process approach, depicted in Figure 2.2, highlights the importance of feedback, or information about how a message is received, and particu-larly nonverbal feedback, which may accompany or substitute for verbal feedback. Consider, for example, the nonverbal messages that students send to instructors during a lecture to indicate their degree of attention and comprehension. While the members of one class may be totally engaged and making consistent eye contact with the teacher, the members of another class may be slouching, fidgeting, and avoid-ing the instructor's gaze. Right or wrong, most teachers will imbue these nonverbal behaviors with meaning and interpret the first class as more engaged and intelligent. The importance of this nonverbal communication is captured by the axiom "You cannot not communicate" (Watzlawick, Beavin, & Jackson, 1967, p. 49). In other words, a person need not speak to communicate; nonverbal messages are conveyed through a person's silence, facial expressions, body posture, and gestures. As a result, any type of observable behavior is a potential message (Redding, 1972).

The transactional-process model differs from the information-transfer approach in terms of the presumed location of the meaning of the message. In the information-transfer model, the meaning of a message resides with the sender, and the challenge of communication is to transmit that meaning to others. In the transactional-process model, in contrast, meanings are in people, not words (Richards, 1936). The model focuses on the person receiving the message and on how the receiver constructs the meaning of that message, as well as what the sender intends. We have also found this model to be useful in teaching health-care providers how to hand off information about a patient to a colleague, for example, when a nurse ending the night shift at a hospital enters information into a patient's chart for the nurse just beginning the morning shift. Rather than simply handing the information off and heading out the

FIGURE 2.2

The Transactional-Process Model of Communication

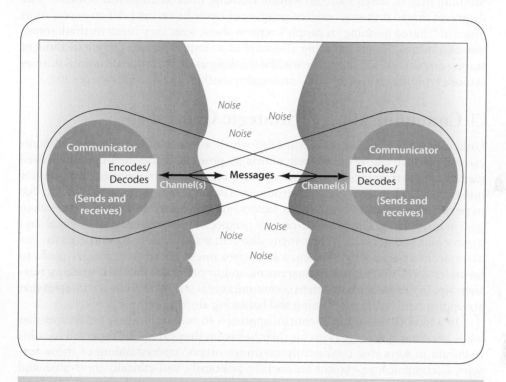

door, senders promote effective communication when they pause and make sure that receivers "grasp" the message. This is also an opportunity for receivers to clarify and ask questions—questions that could be critically important for the health and safety of the patient (Wohlauer, M., et al., 2012).

One area to which the transactional-process model can be usefully applied is organizational leadership. Ideas about leadership have evolved from the simple belief that certain people are born with leadership skills to the acknowledgment that leadership involves a transaction between leaders and followers. Successful leaders can shape the meanings that followers assign to what leaders say or do. In this sense, then, leadership is the transactional management of meaning between leaders and followers. Compare this to the information-transfer model, which instead gauges a leader's effectiveness solely on his or her ability to put across a message. In contrast, the transactional-process model suggests that a common understanding may emerge over time between a leader and his or her followers as a result of a series of communication exchanges.

Many experts criticize the transactional-process view for its emphasis on the creation of shared meaning through communication. This bias toward shared meaning may be based more on wishful thinking than on empirical research. The degree of shared meaning between people can never be verified. All one ever has as proof of "shared meaning" is people's reports about what they mean or think someone else means. Shared meaning also implies widespread convergence of thought among employees, which may be wishful thinking as organizational communication is more typically characterized by ambiguity, conflict, and diverse viewpoints.

☐ Communication as Strategic Control

Unlike the transactional-process model, which assumes that effective communicators are clear and open in their efforts to promote understanding and shared meaning, the **strategic-control perspective** regards communication as a tool for influencing and shaping one's environment (Parks, 1982). It recognizes that, due to personal, relational, and political factors, greater clarity is not always the main goal in interaction. The strategic-control perspective sees communicators as always having multiple goals, as well as many different ways of pursuing those goals. For example, in a performance review, a supervisor might have three primary goals: to be understood, to motivate improvement, and to preserve a positive working relationship. In this view, a competent communicator is one who chooses strategies that are appropriate for accomplishing and balancing among multiple goals.

In addition, the strategic-control approach to communication recognizes that while people may have reasons for their behavior, they cannot be expected to communicate in ways that consistently maximize others' understanding of those reasons. Communicative choices are socially, politically, and ethically motivated, and there are often conflicts between or among those motivations. For example, we all recognize that others may violate the communicative expectations of clarity and honesty in the workplace when they believe it is in their political interest to do so. You may recall a time when a boss asked you how you were doing and you replied, "Just fine!" even when you were feeling tired, frustrated, and stressed. You likely recognized that a completely honest response in that case would not serve your best interests.

The practical limitations of broad generalizations about what constitutes effective communication led to a focus on communication as goal attainment in specific situations, as a means to accomplish one's ends through saying not necessarily what you mean, but instead what is appropriate for the setting and the audience. Viewed this way, communicators must be able to recognize the constraints of the situation, as well as the perspectives of others, and adapt to multiple goals simultaneously by being clear and assertive about personal goals while at the same time being respectful of others (Tracy & Eisenberg, 1991).

The strategic-control approach also makes room for **strategic ambiguity**, an important concept that describes the ways in which people may communicate unclearly—or at a more abstract level—but still accomplish their goals (Eisenberg, 1984). Strategic ambiguity accomplishes the following goals:

- *It promotes unified diversity.* Strategic ambiguity takes advantage of the diverse meanings that different people can give to the same message. For example, Nike's slogan "Just Do It" and Apple's "Think Different," are sufficiently ambiguous to allow consumers to read their own meanings into them. Another example of the use of strategic ambiguity that allows room for multiple interpretations is the invocation of wholesome family values by political parties. Politicians can vary their behavior, beliefs, and promises while still claiming that they endorse this highly abstract concept.

- *It preserves privileged positions.* Strategic ambiguity preserves privileged positions by shielding those with power from close scrutiny by others. A seasoned diplomat or a professor emeritus giving a speech, for example, is traditionally given the benefit of the doubt by supporters who may have to fill in some gaps in their understanding.

- *It is deniable.* By being less than precise (e.g., in providing a lukewarm reference for a mediocre colleague), employees can protect confidentiality, avoid conflict, and conceal key information that may afford them a competitive advantage. In this sense, strategic ambiguity is said to be deniable; that is, the words seem to mean one thing, but under pressure they can appear to mean something else.

- *It facilitates organizational change.* Strategic ambiguity facilitates organizational change by allowing people the interpretive room to change their specific activities while appearing to keep those activities consistent with more abstract goals. For example, the advent of air travel challenged transatlantic ocean liner companies that provided passage by ship. The firms that defined themselves solely as transportation companies did not survive, whereas those that interpreted their business more broadly (and ambiguously) as "entertainment" went on to develop leisure cruise businesses. In a completely different context, community colleges in many states are finding ways to remain true to their locally engaged and targeted vocational missions while at the same time expanding their offerings into broader four-year degree programs.

For an example of the pros and cons of strategic ambiguity, see *What Would You Do?* on page 38.

Unlike the other models of communication, the strategic-control approach challenges the idea of shared meaning as the primary basis or motivation for communication. Rather, it holds that shared meaning is an empirically unverifiable concept (Krippendorff, 1985) and that the primary goal of communication should be organized action (Donnellon, Gray, & Bougon, 1986). If we accept that the meaning one person creates may not correspond to the meaning that another person gives to the same message, it is less important that the two people understand each other than it is that they act in mutually satisfying ways (Weick, 1995).

It's Not Personal, It's Just Policy: Organizational Ambiguity in Action

The strategic use of ambiguity can have positive or negative influences on the quality of organizational life. One arena of organizational communication in which strategic ambiguity plays out is in writing and enforcing organizational policy. Viewed from a positive perspective, strategically ambiguous policy language can open up possibilities in a policy text and help policymakers avoid the creation of overly oppressive rules. From a negative perspective, strategic ambiguity can also be used to justify some fairly insidious communication practices.

Such was the case when a meteorologist from Shreveport, Louisiana, was fired from her position at a local news station. According to a formal statement from KTBS, Rhonda Lee was dismissed for responding to a viewer comment on the station's Facebook page, which the news organization claimed violated its policy on social media (O'Brien, 2012).

The meteorologist was dismissed after defending her choice of hairstyle to a viewer, who claimed that her hair was not something that "looks good on TV" and likened her to a "cancer patient" (Smith, 2012). Rhonda, who is African American, wears a very short, natural hairstyle. In a post to the station's Facebook page, she responded to the comment comparing her to a cancer patient by stating, "I'm in perfectly healthy physical condition." She then turned to the underlying tone of the original comment, which she viewed as a critique of her "ethnic hair." She wrote:

> I'm very proud of who I am and the standard of beauty I display. Women come in all shapes, sizes, nationalities, and levels of beauty. Showing little girls that being comfortable in the skin and HAIR God gave me is my contribution to society. (Smith, 2012).

Rhonda alleged that she was terminated because she defended her "ethnic" hair, but the station maintained that she was fired for violating its social media policy. In support of this position, the station manager posted a copy of an e-mail about the station's Facebook page. The e-mail stated, "When we see complaints from viewers, it's best not to respond at all" (O'Brien, 2012). Rhonda claimed that she was not aware of the rule, and when she pressed for additional evidence about the station's policy, she was informed that the policy "isn't written down" (Smith, 2012).

DISCUSSION QUESTIONS

1. How does Rhonda Lee's termination illustrate the deniability aspect of strategic ambiguity and the strategic-control perspective? Moreover, how does this example demonstrate the ways in which the strategic-control perspective can sidestep issues of ethics?
2. How would you respond to being fired for violating a policy that you did not know existed, or more important, for violating a policy that isn't formally written down? Alternately, what if you were asked to fire someone for violating a policy that you didn't completely understand or did not personally agree with?
3. How might social media sites, like Facebook, Twitter, Instagram, and others perpetuate the problems associated with strategically ambiguous policy statements and the strategic-control perspective as a whole? How would you advise an organization to use (or not use) social media to respond to personal attacks and negative feedback?

Although the strategic-control perspective advances our appreciation of the subtleties of communication, it is not without problems. First, it minimizes the importance of ethics. While strategic ambiguity is commonplace in organizations, it is all too often used in an attempt to escape blame. When called on to testify about their actions in a court of law, many if not most executives will make good use of the wiggle room or plausible deniability afforded by vague or ambiguous language. That way, when positive consequences accrue from their actions they can claim credit, but when bad things happen they can quickly identify an interpretation of events that lets them off the hook.

Another limitation of the strategic-control approach is its emphasis on the behavior of individuals or on individuals controlling their environment through communication, often at the expense of the community. As such, it clouds issues related to cooperation, coordination, power and inequality, empathy, and the interdependent relationships of individuals and groups. The strategic-control model suggests that the world is composed of independent communicators and rugged individualists working to control their own environments.

☐ Communication as a Balance of Creativity and Constraint

Let us now turn to our final definition of communication. We believe that it will offer you a new way of thinking about the choices you make and the actions you take in any for-profit or nonprofit business setting. It will also provide you with a way of talking about communication that will demonstrate to your coworkers, clients, customers, and others the value and importance of communication in everyday work life.

In this text, we define *organizational communication* as a **balance of creativity and constraint**. We believe that communication is the moment-to-moment working out of the tension between individual creativity and organizational constraint. The phrase "moment-to-moment working out of the tension" refers specifically to the balance of creativity, which includes thinking innovatively, being willing to reexamine taken-for-granted routines and practices, encouraging new ideas, and so on; and constraints including the constructions of reality that limit the individual's choice of strategic response, such as deadlines, financial limits, organizational rules, and so on.

Since the late 1960s, the central focus of social theorists has been the relationship between individuals and society, which in our case translates to the relationship between employees and organizations. Two competing perspectives examine this relationship. The *macro* perspective sees individuals as being molded, controlled, ordered, and constrained by society and by social institutions. In contrast, the *micro* perspective sees individuals as active agents who create society and its social systems. Our definition of communication assumes both perspectives are true—simultaneously. This dichotomy has obvious implications for organizational communication, depending on whether the emphasis is on how employees communicate to create and shape organizations or on the constraints organizations place on that communication. In other words, while we no doubt conform to social pressures, rules, laws, and standards for behavior, "we are rule and system users and rule and system breakers as well" (Wentworth, 1980, p. 40).

Although many writers have contributed significantly to this line of thought, Anthony Giddens's (1984) theory of structuration is especially relevant to students of organizational communication. In discussing the relationships between individual communication and social systems and structures, Giddens simultaneously focuses on the creative albeit constraining aspects of structure, or what he calls the **duality of structure**. In this view, the designer of a new product advertisement is both bound by the rules, norms, and expectations of the industry *and* open to the possibility of transcending those structures by designing a creative ad. In this sense, creativity is the design and modification of social systems through communication.

The communication process is not viewed solely as what employees say to one another inside organizations but instead as how people organize real and symbolic resources, deal with conflicting goals in relation to those resources, manage multiple meanings, and contend with an ongoing stream of information, ambiguity, and change, all of which impact organizational outcomes (Barnard, 1968; Farace et al., 1977; Johnson, 1977; Weick, 1979). That is why we say that people create social reality or organize through communication in an ironic sense. They rarely get the reality they set out to create (Ortner, 1980). The process of designing a new restaurant, for example, is necessarily a series of compromises among differing dreams and worldviews. A restaurant owner must accommodate local government policies alongside her desire to make her own decisions; rising food costs alongside a chef who wants to cook innovatively; and a desire to provide consistently excellent customer service alongside servers who call in sick at the last minute. Rarely does one individual get to call all the shots. Both the physical design and the interpretations of that design are the result of negotiation.

The **theory of structuration** sees human behavior as an unresolvable, productive tension between creativity and constraint. William Wentworth (1980) reminds us that thinking of people as either inherently constrained or inherently creative does not offer a complete characterization of the relationships between individuals and society. Instead, he argues, social life is a balance of creativity and constraint—of constructing social reality and of being constrained by those constructions—and it is through communication that balance is achieved.

As an example of how the tension between creativity and constraint is constructed through communication, we can cite the meetings we attended at a company that manufactures hydraulic lifts. These staff meetings were controlled by the company president according to an agenda that he prepared. Most discussions were marked by short briefings on various topics such as new sales, personnel changes, and capital equipment expenditures, and little actual decision making. Although the executives in attendance were veteran decision makers, they knew from experience that the president viewed any opposing viewpoint as a sign of disloyalty. Nicknamed "Little General" by his direct reports, the president routinely embarrassed employees who disagreed with him or who attempted independent action. Over time, employee nonconfrontation was taken for granted by everyone on the senior team, and this dysfunctional pattern became an organizational reality (Berger & Luckmann, 1967). Despite the strong constraints on communication and the norm of passivity at the company, however, occasionally the urge to be creative broke through at meetings. An employee might, for instance, introduce a topic that was not on the president's agenda or present new data (tentatively!) that conflicted with data given by the president. By observing communication in these ways, we saw both creativity and constraint in action, as the company's norms were both applied and challenged.

Notice that this balancing act stimulates creativity as a strategic response to organizational constraints. In our example, the staff members acted on information they already had to guide their choices of when to speak and what to say. Unfortunately, however, the organizational reality of nonconfrontation limited their strategic choices and their ability to respond. Because the president seemed unable to respond to their initiatives positively and because they were unable to alter his construction of reality, the balance was tipped toward constraint and away from creativity. It was this lack of balance that made the staff meetings relatively unproductive, one-sided affairs.

Fortunately, the balance does not always tip in favor of constraint, although some degree of structure is always necessary. A great example of an organization known for encouraging idiosyncratic behavior on the part of its employees is Southwest Airlines. From its inception, Southwest has cultivated an organizational culture that values individual creativity and initiative, most keenly manifested in the employees' dress, informal attitude, and use of offbeat humor. One of their advertising campaigns—which included large posters of employees displaying outrageous facial expressions, hand gestures, and hairstyles—nicely illustrates this culture. But now that Southwest has grown significantly, acquired another carrier (AirTran), and started partnering with a third carrier (Delta), it will be interesting to observe whether it can retain its light-hearted edge. Similarly, companies such as Google, Pixar, and Zappos are nearly as well known for their creative, unique cultures (where employees are given significant freedom and bureaucracy is downplayed) as they are for their products and services.

To better understand the two approaches, reflect on the different classroom climates that you have experienced. More than likely, you will be able to place each on a continuum between those that emphasized constraint (strict rules, centralized control) and those that stressed creativity (flexible rules, tolerance for a range of acceptable behaviors).

Having now reviewed the high points of organizational communication theory — communication as information transfer, transactional process, strategic control, and a balance of creativity and constraint—we use the best concepts from each perspective to develop our own model of organizations as dialogues. A summary of the perspectives appears in Table 2.1. A specific representation of the balance metaphor for understanding organizational communication is shown in Figure 2.3.

TABLE 2.1

Organizational Communication: Preliminary Perspectives

COMMUNICATION AS INFORMATION TRANSFER	COMMUNICATION AS TRANSACTIONAL PROCESS	COMMUNICATION AS STRATEGIC CONTROL	COMMUNICATION AS A BALANCE OF CREATIVITY AND CONSTRAINT
Metaphor: Pipeline or conduit	*Metaphor:* Process	*Metaphor:* Control	*Metaphor:* Balance
Goal: Using communication as a tool to transfer information from sender to receiver.	*Goal:* Adapting messages to the needs and expectations of listeners.	*Goal:* Deploying ambiguous messages to take advantage of the diversity of meanings people often give to the same message to control environments and achieve multiple goals.	*Goal:* Working out the tension between individual creativity and organizational constraint in moment-to-moment interactions.
Measure of effectiveness: Receiver of communication understands (or does) what the speaker intended.	*Measure of effectiveness:* Senders and receivers share meaning.	*Measure of effectiveness:* Coordinated action is accomplished through diverse interpretations of meanings.	*Measure of effectiveness:* A balance between satisfied individuals and a cohesive community.

FIGURE 2.3

Communication as a Balance of Creativity and Constraint

Metaphor: Balance

Assumptions

1. The duality of structure: Individuals are molded, controlled, ordered, and shaped by society and social institutions; individuals also create society and social institutions.

2. Communication is the moment-to-moment working out of the tensions between the need to maintain order (constraint) and the need to promote change (creativity). As such, communication is the material manifestation of

   a. Institutional constraints
   b. Creative potential
   c. Contexts of interpretation

Representative Model

Creativity ————————————△———————————— Constraint

Communication

Description

Creativity	Communication	Constraint
Interpretations of meanings; all forms of initiative; new ways of organizing tasks and understanding relationships; resistance to institutional forms of dominance; uses of storytelling and dialogue to alter perceptions; uses of social constructions of reality to forge new agreements and to shape coordinated actions at work	Reveals interpretations of contexts; asks questions about resources for creativity and the presence of constraints; suggests the possibility of dialogue	Social and institutional forms, laws, rules, procedures, slogans, and management styles designed to gain compliance and limit dialogue at all costs; top-down decision making and problem solving

EVERYDAY ORGANIZATIONAL COMMUNICATION

Online Networking Profiles: Balancing Creativity and Constraint

Balancing creativity and constraint, the metaphor we conceived of as an analytic framework for organizational communication, can also be used to help individuals become more successful in their personal or professional endeavors. Let's consider the challenges of balancing creativity and constraint in an arena that you may already be familiar with: that of successful online networking and self-promotion.

If you are a student who wants to meet new people on campus, a college senior looking for an internship, a single person who wants to find a date, or a member of a new band that wants to be discovered, online networking sites like LinkedIn, Facebook, and Twitter may meet your needs. These sites allow groups and individuals to market themselves to a desired audience, whether a social group, a date, or a company, by posting online profiles that provide personal and professional information.

Some people, however, have trouble establishing the line between their private, personal information and their public, professional profiles. Not only must individuals and organizations negotiate social norms about what is appropriate to post online, they must also pay attention to ever-changing privacy controls. Because it tracks your interests, Facebook is more likely to invade your privacy, causing you to share things publicly that you may wish to keep private, whereas Twitter "is a lot less intrusive and does not force you to share your data, or of those you are associated with (at least so far)" (Wolfe, 2014). In any case, posting on social media requires you to walk the line between creativity and constraint as you seek to market yourself both appropriately and effectively.

The shifting norms of online networking encourage individuals to reveal key pieces of information. Successful dating profiles, for example, typically describe the writer's age, height, weight, hair color, profession, and personal interests as well as desired traits in a prospective date. Without this information, a profile will be entirely overlooked or considered suspect because of its glaring omissions. Sites like Match.com, OkCupid, and eHarmony allow room for creativity. Catchy profile titles attract visitors, as do personal photographs and open responses that allow the writer to relate additional information, from an explanation of a favorite hobby to a description of the ideal vacation.

At the same time, the desire to design a creative and catchy profile is often constrained by social norms about appropriate and inappropriate information. Students have been suspended and employees have been fired over inappropriate images that they have posted on Facebook. Although many sites have instituted privacy settings to protect users' information, these controls are not perfect. In a particularly ironic case, a private family photo of Mark Zuckerberg, the founder of Facebook, went viral on both Facebook and Twitter. While the Zuckerberg's made the picture of their family Christmas available only to their friends, that didn't stop one of those friends from sharing and retweeting that image.

DISCUSSION QUESTIONS

1. Which of the online profiles you've viewed stand out the most? What characteristics do they share? In what ways are they different?
2. How have you had to balance creativity and constraint around issues of privacy when constructing your own online profiles?
3. What are some of the other everyday contexts in which your life is organized through your attempts to balance creativity and constraint? Consider the choices you make about how you dress in various contexts (school, social events, work) or the way you interact in meetings at work, at a religious institution, or in a campus organization.
4. In which organizational environments do you organize your self-presentation in ways that favor creativity? In which environments do you accommodate organizational constraints? Why do you make those choices?

ORGANIZATIONS AS DIALOGUES

As we have discussed, human beings are both social and private beings. As such, we each establish a sense of self that is apart from the outside world (an identity) and that engages in a lifelong conversation with another sense of self that is a part of the outside world (membership in a family and community). The idea that a single person can envision and build a world to inhabit is a total fantasy—even if it were possible, when we were finished we would be totally alone. Conversely, if our contexts for interpretation came entirely from others, we would lose our unique identities. In other words, our very selves can be understood as a result of the balance between social constraints and individual creativity. Our self-concept is formed in part from the social relationships we have with others and from others' responses to what we say and do (Bakhtin, 1981; Blumer, 1969; Jackson, 1989).

According to George Herbert Mead (1934), the **self** consists of two interrelated "stories": (1) the story of "I," or the creative, relatively unpredictable part of a person that is usually kept private; and (2) the story of "me," or the socially constrained, relatively consistent part of a person that is more openly shared with others.

The "I" is impulsive, whereas the "me" strives to fit into society's rules and norms. The creative aspect of the self (the "I") desires meaningful action with others. The constraining aspect of the self (the "me") guides this action by anticipating responses and applying social rules of behavior. For our purposes, we are interested in how organizations provide a context for conversations that we have about ourselves, others, and our social realities. In this section, we discuss how our participation in dialogue is always informed by the contexts in which we find ourselves, as well as the key features of dialogue that cut across all contexts.

☐ Dialogue and the Situated Individual

We grow up and learn about life in multiple organized contexts, each of which has its own constraints (rules, norms, and expected understandings) that make it unique. These constraints play two roles: (1) They limit creativity and individual freedom, and (2) they suggest particular constructions of reality that assist in interpretation. For example, if a coworker leans over and kisses you against your wishes, it would be clear from the business context that such behavior is inappropriate and that a strong negative reaction on your part is warranted. If a family member does the same thing, the meaning would likely be entirely different, as would be your response.

Consider also how interpretation is complicated by multiple contexts in the typical family business or when spouses work together in the same company. You can imagine the conversations: "Dad, you can talk to me that way at home, but not here in front of the other employees!" or "How could you, my own wife, not support me in the faculty meeting?" Different contexts suggest different rules for action and interpretation. Even within a small organization, multiple contexts are always open to interpretation.

Similarly, in conducting performance appraisals, how tough should supervisors be on marginal performers? Seen in the context of the business as a financial entity accountable to shareholders, a supervisor should be direct and tough. In a context that emphasizes the supervisor-employee relationship, however, knowledge of a person's backstory and personal struggles could cause the supervisor to be more understanding. Interpreting and communicating in multiple contexts is one of the hardest things we do in organizations.

In fact, all individuals are situated in multiple contexts. In a broad sense, this means that behavior is both guided and constrained by the types of organizations with which we affiliate, whether they are capitalist enterprises, voluntary associations, nation-states, or families. More specifically, all behavior is situated in smaller, or more local, contexts. The **situated individual** is a person conducting the everyday business of constructing and maintaining the social realities in which he or she lives. As Anderson (1987) notes:

> The situated individual is connected to others through a network of shared, mutually negotiated, and maintained meanings. These meanings provide location, identity, action, and purpose to the individual. They tell me where I am, who I am, what I am doing,

how to do it, and why. . . . The network of meanings is not independent of the situated individual. It is the product of the interaction among situated individuals. (p. 268)

Difficulty is encountered when the multiple contexts impinging on an individual suggest inconsistent or conflicting communication or behavior. A study of Disneyland's corporate culture provides a detailed example of multiple conflicting contexts for interpretation (Smith & Eisenberg, 1987). In the early days of the theme park, employees used two metaphors, "the show" and the Disney "family," which were keyed to larger contexts. The first metaphor—Disneyland as a show—suggested that employees were actors who played important roles. They could thus be told by the "director" to act in particular ways because of "box office concerns" (e.g., to smile more or to style their hair differently). The other metaphor—Disneyland as a family—suggested a different and sometimes opposing context in which management, like a loving and concerned parent, took care of its employees and provided a nurturing environment. These conflicting contexts for interpretation had very different consequences for Disney policy, and in the mid-1980s, company employees called a rare strike in response to a pay cut that was being sold by management as a "sacrifice families are sometimes called upon to make." Recent case studies suggest that the show metaphor—so compatible with business—has won out. The company has continued to make business decisions that negatively impact employees in the name of show business—including in 2015 when they replaced long-term domestic employees with less expensive international employees hired through an outsourcing firm in India and brought to Orlando on temporary visas.

Another example of a struggle between multiple and potentially competing contexts took place in a Midwestern Catholic health-care system that was striving to improve the efficiency of its operations (Goodier & Eisenberg, 2006). Initially, the system adopted the Six Sigma quality-improvement process made famous at General Electric, complete with its vocabulary of "warfare" and "black belts." Almost immediately, there was pushback from longtime employees who felt this approach conflicted with the spiritual values of the institution. After much negotiation, they managed to modify the traditional vocabulary to create a hybrid they dubbed "soulful Six Sigma" that honored the assumptions and beliefs key to each context.

The situated-individual model of organizational communication may be summarized as follows:

1. The individual is an actor whose thoughts and actions are based on the interpretation of contexts.
2. More than one context always exists to guide the individual's actions and interpretations.
3. Communication is a practice that includes both interpretation and action; as such, it can reveal sources of creativity, constraint, meaning, interpretation, and context.

A final example will help clarify this notion of the situated individual. One of the authors of this textbook became involved with a problem facing a customer service manager at a large travel agency. The manager, we'll call her Laura, sought to convince management of her need for a full-time accountant to manage the record keeping of customer service billings. Laura's initial request was met with assurances from her boss that an accountant would be hired, but then management decided to deny her request. The problem, then, was how to interpret the denial and what, if anything, to do about it.

There were various possible ways to contextualize, or make sense of the situation. From Laura's point of view, the problem was the lack of expertise in her department and the need to address it by hiring an accountant. Members of the finance department saw the situation differently. Because they had sought for several years to hire their own accountant, they strongly resisted the idea that one might now be hired in customer service. As a result, rumors surfaced among the finance department staff about Laura's competency as a manager, suggesting that she would not need the new position if she were doing her job properly. Still another view of the situation came from the general manager of the travel agency who resisted the new hiring because none of the companies he had worked for in the past had an accountant in customer service. The board of directors based its disapproval on economic concerns: Shareholders would not be pleased by new hires in a recession. Finally, Laura's peers perceived her as aloof and a loner, rather than as a team player. Consequently, no informal group within the company was inclined to support Laura's agenda to hire an accountant. Laura might not have faced this problem if she had been more involved in informal communication networks or if the company had ways of considering multiple interpretations side by side in conversation—that is, in some form of dialogue.

Keep in mind that this is a *simple* example of how multiple contexts can inform the interpretation of selves, others, and action. Although the facts relating to the issue of whether to hire an accountant remain the same, the meanings of those facts are constructed differently depending on which context is applied. Because no one individual has access to all potential contexts, each individual's interpretation is based on a limited understanding of the reality being constructed. Fortunately, however, the limitations of one person's interpretations are usually offset by others' perspectives. When individuals work to coordinate their contexts, interpretations, communication, and actions, they are said to be organizing. One way of viewing this organizing process is as dialogue, some definitions of which are discussed next.

☐ Definitions of Dialogue

In our working definition of communication as a balance of creativity and constraint, we maintain that dialogue is balanced communication, or communication in which each individual has a chance to both speak and be heard. Dialogue has four features, each representing an increasing degree of collaboration and respect for the other. These include dialogue as (1) mindful communication, (2) equitable transaction, (3) empathic conversation, and (4) real meeting.

Dialogue as Mindful Communication

While many people believe that communication is mostly a conscious activity, studies have demonstrated that this is not the case. (For a comprehensive overview, see Langer, 1998; see also Motley, 1992.) In fact, communication and cognition researchers believe that most of us are somewhat **mindless**—communicating without conscious, purposeful intent—most of the time. This is because we rely on repeated forms of talk—*scripts*—that are easy to perform and whose likely outcomes are well known to us. Consider, for example, the following mindless exchange:

> "Hi, how are you doing?"
> "I'm fine, how are you?"
> "Good, good." Pause. "Well, then, see you later."
> "Okay. See you later."

An advantage of being able to speak mindlessly is that the brain reserves energy for more challenging situations (King & Sawyer, 1998). The disadvantage is the tendency to get locked into rigid habits of thought and action. Physicist and dialogue theorist David Bohm (1980) underscores this tendency in his distinction between "thinking" and "having thoughts." Most of the time, we mindlessly draw on the stories we have been told throughout our lives to make sense of new situations (i.e., we "have thoughts"); in contrast, thinking involves deep reflection on the nature of the situation and a conscious choice of appropriate frameworks. Unlike having thoughts, thinking implies a willingness to listen and be open to beliefs beyond what one already knows.

In contemporary American culture, you may observe mindless conversations about politics or the economy that echo sound bites and arguments drawn from partisan media sources. Rather than treat media claims as hypotheses requiring interpretation and critical analysis, many people accept the messages as presented and consequently "have thoughts" that they pass on to others in conversation. What is missing is careful consideration of the evidence supporting various claims and a willingness to explore compromise positions that could bring people with different viewpoints together through a negotiated understanding of the issues.

Of course, mindless communication can never be eliminated entirely as all of us employ necessary scripts much of the time. We are, however, concerned about how effective we can be in our work and home lives when we rely too much on these forms. Stephen Covey's *The Seven Habits of Highly Effective People* (1990) argues that being successful requires becoming more goal-oriented, focused, and strategic in our dealings with others. His prescriptions for success in the workplace prompt us to become more conscious of our communication and more reflective about the outcomes we wish to achieve.

As you can gather, a **mindful** approach to organizational communication enables us to understand talk "as a mental and relational activity that is both purposeful and strategic" (Goodall & Goodall, 2006, p. 52). Elaine Langer (1998) found that when we become more conscious of our communication, we become more mindful, and that when we become more mindful, we will likely behave with more integrity. We will learn to recognize that we are responsible for our communication goals, our communication choices, and our performance relative to achieving our goals. We are less apt to act thoughtlessly toward others.

Becoming more mindful in organizations requires us to (Goodall & Goodall, 2006):

- Analyze communication situations and develop strategies for accomplishing goals.
- Think actively about possible communication choices, especially those that don't seem like choices, as well as the potential organizational, relational, and personal outcomes of those choices.
- Adapt messages in a timely and thoughtful manner when seeking to inform, amuse, persuade, or otherwise influence listeners and audiences.
- Evaluate the feedback or responses we receive as an indication of how successful we were in accomplishing our purpose.

Mindful communication requires discipline and regular practice. It begins when we catch ourselves behaving mindlessly and decide to become more conscious of our interactions. It improves as we find that by not using scripts as much, we see new possibilities in our relationships with others. It provides us with a foundation for building trust and behaving authentically with others, which, in turn, encourages others to act with greater integrity toward us. Becoming more conscious communicators affords us one additional, crucial benefit: It promotes an environment in which an equitable exchange of ideas is possible.

Dialogue as Equitable Transaction

An **equitable transaction** from a communication perspective is one in which all participants have the ability to voice their opinions and perspectives. In defining dialogue this way, we call attention to the fact that not everyone in an organization has an equal say in making decisions or in interpreting events. In the traditional manufacturing organization, people in low-level jobs were discouraged from "interact[ing] with anybody in the organization unless [they] got permission from the supervisor, and then he wanted to know what [they] were going to talk about. So there's this notion in an organization that talking to people is not what your job is, that talking to people [means] interfering with . . . productivity" (Evered & Tannenbaum, 1992, p. 48). Even in some progressive companies, certain people's opinions are valued more highly than others', as these individuals can back up what they say with rewards or sanctions.

One way to learn about how individuals participate in organizational dialogues is to ask questions about **voice**, the ability of an individual or group to participate in the ongoing organizational dialogue, and to pay close attention to when, where, and for how long individuals speak. In most organizations, a few voices are loud and clear (e.g., those of the owners or senior managers), while others are muted or suppressed (e.g., those of the janitorial and clerical staffs).

In the literature on organizations, voice has a more specific meaning. It refers to an employee's decision to speak up against the status quo rather than keep quiet and stay or give up and leave (Hirschman, 1970). In an ideal world, voice is the preferred option because it raises important issues and encourages creativity and commitment. In most companies, however, many barriers to voice exist. The suppression of employee voice within organizations can lead to **whistle-blowing**, wherein frustrated employees take their concerns to the media, the courts, or others outside of the organization (Redding, 1985). In extreme cases of suppressed employee voice, the results may include sabotage and violence in the workplace (Goodall, 1995; Harris & Ogbonna, 2012).

At a minimum, dialogue requires that communicators be afforded equitable opportunities to speak. While the notion of dialogue as equitable transaction is a good starting point for thinking about organizational communication, it does not explicitly address the quality of that communication.

Dialogue as Empathic Conversation

In defining dialogue as **empathic conversation**, we refer to the ability to understand or imagine the world as another person understands or imagines it. Achieving empathy is difficult for people who believe that their view of reality is the only correct view and that others' perceptions are misinformed or misguided. Indeed, Western communication is largely based on assumptions of what is right. As a result, it becomes much more difficult to accept the validity of a different perspective, especially a radically different one.

Empathy, or perspective taking, is absolutely critical in organizations. It promotes understanding among different departments, makes managing diversity and inclusion possible, and acknowledges that although individuals and groups have different perspectives on the organization, no single perspective is inherently better than others. In this way, we can focus on common problems without immediately turning those who have a different view of these problems into enemies or traitors. The challenge, of course, is learning to appreciate differences in interpretation without feeling pressured to either demonize the other or strive for complete agreement. Put differently: "Can I recognize the value of your [perspective] . . . without us having to somehow merge into something that's less rich than the community of differences?" (Evered & Tannenbaum, 1992, p. 52).

Researchers at the Massachusetts Institute of Technology (MIT) take a similar view of organizational dialogue in their efforts to create learning communities

(Isaacs, 1999; Senge, 1990; Senge, Kleiner, Roberts, Ross, & Smith, 1994). Building on the work of physicist David Bohm that we discussed earlier, the researchers define dialogue as a kind of "collective mindfulness" in which the interactants are more concerned about group effectiveness than about individual ego or position. From this perspective, dialogue affords new opportunities for people in organizations to work together. Not merely a set of techniques, dialogue requires that people "learn how to think together—not just in the sense of analyzing a shared problem or creating new pieces of shared knowledge, but [also] in the sense of occupying a collective sensibility, in which the thoughts, emotions, and resulting actions belong not to one individual, but to all of them together" (Isaacs, 1999, p. 358). The MIT Dialogue Project has attracted the attention of business because it links the fate of whole systems of individuals (e.g., organizations, societies, species) with dialogue, flirting with the idea that our relationships with others can possess a spiritual quality inasmuch as they promote feelings of wholeness and connection.

We know that treating people like inanimate objects is inappropriate, but are understanding and empathy enough? Is it possible to connect with another person in a way that goes deeper than empathizing with their point of view? This question leads us to yet another potential definition: dialogue as real meeting.

Dialogue as Real Meeting

In defining dialogue as **real meeting**, we mean that through communication, a genuine communion can take place between people that transcends differences in role or perspective and that recognizes all parties' common humanity. Communication scholar John Stewart (2000) refers to this state as "letting others happen to you while holding your ground." The notion of dialogue as empathic conversation is insufficient because it assumes that one individual experiences the other as a kind of object, rather than as a fellow interpreter. In other words, once the conversation has ended, even empathic communicators may continue to view the dialogue as mainly instrumental in accomplishing their personal and professional goals. Therefore, one's performance of empathy may be false or even used as a means to a personal strategic end.

Certain types of dialogue are valuable in and of themselves. Buber distinguishes between *interhuman dialogue*, which has inherent value, and *social dialogue*, which has value as a route to self-realization and fulfillment. According to Buber, "We are answerable neither to ourselves alone nor to society apart from ourselves but to that very bond between ourselves and others through which we again and again discover the direction in which we can authenticate our existence" (cited in Friedman, 1992, p. 6). From this perspective, since life exists only in communion with other humans, dialogue is a fundamental human activity. How do meetings in organizations resemble Buber's ideal? Buber sees meeting as a relationship between "I and Thou," wherein two individuals acknowledge that each is an interpreter and that neither reduces the other to an object of interpretation within a context that has already been constructed. For example, we have seen senior managers who have struggled to understand one another move to a higher level of trust and coordination in which their respect and regard for others appear as the foundation of each of their conversations. This respect for another's subjectivity and worldview is the key ingredient in real meeting.

Seeking dialogue because it has value in itself can often result in positive consequences for an organization:

> [Dialogue] is one of the richest activities that human beings can engage in. It is the thing that gives meaning to life, it's the sharing of humanity, and it's creating something. And there is this magical thing in an organization, or in a team, or a group, where you get unrestricted interaction, unrestricted dialogue, and this synergy happening that results in more productivity, and satisfaction, and seemingly magical levels of output from a team. (Evered & Tannenbaum, 1992, p. 48)

This definition of dialogue combines the abstract or spiritual with the more practical aspects of how we communicate. Are we open to the voices of others? Do we recognize that all views are partial and that each of us has the right to speak? Are we open to the possibility of maintaining mutual respect and openness of spirit through organizational communication? Such questions are not easily answered by people in organizations. Although people may desire to maintain an open dialogue, they are too often constrained by learned behaviors that guard against intimate disclosure; by the social, professional, and political consequences of those disclosures; and by the habit of separating emotions from work.

To establish dialogue as real meeting, we must learn to interpret communication as a dialogic process that occurs between and among individuals, rather than as something we do *to* one another. All parties are responsible for the dialogue as well as for the risks taken; only together can they make progress. We engage in dialogue to learn more about the self in context with others. Dialogue helps us attain new appreciations for the multilayered dimensions of every context: "The crucial point is to go into a dialogue with the stance that there is something that I don't already know, with a mutual openness to learn. Through dialogue we can learn, not merely receive information, but revise the way we see something" (Evered & Tannenbaum, 1992, p. 45).

Dialogue as real meeting is difficult to achieve, which is why it does not characterize most interactions either inside or outside of organizations. Most organizations readily acknowledge the importance of equitable transactions and are motivated to create increased empathy across hierarchical levels and professional groups. Still, dialogue as real meeting is an important communicative goal because it can transform organizations into energetic and dynamic, even soulful workplaces. Such organizations are both effective and enjoyable because they encourage the kinds of communication required for real human connection.

There are advantages and limitations associated with promoting dialogue in organizations. It can increase employee satisfaction and commitment, reduce turnover rates, and lead to greater innovation and flexibility within an organization. However, it is also time-consuming, which means that not all issues are worthy of this kind of deep exploration. In addition, promoting dialogue may lead employees to assume that their ideas and opinions will be implemented. Although there may be an equitable distribution of power and voice in the group, within a capitalist system the owners and their agents still retain the right to make the final decisions.

Finally, dialogue may lead to a lack of closure or to the feeling that no right answer can be found. This problem is related in part to the nature of Western society, in which people expect definitive answers from science, medicine, politics, and technology. In an increasingly complex world, the drive for the one "right" answer may give way to making decisions well in the search for "good" answers. Specifically, dialogue may encourage communicators to attend more closely to the ethical implications of their communication practice. In the next section, we address two potential outcomes of dialogue: integrity and ethical communication.

▨ INTEGRITY AND ETHICS IN ORGANIZATIONAL COMMUNICATION

Integrity is a mindful state of acting and communicating purposefully to fulfill the promises and commitments you make to others. We associate integrity with honesty, openness, commitment, and trust. There are some excellent examples of people who have acted with integrity. *Time* magazine's "Person of the Year" issue for 2002 was, for the first time, shared by three women: Cynthia Cooper (WorldCom), Coleen Rowley (FBI), and Sherron Watkins (Enron). Each of them "blew the whistle" on unethical or irresponsible actions in her organization. Each risked her job and reputation to do what she believed was right for her coworkers and for her organization's stakeholders. Each woman made a conscious choice to act in the best interests of others, despite the cost to herself. Because these women were willing and able to speak up, their organizations were given a valuable opportunity to learn from past mistakes and to create a better system for the future.

Another person who acted with integrity was Aaron Feuerstein, the owner of Massachusetts fabric maker Malden Mills. He chose to keep his three thousand employees on the payroll and rebuild his company after a devastating fire that destroyed three company buildings. Feuerstein, the grandson of the founder of the company, said that he never considered shutting down the business after the fire. He believed that his employees deserved to be treated well because without their dedication and hard work the company would not have grown. He made a conscious decision to honor his commitments to them even though it represented a huge personal loss for himself.

The point we are making is simple yet profound. Rather than being an abstract aspect of character, integrity is a core business principle that requires mindfulness, dialogue, and considerable courage to enact (Beckett, 2005).

Integrity is a necessary, but not sufficient, component of ethics. **Ethics** refers to the systems of rules, duties, and morality that we use to guide our behavior.

Put simply, ethics refers to "doing things right" and "doing the right things" in organizational contexts (Kauffman, 2008, p. 10). In organizational communication, this approach to ethics means that we have to consider both the *process* (how we communicate) and the *product* (the material and symbolic results of our communication behaviors). As you will see throughout this book, ethics figures into almost all organizational communication, from everyday interpersonal interactions at the office to how organizations make use of natural resources. Ethical communication is

> fundamental to responsible thinking, decision making, and the development of relationships and communities within and across contexts, cultures, channels, and media. Moreover, ethical communication enhances human worth and dignity by fostering truthfulness, fairness, responsibility, personal integrity, and respect for self and others. We believe that unethical communication threatens the quality of all communication and consequently the well-being of individuals and the society in which we live. (National Communication Association, 1999)

But what are the rules for ethical communication? Some rules exist in the form of cultural aphorisms like the golden rule, found in many world religions, that instructs us to treat others as we would want to be treated. In an organizational context, the golden rule might translate into a very simple bottom line for business relationships: do what you said you would do. In other words, follow through on your commitments, and make sure that others in your organization do the same. This, however, is easier said than done. Bruce Hyde (1995) asked his students to keep track of their verbal commitments over the course of a week and to try to honor each one. He calls this "being your word." The students were shocked by how often they failed to follow through on their commitments.

Ideas about ethical behavior are somewhat culturally bound. In North American business cultures, the organizational values associated with ethical communication suggest that we should

- Trust one another.
- Treat one another with respect.
- Recognize the value of each individual.
- Keep our word.
- Tell the truth; be honest with others.
- Act with integrity.
- Be open to change.
- Risk failing in order to get better.
- Learn; try new ideas. (Harshman & Harshman, 1999, p. 15)

In keeping with these broad guidelines, many professionals, including members of the communication discipline, have developed a professional code of ethics that serves similar functions (see Table 2.2).

Ethical communication involves balancing and negotiating often competing demands. Managers must work to find and communicate an always shifting balance between their roles as organizational experts and equal and engaged partners

TABLE 2.2

NCA Credo for Ethical Communication

Questions of right and wrong arise whenever people communicate. Ethical communication is fundamental to responsible thinking, decision making, and the development of relationships and communities within and across contexts, cultures, channels, and media. Moreover, ethical communication enhances human worth and dignity by fostering truthfulness, fairness, responsibility, personal integrity, and respect for self and others. We believe that unethical communication threatens the quality of all communication and consequently the well-being of individuals and the society in which we live. Therefore, we, the members of the National Communication Association, endorse and are committed to practicing the following principles of ethical communication.

- We advocate truthfulness, accuracy, honesty, and reason as essential to the integrity of communication.
- We endorse freedom of expression, diversity of perspective, and tolerance of dissent to achieve the informed and responsible decision making fundamental to a civil society.
- We strive to understand and respect other communicators before evaluating and responding to their messages.
- We promote access to communication resources and opportunities as necessary to fulfill human potential and contribute to the well-being of families, communities, and society.
- We promote communication climates of caring and mutual understanding that respect the unique needs and characteristics of individual communicators.
- We condemn communication that degrades individuals and humanity through distortion, intimidation, coercion, and violence and through the expression of intolerance and hatred.
- We are committed to the courageous expression of personal convictions in pursuit of fairness and justice.
- We advocate sharing information, opinions, and feelings when facing significant choices, while also respecting privacy and confidentiality.
- We accept responsibility for the short- and long-term consequences for our own communication and expect the same of others.

Source: From "Credo for Ethical Communication," National Communication Association, 1999. Retrieved from http://www.natcom.org/uploadedFiles/About_NCA/Leadership_and_Governance/Public _Policy_Platform/PDF-PolicyPlatform-NCA_Credo_for_Ethical_Communication.pdf

with their employees. In many cases there is no easy solution, no one right way to achieve that ethical balance; instead, skilled and knowledgeable communicators recognize that ethical communication is a lifelong pursuit that is enacted in every-day communicative choices with others.

SUMMARY

There are many competing definitions for and approaches to organizational communication. There is value in learning about them because each offers a different way of understanding communication and of acting on that understanding when at work in organizations.

Researchers commonly encounter four definitions of organizational communication in the literature: communication as information transfer, transactional process, strategic control, and a balance of creativity and constraint. This list is approximately chronological and reveals an increased interest in feedback and two-way interaction. Our own view of organizations as dialogues extends this trend.

Recasting organizations as dialogues, in contrast, say, to economic or political systems, places our focus on the interplay between self and others in multiple, changing contexts and situations. Each of these foundational elements arises in relationship with the others, culminating in the idea that every individual is situated in flows of communication.

When situated individuals come together to organize, they may vary considerably in the sorts of communication in which they engage. On one end of the spectrum is discussion, wherein people seek to dominate others. At the other end is dialogue. Writers on dialogue (Isaacs, 1999) have outlined what we categorize as four levels that increasingly reveal people with a fundamental respect for the subjectivity and differing worldview of the other. The four levels are dialogue as mindful communication, equitable transaction, empathic conversation, and real meeting.

Dialogue is a strategy that can enable us to work with integrity. Working with integrity is important to the well-being of individuals, organizations, society, and our global community. As we have shown in this chapter, working with integrity means refusing to rely on old, mindless scripts and instead making informed choices about how you think, communicate, and act.

Working with integrity is primarily enabled by your willingness to learn how to work collaboratively and to discipline yourself to the habits and practices of ethical communication. In this way, working with ethics asks you to apply the lessons of balancing creativity and constraint through dialogue. It asks you to respect others and to respect yourself, to reach out to others while standing your ground. It asks you to live and work honorably by accepting full responsibility not only for what you say and do, but also for your human connection to the outside world and to people whom you have never met but nevertheless are now—and will always be—affected by the choices you make, the decisions you reach, the words and actions you offer to the world.

QUESTIONS FOR REVIEW AND DISCUSSION

1. What are the four major approaches to communication discussed in this chapter? What insights does each approach provide? What is the point of learning these definitions and approaches to organizational communication?

2. Explain what we mean by our definition of *organizational communication*. What are the sources of individual creativity? What are the sources of organizational constraint?

3. Strategic ambiguity is discussed as a way to encourage empowerment by allowing employees at different levels within a company to interpret the meaning of statements in relation to their own jobs. However, it doesn't always work out that way. What potential problems are associated with using strategic ambiguity?

4. What is dialogue? Of the four types of dialogue described in this chapter, which ones do you believe are most likely to be available to organizational employees? Why?

5. How would you characterize the kinds of communication that are most prevalent in university life, both in and outside the classroom? For example, do students of the humanities and the social sciences follow different definitions of communication than their counterparts in business, engineering, and the natural sciences?

6. Under what circumstances do you behave most mindfully? Think of situations in jobs or classes that required a great deal of mindfulness from employees or students. Did the expected degree of mindfulness cause any problems?

7. What is the relationship between organizational communication and working with integrity?

KEY TERMS

Balance of creativity and constraint, p. 40

Duality of structure, p. 40

Empathic conversation, p. 51

Equitable transaction, p. 50

Ethics, p. 54

Information-transfer approach, p. 31

Integrity, p. 54

Mindful, p. 50

Mindless, p. 49

Real meeting, p. 52

Self, p. 45

Situated individual, p. 46

Strategic ambiguity, p. 36

Strategic-control perspective, p. 36

Theory of structuration, p. 41

Transactional-process model, p. 34

Voice, p. 51

Whistle-blowing, p. 51

CASE STUDY

The Many Robert Smiths

JASON, THE JANITOR

"Smith is a tidy man. I pass by his desk at night when I'm cleaning up, and his area is the only one that's perfect. Nothing is ever out of place. I've made a kind of study out of it. You know, paid lots of attention to it on account of it being so unusual. So I've noticed things.

"I'd say Smith must be a single man. There are no pictures of family on his desk or on the walls. Most people leave clues to their personal life in the office—photographs, items they picked up during vacations, stickers with funny sayings on them. But not Smith. In Smith's area, there is no trace of anything personal. Just some books and the computer. The books never change positions, which tells me he never has to look things up. So I think Smith must be a smart man, too.

"I've never met him. Or if I did, I never knew it. But I see him in my mind as a tall, thin guy with glasses who doesn't smile too often. He may be shy, too. Fastidious people are often shy. Maybe he's an accountant or a computer programmer. It's hard to say. But Smith makes my job interesting. I look at his desk every night to see if anything has changed."

CATHERINE, THE RECEPTIONIST

"Smith is okay, a little shy maybe. He says 'hello' to me every morning. Just a 'hello,' though—nothing more, not even my name. I didn't know his name for months. But then, I didn't say much to him either.

"Then one afternoon he had a visitor. It was a woman—a beautiful woman in her late twenties or early thirties. She asked to speak to Bobby. 'Bobby who?' I asked. She looked confused; then she smiled and said, 'Bobby Smith. I thought everyone knew him as Bobby.' Well, this was interesting. I mean, I suddenly realized Smith had a first name—Robert. I had never thought of him as anyone's 'Bobby' before.

"I paged Smith, and he came downstairs. When he saw the woman, his face turned white like he'd seen a ghost. She called his name, and he stood still. I thought he was about to cry or something, but instead he just shook his head, as if to say, 'No.' He didn't say anything. Just shook his head. Then he turned and walked back upstairs, slowly. The woman just watched him. Then she turned around and walked out. I never saw her again. I don't know if she was a girlfriend, sister, or friend. Smith never said anything about her.

(continued, The Many Robert Smiths)

"In this job, I meet all kinds of people. I've learned a lot about people while working here as a receptionist. But Smith is still a mystery to me. I don't know much about him. All I know is that his first name is Robert but that some people call him Bobby, that he says 'hello' to me every morning like clockwork, and that there was once a beautiful woman in his life. Oh yeah, and he's about 5 feet 7 inches tall, has short hair and a big mustache, wears an earring, and obviously works out a lot."

Wilson, the Boss

"Smith is a strange guy, but a good worker. He never misses a day and is even willing to work nights or weekends to get the job done. His work is always neat and well organized. Personally, I wish he would get rid of his earring and mustache, but that's just him, I guess.

"I hired him five years ago as an entry-level accountant. His work in that position was good. He was promoted to a senior accountant position very quickly, as if someone up there in the company ranks were watching out for him. Usually it takes the best accountant five to seven years to make it to senior status; Smith made it in three. Last fall I asked him to take charge of a major audit, and he's been diligently working on that project ever since.

"Smith never talks about his life outside of work. And I never ask him. He seems to like it that way. But from the way he is built, I'd say he spends a lot of time working out at a gym. He drives a vintage black sports car, a Speedster, and it is always clean. He leaves it open during the day with a pair of Ray-Bans on the dash, always in the same position.

"I figure he comes from a wealthy family. He graduated from Stanford. But he doesn't act like a Californian. I'd say he's from Pittsburgh. I don't know why I say that. Actually, to be honest, Smith scares me a little bit. I don't know anyone who's as calm and collected and perfect as Smith is. In movies it's always the mass murderer who's like that. Not that I think Smith is that way. But I wouldn't be surprised, either. I wish his starched shirts would just one time come back from the cleaners with a rip in them or something. I know that sounds small. I can't help it. Smith does that to me."

Felicia, a Coworker

"Robert is my good friend. He's a warm, sensitive person with a heart of gold. He and I have talked a lot over the past couple of years—mostly about our dreams. We both want to work hard, save a lot of money, and be able to do something else with our lives while we are still young enough to enjoy it.

"Robert came from a poor family. He grew up moving around from town to town while his mother looked for work in construction. He had two brothers and a sister, all older. He was the baby. His father was killed in the Vietnam War. His older brothers are both in the military and don't have much in common with Robert, and his sister is a successful lawyer in Washington. Robert showed me a picture of her once; she's a beautiful woman. They had a big argument a while back. He wouldn't say much about it, except that he hasn't seen her since. His mother died of lung cancer two years ago.

"Robert worked hard in school but won an athletic scholarship to Stanford. He was a gymnast. Or still is, because he spends two or three nights a week working with underprivileged kids downtown, teaching them gymnastics. And he is big in Adult Children of Alcoholics, which I took him to. That's a whole story in itself. He has a lot of hobbies, which, when he does them, aren't exactly hobbies anymore. He is such a perfectionist! Like that car of his, for instance. He built it himself, out of a kit. And you should see his apartment."

JENKINS, THE RETIRED CEO

"Robert Smith is one of the company's finest employees. And he is an exceptional young man. I recruited him at Stanford when I was teaching there right after I retired. Since then, I've followed his career. I asked him not to say much about our relationship because some people might get the wrong idea. I want him to make it on his own, which he has. I put in a good word for him here and there, but never anything too pushy.

"I knew his father in Vietnam. He served in my command and was a good soldier. He was due to be shipped home later in the week when he was killed. It was sad. I wrote the letter to his family myself. When I got out of the Army, I moved into the private sector. You can imagine how odd it was for me to walk into that accounting class at Stanford and see Robert Smith, who looks just like his dad except for the mustache and earring, sitting in the front row. I couldn't believe it. Still can't.

"In a way, I feel related to Robert. He still comes to visit us on the holidays. I like that."

ASSIGNMENT

1. You are the executive recruiter (or headhunter) who compiled the preceding information about Smith from interviews with his colleagues. You also have Smith's résumé and performance appraisal reports to supplement the interviews. Your job is to prepare a personality profile of Smith for a firm that may be interested in hiring him. What would you write? How would you explain the different perspectives on Smith? If you were Robert Smith, what would you say about the interview statements?

(continued, The Many Robert Smiths)

2. We live complex (and often contradictory) lives as situated individuals in organizations. This should make us sensitive to the various ways in which meanings are constructed through communication. Construct an investigation of yourself, using interview statements by others describing who you are. Supplement these statements with your own résumé. What do the statements tell you about yourself? About your construction of others? About yourself as a situated individual in an organization? About the complexities of interpreting meaning?

3. As a student of communication, you are interested in finding ways to improve your own and others' interpretations of meanings. Review the case study as if you were a communication consultant working with the executive recruiter. Your job is to help the headhunter construct better follow-up questions and produce a complete report on Smith. What questions would help explain the different views of Smith?

PART II

Theories of Organizational Communication

Three Early Perspectives on Organizations and Communication

We have so far discussed the pervasiveness of organizational communication in society and provided definitions for thinking about the nature of communication. In this chapter, we hone in on the organizational context and discuss in detail three early theories of organizations that were not developed with a communication focus, but rather with a business focus. We begin with these early theories because they defined, or failed to define, communication and continue to have a significant impact on organizational practice. These three organizational perspectives are:

1. Classical management
2. Human relations
3. Human resources

Before we start, however, we want to make sure that you have a thorough understanding of what is meant by the word *theory*.

◼ WHY THEORY?

Theories of human behavior run the gamut from simple ideas to formal systems of hypotheses that aim to explain, predict, and control. All theories share two features: they are historical, and they are metaphorical. Any theory of organizational communication is historical in that it is a product of the time in which it emerged, reflecting the concerns and interests of the culture that produced it. For example, communication theories emphasizing the importance of self-disclosure arose during the 1960s counterculture. A **theory** is metaphorical in that it uses language to suggest enlightening comparisons between organizational communication and other processes. For example, scientific management theory, which we will discuss in this chapter, compares organizations to machines.

Theories function as thinking tools. They enhance our ability to explain and to act on a wide variety of practical issues, such as what motivates people to want to work. The way we talk about an issue or a problem influences the solutions we can propose. But theories are also historical and cultural narratives. They are goal-oriented stories that emerge during particular historical circumstances and reflect the beliefs and concerns of particular cultures. They develop and are shared for the purpose of explaining those circumstances to other members of the culture. As cultures change, so too do theories purporting to explain them.

We approach theory by considering the three P's of historical writing. Historical writing is always partial, partisan, and problematic. These points provide an important perspective on communication and reveal the limitations of any account. All talk is partial, partisan, and problematic, and theories of organizations and communication are no exception.

☐ Theories Are Partial

An argument could be made that any attempt to trace the history of organizational communication is necessarily incomplete and therefore misleading. Obviously, we have chosen to write this chapter anyway. Our primary condition is **partiality**, as our account tells only part of the story.

However, the inability to articulate a complete account of the history of organizational communication is not unique to our field, nor is it disabling. As French philosopher Jacques Derrida (1972) notes, all thought is inscribed in language, and language is rooted in an inescapable paradox. There is no point of absolute meaning outside of language from which to view—or to prescribe—the truth of the world.

It is logically impossible to say everything about anything; new perspectives are always possible. Because all language is partial regardless of length, there can be no absolute history, no full account, no complete story of organizational communication. From this perspective, our account is necessarily partial, as are the theories themselves.

☐ Theories Are Partisan

The story we tell is **partisan** and it is the one that we favor. Until recently, the history of organizational communication typically emphasized the interpretations of dominant white males in Western culture, with little attention given to how members of oppressed, marginalized, or subjugated groups like women and minorities would tell the story.

Why is this important? Compare, for example, how a Native American might interpret the nineteenth-century expansion of railroads, mining, and manufacturing interests across the Great Plains with the account given in many U.S. history textbooks. Depending on one's interests, or partisanship, this story can be seen as one of tragedy or opportunity. Although there may be disagreement about how the story gets told and who should tell it, there is likely to be agreement on at least some of the story's events and characters. Everyone agrees that Native Americans considered the Great Plains their natural hunting grounds and that westward expansion by white settlers took place. Partisanship, then, is not so much about identifying facts as it is about interpreting their meanings.

All thought is partisan. When we read about theories, then, it is useful to think of each theory as one that tells a particular story. Because each story represents the interests of the storyteller, it is a partisan perspective on broader, more complex stories about the world. In this sense, many theories make up the complex story of organizational communication.

☐ Theories Are Problematic

Finally, we write this chapter knowing that the story itself will be **problematic**. Our emphasis on dialogue asks more questions than it can answer, and the answers it does provide are based on what is currently known rather than on all that could be known. Theorists who generated the philosophies on which we choose to build were operating under similar constraints. In admitting the problematic nature of our narrative, we also invite dialogue, asking our readers to bring to our account their experiences and understandings.

Consider how this concept can inform our understanding of everyday organizational communication. Rather than making ultimate statements, it encourages us to ask more contingent questions and to invite others into the dialogue. Rather than assuming that we know the whole truth about any issue, it urges us to ask for the input of others who may hold different perspectives. This is very much in line with the philosophy and conception of this text—not as a book of answers, but rather as a way of thinking that produces thought-provoking questions across multiple contexts and situations.

Now that you have a clearer understanding of our perspective on theories, it is time to examine some specific theoretical perspectives on organizations with implications for communication.

▧ CLASSICAL MANAGEMENT APPROACHES

Classical management approaches are represented by a collection of theories that share the underlying metaphor of organizations modeled after efficient machines. This section describes the evolution of this idea from the eighteenth century to more recent times, beginning with the nature of preindustrial organizations and concluding with the apex of the classical approaches, the Industrial Revolution.

□ From Empire to Hierarchy

From the eighteenth century to the early twentieth century, organizations functioned much like empires. Corporations were viewed as extensions of governments; they expanded trade, provided employment for the masses, and contributed to economic and social development (Rose, 1989). Cities in North America were even mapped according to the appropriation of territories by organizations.

In the mid-eighteenth century, Benjamin Franklin (1706–1790) popularized some early notions of empire and pragmatism in his *Poor Richard's Almanac*. This book is primarily a collection of parables and quotations that elevate hard work (called "industry"), independence (the accumulation of wealth on individual, corporate, and national levels), and the virtues of planning, organizing, and controlling one's life through work. Here are some sample axioms from Franklin's almanac (reprinted in 2004):

- Industry need not wish—There are no Gains without Pains.
- God gives all things to industry.
- God helps them that help themselves.
- Sloth makes all things difficult, but industry all easy.
- Early to Bed, early to rise, makes a Man healthy, wealthy, and wise.

Although Franklin was not the only writer to express these ideas—similar sentiments are found in Japanese and Chinese proverbs, the Old Testament, and the Talmud—he was the first to popularize them as the foundation for an American work culture. Moreover, the proverbs were influential precisely because they fit neatly into the wisdom of older narratives used in churches, schools, and business.

During this same period, Frederick the Great (1712–1786), the king of Prussia, organized his armies on the principles of mechanics: ranks, uniforms, regulations, task specialization, standardized equipment, command language, and drill instruction (Morgan, 1986). His success served as a model for organizational action, one based on the division of labor and machinelike efficiency. Adam Smith (1723–1790), a philosopher of economics and politics, published *The Wealth of Nations* in 1776, which praised the division of labor in factory production. As Karl Marx (1818–1883) would later demonstrate, this was essential to organizing corporations and societies along class lines.

By 1832, a blueprint for such an organizational form had emerged. Characterized by a strict division of labor (the separation of tasks into discrete units) and hierarchy (the vertical arrangement of power and authority that distinguishes managers from employees), this organizational form would become the "classical theory of management."

As shown in Figure 3.1, the classic bureaucratic organization privileges a top-down, or management-oriented, approach. Two assumptions of this perspective are worth noting. First, the emphasis on developing scientific methods for production is politically and socially linked to providing that information to managers and

FIGURE 3.1

Organizational Charts Illustrating the Principles of Classical Management Theory and Bureaucratic Organization

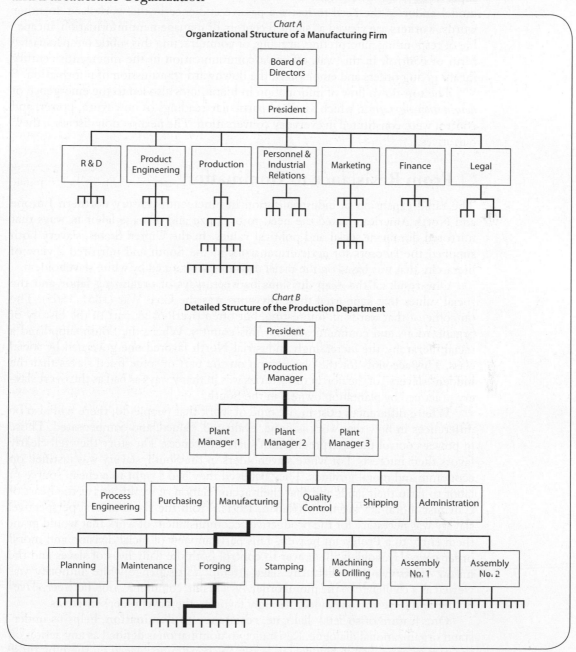

Source: From *Images of organization*, by G. Morgan, 1986, p. 20. Reprinted by permission of Sage Publications, Inc.

supervisors only, who in turn use it to organize and control workers. Second, the model endorses the need to foster a passive audience in the workplace. In other words, workers are viewed as silent receptors of management information, incapable of responding, interpreting, arguing, or counteracting this subtle but persuasive form of control. In this way, effective communication in the nineteenth century meant giving orders and emphasized the downward transmission of information.

The top-down flow of information in hierarchies also led to the emergence of *domination narratives*, which ascribed particular readings of how truth, power, and control were constituted in everyday conversation. The next section discusses these narratives.

☐ From Resistance to Domination

The rapid expansion of industrialization in nineteenth-century northern Europe and North America created the need to organize and manage labor in ways that mirrored dominant social and political values. In the United States, slavery both supplied the laborers for agricultural work in the South and mirrored a view of hierarchy that was based on the racial divisions sanctioned by white slaveholders.

One result of the deep divisions between ways of organizing labor and the social values that supported these divisions was the Civil War (1861–1865). The outcome of that war is an interesting, but often overlooked, part of the history of organizations and communication in this country. Where the South supported a racial hierarchy, the increasingly industrial North favored one governed by social class. This accounts for the observation on the part of some freed slaves that the hidden "slavery" of the northern factories was in many ways as bad as the overt slavery practiced by plantation owners in the South.

Where differences exist in the type of work that people do, there will also be differences in how that work is done, evaluated, valued, and compensated. Those in power control the interpretation of such differences. The story they tell clearly favors their interests. For white slaveholders in the South, slavery was justified on economic and moral grounds. They believed they had a right to a cheap source of labor to farm their lands and that their accumulation of wealth was at the heart of Calvinist moral advancement (Raban, 1991). From the slaveholders' perspective, slavery was necessary for the productive accomplishment of work that would grant them entry to a Protestant heaven. This partisan view of racial division and moral order gave slaveholders the power to control both the daily lives of slaves and the means of resolving conflict. Any slave attempt to challenge white authority was viewed as a challenge to the moral order. As a result, communication between slaveholder and slave was one-sided, strongly favoring the slaveholder's interests.

One feature of societal dialogue, **resistance to domination**, helps us understand organizational dialogue. Resistance to domination is defined as any action on the part of oppressed individuals to lessen the constraints placed on them by those in power. Such resistance takes many forms. For example, there are the narratives of the less powerful and the powerless, of those who ordinarily have little or no voice in organizational and societal dialogue. They provide different accounts of events and the meanings those events had for the participants (Freire, 1968).

James Scott (1990) points out how the accounts of the powerless can function as **hidden transcripts** of the other side of the story. Hidden transcripts include themes and arguments that are well known by members of the oppressed group but are kept out of the public eye for fear of reprisal from those in power. One kind of hidden transcript is the resistance narrative, like those that gave slaves a way to express their outrage to others who were caught in the same situation. Their stories reversed the order of things, placing slaveholders in inferior intellectual, moral, and performance positions. In this "world turned upside down" (Scott, 1990; Stallybrass & White, 1986), those without power could take control of the story and use it as a "performative space for the full-throated acting out of everything that must be choked back in public" (Conquergood, 1992, p. 91). By looking at the dominant narrative alongside the slave narrative, we get a sense of the potential dialogue that might have occurred between the two groups. Unfortunately, however, that dialogue remained mostly implicit because the dominant group's narrative was told in public and the slaves' narrative in private.

In addition to slave narratives, other forms of resistance to domination came with the slave songs, ditties, and dirges that would later become known as "the blues." Similarly, there are accounts of resistance to domination from those who were once among the dominant and powerful. Perhaps the best known of these accounts is the gospel hymn "Amazing Grace," which combines the rhythms and sensibilities of a slave song with words penned in 1779 by a former slave trader turned English minister, John Newton (2011):

> Amazing Grace, how sweet the sound, / That saved a wretch like me.
> I once was lost, but now I'm found, / Was blind, but now I see.

Unfortunately, abuses of power based on hierarchically ordered systems of domination persist, especially in areas under severe political and military occupation, as well as in illegal sweatshops employing immigrant laborers the world over. According to the International Labour Organization's 2014 report, "21 million people are victims of forced labour—11.4 million women and girls and 9.5 million men and boys. Of those exploited by individuals or enterprises, 4.5 million are victims of forced sexual exploitation. Forced labour in the private economy generates US$ 150 billion in illegal profits per year."

According to the U.S. Department of State's Trafficking in Persons Report (2011), different forms of slavery are still practiced:

- Afghanistan: Children are tricked or forced to become suicide bombers.
- Bolivia: Children are subjected to forced labor in mining and agriculture and as domestic servants. Some families actually lease their children for forced labor in these areas.

- Burma: The military engages in the unlawful conscription of child soldiers.
- Fiji: Staff members at hotels procure underage boys and girls for commercial sexual exploitation by foreign guests.
- Greece: Victims from other nations are forced to work in agriculture and construction in debt bondage.
- Sudan: Displaced Sudanese women are forced to work as domestic servants, and Sudanese girls are made to engage in prostitution at restaurants and brothels, sometimes with the assistance of law enforcement.
- United States: Trafficking occurs for commercial sexual exploitation in street prostitution, brothels, and massage parlors.

☐ The Industrial Revolution

Although organizations and communication existed before the steamboat, railroad, and cotton gin, it was not until the Industrial Revolution that modern machinery and methods of production emerged with the rise of the factory bureaucracy (Perrow, 1986).

The rise of the modern factory during the industrial period was an extension of a social and racial class structure that sought to stabilize power relations among people by controlling the means of production and consumption in society (Foucault, 1972, 1979). The organization of work and communication in early factories was highly influenced by the new concepts of division of labor and hierarchy. The rationale was that the work institution should mirror the organization of the ideal society.

The Industrial Revolution is also associated with the rise of science. With science came much more than a highly ordered method of explaining phenomena: from explanation emerged the ability to predict, and from the ability to predict came the potential to control. The underlying theme of the classical management approach to organization is the scientific rationalization of control. Organizations are viewed as the primary vehicle through which our lives are rationalized—"planned, articulated, scientized, made more efficient and orderly, and managed by experts" (Scott, 1981, p. 5).

☐ Scientific Management

The years 1880 to 1920 were characterized by both significant racial and class prejudice, and by unprecedented economic expansion in the United States. With massive industrialization came the ruthless treatment of workers by owners who subscribed to a "survival of the fittest" mentality. Those employees who succeeded were deemed to be morally strong; those who failed were deemed to be unworthy of success (Bendix, 1956).

Born in this era was the middle-class engineer Frederick Winslow Taylor (1856–1915), a pioneer in the development of **scientific management**. His book *The Principles of Scientific Management* (1913) is based on the assumption that management is a true science resting on clearly defined laws, rules, and principles.

Taylor's time and motion studies led to improved organizational efficiency through the mechanization of labor and the authority of the clock. Taylor divided work into discrete units and observed workers as they labored, measuring their productivity and using the output and speed of the top performers to set productivity standards for all doing that job. This principle was then used to plan factory outcomes, to evaluate worker efficiency, and to train less-skilled workers. The production system required divisions of labor and carefully developed chains of command; communication was limited to orders and instructions.

Taylor's goal was to transform the nature of both work and management. He hoped that cooperation between managers and employees would bring a new era of industrial peace: "Under scientific management, arbitrary power, arbitrary dictation, ceases; and every single subject, large and small, becomes the question for scientific investigation, for reduction to law" (Taylor, 1947, p. 211).

But things didn't work out that way. Instead of industrial peace, scientific management led to increased conflict because it reinforced hierarchical distinctions and further objectified the already downtrodden worker. Although Taylor claimed that he was developing his ideas to help the working person, by the end of his life he was cursed by labor unions as "the enemy of the working man" (Morgan, 1986). Even so, Taylor's work ushered in a new focus on the relationship between managers and employees as a key to organizational productivity, and this remains a bedrock principle of contemporary management theory (Braverman, 1974).

More specifically, Taylor's model ushered in a systematic approach to the division of labor that has gone far beyond the design of work for which it was originally developed. Scientific management created a firm division between managers, whose task was to plan and control the design of work, and employees, whose job was to implement those plans. In short, scientific management assumed that some employees are better suited to "thinking" work and some to "doing" work, ultimately laying the groundwork for the class-based distinction between white-collar and blue-collar employees that we know today. Other divisions would follow. White, middle-class male employees were believed to be better managers because they were more "rational" and less "emotional" than their female counterparts. Men also came to be seen as better suited to the demands of public work because they were not burdened with private domestic responsibilities.

Women, who were largely written out of Taylor's theory and out of formal organizational life, soon appropriated scientific management for use in the domestic realm. The emphasis on science and mechanization, the production of new household technologies and so-called conveniences, and the "cult of domesticity" combined to create a scientific management approach to home life at the turn of the century. In 1913, Christine Frederick, an editor for the popular magazine *Ladies' Home Journal*, wrote a "how-to" book for women called *The New Housekeeping*. In it, she outlined the twelve principles of scientific efficiency that applied to the home, including ideals or "the one best way" to complete a task, standardized operation, and scheduling. She encouraged women to adopt the correct attitude toward efficiency because not only the household but also the mind must be "managed" and "organized."

While they may not use the label, many working families today adopt a scientific management approach in their efforts to give order to their busy lives. Consider the working mother who checks her iPhone to scan her color-coded calendar of work, family, and volunteer commitments as she leaves work to pick up her children from school before dropping them off at their various activities. Her constant desire to find the most efficient way to control her work and personal life extends Taylor's theory into the present era.

Scientific management, then, is a management-oriented, production-centered view of organizations and communication. Its ideal, the efficient machine, holds that humans function as components or parts. It also assumes a fundamental distinction between managers and employees: Managers think, workers work (Morgan, 1986). The ideal of scientific management is best realized in straightforward task situations that require no flexibility in responding to contingencies and that offer no opportunities for initiative. This description of an organization does not take into account human motivations for working, personal work relationships, or the flexibility required by the turbulent nature of organizational environments. Moreover, efforts to improve efficiency through aggressive supervision or autocratically derived production standards often alienated workers, as in Henry Ford's automobile plant, which experienced a turnover rate of 280 percent annually under scientific management (Morgan, 1986).

☐ Fayol's Classical Management

At roughly the same time Taylor was working on scientific management in the United States, French industrialist Henri Fayol (1841–1925) was developing his influential theory of "administrative science," or classical management (1949). Fayol was the highly successful director of a French mining company, and his management principles became popular in the United States and elsewhere in the late 1940s. He is perhaps best known for articulating the five elements of classical management: planning, organizing, commanding (goal setting), coordinating, and controlling (evaluating). He was even more specific in detailing how this work ought to be done.

Katherine Miller (2012) groups Fayol's principles into four categories: structure, power, reward, and attitude. Regarding structure, Fayol prescribed a strict hierarchy with a clear vertical chain of command; he called this the *scalar principle*. He believed that each employee should have only one boss and should be accountable to only one plan. Like Taylor, Fayol advocated division of labor through *departmentalization*, the grouping together of similar activities. The resulting organizational structure is the classic hierarchical pyramid.

In terms of power, Fayol advocated the centralization of decision making and respect for authority. He held that authority accrues from a person's position and character and that discipline and obedience could be expected only if both were present. Moreover, he viewed discipline as respect for agreed-on rules, and not solely respect for position.

EVERYDAY ORGANIZATIONAL COMMUNICATION

Scientific Management at the Gym

For many people, exercise is a therapeutic means of escaping the daily grind and a way to work out on-the-job and other stresses. We often hear students talking about the need to hit the gym during finals week as a way of dealing with building pressure and anxiety. Increasingly, however, gyms and exercise routines are becoming as carefully managed (or as "Taylorized") as many work environments. This is not to say that exercise is becoming less enjoyable or relaxing, but rather that gyms and fitness instructors are becoming increasingly savvy about utilizing and marketing a key attribute of scientific management: identifying the most effective way to complete a task, like getting fit or losing weight, in the shortest amount of time while conserving the most energy.

Consider the example of Curves, a women's gym established as a franchise in 1995. Curves is known for its thirty-minute workout, which "gives you a complete cardio & strength-training workout . . . where you can burn up to 500 calories every time". Women work out in a circuit of resistance machines, performing exercises that target different areas of the body. The ultimate goal of this routine is, of course, to offer maximum benefit in a minimal amount of time, especially as would-be gym members often cite "lack of time" for their decision not to commit to regular exercise.

The appeal of scientific management has also affected the very machines that you come across at your local gym. An increasingly popular machine in the fitness world, the Pilates reformer, takes the stretching exercises and breathing techniques made famous by Joseph Pilates in a new direction with a system of strings, pulleys, and movable carriages that help ensure proper body alignment and, therefore, increased effectiveness during exercise. Similarly, weightlifting machines are purposefully designed for users to practice the ideal way to do an exercise with maximum benefit, and stair-climbers, treadmills, and stationary bicycles display the number of calories burned per hour, offering users the chance to track and improve their efficiency in ways that would have made Taylor himself proud.

DISCUSSION QUESTIONS

1. With these examples in mind, what do you feel are the benefits and burdens of a Taylorized approach to fitness?
2. If you work out, do the principles of scientific management influence your workouts? What steps do you take to ensure maximum benefit with minimal time commitment?

(continued, Scientific Management at the Gym)

3. If you do not currently work out, are you attracted to the idea of scientific management at the gym? Would a scientifically managed approach to fitness inspire you to exercise more regularly, or would it make you less likely to work out? Why?

4. Consider other ways in which scientific management plays out in your life. Have you held a professional or volunteer position that stressed maximum benefit in minimal time? What ways did you benefit from such a system, and in what ways did you find it frustrating? What were the pros and cons for the organization or company that employed you?

Mirroring Taylor's view of rewards, Fayol advocated fair remuneration for well-directed efforts, foreshadowing the potential of profit sharing as a compensation system (Tompkins, 1984). Most concerned about the employee's perception of equity in pay and other issues, Fayol believed in the value of a stable workforce. Because of this, he was a proponent of stable tenure for employees as a means of avoiding high turnover rates and recruitment costs.

Finally, regarding organizational attitude, Fayol held that employees should subordinate their personal interests to those of the organization. He also saw rational enforcement of agreements through fair supervision as the method for ensuring this organizational attitude. At the same time, Fayol encouraged employee initiative, or the capacity to see a plan through to completion, and believed that supervisors should work hard to build positive employee morale.

The guidelines Fayol developed for organizational administrations were intended to be useful across a variety of situations. Some of his principles, most notably those related to unity of command and centralization, are specifically focused on organizational communication (Tompkins, 1984). However, as Fayol cautioned, "There is nothing rigid or absolute in management affairs, it is all a question of proportion. Seldom do we have to apply the same principle twice in identical conditions; allowances must be made for different changing circumstances" (1949, p. 19).

☐ Bureaucracy

A final piece of the classical approach fell into place with the development of the idea of **bureaucracy**. In the harsh working conditions of the early twentieth century, job security did not exist, young children worked long hours for meager wages, and workers were hired and fired for reasons that had to do with their race, religion, sex, attitude, or relationship to the boss. This method of dealing with employees, called **particularism**, was expedient for owners and managers but often had dire consequences for employees. Particularism also presented an ideological conflict in the United States: "On the one hand, democracy stressed liberty and equality for all. On the other hand, large masses of workers and nonsalaried personnel had to submit to apparently arbitrary authority, backed up by local and national police forces and legal powers, for ten to twelve hours a day, six days a week" (Perrow, 1986, p. 53).

It was this conflict between ideology and practice that gave rise to a system that protected employees better than particularism. We now call that system bureaucracy.

According to W. Richard Scott (1981), organizational bureaucracy has the following six characteristics:

1. A fixed division of labor among participants
2. A hierarchy of offices
3. A set of general rules that govern performances
4. A rigid separation of personal life from work life
5. The selection of personnel on the basis of technical qualifications and equal treatment of all employees
6. Participants' view of employment as a career; tenure protecting against unfair arbitrary dismissal

Although the well-known German scholar Max Weber (1864–1920) was not a blind advocate of bureaucracy (he feared that its sole focus on instrumental rationality would drive out mystery and enchantment from the world), he saw it as technically superior to all other forms of organization. Furthermore, he was a strong advocate for universalism, or equal treatment according to ability. Most people today associate bureaucracy with the red tape and inflexibility of public agencies. However, these may not necessarily be results of a bureaucratic approach. In his famous defense of bureaucracy, Charles Perrow (1986) argues that the machine itself ought not be blamed, but rather the people who misuse it to further their own interests.

When examining bureaucracy, it is useful to examine it not just in terms of what came before it (particularism), but to consider Weber's goal of universalism, which sought to introduce standards of fair treatment in the workplace. Even today, managers struggle to hold on to the powers to hire, fire, promote, and discipline employees at will. In addition, prebureaucratic decision making is viewed by managers as easier, and more expedient, than decision making in a bureaucracy. The latter makes decisions harder to implement while it protects employees from abuse.

The ideal bureaucracy cannot be fully realized for several reasons: (1) It is not possible to rid organizations of all extraorganizational influences on member behavior; (2) bureaucracy does not deal well with nonroutine tasks; and (3) people vary in terms of rationality (Perrow, 1986). These inadequacies of bureaucracy were the impetus for other theories. Alternative forms of organizing were proposed that loosened the rigid assumptions of classical management theory, and paved the way for new insights into human organization.

☐ Implications for Organizational Communication

Classical management approaches view communication as unproblematic. They suggest that communication is simply a tool for issuing orders, coordinating work efforts, and gaining employee compliance. In a hierarchical world, they view the primary function of communication as the transfer of information through the proper channels. In the classical management approach, any attempt at achieving a balance between individual creativity and organizational constraint through dialogue will tilt in favor of constraint.

It is important to recognize that many of the tenets of the classical approach to management are alive and well in organizations today. The military still maintains strict divisions of labor and a scalar chain-of-command hierarchy, and Taylor's ideas about designing jobs scientifically, making work routine, and hiring people fit to accomplish a specific task are evident in contemporary corporate concerns with organizational efficiency. In applications ranging from software design to fast-food sales to the creation of computerized accounting systems, the goal of reducing the number of steps involved to reliably produce a quality result is still paramount (Miller, 2003). Additionally, the classical management objective of fitting the right person to the right job is now called "individualizing the organization" (Lawler & Finegold, 2000), where physical criteria have been replaced by psychological profiles that focus on individual differences in abilities, needs, and career aspirations.

In the next section, we will explore the origins of many of these challenges to, and modifications of, the classical approach.

◨ THE HUMAN RELATIONS APPROACH

Noted communication theorist Kenneth Burke was once asked how he became interested in the study of human communication. He replied, "People weren't treating each other very well. I wanted to help find a way to make relationships better" (cited in Goodall, 1984, p. 134). Burke's comment was made during a time of unparalleled economic depression when models of bureaucracy were questioned and theories of human relations first emerged.

☐ Historical and Cultural Background

Two major events—the Great Depression and World War II—came at a time when the perceived limitations of scientific management were at their peak. The Great Depression created economic and social hardships for millions of people and led to major changes in government policies regarding Social Security, public assistance, and the funding of public improvement projects. The Depression also contributed to major migrations of workers—from the drought-ridden central farming states to the West Coast and from the impoverished rural South to northern cities—as people went in search of jobs. A surplus of available workers and a lack of employment opportunities meant keen competition for work and widespread abuse of workers by employers. It is not surprising, then, that this period was also marked by the expansion of powerful labor unions. These organizations advocated human rights, fair wages, and improved working conditions.

Divisions between managers and workers became more intense during the Depression. Demands for improved working conditions were accommodated only when the improvements increased productivity and profits. Wages were determined by factory output, but increased output achieved through longer hours and relentless pressure to produce tended to increase the incidence of work-related injury, illness, and death. In addition, the typical workweek, which consisted of 6 twelve-hour days with one daily half-hour meal break, contributed to the strained relationship between workers and managers.

With World War II, however, came an enormous expansion of new jobs in both the military and the private sector. The war also placed academic researchers, managers, and military personnel in direct communication with one another for the first time. W. Charles Redding (1985), a pioneer of organizational communication and one of its leading historians, refers to this trinity as the "Triple Alliance." He argues that through the alliance, managers and military officers benefited from new ideas about organizing work and developing trust among workers, while academic researchers benefited from their access to industrial plants and their involvement in training workers, military personnel, and managers. The effects of this war-formed alliance would have a lasting impact, particularly on the subdiscipline that was created out of that alliance: organizational communication (Redding, 1985).

☐ What Is Human Relations?

Although Frederick Taylor had hoped to emphasize the importance of cooperative relationships between managers and employees, his methods did little to contribute to the quality of those interactions in the early twentieth century. It was not until the 1920s and 1930s that Mary Parker Follett, Elton Mayo, and Chester Barnard would examine the employee-manager relationship in an entirely new way. Their work would provide the foundation for the human relations approach and would become a precursor of contemporary thinking about management and leadership. **Human relations** thinking emphasized the interpersonal and social needs of individuals and marked a clear break from earlier points of view. The human relations approach starts with the assumption that all people "want to feel united, tied, bound to something, some cause, bigger than they, commanding them yet worthy of them, summoning them to significance in living" (Bendix, 1956, p. 296).

Mary Parker Follett (1868–1933) was a Boston social worker who used her experience running vocational guidance centers to develop new ideas about leadership, communication, social processes, and community. In contrast to the dominant scientific management preoccupation with efficiency and strict divisions of labor and decision making, Follett was a democratic pragmatist who believed that only cooperation among people working together in groups under visionary leadership produced excellence in the workplace, the neighborhood, or the community (Dixon, 1996; McLarney & Rhyno, 1999). She advocated what we would consider today a feminist view of management that focused on empowering workers by sharing information with them, emphasizing cooperation to solve problems, and organizing teams to accomplish tasks. She believed that "genuine power can only be grown . . . for genuine power is not coercive control but coactive control" (cited in Hurst, 1992, p. 57), and that workers at all levels in any organization were sources of creativity whose loyalty "is awakened . . . by the very process that creates the group" (cited in Hurst, 1992, p. 58). The democratic ideal, she believed, was achieved by integrating organizations, neighborhoods, and communities through teamwork and by encouraging individuals to live their lives fully. These ideas, considered radical in their time, marked the start of a new way of thinking about leadership, groups, communication, and relationships between managers and workers that still holds sway today (Graham, 1997).

Elton Mayo (1880–1949), a Harvard professor, also set out to critique and extend scientific management. Like Follett, Mayo did not share Taylor's view of organizations as comprising wage-maximizing individuals. Instead, Mayo stressed the limits of individual rationality and the importance of interpersonal relations. In contrast to scientific management, Mayo (1945) believed:

1. Society comprises groups, not isolated individuals.
2. Individuals are swayed by group norms and do not act alone in accord with self-interests.
3. Individual decisions are not entirely rational, but are also influenced by emotions.

Chester Barnard (1886–1961), a chief executive at Bell Telephone Company in New Jersey, the author of the influential book *The Functions of the Executive* (1968), and a man very much influenced by Follett, asserted the importance of cooperation in organizations: "Organizations by their very nature are cooperative systems and cannot fail to be so" (cited in Perrow, 1986, p. 63). The key to cooperation, he argued, lay in persuading individuals to accept a common purpose, from which all else would follow. Unlike Taylor's emphasis on economic inducements, Barnard viewed the role of management as largely communicative and persuasive. Effective managers strived to communicate in ways that encouraged workers to identify with the organization. Barnard also valued the contributions of informal contacts to overall organizational effectiveness. For the first time, then, the purpose of management was seen as more interpersonal than economic.

☐ The Hawthorne Studies

While Barnard was running New Jersey Bell, a landmark event was taking place at another subsidiary of the American Telephone and Telegraph Company (now AT&T), the Hawthorne plant of Western Electric in Cicero, Illinois. Mayo and F. J. Roethlisberger (also a Harvard professor) were called to the Hawthorne plant by W. J. Dickson, a manager and industrial engineer concerned about widespread employee dissatisfaction, high turnover rates, and reduced plant efficiency. Previous efforts to correct these problems by using principles of scientific management had failed. Perrow (1986) picks up the story:

> The researchers at Western Electric took two groups of workers doing the same kinds of jobs, put them in separate rooms, and kept careful records of their productivity. One group (the test group) had the intensity of its lighting increased. Its productivity went up. For the other group (the control group), there was no change in lighting. But, to the amazement of the researchers, its productivity went up also. Even more puzzling, when the degree of illumination in the test group was gradually lowered back to the original level, it was found that output still continued to go up. Output also continued to increase in the control group. The researchers continued to drop the illumination of the test group, but it was not until the workers were working under conditions of bright moonlight that productivity stopped rising and fell off sharply. (pp. 79–80)

Mayo and his colleagues realized that the productivity improvements they had measured had little to do with the level of illumination or other physical conditions in the plant. Instead, they found that the increased attention given to the workers by management and researchers was the key to increased productivity. This finding—that increased attention raises productivity—has come to be known as the **Hawthorne effect**.

☐ Reflections on Human Relations

It is difficult to criticize the primary goal of the human relations approach: to restore whole human beings and quality interpersonal relationships to their rightful place in what had become an overly rational view of organizations. In this spirit, the work of Chris Argyris (1957) has been influential. According to Argyris, the principles of formal organization, such as hierarchy and task specialization, are incongruent with the developmental needs of healthy adults. But do real alternatives exist? Critics have labeled Argyris and others who share his views as "romantics," arguing that alienation is an inherent part of organizational life (Drucker, 1974; Tompkins, 1984).

Indeed, there is little empirical evidence to support the effectiveness of the human relations approach, particularly the claim that positive employee morale fosters productivity (Miller & Form, 1951). Nevertheless, the approach, reflecting the romantic ideals of the time, has played an important role in further research on organizational behavior. Table 3.1 on page 82 summarizes the move

TABLE 3.1

Summary of Historical and Cultural Influences on the
Classical Management and Human Relations Approaches
to Organizations and Communication

CLASSICAL MANAGEMENT	HUMAN RELATIONS
Theme: Scientific rationality leads to improved efficiency and productivity	*Theme:* Improved human relations leads to improved efficiency and productivity
Enlightenment ideals	Romantic ideals
Industrial Revolution	Development of psychology
Scientific methods	Social scientific methods
Dominant metaphor: Organization as an efficient machine	*Dominant metaphor:* Organization as the sum of relationships
Supporting principles: *Ideal form of society* is authoritarian and values hierarchical organization	*Supporting principles:* *Ideal form of society* is democratic and values open and honest relationships
Divisions of labor/social classes/races/sexes/nations; if "the rules" were applied equally to everyone, individuals who worked hard and obeyed instructions could better themselves	*Divisions* of labor/management honored; negotiation of differences through open communication valued
Conflict based on divisions; dialectical relationships between management and labor based on power and money	*Conflict* based on lack of shared understanding; dialogic model of relationships between management and labor based on trust, openness, honesty, and power
Application of the principles of mechanics to organizations and communication led to operationalizing the machine metaphor (e.g., "This business runs like clockwork.")	*Application* of humanistic and behavioral psychology to organizations and communication led to operationalizing relational metaphors (e.g., "This business is like family.")
Communication is top-down and procedurally oriented; following "the rules" is valued, and opposing them calls into question the whole moral order	*Communication* is relational and needs-oriented; self-actualization is valued if it occurs through work
Dominant form of organizing: Bureaucracy	*Dominant form of organizing:* Teams or groups within bureaucracies
Stability best obtained through adherence to procedural forms of order	*Stability* best obtained through relational and personal happiness
Limitations: Too constraining; encourages mindless adherence to details and procedures and discourages creativity	*Limitations:* False openness, abuse of trust and/or honesty; equation of employee happiness with efficiency or productivity

from classical management to human relations in the study of organizations and communication.

Research that applies human relations thinking to the relationship between management and organizational effectiveness has been inconclusive and disappointing. Its underlying ideology has been interpreted as an unacceptable willingness to trade profitability for employee well-being. William Whyte (1969), in his classic critique, criticizes the human relations approach for attempting to replace the Protestant work ethic and entrepreneurialism with a social ethic of complacency that emphasizes dressing well, acting friendly, and "fitting in." Another critic has referred to human relations as "cow sociology": "Just as contented cows [are] alleged to produce more milk, satisfied workers [are] expected to produce more output" (Scott, 1981, p. 90).

A similar critique of a simplistic connection between good feeling and organizational effectiveness has been offered by communication scholars (Eisenberg & Witten, 1987). Although we would all like to believe that openness, self-disclosure, and supportive relationships have positive effects on organizational productivity, research does not support that ideal. Instead, models of employee motivation have become increasingly complex, causing us to revise what is meant by good leadership and the conditions under which a focus on interpersonal relations may be desirable. However, the applicability of these contingency models is limited to specific situations, resulting in a body of research with limited implications for practice.

Finally, an emerging line of historically based research asks how much of human relations theory is best understood as a manifestation of the Cold War mentality. The Cold War (circa 1947–1991) was a time of high tension underscored by the threat of nuclear war among the former Soviet Union, China, and the West. It was characterized not only by a widespread fear of nuclear annihilation and a war in Southeast Asia, but also by a preoccupation with psychological assessments of identity, anxiety, relationships, leadership, and hierarchy, particularly as these concepts related to decision making and emotional states. As we noted earlier, theories are as much a product of the times in which they were produced as they are the natural extensions of existing lines of scientific research. In the post-9/11 war-on-terror discourse about organizations and society, the resurgence of national interest in common human relations themes—identity, anxiety, relationships, and leadership—deserves assessment with its historical predecessor, the Cold War. It also raises the question: What topics would seem important to us today about communication in organizations if the Cold War and the war on terror had not intervened to shape our thinking (see Trethewey & Goodall, 2007)?

◻ THE HUMAN RESOURCES APPROACH

In retrospect, the human relations approach identified many important issues (e.g., that informal communication is important and that human decision making is emotional as well as rational) but fell short of truly valuing employee perceptions, worldviews, and voice. Where human relations encouraged employee communication mainly to "blow off steam," it took another set of thinkers to fully assert the crucial role all employees can play in promoting organizational effectiveness. While incorporating most of the assumptions of human relations, the **human resources** approach is concerned with the total organizational climate as well as with how an organization can encourage employee participation and dialogue. Three theorists best capture the spirit of the original human resources movement: Abraham Maslow, Douglas McGregor, and Rensis Likert.

☐ Maslow's Hierarchy of Needs

According to Abraham **Maslow's hierarchy of needs**, people's basic needs for food, shelter, and belonging must be satisfied before they can move toward achieving their full human potential, which Maslow calls "self-actualization" (Figure 3.2).

FIGURE 3.2

Maslow's Hierarchy of Needs

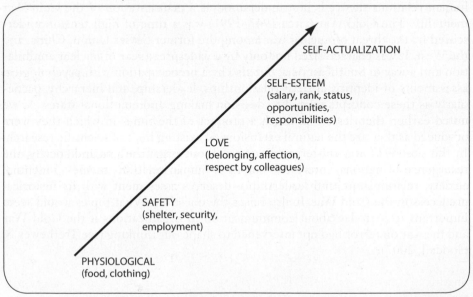

In Maslow's model, lower-level needs cease to be motivating as soon as they are fulfilled. If, for example, someone is satiated, food will not serve as a motivating force. Self-actualization, however, continues to motivate even as the need is being satisfied.

In *Eupsychian Management* (1965), Maslow poses the question: What are the conditions, including managerial approaches and employee rewards, that will enable self-actualization? He concludes that the conditions that foster individual health are often surprisingly good for the prosperity of the organization as well. He defines the problem of management as that of setting up social conditions in the organization so that the goals of the individual merge with those of the organization.

A quick perusal of corporate websites reveals that many organizations recruit the best and brightest candidates by highlighting opportunities for personal growth, fulfillment, and self-actualization. For example, Google's online career page simply states: "Do cool things that matter." Zappos's career page says, "Where culture thrives, passion follows." And Microsoft's page says, "Empower your future."

Maslow's ideas permeate contemporary management theory and practice. Jim Collins, one of the best-selling management authors today, argues that managers, entrepreneurs, and CEOs in great organizations are never satisfied with the status quo; rather, they yearn to be the best of the best. If designed correctly, the workplace becomes a site where individuals can realize their full potential and remain continually motivated.

Employees of award-winning organizations who work in rewarding and challenging positions may find it possible to align their personal development goals with customer service, intelligence gathering, or software engineering. However, it is unlikely that *all* employees will have the opportunity to self-actualize. The maintenance crew, cafeteria employees, and mail room staff, for example, may find it difficult to "be all that they can be" while working monotonous or otherwise unsatisfying jobs. Underlying Maslow's theory, then, is an undercurrent of the same class-based divisions that characterized Taylor's thinking, namely, the rather elitist notion that some members of society and organizations are more likely to become self-actualized than others.

The tension between the "non-actualized masses and the actualized few" is one that permeates Maslow's work (Cooke, Mills, & Kelley, 2005, p. 134). That said, Maslow's work is still current and paved the way for more recent theories of performance, including work on employee engagement and emotional intelligence (Sala, Drusket, & Mount, 2006).

☐ McGregor's Theory Y Management

Sharing Maslow's view that classical management theory fails to address important individual needs, Douglas McGregor (1960) argued that classical approaches are based in part on an assumption that the average employee dislikes work and avoids responsibility in the absence of external control. He calls the control-oriented, bureaucratic style of management **Theory X**, which he summarizes as follows:

1. The average human being has an inherent dislike of work and will avoid it if he [or she] can.
2. Because of [their] . . . dislike of work, most people must be coerced, controlled, directed, [or] threatened with punishment to get them to put forth adequate effort toward the achievement of organizational objectives.
3. The average human being prefers to be directed, wishes to avoid responsibility, has relatively little ambition, and wants security above all. (pp. 33–34)

Although Theory X may seem quite limited, it helps to identify some of the implicit and explicit assumptions of the traditional organization.

McGregor (1960) advances an alternative set of assumptions or principles in his **Theory Y**:

1. The expenditure of physical and mental effort in work is as natural as play or rest.
2. External control and threat of punishment are not the only means for bringing about effort toward organizational objectives. [People] will exercise self-direction and self-control in the service of objectives to which [they are] committed.
3. Commitment to objectives is a function of the rewards associated with their achievement (including the reward of self-actualization).
4. The average human being learns, under proper conditions, not only to accept but [also] to seek responsibility.
5. The capacity to exercise . . . relatively high degree[s] of imagination, ingenuity, and creativity in the solution of organizational problems is widely, not narrowly, distributed in the population.
6. Under the conditions of modern industrial life, the intellectual potential . . . of the average [person is] only partially utilized. (pp. 47–48)

In Theory Y, McGregor builds on the best of the human relations approach to offer a fundamentally different view of employees and of their relationship with management. Employees are viewed as possessing a high capacity for autonomy, responsibility, and innovation. Unlike the Theory X manager, the Theory Y manager has a more participative and facilitative management style that treats employees as valued human resources. Optimistic about incorporating the individual's desires in an organizational framework, McGregor argues that "the essential task of management is to arrange things so people achieve their own goals by accomplishing those of the organization" (cited in Perrow, 1986, p. 99). In contrast to the scalar principle of classical management, in which decision-making ability is centralized within management, McGregor offers the principle of integration, where employees are self-directed as a result of their commitment to organizational goals.

Managing the Kitchen

Most descriptions of management styles begin, as we did in this chapter, with an overview of scientific management, followed by a discussion of human relations and human resources management. This is not to say that management styles have followed a natural progression from scientific management to the human resources approach, nor that one approach to management is always better than another simply because it was developed first or last. In fact, examples of organizations that thrive under a more scientific management style continue to abound.

Consider the ways in which modern, professional kitchens are organized. Most continue to follow the rules established by the noted French chef Auguste Escoffier in the early twentieth century. Escoffier's approach is often referred to as a kitchen brigade and involves a strict hierarchy of the following positions:

- *Chef de cuisine*. Sometimes referred to as the head chef or the executive chef, the *chef de cuisine* is the overall manager of the kitchen who is responsible for the menu, ordering food, and leading the restaurant operation.
- *Sous-chef*. The second in command, the *sous-chef* takes orders from the *chef de cuisine* and oversees the executions of those orders.
- *Chef de partie*. Sometimes referred to as a station cook or a line cook, the *chef de partie* is in charge of a specific type of cooking, like a sauté chef. Station chefs are sometimes organized within their own hierarchy of first, second, and third chefs at the different cooking stations (e.g., fish chef, grill chef).
- *Commis*. This basic chef works under the *chef de partie* to learn the different stations in the kitchen.
- *Kitchen assistants*. Dishwashers and other individuals assist the chefs.

These hierarchies are evident not only in fine dining restaurants but also in television cooking shows like *Hell's Kitchen*. The repeated chorus of "Yes, Chef!" every time Chef Gordon Ramsay barks an order shows just how ingrained the contestants are to follow this brigade style of management.

The brigade approach most resembles a scientific or classical style of management, primarily as a way to ensure efficiency and effectiveness in the kitchen. Efficiency is required when chefs must feed many people each day, and effectiveness is required to ensure food quality and food safety.

Newer restaurant models have experimented with organizational and management styles. A new type of restaurant encourages people to take the food they need and leave what they see as a fair price in return. Some establishments even

(continued, Managing the Kitchen)

let patrons wash dishes or bus tables (i.e., engage in kitchen assistant roles) as a way to "pay" for their meal. While the brigade style of managing kitchens is still preferred, these new types of restaurants demonstrate that other styles are possible.

DISCUSSION QUESTIONS

1. Have you ever worked in a kitchen or restaurant? If so, how closely did the kitchen follow the brigade style of management? What kind of management style would you prefer as a kitchen or restaurant employee?
2. Even though more classical and scientific approaches to management help ensure efficiency and safety in the kitchen, how ethical is it for chefs like Gordon Ramsay to communicate with employees by barking orders and publicly shaming subordinates?
3. Alternative restaurant structures may be growing in popularity, but they also give us the opportunity to examine the relationship between what is ethical and what is fair. Is it fair for someone to eat a lot of food and leave a small amount of money or even no money at all? What if that person hadn't eaten in a couple of days? Why might the success of these restaurants be growing, even though they're working under a fairly unpredictable structure?
4. You have just been hired as a hotel manager for a five-hundred-room hotel that has a five-star restaurant serving breakfast, brunch, lunch, dinner, and room service. You manage both the hotel staff and the kitchen staff. The restaurant has a *chef de cuisine* to focus on the daily needs of the kitchen. The *chef de cuisine* oversees more than one hundred members of a formal brigade-style kitchen and restaurant. You have a very successful background in management, but you tend to prefer the human resources approach. What would you do to develop a good relationship with your *chef de cuisine*, even though you have different management styles? How might you integrate different management strategies that would help you meet both of your needs?

□ Likert's Principle of Supportive Relationships

Continuing the trend toward employee participation in decision making, the work of University of Michigan professor Rensis Likert has contributed to our understanding of high-involvement organizations. Likert's (1961) **principle of supportive relationships** holds that all interactions within an organization should support individual self-worth and importance, with an emphasis on the supportive relationships within work groups and open communication among them.

Likert divides organizations into four types, or "systems," based on degree of participation:

System I—exploitative/authoritative
System II—benevolent/authoritative
System III—consultative
System IV—participative

The principle of supportive relationships considers open communication to be among the most important aspects of management. It also prefers general oversight to close supervision and emphasizes the role of the supportive peer group in fostering productivity. Therefore, Likert's principle supports System IV, participative management.

Research on Likert's systems has been inconclusive (Perrow, 1986). Many studies have shown that good classical changes in organizations (e.g., improved work procedures and plans) are as important as participation in increasing organizational effectiveness. The human resources approach continues the human relations tendency to treat all organizations the same, which opponents in the institutional school and the cultural approach (see Chapter 5) view as inappropriate.

While the human resources approach emphasizes employee participation in organizational decision making, it does not explain the pragmatics or politics involved in establishing such a voice for employees. As a result, its prescriptions for participation tend to have limited use. Nevertheless, the quest for effective forms of participative decision making continues (Miller & Monge, 1986).

Summary

Three general approaches—classical management, human relations, and human resources—have greatly impacted the development of communication theories and organizational practice, and they continue to shape current thinking. When striving to understand organizational communication, remember that all historical narratives and all human communication exhibit the three *P*'s: they are partial, partisan, and problematic.

The classical management approach emerged during the Industrial Revolution, a period characterized by a quest to adapt the lessons of science and technology to make perfect machines. These early organizations were built on the model of the efficient machine, and so-called scientific management was characterized by a machinelike dependence on hierarchy, divisions of labor, strict rules for communication between management and workers, and formal routines. The term *bureaucracy* is often used to describe the structure of these early organizations. In some industries, similar attempts to rationalize organizations continue today.

In the image of the ideal machine, communication happens *before* the machine is turned on, such as when a manager explains how to operate the machine to the workers responsible for the labor. Communication that occurs *during* work tends to slow down production; therefore, informal talk is considered unnecessary and costly. Morgan (1986) suggests that the machine metaphor is useful for organizing work that is straightforward and repetitive in nature and is performed in a stable environment by compliant workers. He attributes the limitations of this approach to its narrow focus on efficiency: It does not adapt well to changing circumstances, and it can have a dehumanizing effect on employees. When opportunities for dialogue do not exist, employees' resentment may be expressed as resistance, leading to work slowdowns or even sabotage.

In the classical management approach, any attempt at achieving a balance between individual creativity and organizational constraint through dialogue will tilt in favor of constraint. The individual needs of workers are largely ignored, communication is limited to the giving of orders, and the strict imposition of rules and routines seeks to maintain order above all else. When such strict adherence to hierarchical power remains in place for too long, underground opposition or resistance is likely to emerge.

The human relations approach to organizations and communication emerged against the cultural and economic background of the Great Depression. Studies demonstrating a positive correlation between improved productivity and managers who paid attention to workers led to new theories about the role of communication at work. The balance in the organizational dialogue then tipped back toward a concern for individual creativity and the satisfaction of needs. However, critics argued that the balance had tipped too far and that making workers happy did not necessarily make them more productive. They saw the new social ethic as a threat to the Protestant work ethic with its emphasis on achievement and entrepreneurship.

Refinements in human relations theory led to the human resources approach. Through this approach, advances were made in our understanding of the relationship between individual needs for creativity and organizational structures. In the period following World War II, studies of leadership style, decision making, and organizations as institutions served to redefine the individual in organizations as socially situated and rational only within limits.

This highly contingent and dynamic view of the individual suggests a new role for communication: The construction of definitions of the situation and of decision premises that shape individual behavior. It also suggests a new view of employee motivation and performance: The employee's motivation is derived from his or her interests, which constitute the individual's definition of the situation. Situations are symbolic constructions of reality that are individualized according to personal needs, desires, and interests. Many employees are motivated as much by symbolic rewards as they are by their paychecks.

The human resources movement is a precursor of many of today's most common management practices. Employees are given more freedom to construct organizational reality through opportunities for dialogue. Their increased involvement, however, also means greater responsibility and accountability for decisions and actions. Of all the approaches to management that we have observed in action, participative management is the most difficult to implement. However, when applied successfully, it fosters more satisfied, committed employees and more productive organizations.

Two extremes of thought on organization and management—tightly controlled formal bureaucracies versus a looser, more empathic view of employees as valuable human resources—are at the opposite ends of our theoretical continuum for understanding organizational communication. At the far right is bureaucracy, which holds that formal structure and communication that respect the chain of command ensure productivity and stability. At the far left is the human resources approach, which holds that open communication between managers and employees ensures creativity, adaptability to change, and satisfaction of the individual's needs and motivations. We have discussed the problems associated with an organizational dialogue that is tipped too far in favor of either approach. In the following chapters, we will examine new theories that propose solutions to these problems.

QUESTIONS FOR REVIEW AND DISCUSSION

1. Why do we need theory to study organizational communication? What do we mean by the idea that all theories are metaphors?

2. Why is all communication partial, partisan, and problematic?

3. What is the classical management approach? What does the machine metaphor imply about communication in organizations based on classical management? What is "scientific" about Henri Fayol's approach to decision making?

4. What is useful about the idea of resistance to domination when it is applied to classical management theories? Does this idea have relevance in today's organizations? If so, why and how?

5. Why were Mary Parker Follett's ideas about management considered "radical" in her day? What specific influences of her work can you see in human relations and human resources theories?

6. What are the principles of the human relations and human resources approaches to organizational communication? What was the influence of the Triple Alliance on the historical development of organizational communication? Why did Elton Mayo's work have so much impact?

7. Why has Abraham Maslow's hierarchy of needs had such far-reaching implications for the development of human resources approaches to management and communication? What are the fundamental differences between McGregor's Theory X and Theory Y when applied to human communication at work?

KEY TERMS

Bureaucracy, p. 76
Classical management, p. 67
Hawthorne effect, p. 81
Hidden transcript, p. 71
Human relations, p. 79
Human resources, p. 84
Maslow's hierarchy of needs, p. 84
Partiality, p. 66
Particularism, p. 76

Partisan, p. 66
Principle of supportive relationships, p. 87
Problematic, p. 67
Resistance to domination, p. 70
Scientific management, p. 72
Theory, p. 65
Theory X, p. 86
Theory Y, p. 86

Riverside State Hospital

BACKGROUND

Riverside State Hospital is a five-hundred-bed, state-supported psychiatric facility located along the scenic banks of the Tennessee River. Admission to the facility requires a physician's order or a court referral. The hospital staff consists of physicians, psychologists, psychiatrists, nurses, dietitians, pharmacists, therapists, technicians, and general housekeeping and groundskeeping personnel, all of whom are state employees. The hospital is run primarily as a bureaucracy, with levels of authority and salary based on seniority and rank.

All employees hold a government service (GS) rank, the lowest being GS-1 (groundskeeping trainee) and the highest, GS-15 (administrator or CEO). In addition, within each rank are seven to ten steps, which are determined by seniority and achievement. Performance reviews are conducted annually, at which time promotions in steps or in GS rank may occur. Employees are given annual salary adjustments for inflation or cost-of-living increases. Full state benefits are provided to all workers.

Riverside employees work eight-hour shifts. Employees below rank GS-12 (head or chief) take a thirty-minute lunch break and 2 fifteen-minute breaks during each shift. Members of the professional staff (physicians, nurses, pharmacists, and the like) work on a three-shift schedule: 7 a.m. to 3 p.m., 3 p.m. to 11 p.m., and 11 p.m. to 7 a.m. The hospital operates year-round.

THE PROBLEM

A few days ago, a resident patient at Riverside State Hospital was killed when part of the wall next to his bed collapsed. Horace James Wilcox Jr. was fifty-six years old when he died. He had no family and had been a resident at the hospital for three years. He suffered from traumatic amnesia and scored in the borderline range on intelligence tests. He was otherwise in good health. He was also well liked and seemed to be responding to treatment.

In statements made to state investigators and the news media, hospital administrators called the accident a "tragedy." They explained, "There had been no indication that the wall was weak or that Wilcox was in any danger." You are the government investigator assigned to the Wilcox case. Your job is to determine whether any evidence exists that would make Riverside State Hospital liable for Wilcox's death.

(continued, Riverside State Hospital)

THE INVESTIGATION

You learn from your investigation that Wilcox was a quiet man who tended to keep to himself, although he did join the other patients on the ward for scheduled games and activities. During these times, he talked a lot about current news events. Watching television news was his favorite source of entertainment. He was known among the staff as the most informed patient on the ward.

Your investigation also reveals that Wilcox's amnesia was complicated by his belief that he was directly affected by whatever he saw on television. News events—particularly family tragedies—affected him deeply. The hospital staff had tried reducing his television viewing time to prevent further complications, but he became depressed. His television privileges were restored as a result, and the staff tried instead to use the emotions he displayed about news shows in his therapy. Perhaps, they reasoned, some family tragedy had produced the traumatic amnesia.

In addition, for the past month, Wilcox had repeatedly exclaimed, "The sky is falling," especially when he was confined to his bed at night and in the morning upon awakening. He would also point at the ceiling and walls of his room and cry out, "There is trouble here, trouble from the sky." On several such occasions he had to be physically restrained and calmed with drugs. During this same month, an Air Force fighter plane had exploded in the sky during an air show, and videotape of that event had appeared frequently on the television news. Given Wilcox's past history of responding emotionally to tragedies reported in the news, the staff linked his most recent behavior to the air show disaster. However, you think there may be more to it. Considering Wilcox's unwillingness to go to bed at night, his complaints about an impending tragedy may have had an altogether different meaning: Perhaps "the sky" was a reference to perceived structural defects in the walls and ceiling of his room. You wonder whether Wilcox was trying to direct attention to the actual physical deterioration of his room. Moreover, his psychiatric history may have led those in charge of his care to dismiss his allegations.

Upon further investigation, you learn that the walls and ceiling in Wilcox's room had been repainted three times during the past twelve months due to stains from a leaking water pipe. You think the leak may have seriously weakened the wall, and you feel that hospital personnel should have followed up on this situation. You also discover that state funding for maintenance had been cut back severely during the previous summer and that although there was structural damage to the wall, there was no indication that it was unsafe. From the hospital administrators' perspective, then, the culprits were an aging building and insufficient state funding to repair it. Even so, they maintain that the collapse of the wall was "an unforeseeable accident." You obtain copies of the building inspection reports for the past three years. You note that in the past year, state inspectors recorded the deteriorating condition of the wall and ceiling that eventually collapsed. These forms were signed by Hillary Hanks, the head of resident life.

In an interview with Hanks, you discover that although her name appears on the state inspection forms, she did not actually sign them. She explains that her secretary, Nancy Ellis, regularly signs her name on state forms to save time. She adds, "There are so many forms to sign that if I signed them all, I wouldn't get any real work done." When you speak to Ellis, she confirms Hanks's story. Furthermore, Ellis is annoyed because the man who delivered the forms to her was supposed to point out any problems that required attention. The problem with the walls and ceiling in Wilcox's room had not been reported verbally to Ellis, and therefore she didn't notify Hanks. Now Hanks is in trouble with her superior, and that means Ellis will lose her chance at a promotion. Any trouble for Hanks generally means trouble for Ellis, too. Ellis admits that she regularly avoids telling her boss any bad news for exactly that reason, but this time, Ellis claims, she was unaware of the bad news. You ask Ellis what she did with the inspection report. She points to the overstuffed filing cabinet behind her. "That's where I put it," she says, "along with all the other paperwork that never gets read around here."

You find out that the report was prepared by state inspector Blake Barrymore, who gave it to a groundskeeper for delivery to the appropriate hospital administrator because "it was raining that day, and I was late for another inspection." He adds that it is not his official responsibility to deliver the report himself or to follow up on it. You discover that the inspection report was delivered by Jack Handy, a reliable and well-liked groundskeeper, but you also discover that Handy is illiterate. He did not know what the forms contained because he could not read them. He did not report any problems with the walls or ceiling because Barrymore didn't tell him there were any problems. Besides, Handy added, "Nobody listens to a groundskeeper anyway. I could tell the administrators that there was a bomb in the hospital, and because I'm just a groundskeeper, they'd let it pass. So I just do what I'm told to do." You file your report. The insurance company claims that gross negligence on the part of Riverside State Hospital indirectly caused the death of Horace James Wilcox Jr. At a press conference, the hospital spokesman places the blame for Wilcox's death on Nancy Ellis, claiming that it was her responsibility to report the problem to her superior, Hillary Hanks. He adds that Hanks has been "reassigned" to other duties and is unavailable for comment. In a final statement, the spokesman says, "The hospital deeply regrets this tragic accident and reminds the state legislature that until the requested funds for structural repairs are made available, the hospital administration cannot be held accountable for structural defects that are beyond its control."

(continued, Riverside State Hospital)

Assignment

1. What management approach does Riverside State Hospital's style of management most resemble?
2. How does the management approach influence communication at the hospital?
3. Should Ellis be held responsible for Wilcox's death? Why or why not? In what ways did the hospital's organizational structure contribute to Wilcox's accidental death?
4. What recommendations would you propose to help Riverside State Hospital avoid similar occurrences in the future? How can organizational communication be improved?

CHAPTER 4

The Systems Perspective on Organizations and Communication

In this and the following chapter we continue our story of organizations and communication by considering two prominent metaphors—systems and cultures—through which we seek to describe the contemporary world. According to one well-known observer of business, "The unhealthiness of our world today is in direct proportion to our inability to see it as a whole" (Senge, 1990, p. 168). By thinking in terms of systems and cultures, we find ways of thinking about wholes, and in so doing we may learn how to survive in an era of economic, political, and environmental limits. Unlike the machine metaphor of classical management theory, the focus of the systems and cultural approaches is not on individual parts or people but on relationships, on the pattern that connects (Bateson, 1972). As such, these approaches give supreme emphasis to communication—that is, to the development of meaning through human interaction.

We begin with the systems approach, which broadens our way of looking at organizations by borrowing concepts from other areas of study, including engineering, biology, chemistry, physics, economics, and sociology. Associated with the nature of a system are such components as environment, interdependence, goals, feedback, and order. In addition, the systems approach has important implications for the situated individual striving to balance creativity and constraint.

◩ THE SYSTEMS PERSPECTIVE

A classic advertisement for BMW poses this question: "What makes the BMW the ultimate driving machine?" Is it the car's superb handling and braking? Aerodynamic design? Powerful engine? According to the advertisement, no single feature makes the BMW special; rather, the car is unique in the way that all its qualities work together as a whole to create "the ultimate driving machine."

This advertisement nicely illustrates the **systems approach**, which emphasizes the important difference between a disconnected set of parts versus a collection of parts that work together to create a functional whole. That functional whole is called a "system," and in a system the whole is more than the sum of its parts. Sociologist Walter Buckley (1967) translates this expression as follows: "The 'more than' points to the fact of organization, which imparts to the aggregate characteristics that are not only different from, but [also] often not found in the components alone; and the 'sum of the parts' must be taken to mean, not their numerical addition, but their unorganized aggregation" (p. 42). In other words, organization makes a social system more than just its individual pieces. In a marriage, family, team, or business, the *relationships* that exist among people are what make the group a system.

Although it has come to be applied broadly to social systems, the systems approach has its roots in the natural sciences, notably physics and biology, as we discuss in the following sections.

☐ The Origins of Systems Theory in the Natural Sciences

Before the groundbreaking work of Albert Einstein, Isaac Newton's concepts of the universe prevailed. Space and time were viewed as distinct entities operating "in a fixed arena in which events took place, but which was not affected by what happened in it. . . . Bodies moved, forces attracted and repelled, but time and space simply continued, unaffected" (Hawking, 1988, p. 33). There is a parallel between this view of the physical world and classical approaches to organization. Scientific management, for example, relied heavily on time and motion studies (whose principles were drawn from Newtonian physics) to provide data to managers about worker productivity and efficiency.

Einstein's theory of relativity radically transformed how we saw our world. This new way of seeing brought new questions: What if time and space are not fixed but relative? If, as Einstein's general theory of relativity suggests, time runs slower nearer the earth due to the influence of its gravitational pull, does this imply that observations of what appears to be a fixed reality are skewed by the observer's position? For example, a commercial jetliner passing overhead often appears to be floating, almost standing still, when in fact it is traveling at hundreds of miles an hour. Relativity theory explains what is wrong with the assumption of a fixed universe:

> Space and time are . . . dynamic quantities: when a body moves, or a force acts, it affects the curvature of space and time—and in turn the structure of space-time affects the way in which bodies move and forces act. Space and time not only affect but also are affected by everything that happens in the universe. (Hawking, 1988, p. 33)

In other words, rather than conceptualizing time and motion studies within the limited framework of a specific task, the interpretation of the task is expanded to include how it functions as part of a dynamic interdependent system. For example, a company can work hard to lower the cost of its product through more efficient production, but if it fails to closely monitor consumer tastes, it may end up failing anyway. So, the technology for making high-quality, inexpensive compact discs has never been better, but they are quickly becoming obsolete in an era of digital downloads. Systems theory encourages us to explore how organizational effectiveness depends on the coordination of the total enterprise. Appropriate questions might include: What are the intended and unintended consequences of increased or decreased efficiency? How do pressures to reduce time and eliminate unnecessary steps in production affect employee morale, absenteeism, commitment, and turnover? How, in turn, do these factors affect productivity in important but potentially unexpected ways?

This shift in our understanding of the laws of the universe does more than simply call into question the rationality of time and motion studies. It also brings to our attention the idea of dynamic systems of interacting components, whose relationships and interactions point to a new kind of order based on patterns of interaction. The ideas of dynamic systems were applied to atomic physics, navigational science, aerospace engineering, and electronics, but it was not until World War II that a *general* systems paradigm emerged with applications to organizations. Indeed, today we don't have to look far to see the impact of systems theory on the field of communication. Consider some of the terms we routinely use to describe communication: *sender*, *message*, *channel*, *receiver*, and *feedback*. Before 1948, the vocabulary of communication developed by the ancient Greeks was still in use (e.g., *speech*, *speaker*, *audience*, *ethos*, *pathos*, and *logos*). Since then, our language about communication processes has been transformed by the information revolution. As Stuart Clegg (1990) puts it, "Systems ideas are now so much a part of the modernist consciousness that they barely require elaborate iteration" (p. 51).

In addition to theoretical advances in physics, new technologies have been spawned by industries capitalizing on scientific advances. Primarily an outgrowth of the transistor and, later, the microchip, communication technologies like television, satellites, computers, and smartphones have contributed to the emergence of what Marshall McLuhan called the "global information society" (1964). McLuhan's idea is simple but profound. The instantaneous transfer of information across cultural boundaries means that our perceptions of reality, of cultural differences, of political and social events, and even our views of what constitutes "the news" cease to be mediated by fixed notions of space and time. Because information now connects us in ways not possible before, the world has become—in McLuhan's famous phrase—a "global village."

☐ Biology and General Systems Theory

Within the broad context of the information revolution there emerged a more specific contributor to systems theory—the natural sciences, and especially biology. It is easy to see why. A living system is alive not because of any particular component or component process (e.g., a respiratory or digestive system), but because of the relationships and interchanges among processes. Within any system there are subsystems, and it is the *connections* between subsystems (e.g., how oxygen gets from the lungs into the blood, then into the muscles and synapses) that define the characteristics of biological or living organisms. To take a holistic approach means to consider the properties of systems that come out of the relationships among their subsystems or parts.

Biologists Ludwig von Bertalanffy (1968) and J. G. Miller (1978) are credited with advancing the study of living systems, and von Bertalanffy pioneered the development of general systems theory. **General systems theory** applies the properties of living systems—such as input, output, boundaries, homeostasis, and **equifinality** (the idea that there is more than one right way to accomplish the same goal)—to a dazzling array of social phenomena. Table 4.1 on page 101 provides an overview of the hierarchy of general systems theory. As biologist Lewis Thomas explains in his landmark work *The Lives of a Cell* (1975):

> Although we are by all odds the most social of all social animals—more interdependent, more attached to each other, more inseparable in our behavior than bees—we do not often feel our conjoined intelligence. Perhaps it is in this respect that language differs most sharply from biological systems for communication. Ambiguity seems to be an essential, indispensable element for the transfer of information from one place to another by words, where matters of real importance are concerned. It is often necessary, for meaning to come through, that there be an almost vague sense of strangeness and askewness. Speechless animals and cells cannot do this. . . . Only the human mind is designed to work this way, programmed to drift away in the presence of locked-on information, straying from each point in the hunt for a better, different point. (pp. 89–94)

In other words, the ambiguity inherent in all human communication makes the interdependencies between members of a social system (i.e., among people) looser than those found in biology or those that connect the parts of a car. The fact that words are open to interpretation means that while we may think we understand one another, there may in fact be a wide gap in interpretation of which we may not be aware. Put another way: "Social organizations, in contrast to physical or mechanical structures, are loosely coupled systems" (Scott, 1981, p. 103).

TABLE 4.1

The Hierarchy of General Systems Theory

LEVEL	DESCRIPTION AND EXAMPLES	THEORY AND MODELS
Static structures	Atoms, molecules, crystals, biological structures from the electron microscope to the macroscopic level	Structural formulas of chemistry; crystallography; anatomical descriptions
Clockworks	Clocks, conventional machines in general, solar systems	Conventional physics, such as the laws of mechanics (Newton and Einstein)
Control mechanisms	Thermostats, servomechanisms, homeostatic mechanisms in organisms	Cybernetics; feedback and information theory
Open systems	Flames, cells, and organisms in general	Expansion of physical theory to systems maintaining themselves in flow of matter (metabolism); information storage in genetic code (DNA)
Lower organisms	Plantlike organisms: increasing differentiation of system (so-called division of labor in the organism); distinction of reproduction and functional individual ("germ track and soma")	Theory and models mostly lacking
Animals	Increasing importance of traffic in information (evolution of receptors, nervous systems); learning; beginnings of consciousness	Beginnings in automata theory (stimulus-response relations), feedback (regulatory phenomena), autonomous behavior (relaxation oscillations)
Humans	Symbolism; past and future, self and world, self-awareness as consequences; communication by language	Incipient theory of symbolism
Sociocultural systems	Populations of organisms (humans included); symbol-determined communities (cultures) in humans only	Statistical and possibly dynamic laws in population dynamics, sociology, economics, possibly history; beginnings of a cultural systems theory
Symbolic systems	Language, logic, mathematics, sciences, arts, morals	Algorithms of symbols (e.g., mathematics, grammar); "rules of the game," such as in visual arts and music

Source: From *General system theory*, by L. von Bertalanffy, 1968, pp. 28–29.

With the advent of relativity and the use of analogies between organic systems and human societies, the concept of dynamic systems was born, offering innovative ways of understanding the relationships among functioning components in space and time. However, applying systems theory to human language would prove to be challenging. The work of chemist Ilya Prigogine (1980) has helped to expand the potential application of systems thinking to social organization. By studying chemical reactions, Prigogine found that in open systems, defined as those systems that *must* interact with their environments to survive, a movement toward disorder often precedes the emergence of a new order. In contrast to the Newtonian vision of a universe constantly falling apart, Prigogine's findings suggest that both living and nonliving systems have the potential for self-organization or self-renewal in the face of environmental change, and that disorder is a natural part of the renewal process.

More recently, biological concepts and processes have gained greater prominence in organizational theory and practice. Most notably, manufacturing and information (computer) system designs are now being fashioned after robust biological systems. Abandoning the top-down, "central-processing" model implicit in classical approaches, all manner of new organizational structures and processes are being modeled after living systems, which tend to exhibit distributed intelligence. By **distributed intelligence** we mean that all members of the system—whether people or cells—play an important role in the system's ongoing self-organization. Imagine for a moment what life would be like under a central processing unit (CPU) in which the brain was in charge of everything that happened in your body. What would happen if your brain had to "turn on" the rest of the body's systems each morning? Our tendency to equate rationality with intelligence has caused us to miss the very real, but nonlinguistic, forms of intelligence that are distributed throughout our bodies.

The advantage of modeling organizations after living systems is that living systems—which exhibit distributed intelligence and seek to organize—are far more adaptive to a changing environment than are closed systems such as machines. Even theories of artificial intelligence have moved from centralized models to linked computers that share information in a weblike fashion. Echoing our earlier discussion of participation and voice, the tentative conclusion appears to be that people learn best in a complex environment when they are loosely connected and free to initiate action from anywhere in an organization.

☐ From Biology to Organizational Communication

Academic disciplines whose traditional focus had been on complex processes of information exchange embraced systems theory. Sociologist Albion Small (1905) used concepts of systems theory in his field-defining work at the University of Chicago, and other prominent social theorists, such as Talcott Parsons (1951) and

George Homans (1961), followed suit. Similarly, the initial popularity of the systems approach to organizational communication studies was enormous. Daniel Katz and Robert Kahn's *The Social Psychology of Organizations* (1966), a landmark application of systems theory to organizations, argued that organizations are fundamentally open systems that require a constant flow of information to and from their environment. In the field of organizational communication, then, systems theory provided a new connection between communicating and organizing.

Following the collapse of the Berlin Wall in 1989 and the opening of the republics that made up the former Soviet Union, new systems of PC-based communication—combined with the new technology of powerful search engines—created new business relationships and global markets via the Internet. One search engine in particular—Google—has as its corporate mission to "organize the world's information and make it universally accessible and useful." Never before has knowledge of systems, and particularly of communication systems, been more highly prized worldwide.

◻ WHAT IS A SYSTEM?

As you can tell from the preceding discussion, a system may be defined as a complex set of relationships among interdependent components or parts. In the study of organizational communication, we are concerned both with the nature of those components in organizations and with the relationships among them.

☐ Environment and Open Systems

According to systems theory, organizations do not exist as entities isolated from the rest of the world. Rather, organizations exist in increasingly turbulent environments that both provide inputs to the organization and receive outputs in the form of products and services. For a company to succeed, some of its members must spend a significant amount of time engaged in environmental scanning, the careful monitoring of competitors, suppliers, government legislation, global economics, new technologies, political developments, and consumer preferences. Failure to do so leaves an organization vulnerable to unexpected environmental jolts, which can have disastrous consequences. In most successful companies, environmental scanning is done by organizational **boundary spanners**, employees who have regular opportunities for interaction with people outside of the company.

An organization's relationship with its environment, however, is not limited to scanning. As open systems, organizations must also work *with* their environments to be successful, for example, by establishing joint ventures and strategic partnerships. This is a significant change from traditional "us-against-them" theories of competition. It is often difficult for companies to know who is a potential adversary or friend, so the best strategy is usually **coopetition**, a blend of cooperation and competition that tries to reap the best of both worlds (Brandenburger & Nalebuff, 1996). Within a state higher education system, universities sometimes come together to coordinate program offerings and work together to create online offerings. A landmark example of coopetition is SEMATECH, a semiconductor consortium formed by the U.S. government to improve the global competitiveness of the entire semiconductor industry (Browning & Shetler, 2000). At first, participating companies (e.g., Intel, HP, Motorola) were uncomfortable sharing information with their "enemies," but they later came to the important realization that their individual competitiveness was enhanced, not hindered, by a certain level of cooperation.

This critical insight can be useful in the development of cross-functional collaboration within social networks and organizations. **Open systems theory** encourages individual members (whether people, departments, or organizations) to be mindful of the importance of the overall health of their industry "ecosystem" (Lewin, 1997). For an example of how this theory applies to the local food movement, see *What Would You Do?* on page 105. The analogy between organizations and living organisms helps further explain the concept of open systems. Organisms are open systems in that they rely on exchanges with their environment to survive. Human beings, for example, need food, air, water, and sunlight to live. Similarly, organizations rely on communication with their environments. As Walter Buckley (1967) explains, "That a system is open means, not simply that it engages in interchanges with the environment, but that this interchange is an essential factor underlying the system's viability, its reproductive ability or continuity, and its ability to change" (p. 50). Therefore, an open system that interacts productively with its environment tends to create structure or, more simply, to organize, whereas in a closed system there is little or no interaction with the environment and the organization may approach entropy or disorder.

☐ Interdependence

Another essential quality of a system, **interdependence**, refers both to the wholeness of the system and its environment and to the interrelationships of individuals within the system. These relationships can vary in terms of their degree of interdependence.

For example, the student-teacher relationship is generally one of dependence— the teacher's feedback about the student can affect his or her success in the class, but the student's feedback about the teacher is much less likely to have any impact. The lack of mutual interdependence results from a significant power imbalance. In contrast, because most marriages are characterized by a high degree of interdependence, the decision of one partner to withdraw emotionally from the relationship puts the whole system at risk. In systems theory, then, the interdependent relationships between people not only give an organization its character, but also are established and maintained through communication.

Locavores, Sustainability, and Systems

The term *locavore* was coined in 2005 by four women in San Francisco who organized a sustainability group on behalf of locally grown foods, or foods grown within a hundred-mile radius of the city. By 2007, the word *locavore* had become so popular that Oxford University Press named it "Word of the Year." This is certainly a testament to how quickly the organic and systemic approach to encouraging local food production and consumption grew into a global social movement contributing to sustainable environments (Cloud, 2007, p. 3).

As the world becomes more conscious of the real costs—the carbon footprint—created by importing and marketing food grown thousands of miles from home, there has been increasing interest in finding better ways of protecting our environment and improving our health. For example, "shipping a strawberry from California to New York requires 435 calories of fossil fuel but provides the eater with only 5 calories of nutrition" (Cloud, 2007, p. 3). Furthermore, the longer food—even organic food—remains in transit or on the supermarket shelf, the lower its nutritional value. Adding to the appeal of consuming organic foods grown from sources close to home is the fact that a growing number of shoppers shy away from produce that has been genetically modified or grown with pesticides and avoid meat and poultry that has been injected with hormones. One study by Packaged Facts (2015) reports that in 2014, non-GMO products accounted for $550 billion of the total $5 trillion global food and beverage market. They also predict that the global market for non-GMO products will double by 2019.

There is a growing desire on the part of many individuals to better understand the impact of their food choices on their natural and economic environment. These connections can be made through various applications of systems theory, in which ecological thinking is central. In fact, there are several websites that allow you to measure your carbon footprint as well as to gauge how you can lower it by making a few changes in your lifestyle, including your food-purchasing habits. (You can use the Nature Conservancy's carbon footprint calculator, for example.)

Locavores are significantly impacting the ways we learn about the complex relationship between sustainable environments, economics, nutrition, and health. By emphasizing the interdependent and evolving connections among environment, goals for health, and the ecology of the planet, locavores enact the basic tenets of a systems approach to organizing and problem solving. Their approach also serves as a good example of how to apply systems thinking to the

(continued, Locavores, Sustainability, and Systems)

food we produce and consume. Just as systems theories are often perceived as difficult to apply because of their complexity, changing our lives and our eating habits to reduce our carbon footprint may be seen by some skeptics as unrealistic.

DISCUSSION QUESTIONS

1. What story do you tell your friends about what you eat? Does that story connect your eating habits to larger environmental or health issues (e.g., does it degrade the environment or shorten your life span)? If so, what effect does that connection have on listeners? If not, what might you do to connect your story to those concerns?
2. Given what you have read about systems theories and sustainability, does personal preference for taste, color, and even price trump ecological concerns? Do our food choices have ethical implications that go beyond our ability to pay for food?
3. What connections do you see between the decisions one makes in choosing to be a locavore, and the effects of these decisions on other aspects of a person's life? How do decisions about food—made in the context of ecological sustainability and healthy living—affect other relationships and commitments that a person may have?

The failure to recognize interdependence in dynamic systems leads to what ecologist Garrett Hardin (1968) calls "the tragedy of the commons." The tragedy of the commons, for example, the destruction of rain forests, the exploitation of grazing land, the pollution of major waterways, occurs when a group of people (or organizations or departments within organizations) with access to a common resource use it in ways that focus on personal needs rather than on the needs of the whole. While each individual's actions may make sense from his or her perspective, the failure to recognize the interdependence and consequences of one's actions can be devastating to both the individual and the system.

In organizations, division of labor can cloud people's perceptions of the interdependent nature of their work. For example, when we toured a company that manufactures high-technology radio transmitters, we asked employees to describe the various kinds of jobs available in the company and whether they had considered cross-training or moving to a different department. We found that most employees in the company were ignorant of the nature of their coworkers' jobs. Even employees within the same work group had little knowledge of one another's jobs, despite their daily contacts. One employee, who for fifteen years had been handing over his finished parts to a coworker through a small window in an interior wall, had no idea what the coworker did with those parts. A worst-case scenario from a systems perspective, the company's employees did not see themselves as part of an interdependent system because of the strict division of labor. In an interdependent system, no part of the system can stand alone; each relies on the other parts to do its job effectively.

Health-care organizations often recognize the importance of building system interdependence into their everyday practices. In the context of health care, **communication breakdowns** are a common cause of surgical errors and other adverse events for patients (Nagpal et al., 2010). These communication breakdowns, or instances where information was not appropriately delivered, received, or interpreted, can happen across the preoperative, intraoperative, and postoperative phases of care. According to one review, most "breakdowns" occur between a single sender and a single receiver, and surgeons were the most common "transmitters and receivers" in communication breakdowns (Greenberg et al., 2007). One explanation for these breakdowns may be that surgeons often rely on assumptions, rather than check those assumptions through communication with team members. For instance, surgeons may assume that particular instruments or equipment will be on hand in the operating room. If not, the surgeon may cut corners, use whatever tools are available, and potentially jeopardize the patient's care. Alternatively, health-care team members may have different expectations for communication. Nurses may believe that preoperative briefings increase patient safety, while surgeons may view such briefings as taking valuable time away from surgery to tell people what they should already know (Nagpal et al., 2010). Checking assumptions and building in more standardized procedures for delivering preoperative information are two simple steps that could increase interdependence and improve patient outcomes in health-care organizations.

☐ Goals

Organizational goals are defined in various ways in theories of organization and communication. From a scientific management perspective, goals are central: Both individuals and organizations direct their activities toward goal attainment. Increasingly, corporations rely on acronyms like SMART—specific, measureable, attainable, realistic, and timely—as a way to move individuals toward strategically set goals. At the same time, institutional perspectives also show that organizations and their members may espouse goals, but quite often these same goals do not guide their behavior (Scott, 1981).

Michael Keeley (1980) makes an important distinction regarding organizational goals. Examining the traditional view of organizations as being mobilized around common goals, he distinguishes between the goals *of* individuals, which are personal and highly variable, and the goals individuals have *for* their organization, which are more likely to be shared. One of the primary functions of leadership is to focus employee attention on a limited number of top priorities that individuals are interested in pursuing. One version of these compelling organizational aspirations are what Jim Collins calls big, hairy, audacious goals (BHAGs): Priorities that are clearly articulated and broadly shared with employees.

Goals may differ across system levels. For example, a department at one level within a large corporation may seek to be profitable. At the next level, however, the corporation may be under pressure from stakeholders to raise cash, and this corporate goal may result in selling the business unit (a decision that is unfavorable to the unit). At the same time, the first unit's goal of profitability may conflict with the individual goals of employees or managers within the unit, who advocate goals such as improving product quality or focusing on strategic products at the expense of others. Systems theory emphasizes that what is good for one level of the system may not be good for the other levels.

☐ Processes and Feedback

A system is not simply an interdependent set of components; it is also an interdependent collection of processes that interact over time. For instance, the production of this textbook is the result of many rounds of development and revision. Editors respond to customer concerns and must somehow bring together the authors as well as the design, production, digital, advertising, marketing, and sales teams. Moreover, these collaborative processes involve numerous handoffs, the timing and quality of which will shape, if not determine, the nature of the finished product. Whereas classical theories directed our attention to the individual employee, systems approaches lead us to focus on core processes.

Suppose that an instructor is dissatisfied with the coverage in a textbook and cancels future orders, or that he or she is generally pleased with the product but requests changes in its design. These are examples of **feedback**, which can be defined as a system of loops that connect communication and action. Individuals provide messages to others, who then respond to those messages in some way. In systems theory, there are two main types of feedback: negative and positive. Negative, or deviation-counteracting, feedback is illustrated by the instructor's complaint about the textbook. The negative feedback seeks to reestablish the goals or quality levels that were initially established for the product. This type of feedback is sometimes referred to as "cybernetic," after the Greek word for "steersman," or someone who used oars to stay on course. The other type of feedback—positive, or deviation-amplifying, feedback—is illustrated by the consultant who suggests changes in product design. It seeks to find new avenues of growth and development.

In their work on learning organizations, Chris Argyris and Donald Schon (1978) assert that businesses need both deviation-counteracting and deviation-amplifying feedback to achieve success. While deviation-counteracting feedback encourages adherence to an established strategy or course of action, deviation-amplifying feedback ensures that alternative strategies or courses of action are considered. Argyris and Schon call the latter practice "double-loop learning," or the ability to "learn how to learn" by using feedback to reexamine established assumptions and decision premises.

An intriguing contemporary application of this type of complex thinking is found in organizational communication scholar Steve Corman's (2006) notion of **counter-networking**. The term refers to any approach that seeks to impede an adversary's performance through modification of its communication network (p. 93). Corman's interest is in countering terrorist networks by using **reverse organizational science**, which means turning around the usual advice given to business leaders about making their organizations more successful. In this way, counter-networking is a process for using a systems approach to create negative feedback that promotes "un-learning" and chaos among terrorists. One example is the introduction of urgently needed but false information (e.g., the time of a scheduled meeting prior to a suicide bomber attack) through a credible source within the terrorist network. The misinformation would then travel throughout the network, the ability of the terrorist team to coordinate their work would be impaired, and the likelihood of capturing the team members would be increased by tracking the message backward through the network.

☐ Openness, Order, and Contingency

Systems theory evokes the image of a complex, interdependent organization that operates within a dynamic environment and is engaged in an ongoing struggle to create order in the face of unpredictability (Clegg, 1990; Thompson, 1967). In retrospect, it is indeed surprising that classical management theories paid so little attention to an organization's environment, focusing instead on treating organizations equally and directing management to conduct careful studies of the "one best way" to accomplish work within the boundaries of the organization.

By contrast, today's open systems are less reassuring and much more unpredictable. Environmental openness helps organizations see themselves as part of a dynamic system of intricate interdependencies and relationships. Openness in the organization-environment relationship also has implications for some of the more prescriptive aspects of organizational theory. The existence of diverse environments across industries, companies, and even geographic regions means that the same organizing principles and solutions cannot be applied in all situations; rather, they are contingent on various factors. For example, the health of our global economy continues to be a major challenge for governments and organizations worldwide. The complexity and interconnectedness of the global economic system was made frighteningly apparent when the falsely inflated global housing bubble burst in 2007, which in turn led to an unprecedented, rapid insolvency among banks and investment houses during 2008. (These events were dramatized in the Oscar-nominated film *The Big Short* in 2015.) Motivated by high rates of return and hiding behind complex financial structures, some of the most well-respected and established financial institutions in the world made millions of uncollectable loans and eventually collapsed. These banking and financial failures, an inability of leading nations to generate credible solutions, and repeated calls for multibillion-dollar bailouts, combined with massive layoffs and a dramatic downturn in consumer confidence, in turn spawned a deep recession worldwide.

Clearly the weakness of our global economy is unlikely to be resolved by the actions of any one government or industry. Because this is a systems problem, it requires a systems solution that involves input from coalitions of governments and industries, as well as a general rethinking of how best to create wealth and prosperity, manage resources and business, and position governments and regulatory agencies in our complex global economic environment. Yet as systems theory has taught us, the term *equifinality* means that the same goal may be reached in multiple ways. Jay Galbraith (1973) summarizes the two basic tenets of **contingency theory** as follows:

1. There is no one best way to organize.
2. All ways of organizing are not equally effective.

These principles imply not only that the forms of organizing which will work best depend on the environment, but also that the match between certain organizational approaches and specific environments should be explored because some approaches will indeed work better than others. Think about two different but related organizational challenges, the first having to do with preparing for an approaching hurricane; and the second with developing construction standards to prevent hurricane damage in the distant future. The first challenge leaves no time for careful deliberation—centralized communication and quick decision making are needed to save lives. The second allows for a more deliberate and inclusive dialogue, which will increase the likelihood of buy-in and long-term success. Different challenges suggest different organizational approaches. In addition, organizations that exist in complex and highly turbulent environments (e.g., Homeland Security, Centers for Disease Control and Prevention) require very different forms of leadership, interpersonal communication, decision making, and organizational structure than those in somewhat more predictable environments (e.g., chain restaurants, car dealerships) (Lawrence & Lorsch, 1967; Weick & Sutcliffe, 2001).

▧ THE APPEAL OF SYSTEMS THEORY FOR ORGANIZATIONAL COMMUNICATION

Systems theory appeals to those who are interested in organizational communication because it highlights communication processes in organizing. In addition, it is theoretically capable of capturing much of the complexity of these processes. While experience teaches us that communication is complex and takes place over time, earlier theories were based on the overly simplistic idea that communication only involved the sending and receiving of messages.

Research on systems theory so far has been somewhat disappointing. Historically, researchers have had difficulty translating the concepts of systems theory into research designs, partly because they emphasize change over time and up until recently most statistical models in the social sciences have been static (e.g., regression analysis). Systems theories are ideally tested using statistical methods that accommodate multiple factors interacting over time. Fortunately, these methods (time series analysis) are increasingly available in graduate schools, so we can expect better application of them to systems theories in the future. For now, because actual studies of complex human systems are rare, systems theory has been characterized as an appealing but abstract set of concepts with limited applicability to actual theory or research (Poole, 1996). However, efforts have been made to reinvigorate systems theory in ways that are compatible with organizational communication. We are referring specifically to the innovative theories of Peter Senge and Karl Weick, which we discuss next.

☐ Peter Senge's Learning Organization

Management theorist Peter Senge (1990) has succeeded in bringing systems thinking to those who manage corporations under the umbrella idea he calls **learning organizations**. These organizations exhibit the following five features:

1. *Systems thinking.* Combining holism and interdependence, systems thinking claims that for any one member to succeed, all members must succeed.
2. *Personal mastery.* All members share a personal commitment to learning and self-reflection.
3. *Flexible mental models.* Mental models are those patterns of belief that shape and limit an individual's interpretations and actions. In a learning organization, members engage in self-reflection, allowing them first to understand and then to change the mental models that tend to guide their thinking.
4. *A shared vision.* In learning organizations, tight hierarchical control is replaced by "concertive control" (Tompkins & Cheney, 1985), whereby members act in concert because they share a common organizational vision and understand how their own work helps build on that shared vision.
5. *Team learning.* Team members in a learning organization communicate in ways that lead the team toward intelligent decisions, with an emphasis on dialogue as the key to team learning.

According to Senge (1990), developing a learning organization requires a major "shift of mind" toward a more participative and holistic notion of effective organizing. What one does with differences in mental models—and how one moves on to team learning—is critical to Senge's approach and our interest in it.

As mentioned in Chapter 2, Senge (1994) and his colleagues at the MIT Dialogue Project (Isaacs, 1999) build on physicist David Bohm's (1980) exploration of the role of consciousness in communication problems. Bohm is critical of the human tendency to see ourselves as separate from the rest of the world. He argues that the result of such thinking is "discussion," wherein we feel free to advocate our opinions, but because we are unwilling to suspend our certainty about our own worldview, no real learning takes place. In contrast, dialogue "starts with the willingness to challenge our own thinking, to recognize that any certainty we have is, at best, a hypothesis about the world" (Senge, 1990, p. 277). From this point, dialogue progresses through a combination of advocacy and inquiry, wherein we collectively offer and expose our ideas to rigorous scrutiny by others. The primary distinction between dialogue and the typical problem-solving meeting in business is that the former places more value on the communication process, and group members are thereby more willing to distance themselves from their own opinions and ideas.

☐ Karl Weick's Sense-Making Model

Karl Weick's exploration of *sensemaking*, developed in his books *The Social Psychology of Organizing* (1979) and *Sensemaking in Organizations* (1995), has greatly influenced the fields of organizational behavior and communication. In particular, his work has reinvigorated systems theory by connecting it with issues of sense making, meaning, and communication while also providing a bridge for the development of cultural studies of organizations (see Chapter 5).

According to Weick (1979), organizations exist in highly complex and unpredictable environments. The job of organizing involves making sense of the uncertainties in environments through interaction, a process that Weick calls **equivocality reduction**. In the process of identifying the meaning of a given situation or event, the same facts can be interpreted in various ways by different observers. How the members of an organization communicate to make sense of equivocal situations is central to Weick's approach.

As illustrated in Figure 4.1, Weick's (1979) model of organizing has three parts: enactment, selection, and retention. In enactment, organizational members create environments through their actions and patterns of attention, and these environments can vary in terms of their perceived degree of equivocality or uncertainty. For example, college presidents and their staffs are struggling these days to decide what to include in their **enacted environment**, the sum total of external parties to which they regularly pay attention. The usual stakeholder list of current students and alumni is now being augmented by local communities, governments, senior citizens, and foreign governments. School administrations vary greatly in the degree to which they pay attention to any of these forces.

Once an environment is enacted, the organizing process requires participants to select the best explanation of the environment's meaning from a number of possible interpretations. Once an explanation is selected, collective sense making

FIGURE 4.1

Weick's Model of Organizing

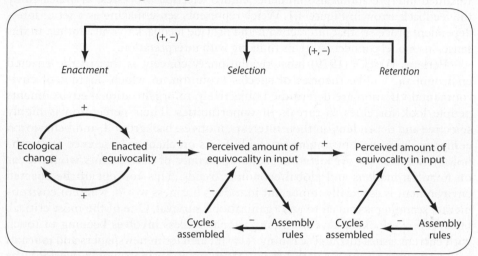

Source: From *The social psychology of organizing*, by K. Weick, 1979. Reprinted by permission.

is accomplished through communication. In other words, people interact about what an external trend may mean for the organization. In the case of higher education, universities like Portland State University, Arizona State University, and the University of Alabama at Birmingham have chosen to interpret their purpose and mission as being in close partnership with the local community and have even redesigned their faculty evaluation systems to align with this interpretation. For example, one of the design imperatives of Arizona State University (ASU) is to "be socially embedded." A socially embedded university is one that builds "mutually beneficial partnerships with communities" and responds to the communities' needs for research and education. ASU rewards students and faculty who successfully build partnerships (such as service learning courses or applied research projects) and reach out to community members. These partnerships may help to build the community's capacity for the provision of services, invigorate the local community's economic vitality, enhance the well-being of community members, or advance research that directly addresses the community's needs.

Finally, by "retention" Weick means that successful sense-making strategies get saved for future use. Each year, ASU recognizes and rewards faculty and staff who embody the goal of social embeddedness with a President's Medal. Profiles of past medal recipients are archived on the university's website to inspire others. In the case of ASU, time will tell what lessons are learned from the university's choice to highlight social embeddedness. Success will not only reinforce their selection but also allow others to see this model as a legitimate option for their institutions. Retained interpretations also influence future selection processes, as indicated by the feedback arrow in Figure 4.1. Weick represents sense making as a set of interdependent processes that interact with and provide feedback to one another. In this sense, his model connects systems thinking with interpretation.

Perhaps Weick's (1979) most revolutionary concept is that of the enacted environment. Unlike theories of species evolution, in which degrees of environmental variation are determined objectively, in organizational environments people look for clues to threats or opportunities. Their perception is highly selective and dependent on their interests, motives, background, and behavior. A company dominated by engineers would focus on changes in science and technology, whereas an organization made up mainly of accountants would focus on financial markets and global economic trends. This concept of the enacted environment is especially important in today's business world, wherein environmental scanning is crucial to an organization's survival. One of the most critical, but often overlooked, keys to organizational success involves keeping in touch with current issues through scanning relevant articles in newspapers and journals and maintaining contacts with others. Many times businesspeople overlook the importance of environmental scanning and miss information that has a direct bearing on their company. Because the enacted environment is always limited by subjective perception, organizational success requires an ongoing examination of current issues.

Weick extends his model of organizing through three important concepts: retrospective sense making, loose coupling, and partial inclusion.

Retrospective Sense Making

An underlying assumption of Weick's model is that decision making is largely **retrospective sense making**. In other words, although people in organizations think they plan first and then act according to the plan, Weick argues that people often act first and later examine their actions in an attempt to explain their meaning. He sums this up in what he calls a "recipe": "How can I know what I think until I see what I say?" (1979). Weick (1995) goes on to identify seven "properties of sense making":

1. *Identity construction.* Who I am is indicated by how and what I think.
2. *Retrospection.* To learn what I think, I look back over what I said earlier.
3. *Enactment.* I create an object to be seen and inspected when I say or do something.
4. *Socialization.* What I say, single out, and conclude are determined by who socialized me and how I was socialized, as well as by the audience I anticipate will audit the conclusions I reach.

5. *Continuation*. My talking is spread across time, competes for attention with other ongoing projects, and is reflected on after it is finished (which means my interests already may have changed).

6. *Extracted cues*. The "what" that I single out and embellish as the content of the thought is only a small portion of the utterance that becomes salient because of the context and personal dispositions.

7. *Plausibility*. I need to know enough about what I think to get on with my projects, but no more, which means sufficiency and plausibility take precedence over accuracy. (pp. 61–62)

The seven properties also apply if we change the pronouns in the recipe to include collective reflection (e.g., "How can we know what we think until we see what we say?").

The important point in Weick's argument is that the balance between planned and unplanned behavior is often the reverse of what we assume it to be. For example, as Malcolm Gladwell demonstrates in the case studies that make up his book *Blink* (2007), having ample time available and a wealth of resources and technologies at our fingertips to plan for decisions doesn't always mean a better decision will be the outcome. Instead, it may be our **adaptive unconscious**, which allows us to focus on what's most important and respond accordingly, that provides a better result.

Loose Coupling

At the same time that Weick stresses the importance of communication at work, he points out that unlike the connections among biological systems, the communication connections among people in organizations vary in intensity and are often loose or weak. Weick's (1976) concept of **loosely coupled** systems has had a major impact on our understanding of organizations as communication systems.

Consider, for example, the typical college or university, in which a great deal of interaction occurs within departments but not across various fields of study. The activities of the history department have little effect on those of the engineering department, for example. Similarly, loose or weak connections usually exist among the university's nonacademic units (staff, administration, and faculty). The university is a classic example of a loosely coupled system.

Whereas strictly rational approaches maintain that loose connections deter people from working together to achieve a common goal, Weick (1979) argues that such connections can sometimes be advantageous. The multiple goals of an organization can be coordinated without extensive communication or consensus (Eisenberg, 1984, 1986, 1990, 1995). In addition, a loosely coupled system is better able to withstand environmental jolts. In a system of close or tight connections, environmental jolts can affect the entire system, whereas in a loosely coupled system, the whole is less affected because of the weak connections among units. Although it is subject to redundancy and inefficiency, a loosely coupled system may still be more effective in the long term.

EVERYDAY ORGANIZATIONAL COMMUNICATION

Making Sense of Your Equivocal Past

There is often a stark contrast between the tumultuous path we travel in life and the story we tell about the journey. As we discuss in this chapter, Weick (1995) terms this phenomenon *retrospective sense making* and argues that people act first and later examine those actions in an attempt to explain their meaning. Have you ever considered how your own life story might be an attempt to come to terms with your equivocal past?

Consider the example of the late Steve Jobs, cofounder of Apple Computer and former CEO of Pixar. At age eighteen, Jobs didn't know what he wanted to do with his life. Imagine his parents' reaction when he decided to drop out of Reed College! Although at the time this choice may have seemed rash, the benefit of hindsight allowed Jobs to state that dropping out of school was one of the best decisions he ever made (Jobs, 2005, para. 5). And thank your iPad that he did—this was when Jobs joined up with Steve Wozniak to sell personal computers assembled in Jobs's garage. Despite the immediate consequences of Jobs's decision (sleeping on the floor in friends' dorm rooms and returning soda bottles for the five-cent deposits to buy food), he became a multimillionaire less than ten years later (para. 6). Told retrospectively, it all makes sense.

Examples of retrospective sense making are not usually as dramatic as Jobs's story. The way that you ended up declaring your current major is a story worth examining, for example. In one case, a student began her postsecondary education as a biology major with a chemistry minor, intent on fulfilling a lifelong dream to become a pediatrician. Poor grades in a required physics course, as well as a newfound passion for a general education course in literature, caused her to switch her major to English. How did her interest in the sciences and earlier experiences enter into the story of her life? She indulged by studying medicine and illness in literature—and even the chemistry of illuminated manuscripts. Today she holds a PhD in English and works at a liberal arts college. Looking back over her years of formal education, it makes sense to her now that she arrived where she did.

For most of us, the experience of college and career is often a series of fortunate and unfortunate accidents and opportunities. Told retrospectively, however, they are most often presented as a series of logical choices that led to an inevitable conclusion. Or as Steve Jobs said: "You can't connect the dots looking forward; you can only connect them looking backwards. So you have to trust that the dots will somehow connect in your future" (2005, para. 9).

DISCUSSION QUESTIONS

1. Think back on how you arrived where you are today. How did you come to attend your current university? What factors led to your decision to declare your current major?
2. If you are currently employed, how does your job fit into your life story? For most people, jobs are primarily a source of income, but they often turn into steps on a long-term career path. Alternatively, an intense dislike of a particular job might lead someone down a completely different path than expected. Have you experienced either scenario?
3. Conduct a brief informal interview with a person you think of as successful (face-to-face, by phone, or by e-mail) and ask about the path that person took to where he or she is today. Ask the following questions: *What were the crucial decisions or turning points in your life? To what extent were you aware of your final destination when you were making those crucial decisions? Do you think of yourself as a success, why or why not?* The person's answers should clearly reveal the difference between the experience of decision making and retrospective sense making of those decisions.

Partial Inclusion

In analyzing the balance between work and other activities, Weick (1979) uses the theory of **partial inclusion** to explain why certain strategies for motivating employees are ineffective. He holds that employees are only partially included in the workplace; that is, at work we see some but not all of their behaviors. An unmotivated employee at work may be a church leader or a model parent, whereas the top performer at a company may engage in few outside activities. In either case, simple theories of organizational behavior are limited when they fail to consider the employee's activities, roles, and interests outside of the workplace. Every individual is a member of multiple systems, and this multiple membership shapes and limits the individual's degree of commitment to any one particular system.

Weick (1979) mainly differentiates himself from those who value profitability above all else. He sees organizations as communities or social settings in which we choose to spend most of our adult lives. As such, organizations provide opportunities for storytelling and socializing; according to Weick, "they haven't anything else to give" (p. 264). A closer analysis of organizations as communities is the primary goal of the cultural approach, our focus in Chapter 5.

☐ A New Look at Systems Theories

Although research using systems theories has left many organizational communicators wanting more, Senge's and Weick's frameworks provide us with some useful ways of thinking about systems and how to integrate their thinking into everyday organizational practices. But what about the relevance of systems approaches to more current organizational communication research? One emerging area of inquiry that makes important use of systems concepts is the study of **policy communication**.

Policies are important texts that help members make sense of the relationships, structures, individuals, rules, and resources that make up an organization (Peterson & Albrecht, 1999). Policies give individuals the means to understand their relationship to the organization for everything from membership to workload to health insurance to financial commitments to vacation time, and so on. In other words, policies are the tangible documents that outline the social and material relationships that make up an organized system.

For organizational communication scholar Heather Canary, the relationship between policies and systems comes together around the concept of **policy knowledge** (Canary & McPhee, 2009). How individuals and groups construct knowledge is an important part of organizing, and Canary argues that organizational policies coordinate actions across social systems. People construct organizational knowledge in the ways they use policy. Policies help individuals make sense of organizational rules, but individuals also use policies to secure resources and rights within an organization.

Think about a 2015 decision in New York State to raise the minimum wage of fast-food employees to $15 an hour. The state-level policy creates certain expectation about how workers should be paid, as well as how social systems should value certain kinds of work. In response to the policy change, several advocates and opponents started arguing for an increase in wages for other professions—namely health-care workers like paramedics and EMTs—and Governor Andrew Cuomo announced that he would begin working on legislation to raise the minimum wage for all industries to $15 an hour. Coordinating actions—like securing a living wage, using vacation time, or taking family leave—requires interdependence across systems. Policy knowledge is important, because it encourages us to think about how we coordinate those activities across social systems through the ways in which organizations and their members implement policies.

In many ways, policies are documents that outline the balance between creativity and constraint—particularly when it comes to approaching organizational communication from a systems perspective. Moreover, policy communication scholars have started to fill some of the methodological gaps in the study of systems theories. For example, Canary's policy work has also led to the development of the Policy Communication Index, which provides organizations with a practical survey tool to measure policy communication practices (Canary, Riforgiate, & Montoya, 2013).

Other methodological resources, including discourse tracing (LeGreco & Tracy, 2009), have provided not only ways of studying policy but also new ways of thinking about systems, their theories and methods, and the ways in which we rely on policy to enact systems-level concepts like interdependence, distributed intelligence, and even partial inclusion.

SUMMARY

The broad term *systems approach* encompasses many theories with various assumptions and implications for action. In contrast to earlier organizational theories—many of which can be classified according to their underlying view of the goals of organizing and of workers—systems theory is more open-ended. Adopting a systems approach requires acknowledging the openness and complexity of social organizations as well as the importance of relationships among individuals over time. Table 4.2 on page 120 provides an explicit comparison of scientific management and systems theories.

In practice, a systems approach can either help or hinder situated individuals. It can help individuals better understand the overall workings of an organization. It can emphasize the importance of relationships and networks of contacts in allowing groups and organizations to achieve goals that are greater than those of the individual. A systems perspective can also reveal important interdependencies, particularly the connections with organizational environments that can affect an organization's survival. Despite its focus on communication and relationships, however, systems theory does not help explain the meanings constructed by interactions. It can identify the potential participants in a productive organizational dialogue, but it cannot tell us about the content of that dialogue. It is in this area that Weick augments systems theory with issues related to sense making, arguably the central process of organizing.

Systems theory is likely to continue to exert significant influence on the field of organizational communication. Particularly in organizations that produce complex products or provide complex services, systems theory is evident in discussions of work-flow analysis, internal customers, and cross-functional work groups, as well as in the use of control charts and process maps. Businesses are increasingly recognizing the critical role of markets and environments in their survival. In Chapter 7, we will return to the discussion of systems theory and see how it applies to the development of network forms of organizing.

TABLE 4.2

Comparison of Scientific Management and Systems Theories

SCIENTIFIC MANAGEMENT	SYSTEMS THEORIES
Metaphor: Machines	*Metaphor:* Biological organisms
Theme: Efficiency—a machine is the sum of its parts	*Theme:* Complexity—a system is greater than the sum of its parts
Influences: Industrial Revolution, modernity, capitalism, and empire; assembly-line production and management; division of labor, interchangeable parts, coordination of many small, skilled jobs	*Influences:* Einstein's theory of relativity; McLuhan's global information society; Miller's biological systems; von Bertalanffy's general systems; information engineering model of communication
Focus of management principles: "The only things that count are the finished product and the bottom line"; time and motion studies	*Focus of management principles:* "Everything counts"; studies of interdependent processes, information flows and feedback, environments and contingencies
Management of individuals as interchangeable parts	*Management of relationships* among components; focus on groups and networks
Planning the work, working the plan	*Planning* the work, using feedback to correct the plan
Motivation by fear and money	*Motivation* by needs and contingencies
Theory of communication:	*Theory of communication:*

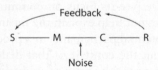

Systems theories diagram:

Feedback

S —— M —— C —— R

Noise

Sender— Message— Channel— Receiver

Noise

Scientific Management diagram:

```
S     M     C     R
e     e     h     e
n     s     a     c
d     s     n     e
e     a     n     i
r     g     e     v
      e     l     e
                  r
```

Sender— Message— Channel— Receiver

Theory of leadership: Trait (tall, white males with blond hair and blue eyes, who come from strong moral backgrounds)	*Theory of leadership:* Adaptive (rhetorical contingency)—anyone can learn the skills of leading by attending to the requirements of behavioral flexibility
Limitations: (1) Forgets that humans are more complex than machines; (2) encourages individual boredom and deep divisions between managers and employees; (3) discourages communication, individual needs, job initiative, task innovation, personal responsibility, and empowerment	*Limitations:* (1) Forgets that humans are symbolic as well as biological; (2) encourages mathematical complexities that are difficult to put into everyday practices; (3) equates communication with information

QUESTIONS FOR REVIEW AND DISCUSSION

1. How has the information revolution influenced the development of systems theory?

2. How are biological systems and organizational communication systems similar? How are they different?

3. In what ways is the environment of a system just as important as the system itself? Why is it crucial for an organization to engage in its environment? Give an example of an organization that has been successful because of openness to its environments, and one which failed because it was not able to establish that engagement.

4. In open systems, interdependence can be a highly adaptive feature of an organization. Can you envision how interdependence might enable organizations to meet their goals? What about the alternative? Can you imagine how system interdependence might inhibit organizational goals? What about individual goals?

5. Think about your own life experience. When have you received negative or deviation-counteracting feedback? How did you use that information to reestablish your own "homeostasis," or steady state? Can you remember a time that you received deviation-amplifying feedback? How did that information change your course of action?

6. In what ways is organizational learning connected to the processes associated with systems thinking?

7. How has the sense-making model reinvigorated the application of systems theory to organizational communication?

8. How does a knowledge of policy communication illuminate our understanding of an organizational system?

9. Why has it been difficult to operationalize systems thinking? What are the major challenges for those doing systems research in an organization?

KEY TERMS

Adaptive unconscious, p. 116
Boundary spanner, p. 103
Coopetition, p. 103
Communication breakdown, p. 107
Contingency theory, p. 110
Counter-networking, p. 109
Distributed intelligence, p. 102
Enacted environment, p. 112
Equifinality, p. 100
Equivocality reduction, p. 112
Feedback, p. 108
General systems theory, p. 100

Interdependence, p. 104
Learning organization, p. 111
Loosely coupled, p. 117
Open systems theory, p. 104
Organizational goal, p. 107
Partial inclusion, p. 117
Policy communication, p. 118
Policy knowledge, p. 118
Retrospective sense making, p. 114
Reverse organizational science,
  p. 109
Systems approach, p. 98

CASE STUDY

Crisis in the Zion Emergency Room

For many years now, the emergency rooms in the United States have been in crisis. Part of the problem is a lack of qualified nurses. Everywhere nurses are in short supply, and those who can work effectively in the emergency environment are even rarer. But there are other reasons for the widespread overcrowding of ERs. A large and growing population of people without medical insurance continues to make use of them for primary care needs. Emergency rooms, staffed primarily to serve the victims of trauma or acute illness, are increasingly overburdened by mothers and infants without adequate prenatal and pediatric care, the chronically ill and disabled, patients with HIV/AIDS, individuals with mental illness or drug or alcohol addiction, and the homeless. The end result is excessive wait times, angry patients, and substandard care. The ER at Zion Hospital is no different.

On any given night, Zion's ER looks like a war zone. The halls of the ER are lined with twenty to twenty-five patients on gurneys, lying in limbo until one of the forty-five regular ER beds opens up. Just walking through the ER can be tricky. The overcrowding of the ER results in a distinct lack of privacy, and more important, it creates confusion about the location and status of patients, which increases the potential for serious errors.

You have recently accepted the position of director of emergency medicine at Zion. Expectations are high that you will be able to do something quickly about the dreadful patient satisfaction ratings that have appeared in recent months. Your initial assessment of the situation, however, is discouraging. For the reasons just described, there appears to be an endless and growing stream of new patients into the ER, and the hospital financial committee looks unfavorably at turning people away. Meanwhile, all of your beds are taken, half of them by people who have already been admitted to Zion but have yet to be assigned a bed upstairs in one of the hospital units. Your staff has to find a way of serving these bored and hungry patients while handling the more critical patients lined up in the hall.

Further investigation reveals that your patients are waiting for beds for a number of reasons: (1) Other units in the hospital, such as the heart center and the pediatric unit, have priority over the ER in getting beds; (2) all of the beds in the hospital are full, and those that are physically empty are locked in units that have been temporarily closed due to the lack of qualified nurses to staff them; and (3) there are long delays from the time a viable bed actually becomes empty to when housekeeping can clean the room for the next patient and floor nurses can accept the new patient to their unit.

The situation is miserable and deteriorating. The nursing shortage is not going to end anytime soon, your current nurses are all threatening to quit, patients are furious, and hospital administrators are urging you to "think outside the box" to find some relief.

ASSIGNMENT

Using what you know about systems theories of organization, answer the following questions:

1. How would you define the problem systemically? How does your choice of definition affect your likely course of action?
2. Using the language of systems theories, which "realities" in this case would be most difficult to change, and which are more malleable?
3. What role does communication play in perpetuating the current situation? How does your understanding of the systems approach help you identify specific communication issues?
4. Using your knowledge of systems, what kinds of communication might you use to address the situation? What obstacles would you expect to encounter, and how would you deal with them? Wouldn't dealing with those obstacles—in whatever way you choose to deal with them—also necessarily create new systemic issues? Given your choice of how to deal with the obstacles, what might these new issues be?
5. What role might communication technology play in developing a systems approach to your solution or solutions?

CHAPTER 5

Cultural Studies of Organizations and Communication

This chapter introduces the idea of organizations as cultures. The cultural approach departs from the more rational and formal approaches that preceded it, such as the systems approach. It brings a new focus on the language of the workplace, the performances of managers and employees, the formal and informal practices that mark an organization's character (such as rites and rituals), and the display of meaningful artifacts like architecture, interior design, public artwork, and furniture. Moreover, the cultural approach concentrates on the human desire to see organizational life as an opportunity to do something meaningful (Gendron, 1999). In this chapter, we will trace the history of the cultural approach; explore the practical, methodological, and social reasons for its popularity; and look at some of the ways researchers and managers have applied it in the context of organizational socialization. Finally, we will outline a communication view of organizational culture to show how an organization's unique patterns of interaction and sense making work together over time to create its distinct culture.

▧ THE CULTURAL APPROACH

When you hear the term *culture*, you most likely think about it in a broad sense, such as the differences between American culture and French culture. A closer view, however, reveals that within every national culture there are thousands of smaller cultures based on religion, ethnicity, geography, and a myriad of other factors. Whenever people create groups or communities, a culture inevitably develops.

The same is true for organizations. But what precisely do we mean by "culture"? How can one word serve to describe so many different kinds of social groups?

Anthropologist Marshall Sahlins (1976) defines culture as meaningful orders of people and things. We learn about a culture not only by what its members say, but also by what they do regularly (e.g., staff meetings, performance reviews, softball tournaments) and the things they choose to display in connection with their work. Sloan Fellows Professor of Management Emeritus Edgar Schein (1992) offers this variation: "An organizational culture is a pattern of shared basic assumptions that have been invented, discovered, and/or developed by a group as it learns to cope with problems of external adaptation and internal integration" (p. 247). A culture is also something like a religion, in that both locate a set of common beliefs and values that prescribes a general view of order (the way things are) and explanation (why things are that way). The tie between religion and culture is important to organizational studies because it indicates how the search for order and explanation compels beliefs.

However, not all members of a culture accept or practice those beliefs in the same way. Culture is never as much about agreement as it is about a common recognition or sensibility. Like religions, most cultures include various sects or subcultures that share a common order but whose ways of understanding or carrying out their beliefs differ. This point underscores the importance of understanding an organization's culture or cultures as a dialogue with many different voices.

☐ Cultures as Symbolic Constructions

To say that a word or thing is "symbolic" means that it stands for something other than itself. This is easy to see with words, which as symbols refer to ideas and things in the world, also known as referents. But symbols also take other forms, such as office size and design, displays of meaningful physical **artifacts**, how managers and employees dress, and what hangs on (or is absent from) the walls. For our purposes, then, the term **organizational culture** stands for the actions, ways of thinking, practices, stories, and artifacts that characterize a particular organization. We study the culture of an organization through close examination of its environment (e.g., the arrangement of parking lots, office cubicles, and conference rooms) as well as through its use of symbols (e.g., topics of conversation, key vocabulary and jargon, and treasured accomplishments and awards).

The study of organizational culture involves interpreting the meanings of these symbols. Viewing organizations as symbolic requires several assumptions. First, all cultural studies begin with a focus on the centrality of language in shaping human perception. Consequently, a large part of any cultural analysis devotes considerable attention to the names of things and how these names are invoked in conversation. For example, from a cultural perspective it is significant when an organization refers to its people as "human resources" or even more dramatically as "heads" to be added or cut. Similarly, a company that speaks of facing its competition using the language of war is different culturally from one that makes broad use of spiritual metaphors such as communion or servant leadership (Goodier & Eisenberg, 2006). In much the same way that we have come to appreciate the importance of nonsexist language in shaping basic assumptions, the terms that organizational members use to describe their worlds are both crucial and largely unexamined. A cultural approach brings them into the light. A comprehensive guide to studying organizational cultures is offered in this text's appendix, "A Field Guide to Studying Organizational Communication."

Another source of inspiration for viewing organizations as symbolic constructions involves defining human beings as symbol-using animals, as Kenneth Burke does in his classic essay "Definition of Man" (1966). Burke's view helps us understand why symbols both represent other things and evoke other symbolic possibilities. For example, an organizational chart simultaneously provides information about hierarchy and relationships (e.g., formal lines of communication and formal status relations) and suggests possibilities for future action (e.g., getting promoted). That is, symbols stand not only for other things but they also shape our understandings of those things and help us identify their meanings and uses. As such, symbols are instruments of human understanding and action. A company that anticipates being sold, for example, begins to "talk" differently to itself (e.g., in terms of "exit strategies" and the use of "multiples" in determining its value), and these new ways of communicating in turn affect action, as a culture of apathy, cynicism, or optimism may develop. The culture of an organization induces its members to think, act, and behave in particular ways.

☐ Cultural Elements

Organizational cultures emerge from members' individual and collective symbol-using practices. These various symbolic expressions combine to create a "unique sense of place" that defines an organization's culture (Pacanowsky & O'Donnell-Trujillo, 1983). Scholars and practitioners often focus on one or more of those symbolic expressions, or *cultural elements*, to learn more about or to transform an organization's culture. Cultural elements include metaphors, rituals, stories, artifacts, heroes and heroines, performances, and values.

- **Metaphors** are figures of speech that define an unfamiliar experience in terms of another, more familiar, one. From a cultural perspective, when members describe their organization as a "family," a "machine," or a "ship," or compare their approach to decision making to "improv comedy" as the folks at Pixar do, they are not simply using flowery language; instead, they come to construct and experience their organizations in relation to those metaphors (Smith & Eisenberg, 1987). Similarly, a study examined bankers' use of "victim" metaphors to explain their role in the banking failures that swept the United Kingdom during the global recession. These metaphors worked to frame public debates in ways that minimized the banks' own responsibility for the crisis (Tourish & Hargie, 2012).

- **Rituals** "dramatize" a culture's basic values and can range in scope from personal, day-to-day routines for accomplishing tasks to annual organization-wide celebrations of top performers (Deal & Kennedy, 1982; Pacanowsky & O'Donnell-Trujillo, 1983) and public meetings (McComas, Besley, & Black, 2010). New product launches, office birthday celebrations, sales conferences, and performance evaluations are all ritualized practices aimed at reinforcing organizational values.

- Storytelling is an important cultural activity because **stories** convey to members what and whom the culture values, how things are to be done, the consequences for cultural compliance or deviation, and the role and meaning of leadership in the organization (Humphreys, Ucbasaran, & Lockett, 2012). Stories have been described as a particularly powerful means of creating and recreating cultures (Smith & Keyton, 2001). The Walt Disney Company, for example, uses formal organizational texts, advertising, and informal channels to narrate a sense of community among its stakeholders.

- Artifacts, or the tangible and physical features of an organization, contribute to its culture. Office decor, spatial arrangements, corporate art, dress codes, and even graffiti are markers of culture (Scheibel, 2003). For example, the creativity and innovation that Pixar holds dear are evident in the fact that employees are permitted to decorate their office space any way they choose.

- **Heroes and heroines** are members of an organization who are held up as role models. They embody and personify cultural values. Heroic figures often are organizational founders or hail from the managerial ranks (Deal & Kennedy, 1982; Fairhurst & Sarr, 1996). The late Steve Jobs, former CEO of Apple and Pixar, began his climb to the top when he and his partner created their first computer in his family's garage. Jobs embodied the innovative leader with a passion for making technology accessible. Similarly, leaders as diverse as the former CEO of Southwest Airlines, Herb Kelleher, and the current CEO of Zappos, Tony Hsieh, have developed near cult status as a result of their consistent advocacy for the core cultural values of their companies.

- Members often engage in dynamic, ongoing, and creative communication behaviors as they construct cultures. **Performances** center on rituals, passion, sociality (or organizational etiquette), politics, socialization of new members, and identity (Pacanowsky & O'Donnell-Trujillo, 1983). A great example of the performance of identity can be seen during hospital rounds, where less experienced physicians are called on to describe specific cases and receive immediate feedback regarding how well they "talk like a doctor."

- **Values** represent a (more or less) shared set of beliefs about appropriate organizational behaviors. They are often derived from charismatic leaders or founders or from organizational traditions (Schein, 1991).

For example, Southwest Airlines values a fun, casual work environment, while General Electric values innovation above all else. The result is a pervasive emphasis on "what matters most" that employees and customers consistently feel. And commitment to these cultural values can be very powerful in boosting employee loyalty and satisfaction as long as the values are aligned with company goals.

These elements of organizational culture are understood differently depending on the approach one takes. To understand the ways various scholars and practitioners unpack and make use of these cultural elements, we must first consider the historical and social trends out of which the cultural approach emerged.

◪ HISTORICAL AND CULTURAL BACKGROUND

The first known reference to organizational culture appeared in a 1979 article by Andrew Pettigrew published in *Administrative Science Quarterly*. The concept became immediately popular for a variety of reasons, including competitive pressures, the coming of age of interpretive research methods, and trends in the wider society. Each of these is discussed in the following sections.

☐ Competitive Pressures

The business climate of the 1970s was characterized by a significant increase in global competition that highlighted productivity problems in the United States. Although for many years the United States had been the world leader in several industries, it suddenly found itself eclipsed by other nations, most notably Japan. In many industries, Japanese manufacturing techniques threatened to prevail, and many wondered what made Japanese companies so successful.

Based on observations of common Japanese management techniques in the 1970s, William Ouchi's (1981) **Theory Z** holds that the survival and prosperity of organizations depend heavily on their ability to adapt to their surrounding cultures. He used the term *culture* to refer to national standards of organizational performance. In comparing those standards in the United States and Japan, he found some major differences. For example, he contrasted the American emphasis on individual achievement with the Japanese emphasis on the performance and well-being of the collective. Ouchi proposed a Theory Z type of organization that would integrate individual achievement and advancement while also developing a sense of community in the workplace. Theory Z organizations, according to Ouchi, would be capable of reducing negative influences and segmented decision making by incorporating new cultural values into the work environment.

Asia's economic troubles at the close of the twentieth century came as a surprise to most people and caused many theorists to question the seemingly "magical" Japanese formulas. In hindsight, it appears that much of Japan's success was gained the old-fashioned way: through spectacular individual efforts, close informal contacts and partnerships, research and development of new products and services, and clever competitive tactics and strategies.

By the mid-1980s, many traditional organizations in the United States were failing financially or were in danger of doing so. The old prescriptions—more hierarchy, bureaucracy, division of labor, and standardization—were no longer effective, and it became clear that radical changes were required for companies to remain competitive. As business leaders began speaking of organizational change— in attitudes, values, and practices—they also began thinking about a holistic transformation in terms of organizational culture. One of the authors of this textbook received a phone call in 1983 from a CEO in search of someone who could "install a new culture" at his company. Managers were attracted to the idea even without much knowledge of how culture develops, much less how it could be altered. Many questions remained: What types of cultures are most productive? What aspects of culture are most closely associated with business success?

☐ Interpretive Methodology

While practitioners were looking for new models of effective organizations, scholars were becoming disenchanted with the overly rational, mechanistic view of communication that characterized the field of organizational communication. As a result, research in organizational communication took an "interpretive turn" in the early 1980s (Putnam & Pacanowsky, 1983). Previously, the dominant vocabulary—derived from the fields of psychology, sociology, and management—covered such topics as performance, motivation, and rewards, as well as work units, hierarchies, and the outcomes of group problem solving, decision making, and leadership. Interpretive theorists became less concerned with these specific topics and more interested in understanding the complex, dynamic nature of organizational life as members experience it. The new focus on organizational cultures required a new vocabulary and new approaches for analyzing organizations and communication.

The anthropological vocabulary of the cultural approach gave organizational researchers, managers, and members new ways of viewing organizations, applying long-standing cultural concepts like values, rituals, and socialization. Today, organization members themselves commonly use this language. The cultural approach has both broadened the scope of what is considered important about organizations and communication and complicated our thinking about organizational communication processes. For example, the study of an organization's values is no longer limited to those stated in the company's formal publications; values may also be found in artifacts and cartoons, in the layout of work space, and even in the arrangement of cars in the employee parking lot (Goodall, 1989). Moreover, interpretive researchers are not interested in treating culture as simply another variable that the organization *has*; culture is not a variable that can be managed or manipulated by leaders. Rather, interpretive researchers are driven to treat culture as something an organization *is*. As a culture, an organization requires exceedingly detailed and nuanced observation of daily life to produce what pioneering anthropologist Clifford Geertz (1973) called a "thick description" of the culture. These highly descriptive accounts provide rich and complex portraits of members' organizational sense-making experiences.

How does one analyze organizational culture in a systematic way? The most common methodology has its roots in anthropology and is called **ethnography**, or the writing of culture (Clifford & Marcus, 1985). Because anthropologists have long studied cultures, researchers sought to integrate anthropological research methods into cultural studies of organizations and communication (Goodall, 1989, 1991; Van Maanen, 1979, 1988). Successful organizations hire ethnographers to review and evaluate their company cultures (e.g., Xerox). In writing an ethnographic account of Disneyland, John Van Maanen (1991), a management professor at the Massachusetts Institute of Technology with an interest in anthropology and communication, relied on his recollections of working there while he was a student as well as his more recent observations of and interactions with employees and guests. Unlike traditional research methods in the social sciences, in which the researcher maintains distance from the group under study, ethnography requires the researcher to become immersed in a culture by experiencing it firsthand.

Organizational ethnography provides "thick" descriptions of organizational life, often capturing subtle points that are overlooked by traditional research methods (Tracy, 2012). For example, consider the difference between a traditional written survey of patient satisfaction in a hospital and an ethnography of a hospital unit (Eisenberg, Baglia, & Pynes, 2006). Whereas the findings of the survey would likely be cut-and-dried and limited to the questions the researchers posed in advance, the ethnography—told in the form of a story—would reveal more about the communication and sense-making processes of all parties involved, including many observations and findings that might surprise the researcher.

Ethnography is a stimulus for cultural change and dialogue as it can expose sources of power and resistance and reveal values and beliefs that might otherwise be taken for granted. Moreover, organizational ethnography encourages us to look beyond the managerial and profitability aspects of organizations and toward a definition of the workplace as a community. Office parties, softball games, and oft-told stories, rumors, and jokes can reveal as much or more about the nature of an organization as a community as employee satisfaction surveys, annual reports, and formal organizational policies.

Although there are many ways to conduct interpretive research, the best studies capture the spirit and diversity of an organization's values and practices through evocative vocabulary or metaphor. For example, Van Maanen (1991) uses the metaphor of a "smile factory" in his cultural study of Disneyland. The image of smiles (friendly, fun, courteous) being manufactured (e.g., the products of a rigid factory assembly line) establishes the tensions of a cultural dialogue between Disney management and

Disney employees. By using this language, Van Maanen delineates the interplay of a staged performance: Employees are "members of a cast" who wear "costumes," not uniforms, and who exhibit onstage, offstage, and backstage behaviors. He also uses the image of the factory to discuss the production of smiles, formal rules about informal behaviors, and the prevalence of supervisory spies who note every infraction. The result is an account of a strong culture's everyday use of language that constructs a metaphor which, in turn, becomes its unique sense of place.

Organizational culture is the result of the cumulative learning of a group of people. This learning manifests itself as culture at a number of levels. According to Edgar Schein (1991), culture is defined by six formal properties: (1) shared basic assumptions that are (2) invented, discovered, or developed by a given group as it (3) learns to cope with its problems of external adaptation and internal integration in ways that (4) have worked well enough to be considered valid and therefore (5) can be taught to new members of the group as the (6) correct way to perceive, think, and feel in relation to those problems.

☐ Social Trends

The economic environment in the United States after World War II also contributed to the popularity in the Western nations of the cultural approach to organizations. After the close of the war, the United States experienced a sense of renewal and promise, both economic and political. As sociologist Todd Gitlin (1987) explains, "The boom was on, and the cornucopia seemed all the more impressive because the miseries of the Depression and war were near enough to suffuse the present with a sense of relief" (p. 13). As Gitlin goes on to point out, these sources of renewal and promise were balanced by the powerful threat of nuclear holocaust in an atomic age. The tension created by these opposing influences helped shape the values of the new, postwar generation. Social, ethnic, racial, political, sexual, and economic tensions contributed to the complexity of the post–World War II climate, as did the new role of science in society, industry, and ideology. Since the Enlightenment, science had delivered on its promise of creating a more progressive and rational society. In the twentieth century, however, science demonstrated a new ability to create weapons that could destroy humanity. Although industry, since the Industrial Revolution, had delivered the products and services that made life easier and more humane, it also sanctioned inequalities between women and men and among ethnic and racial groups. At the same time, fierce competition for scarce natural resources and commodity markets contributed to worldwide tension. Similarly, new communication technologies like radios, stereos, televisions, and satellites made information more accessible as well as more open to commentary. Ideological battles among capitalism, socialism, and communism threatened world peace and led to the Cold War (Taylor, 2003; Taylor, Kinsella, Depoe, & Metzler, 2005).

In many ways, our current historical moment shares much with its post–World War II predecessor (Goodall, 2008). We are witnessing sources of renewal and promise in the form of green organizations, sustainable products, and the hope for renewable energy, yet we are also facing threats of terrorism, global climate change, and economic unrest.

After World War II, the political landscape was changing as well. The mid-1960s are commonly referred to by anthropologists, historians, and literary critics as the end of Western colonialism; European countries like England and France were forced to give up their colonies in Africa and elsewhere (Greenblatt, 1990; Said, 1978, 1984). With the end of colonialism came a redefinition of the role of Western interests in the political and economic subordination of Third World countries (Bhabha, 1990; Clifford & Marcus, 1985; Marcus & Fischer, 1986; Minh-Ha, 1991; Schwartz-DuPre, 2013).

New global economic and political concerns also increased critical scrutiny of organizations. The emergence of multinational firms and a world economy dominated by capitalism and a dependence on cheap labor in Third World countries exposed global problems and inequities, and the management of cultural differences in the workplace became important to firms doing business in other countries. Finding ways to improve cross-cultural understanding and communication skills was an integral component of the cultural approach to organizational communication.

In this turbulent social environment, new questions about organizations addressed such topics as power, participation, domination, and resistance in the workplace. For example, men exerted power over women by defining "real work" as that which was done outside the home (by men) and "housework" as less worthy of compensation or respect. Housework was not valued for its major contributions to the ideals of family and society. As a result, it brought women less status than men received for performing "real work." Furthermore, when women began to assert their right to work outside the home and to assume positions of responsibility in the workforce (in secretarial, food preparation, elementary school teaching, and custodial jobs), they encountered widespread opposition by men.

Similarly, in the 1950s to 1970s, members of minority groups began to seriously challenge the dominant elite that had long controlled their access to equality, the civil rights movement in the United States being a well-known example. These groups included people whose racial, ethnic, or religious heritage distinguished them from the dominant white majority, people with physical and mental disabilities, people who had served in the armed forces, and the elderly. They protested against unfair social and professional practices, discrimination, and oppression.

The social climate in which cultural studies of organizations emerged, then, was characterized by increased participation, globalization, diversity, and resistance to domination on the part of minority groups. The popularity of the cultural approach was thus tied to its focus on cultural differences within organizations or societies.

◪ THREE VIEWS OF ORGANIZATIONAL CULTURE

As we have shown, competitive pressure, interpretive methodology, and social concerns contributed to the rise of the cultural approach. These concerns are more specifically reflected in three broad perspectives that characterize culture studies in organizations today: the practical, interpretive, and critical and postmodern views.

☐ The Practical View

The **practical view** responds to managers' desire for actionable advice and specific communication strategies for enhancing competitiveness and increasing employee satisfaction. From the practical perspective, culture is an organizational feature, like technology or management style, that managers can leverage to create more effective organizations. Adherents believe that quasi-causal relationships can be created between cultural elements (like stories or rituals) and organizational outcomes (like employee commitment). Two successful and germinal books, both sponsored by McKinsey & Company, a management consulting firm, provided the foundation for this view. The first, Terrence Deal and Allan Kennedy's *Corporate Cultures: The Rites and Rituals of Corporate Life* (1982) defined the elements of strong cultures as

- a supportive business environment,
- dedication to a shared vision and values,
- well-known corporate heroes,
- effective rites and rituals, and
- formal and informal communication networks.

The other book, *In Search of Excellence: Lessons from America's Best-Run Corporations* (1982) by Thomas Peters and Robert Waterman, made the *New York Times* best-seller list for nonfiction. Its authors studied sixty-two financially successful companies and found eight common characteristics of their cultures:

1. *A bias for action.* Top-performing companies are characterized by active decision making; they are not characterized by thinking about decisions for long periods of time or relying on a lot of information to make decisions. If a change occurs in the business environment, they act.
2. *Close relations to the customer.* Top-performing companies never forget who makes them successful: their customers. One of the basics of excellence is to remember that service, reliability, innovation, and a constant concern for the customer are vital to any organization.
3. *Autonomy and entrepreneurship.* Top-performing companies empower their employees by encouraging risk taking, responsibility for the decisions they make and the actions they perform, and innovation. If an organization is too tightly controlled and worker performance is too tightly monitored, initiative, creativity, and willingness to take responsibility all tend to decay.

4. *Productivity through people.* A quality product depends on quality workers throughout the organization. Good customer relations depend on valuing service throughout the organization. Top-performing companies recognize these factors and rally against us/them or management/labor divisions.

5. *Hands-on, value-driven.* Top-performing companies are characterized by strong core values that are widely shared among employees and by an overall vision— a management philosophy—that guides everyday practices. Achievement is dependent on performance, and performance is dependent on values.

6. *Stick to the knitting.* Top-performing companies tend to be strictly focused on their source of product and service excellence. They tend not to diversify by going into other product or service fields. They expand their organization and profits by sticking to what they do best.

7. *Simple form, lean staff.* Top-performing companies are characterized by a lack of complicated hierarchies and divisions of labor. None of the companies surveyed maintained a typical bureaucratic form of organizing. Many of them employed fewer than one hundred people.

8. *Simultaneous loose-tight properties.* Top-performing companies are difficult to categorize. They encourage individual action and responsibility and yet retain strong core values; they encourage individual and group decision making. They are neither centralized nor decentralized in management style because they adapt to new situations with whatever is needed to get the job done.

In addition, management theorists Jim Collins and Jerry Porras (2004) suggest that an organization's longevity can be sustained by a culture that preserves its core purpose and values while remaining open to change and opportunity in a dynamic world. This type of corporation creates a strong, homogenous culture characterized by the following:

- *Fervently held ideology.* Strong cultures explicitly articulate their overriding goals and values and ensure that employee behavior is guided and consistent with the ideology. Both Nordstrom's and Zappos's core ideologies, for example, center on customer service, and employees are expected and empowered to provide stellar service.

- *Indoctrination.* Organization with strong cultures seek to instill their core ideology through orientation programs, training, company newsletters and other publications, corporate songs, organization-specific language, and socialization by peers into the culture. At Disney, "cast members" are steeped in the company's history, special language, mythology, wholesome image, and core ideology.

- *Tightness of fit.* Strong organizational cultures employ an extensive screening process to ensure that those hired are good fits with the culture. They also have very clear norms of behavior. Those who fit in with the culture are attracted to it and supportive of it; those who do not fit in with the culture are penalized and are "ejected like a virus" (p. 121). More recent examples of this include Netflix and Amazon who offer employees who are unhappy or whose performance is less than stellar a bonus if they are willing to leave.

- *Elitism.* Belonging, specialness, superiority, and secrecy are the hallmarks of strong cultures. The elitism at Procter & Gamble is reinforced by its secretive culture. Employees are prevented from discussing work in public or working on airplanes where other travelers may see company information. One stock option plan even stipulated that if an employee revealed "unauthorized information" about the company, his or her stock options would be revoked.

Cultures built on these principles can be seen as effective or "strong" because they reproduce the core ideology for their members to see, feel, and internalize in very concrete, explicit, and purposeful ways. In all the previous examples, culture is "a rational instrument designed by top management to shape the behavior of the employees in purposive ways" (Ouchi & Wilkins, 1985, p. 462). PepsiCo, Hyatt, McDonald's, Microsoft, Disney, and Google, for example, are noted for their strong corporate cultures. Each invests tens of millions of dollars annually in the selection and indoctrination of employees into the company's way of doing things. Companies with strong corporate cultures tend to encourage a deep sense of commitment among their employees. However, such companies may require employees to give up significant freedoms (even in the area of personal appearance—Disney "cast members," for example, are barred from having visible tattoos and body piercings or unnatural hair coloring) in exchange for membership.

Strong corporate cultures can lead to positive or negative consequences for employees and other stakeholders. For example, many successful companies today are in the process of replacing top-down management processes with management that is driven by a vision of the future and a set of corporate values.

Creating a strong values-driven culture within a multinational organization is a particular challenge in today's landscape. Yet the practical view suggests that managers can create a seamless, strong culture that blends the "home" (corporate) with the "host" (international) culture (Meyer, 2015). Specifically, Meyer (2015), writing in the *Harvard Business Review*, encourages leaders to do the following:

1. "Identify the dimensions of difference" (p. 71): By understanding the key cultural differences that underlie the home and host cultures, managers will be better able to anticipate and mediate potential conflicts. For example, if the host culture assumes that consensus decisions are most productive, and the home culture assumes that decisions are made at the top of the hierarchy and shared, then decision making may be a key cultural dimension that needs to be explicitly articulated and modeled.
2. "Give everyone a voice" (p. 71): Managers need to be sure that all groups have an opportunity to be heard and a comfortable way to express their interests and concerns.

3. "Protect the most creative units" (p. 71): Those functional organizational units that require flexibility, conditions of strategic ambiguity, and creativity to succeed should have them. Units that can function best with less "room for interpretation," should have the processes, practices, and modes of communication more formalized and codified.

4. "Train everyone on key norms" (p. 71): Leaders should make explicit and train members on key cultural norms, whether those have to do with decision making, customer service, or conflict management.

5. "Be heterogeneous everywhere" (p. 72): According to Meyer, a "culture is likely to have a more integrated culture if all units are diverse" (p. 72). From software engineers to frontline service providers, a diverse workforce can help to "build bridges of cultural understanding" (p. 72).

Whether it is in a large, multinational corporation that spans national boundaries or in a local, family-run business, under this practical approach to culture, leadership's main role is to help employees understand and work according to the organization's vision and values (Deetz, Tracy, & Simpson, 2000; Eisenberg & Riley, 2001).

Of course, left unchecked, strong cultures can become cultlike, dysfunctional, and even dangerous. Indeed, the indoctrination practices of terrorist and other ethically questionable groups look very similar to those outlined by Collins and Porras (Arena & Arrigo, 2005). A worst-case scenario is a company culture that supports unethical behavior. The following kinds of cultures are most likely to encourage questionable ethical practices:

- A culture of broken promises
- A culture where no one takes responsibility
- A culture that denies participation and dissent

In our current economic environment, some organizational leaders are rethinking the ethical dimensions of developing strong cultures, particularly those based exclusively on positivity. Critical management scholar David Collinson (2012) argues that many contemporary leaders use "excessive positivity"—or what popular management texts might refer to as "passion," "zeal," "infectious optimism," and "enthusiasm"—to frame organizational events and to make sense of organizational environments. Leaders' positivity may well inspire followers and build a consistent or strong culture. "However," warns Collinson, "problems can occur, particularly if this positivity is seen to be discrepant with [members'] everyday experience" (p. 88). Indeed, he argues, such overly upbeat attempts to manage culture are often met with employee skepticism, cynicism, and resistance. Moreover, such an approach may prohibit leaders' ability to hear alternative, but necessary, views.

Despite this warning and the sustained criticism of the practical view over the past several years as too controlling and naïve in its inattention to the role that members play in creating cultures, it clearly continues to have currency in contemporary organizations and has brought certain benefits, such as introducing a useful vocabulary for directing managers' attention toward communication practices and the human side of business (Alvesson, 1993; Smircich & Calas, 1987).

☐ The Interpretive View

While the practical assumption that culture can simply be imposed from above or engineered by well-meaning managers may be appealing to organizational leaders, interpretive organizational scholars believe that culture is too complex, holistic, and pervasive to be managed or controlled by any single individual or management team. The *What Would You Do?* box on page 138 asks you to assess how well managers can, in fact, impose a culture from the top down. Those who subscribe to an **interpretive view** treat culture as a process that is socially constructed in everyday communicative behaviors among all members of an organization. They "find it ridiculous to talk of managing culture. Culture cannot be managed; it emerges. Leaders don't create cultures; members of the culture do" (Martin, 1985, p. 95).

From this perspective, culture emerges in the symbolism or discourse of everyday organizational life (Fairhurst & Putnam, 2004). Where the practical view was primarily interested in the meanings of such things as corporate logos and value statements, interpretive scholars focus on a broader view of symbolism in organizations. They focus on the subtle ways in which communication works to build, reproduce, and transform the taken-for-granted reality of organizational culture. How people dress, the stories that they tell, the layout of offices and parking areas, the design of security badges, and the length and tenor of staff meetings each communicate richly about an organization's unique culture. Research taking this perspective can be traced to a group of management and communication scholars who first met at a conference in Alta, Utah, in 1983.

Organized by Linda Putnam and Michael Pacanowsky, this conference and a resulting book, *Communication and Organizations: An Interpretive Approach* (1983), helped legitimize interpretive and cultural studies of organizational communication. Around the same time, an influential article by Pacanowsky and Nick O'Donnell-Trujillo (1983) helped establish organizational communication as a form of cultural performance. Some writers have argued that organizations are mainly storytelling systems (Boje, 1991, 1995). The stories or narratives about the organization's culture convey information about its current state of affairs, and as such the stories serve as resources for everyday sense making (Wilkins, 1984). As noted in Chapter 4, when an organization is viewed as a system—in this case, a storytelling system—modifications represent feedback. Paying attention to stories and how they change can be important for employees and managers alike (Mitroff & Kilmann, 1975).

Organizational stories may be found in speeches and casual conversations, as well as in employee newsletters, company brochures, strategic planning statements, corporate advertisements, fund-raising campaigns, and training videos (Goodall,

A "Shot" of Motivation

Management consultants and trainers who deal with improving an organization's culture often try to bring current scientific research into their work, usually by creatively linking those findings to "best practices," but sometimes by extending a scientific study to unwarranted generalizations about the workplace.

For the past several years, neuroscientists have been interested in seeing how the human brain functions at work. The findings they report are still preliminary in most cases, but they are also quite appealing as potential keys capable of unlocking the secrets of everything from handling stress to stimulating employee motivation. An article by Fox (2008), for example, shared some interesting research about employee motivation and its link to brain function. It said that if a manager shows interest in employees, supports them, and genuinely praises them, the manager is essentially sending a "shot" of serotonin into the employees' brains. Serotonin is the chemical that makes us feel good. It opens our minds to new ideas and creates a desire to support others. Serotonin leads to enhanced levels of motivation. Indeed, one leadership author in the popular press refers to serotonin as the "leadership chemical" (Sinek, 2014). Likewise, a manager can inadvertently send a "shot" of the chemical cortisol into employees' brains by treating them unfairly or by diminishing their efforts. In turn, the cortisol leads the employees to shut down any willingness to help or to be open to new ideas. It's a demotivator.

This brain research naturally leads us to ask, How can a manager consistently send a "shot" of motivation into employees? A few suggestions might be to add some fun and variety into the daily routine, such as starting a "March Madness" pool or beginning each staff meeting with a "fun fact"; provide employees with input and choices to help them feel more empowered and more in control of their own work; and develop goals and challenges for employees so that they are clear about what they are working to achieve and what steps they need to take to get there. Managers should be aware that even a little "shot" can make a big difference in the daily lives of employees.

Let's say that you are an organizational consultant and an expert on organizational culture. An organization approaches you to provide insight into how best to motivate employees in the wake of mandatory pay cuts and layoffs due to an economic downturn. The organizational leaders are particularly interested in discovering how to motivate employees and reward high-performing staff without using monetary incentives. They want you to help them make their office environment more "fun and cool." The corporate culture has always been somewhat formal, which once worked perfectly well for the employees and the organization. What would you do?

DISCUSSION QUESTIONS

1. Would you be concerned about using the preliminary scientific results on "shooting" motivation to help this organization find alternative ways of motivating employees? Why or why not?
2. Can you dictate "fun" in an organization? If so, how? If not, why not? Is there a difference between "organic" fun and "prescribed" fun? Do you think managers can install culture—in this case, "shoot" motivation—from the top down? Should they?
3. In the context of a general economic downturn, wage stagnation, and in the absence of real material rewards, how can leaders inspire and motivate a positive work environment? What tools and resources might be productively deployed toward that end?

1989; Keyton, 2011; Pacanowsky, 1988; Smith & Keyton, 2001). These forums provide opportunities for an organization to talk about its values and aspirations. However, different stories about the organization are told by different narrators. The corporate or official story about the organization may be told by advertising agents working in conjunction with high-level managers and stockholders. The inside stories are told by employees of the organization, who may offer different accounts. In two recent investigations into the working conditions of fruit pickers and manufacturing plant workers in the Carolinas, the accounts given by the business owners and managers differed greatly from the accounts given by the employees. The story told by the owners and managers focused on the number of people employed by the companies, product quality, and reasonable cost to consumers. In contrast, the story told by employees focused on low wages (sometimes paid in the form of alcohol or illegal drugs) and unsafe workplaces.

Clearly, organizational stories represent the interests and values of the storytellers. In the preceding example, neither side's narrative captured the whole story. Usually, multiple stories or interpretations are needed to describe an organization's culture. These stories represent different voices as well as potential dialogues among individuals and groups within the organization. Therefore, we can think of an organization's culture as a potential dialogue of subcultures or as a many-sided story (Boje, 1995).

The interpretive approach to understanding culture has shifted our focus toward how people communicate and create meaning in dialogue. However, symbolic displays must be considered in practical contexts, not as isolated events. Just as a joke, a story, a choice of words, or a ritual can be misleading out of context, symbols should be studied in ways that link them to the realities of work (Alvesson, 1993). In so doing, this view of culture gives us access to the social construction of meaning as well as its consequences.

As a case in point, in 1993, Gideon Kunda, professor of labor studies at Tel Aviv University, published an award-winning interpretive ethnographic study on the power relationships affecting workers' lives in a high-tech engineering firm. His study challenges many of the practical assumptions about corporate culture identified earlier by Peters and Waterman (1982). From interviews, observations, and a close reading of the culture's everyday activities, Kunda concludes that the control and commitment features of strong cultures are the most problematic. Specifically, leadership's attempts to "engineer culture" to look a certain way are flawed. Over time, workers may come to question the authenticity of any emotions and beliefs associated with company slogans and proclamations. Moreover, workers may learn the lessons of strong cultural performances so well that they seem driven to make irony of "the dominant mode of their everyday existence" (Kunda, 1993, p. 216). In such an organization, employee talk is uniformly cynical and sarcastic, reflecting a deep discomfort with commitment to the "party line" that is continually pushed and endorsed by the organization. This has happened to a degree in the way some Disney employees talk about their "loyalty" to "the mouse." Kunda's interpretive study is valuable because it offers balance to what can seem at times to be a one-sided conversation about the benefits of a strong culture.

In his study, Kunda also describes the time-consuming, iterative process he used both to study and "write up" the culture. He makes clear that as symbols or texts, cultures can be interpreted in many different ways, and thus there are often many potential tales to be told about the same culture (Van Maanen, 1988). Interpretive scholars are particularly interested in the form their studies take because they believe that the "tale" is as important as the culture it represents (Goodall, 2000). A volume edited by Purdue University organizational communication professor Robin Patric Clair (2003) highlights the engaging approaches to ethnography that interpretive scholars employ to bring organizational cultures to life on the page. Authors describe, in artful detail, how social and organizational cultures affect the birthing process and the stories mothers are able to narrate about their experience of childbirth, how corrections officers manage the dilemmas that characterize their everyday work worlds, and even how one workplace and community site, Comiskey Park, provided a context for and shaped a family's relationships (Krizek, 2003; Tracy, 2003; Turner, 2003). These cultural tales offer their readers new, engaging, and meaningful ways of "studying and speaking about culture" and, in turn, our lives (Goodall, 2003, p. 63).

Though interpretive studies provide insightful accounts, some have been critiqued for failing to adequately explore the power dimensions of organizational cultures, to address the relationship between the larger social context and the particular culture in question, and to offer prescriptive guidelines for improving cultural performance or facilitating change. Critical and postmodern scholars take up these criticisms directly.

☐ Critical and Postmodern Views

Research on organizational culture has moved significantly in the direction of the **critical and postmodern views**, each of which focuses on challenges to power relationships and the status quo. (Chapters 6 and 7 are devoted to more detailed discussions of these topics.) Two researchers who have made significant contributions to this line of research are Stanley Deetz and Joanne Martin.

Deetz and others (Atkouf, 1992; Smircich & Calas, 1987) argue that the managerial bias in culture research reinforces the "corporate colonization of the life-world" through which the interests of corporations frame all aspects of daily living for their employees (Deetz, 1992, 1995). These critics call for organizational ethnographers to examine issues of power and domination associated with the development, maintenance, or transformation of a particular culture. To do so, critics must expose how cultural elements, including stories, rituals, jokes, and mission statements, function to support and reproduce the power structure that privileges the interests of dominant organizational groups over others. Specifically, critics must reveal the cultural processes through which one particular and privileged social construction of reality comes to hold sway over other equally plausible constructions—that is, how the party line gets established and why employees accept it (Mumby, 1987). Further, they believe the transcripts chronicling the lives of those with less power in organizations should be exposed and read, so that alternatives to the dominant culture can be considered.

Communication scholar Joanne Martin has developed a taxonomy of perspectives on organizational culture that takes into account the movement toward a postmodern view. According to Martin (1992), perspectives on culture can be characterized as highlighting integration, differentiation, or fragmentation. Although studies of organizations typically take one perspective, most organizations contain all three. Each perspective reveals a different orientation to three key features of cultural study: orientation to consensus, relations among divergent manifestations, and orientation to ambiguity. Let us consider each perspective in detail.

Integration

The **integration perspective** portrays culture in terms of consistency and clarity. From this perspective, it appears that cultural members agree about what they need to do and why they need to do it. There appears to be no room for ambiguity. In addition, an organization's culture is portrayed as a monologue, not a dialogue (May, 1988). This tradition in the cultural study of organizations is evident in Tom Peters and Robert Waterman's (1982) descriptions of excellent companies with strong cultures that adhere to a narrow set of shared values, meanings, and interpretations. Similarly, studies that analyze the influence of an organization's founder tend to trace those influences throughout the organization (Barley, 1983; Pacanowsky, 1988; Schein, 1991), sometimes to the neglect of competing values within the company (McDonald, 1988). Indeed, the integration perspective typically favors the story of those in power over other competing stories.

Differentiation

While an integration perspective focuses on agreement, a **differentiation perspective** highlights differences across organizational units or subcultures. The differentiation perspective portrays cultural manifestations as predominantly inconsistent with one another (such as when the responsible party on an organizational chart is different from the person whom "everyone knows" is in charge). Furthermore, when consensus does emerge, the differentiation view is quick to point out its limitations (e.g., that agreement may only exist among a group or subculture of members). From the standpoint of the total organization, differentiated subcultures can coexist in harmony, conflict, or indifference to one another. These subcultures are viewed as islands of clarity, and ambiguity is channeled outside of their boundaries (Frost, Moore, Louis, Lundberg, & Martin, 1991). Of course there is always the possibility that too much differentiation can create wide gaps among parts of the organization. At many multicampus university systems, for example, a great deal of effort is spent both preserving differences among campuses and at the same time ensuring that there is an overarching cultural umbrella under which they all fit.

The differentiation perspective sees organizational cultures as contested political domains in which the potential for genuine dialogue is often impaired. The various subcultures may seldom speak to one another, instead reinforcing their own accounts of organizational meanings without seeking external validation. As a result, they do not actively participate in the broader interests of the organization.

For example, one study revealed that a computer software firm had created barriers to the communication of its subcultures when it moved to a new location (Goodall, 1990). Work groups were physically separated from one another, promoting competition for resources. Another study (Rosenfeld, Richman, & May, 2004) demonstrated how a health-care organization developed a "dispersed network culture," in which two very different understandings of the organizational culture emerged. In this organization, those employees working in the field providing direct care to patients and those employees working in the home office performing clerical duties created two loosely coupled subcultures. According to Rosenfeld, Richman, and May (2004), in a differentiated culture like this one:

> The goal is not necessarily to create one culture through integration or to maintain two separate cultures. . . . Rather, the goal may be to create a unified diversity [Eisenberg, 1984], an organization in which there is a shared understanding and agreement among employees regarding such matters as organizational objectives and policies, while also acknowledging that to meet organizational objectives requires having employees with diverse skills, making organization-wide consensus on issues difficult to achieve. (pp. 48–49)

Divisions among classes of employees, such as those in the field and those in the home office, often occupy the interests of subcultures, and the differentiation perspective can show how conflict among subcultures may be masked or brought in alignment through unified diversity.

Fragmentation

From a **fragmentation perspective**, ambiguity is an inevitable and pervasive aspect of contemporary life. Studies in this area focus on the experience and expression of ambiguity within organizational cultures, wherein consensus and dissensus coexist in a constantly fluctuating pattern of change. Any cultural manifestation can be interpreted in a myriad of ways because clear consensus among organizational subcultures cannot be attained.

Consistent with newer theories of organizations and society as discussed in Chapter 6, the fragmentation perspective replaces certainty with ambiguity, contradiction, tension, and irony as models for interpretation. Ambiguity can be manipulated by management to support its interests and by disempowered employees to cope with their interests (Ashcraft & Trethewey, 2004; Eisenberg, 2007; Harter, 2004; Myerson, 1991; Stohl & Cheney, 2001; Trethewey, 1999b). Researchers have applied ambiguity to organizational communication in a variety of ways. For example, it has been used to explain the divergent accounts of an airline disaster given by eyewitnesses (Weick, 1990) and the ways in which farmers in Nebraska negotiate their simultaneous but competing needs for rugged independence and collective interdependence and survival (Harter, 2004). Recently, the fragmentation perspective, with its emphasis on cultural ambiguity, has been used to explore and explain how faculty and staff at universities create highly individualized, localized, and context-based meanings for work-life symbols, policies, and practices at their institutions, even while their organizational leaders are working to build integrated cultures that embrace work-life balance (Lester, 2015).

The meaning of ambiguity for our concept of organizational cultures as dialogue depends on how we define *dialogue*. If dialogue is viewed as a means of generating consensus, then ambiguity makes dialogue unlikely. Conversely, if dialogue is thought of as embodying a respect for diversity—and perhaps a form of consensus based on acknowledgment of differences—then ambiguity is a necessary component of dialogue. Unlike ambiguity about shared meanings or interpretations of culture, multiple meanings are inevitably found in ambiguities about shared practices (Taylor, Irvin, & Wieland, 2006). Recall that from the interpretive perspective, shared practices and multiple interpretations of meaning for those practices are highly valued. For us, then, ambiguity is a necessary component of dialogue. Indeed, genuine dialogue probably would not exist without ambiguity, for if everything were clearly understood, there would not be much left to talk about (Boje, 1995).

An ethnography focusing on how one university selected its chief academic officer shows the usefulness of Joanne Martin's taxonomy (Eisenberg, Murphy, & Andrews, 1998). In this yearlong study, the participants and the researchers offered various interpretations of the university's search process, and these accounts reflect all three of Martin's perspectives. Some saw the search process as highly rational, with the choice of the leading candidate an inevitable result. Others described the process as highly political, a struggle for power among competing groups on campus; still others saw it as rife with ambiguity and confusion from the outset, lacking explicit decision-making criteria from the beginning of the process. A traditional researcher might ask, "Who is right?" The authors chose instead to describe the ways in which participants selected their interpretation with their audience in mind and felt free to offer different interpretations on different occasions. The authors concluded that using all three perspectives provided a richer view of the search process and the organization's culture than any one view taken alone.

These three frames were also useful for discovering how an organization's cultural values are shared among a contingent and changing workforce. Management scholar Vanessa Hill and organizational network scholar Kathleen Carley's (2011) analysis of a temporary agency that used Martin's taxonomy as a guiding heuristic found that the most successful "purveyors" of cultural values were those who were both well liked and perceived as useful to their coworkers' success. These characteristics were more important to culture building than their hierarchical position or their enactment of policies.

▨ SOCIALIZATION: INTEGRATING NEW MEMBERS INTO ORGANIZATIONAL CULTURES

A cultural approach acknowledges that transitioning new members into an organization requires much more than simply providing necessary task information. Successful socialization demands that organizations help new members feel integrated into the culture. "Workers who remain apart from the prevailing culture rather than becoming a part of it are unlikely to be as effective or as satisfied with the job as they could be" (Hess, 1993). **Socialization** is the process by which people learn the rules, norms, and expectations of a culture over time and thereby become members of that culture. We are all, to some extent, assimilated into a national culture and local cultures. As children, we were most likely taught by parents and others how to become members of a family, community, religion, or country. Socialization involves learning the rules that guide what members of a culture think, do, and say. Socialization of members is essential in any culture and begins at an early age.

In organizations, describing the socialization process helps us understand how the new employee learns about and makes sense of the organization's culture (Jablin, 1987; Kramer & Miller, 1999). Although the employee's first week on the job is filled with surprises, over time the employee learns the formal and informal rules that govern behavior in the organization. This learning process has broad stages including anticipatory socialization and organizational assimilation. See *Everyday Organizational Communication* on page 145 to explore the role of college radio stations in community socialization.

EVERYDAY ORGANIZATIONAL COMMUNICATION

College Radio and Community Socialization

Stanford University's campus radio station, KZSU, has served the student body for nearly seventy years. For more than fifty of those years, Mark Lawrence (Class of '67) has worked as the station's faithful sound engineer. He works with students, takes care of the technical equipment for the station's three studios, and keeps KZSU up-to-date on new gadgets and other sound-engineering advancements. As the station's longest-term employee, Mark has taken on an iconic role at KZSU, and most students couldn't imagine the station without him.

For many academic institutions, college radio stations provide key insights into important elements of culture. Not only do they advance new trends in music, they are also home to organizational heroes and heroines, metaphors, and stories about the college or university, and daily performances by students.

As potential hotbeds of organizational culture, college radio stations also create a space that connects students to opportunities on their campuses and in the larger communities that surround them. For example, the University of North Carolina at Greensboro's college radio station, WUAG, features a program entitled "Greensboro Radio Outlooks on the World" (GROW). In addition to providing a student perspective on local and global topics, the show also gives community members and organizations an opportunity to raise awareness about Greensboro-centered issues like public transportation and locally grown food. Similarly, John Carroll University's student-run station, WJCU, devotes airtime to a daily program called "The Heights." This show has the dual purpose of playing alternative music and keeping students connected to events and issues important to the local Cleveland community.

These campus radio stations and their community-based shows provide the first opportunities for many students to learn about the social, cultural, and institutional concerns that they will encounter at school and beyond.

DISCUSSION QUESTIONS

1. Does your college or university have a campus radio station? If so, how does your campus's station illustrate the everyday elements of organizational culture that help construct your school? If not, can you think of other campus organizations that play a key role in constructing your campus's culture? How do people like Mark Lawrence serve as heroes and heroines in the construction of your school's culture?

(continued, College Radio and Community Socialization)

2. How do campus radio stations connect students to cultural practices outside of the college or university? How do campus radio stations provide resources for socializing students into the cultural practices of the larger community?

3. College radio stations have navigated many structural and cultural changes since they first hit the airwaves. Many stations have faced significant budget cuts, and most are now student-run organizations. Moreover, social media sites like Facebook, Twitter, Instagram, and Snapchat have emerged as communication resources that can connect students with their communities. Considering shrinking financial resources and the rise of social media, how do college radio stations stay relevant, especially as a resource for socializing young people into their communities?

☐ Anticipatory Socialization

Some lessons about the nature of work are learned long before a job begins. In the **anticipatory socialization** stage, people learn about work through communication. There are two forms of anticipatory socialization: vocational and organizational. The vocational type, which begins in childhood, involves learning about work and careers in general from family members, teachers, part-time employers, friends, and the media. Children and adolescents acquire a general knowledge of accepted attitudes toward work, of the importance of power and status in organizations, and of work as a source of meaningful personal relationships (Atwood, 1990; Gibson & Papa, 2000; Jablin, 1985).

Later in life, the organizational type of anticipatory socialization involves learning about a specific job and organization. It takes place before the first day of work and is typically accomplished through company literature, such as brochures, personnel manuals, and websites, as well as through interactions between job applicants and interviewers. Through such communication, individuals develop expectations about the prospective job and organization. However, their expectations are often inflated and unrealistic due to interviewers' tendency to focus on positive aspects of the job and the company.

☐ Organizational Assimilation

The experience of **organizational assimilation** involves both surprise and sense making (Louis, 1980). As new employees' initial expectations are violated, they attempt to make sense of their job and the organization. "The newcomer learns the requirements of his or her role and what the organization and its members consider to be 'normal' patterns of behavior and thought" (Jablin, 1987, p. 695).

For example, presidents and CEOs of companies often attend orientations for new employees and deliver the message that their "door is always open" to employees who want to talk. In most cases, the employees who take this invitation seriously are surprised by the likely reality that the president or CEO is either unavailable or unhelpful or that such conversations are not much appreciated by line and middle managers. After a few weeks, these employees come to make sense of "how things really work around here."

Newcomers' search for information carries a sense of urgency. Typically, new employees have some difficulty performing their jobs and getting along with others until they reach a level of familiarity. Potential sources of useful information for newcomers include (1) official company messages (e.g., from management, orientation programs, and manuals); (2) coworkers and peers; (3) supervisors; (4) other organizational members, including administrative assistants, security guards, and employees in other departments; (5) customers and others outside the organization; and (6) the employee's assigned tasks. Because employees do receive information from multiple sources and look for many opportunities to identify with their new culture, recent studies indicate that organizations should treat orientation programs as a set of multiple activities spread across time and space rather than a discrete and formal event (Stephens & Dailey, 2012).

Newcomers attempt to "situate" themselves in an unfamiliar organizational context, but to do so they must first learn a great deal about how existing members define the organization's culture. To solicit the information they need, new employees tend not to rely on direct questioning because substantial risks may be associated with asking irrelevant questions. Instead, they use other tactics to solicit information about the organizational culture (Miller & Jablin, 1991; see Table 5.1). One of the more interesting tactics, "disguising conversations," involves making jokes about people, procedures, or activities and watching to see whether others think they're funny. Similarly, organizational veterans may use "teasing" to say, "'You're doing something wrong' without saying it" (Heiss & Carmack, 2012, p. 117). Indeed, organizational communication scholars are becoming increasingly interested in how both newcomers and veterans use humor to make sense of and negotiate job expectations and culture in the entry process (Lynch, 2002, 2009; Lynch & Schaefer, 2008; Tracy, Lutgen-Sandvik, & Alberts, 2006).

Over time, employees may evolve from newcomers into full-fledged members of the organization (Jablin, 1987). This period of transition may or may not be lengthy, depending on the organization and the industry involved. In hotels and restaurants, for example, employees may feel like old-timers after only six months on the job, whereas in universities and professional associations, the transitional period may last nearly a decade. Of course, not everyone makes the transition to member. If there is a poor fit, either the organization or the individual may opt out of the relationship. Moreover, the assimilation process is rarely as neat as these "stages" make it sound; large organizations in particular often make room for numerous diverse voices and definitions of membership (Bullis, 1999).

TABLE 5.1

Newcomer's Information-Seeking Tactics
Tactic Example

- Overt question: "Who has the authority to cancel purchase orders?"
- Indirect question: "I guess I won't plan to take a vacation this year." (Implied: "Do we work through the holidays if we don't finish the project?")
- Third parties: (To a coworker) "I'm making a presentation to the president. Does she like it if you open with a joke?"
- Testing limits: Arriving at work wearing casual clothes and observing others' reactions.
- Disguising conversations: "That safety memo sure was a riot. Can you believe the gall of those guys?" (Waiting for reaction to see whether others also think it was funny.)
- Observing: Watching which employees get praised in meetings and emulating those who do; paying attention to specific individuals.
- Surveillance: Eavesdropping on peer conversations; paying careful attention at office parties; monitoring the environment for clues.

During the transitional period of organizational assimilation, employees begin to differentiate between rules and norms that must be followed and those that can be ignored. Feeling more comfortable with the rules of the organization, employees begin to individualize their job, develop their own voice, and behave in ways that both conform to and transform the existing rules. For example, a new supervisor who makes minor changes in how work is delegated distinguishes his or her department from others in the organization. While newcomer behavior focuses on discovering constraints, the transition toward assimilation is marked by a greater degree of creativity. The degree of balance between the two—and of the employee's satisfaction with his or her role in the organization—largely determines patterns of cooperation, resistance, and exit.

☐ New Directions in Organizational Socialization

Over the past several decades, communication scholars have provided more nuanced explorations of the socialization process. These scholars have, for example, explored socialization in **high-reliability organizations (HROs)**, such as nuclear reactors, air traffic control towers, military organizations, and fire departments (Myers, 2005). In HROs, members continually operate in dangerous conditions where even a small misstep can lead to disaster. HROs avoid catastrophe by adhering to meticulously planned and coordinated safety rules and cultures; successful socialization can literally mean the difference between life and death. These studies are for the most part guided by an assumption that anticipatory socialization, assimilation, and organization exit follow a fairly singular and linear process.

More recent scholarship seeks to complicate our understanding of socialization by broadening the context, contributing factors, and temporal variability of socialization into organizational culture(s). Leading this effort is communication scholar and University of Texas professor Brenda Berkelaar (2013), who argues that "political, economic, and technological changes are reshaping how people join and leave organizations" (p. 33). From broad, international, political dynamics to changing interpersonal and familial relationships, there are many factors that currently influence how members' anticipate, join, experience, and exit organizations. Drawn from Berkelaar (2013), Table 5.2 provides a summary of the factors that likely influence organizational socialization and warrant further exploration by organizational communication scholars and practitioners interested in how members learn about, enter, contribute to, and exit organizational cultures.

As organizational scholars begin to explore these yet understudied aspects of organizational socialization, we will learn more about how members' experiences of joining, moving through, and exiting an organizations impacts their cultures and how those organizational cultures, in turn, influence their members.

TABLE 5.2

Understudied Factors Influencing Organizational Socialization

MACRO-LEVEL FACTORS

Macro-level factors include those broad, higher-order communicative processes that can impact organizational communication.

FACTOR	EXAMPLE
Increased Intercultural Contact	
Globalization and increased intercultural contacts can complicate the "assimilation and personalization of organizational, values, rules and norms" that constitute socialization (p. 45).	A regional university is committed to diversifying its student population, but successful recruitment and retention of diverse international students are sometimes challenged when students perceive incongruities between their new organizational values and their cultural, familial, or personal values.
Changing Workforce Conditions	
As the employment model of a single, upwardly mobile career track shifts, in response to the global economic downturn, to a model of more contingent, temporary, and shifting workforce, the socialization process may happen differently than traditional models predict.	A single father of two children works multiple part-time jobs to make ends meet and must simultaneously socialize in the context of multiple organizations whose values, norms, and practices may vary greatly.

(continued)

TABLE 5.2 *(continued)*

FACTOR	EXAMPLE
Understudied Work Contexts Family-owned business and organizations that constitute informal economies, those that are not taxed, regulated, or overseen by a government agency, are a significant portion of the employment landscape across the globe. We currently know little about the socialization process and practices in these types of organizations.	A child born into a family business may experience socialization from the time he is old enough to become aware of the relationship between and among work and family.
New Affordances and Uses of Information Communication Technologies (ICTs) While social media and Web 2.0 tools and practices have altered the ability of individuals to learn about organizations and organizations to learn about individuals, the use and influence of these new technologies in the context of socialization remains relatively understudied. We know little about how social networking sites, data analytic tools, and search engines "change when, how, and what people learn about individuals, organizations, and organizational roles: when and how they enter organizations; how they might engage in ongoing socialization; and when and how they disengage" (Berkelaar, 2013, p. 49).	An admitted, though not yet committed and registered, college student may learn a great deal about a university's values and goals, and her possible role in the academic and extracurricular communities on campus through engaging its social media, thus hastening her socialization.
Protest and Political Instabilities The same communication technologies that enable individuals to learn about organizations also provide them with tools to engage in political movements, protests, and other forms of organizing. Over the past several years, political instability has increased globally and, as a result, many people have voluntarily or involuntarily (in the case of displaced people, refugees, political asylum seekers) become members of new communities.	NGOs, social service organizations, and state agencies may need to understand the unique features of socializing refugees whose socialization is likely complicated by trauma, loss, and intercultural communication challenges.

Meso-level Factors

Meso-level factors refer to group, organizational, and interorganizational communicative processes that can impact organizational communication.

Factor	Example
Changing Organizational Forms ICTs can also encourage new organizational forms such as flash mobs, multinational corporations, and multi-organizational, networked partnerships. These new forms create conditions where the traditional, upward, linear model of socialization gives way to "transitional, internal and ongoing socialization" as people move "over and across, under and through interconnected groups within or across organizations, countries, time zones and newcomer/incumbent boundaries" (Berkelaar, 2013, p. 53).	An individual who recently joined an online support group and is also a long-term warehouse employee may simultaneously experience both newcomer and incumbent status.
"Forced" Socialization We know relatively little about how socialization unfolds when individuals enter organizations with little personal agency or choice (e.g., prison) or when entry is highly structured and determined (e.g., public education).	An eighth-grade student who moves to a new school because his parent got a new job in a different state will be socialized into his new academic home whether or not he choose to make the move.

Micro-level Factors

Micro-level factors refer to interpersonal communicative processes that can impact organizational communication.

Factor	Example
Changing Notions of Work and Career Scholars are recognizing that anticipatory socialization occurs across the life span, not just in childhood, as people shift occupations and careers over time. Additionally, as the social contract has shifted, individuals feel more responsibility for their own career trajectories, rather than relying on organizations to provide them with lifelong employment. Therefore, activities like personal branding (Lair et al., 2005) and other anticipatory socialization strategies take on greater significance.	A woman who left the workforce while her children were small may anticipate reinventing herself and her "brand" when she attempts to rejoin the workforce.

(continued)

TABLE 5.2 *(continued)*

Factor	Example
Changing Family Structures	
As family structures change and grow more diverse to include foster children, blended families, distributed families, and chosen families the socialization of members into these families may shed light on the organizational socialization process.	The blending of two families may serve as a microcosm of the socialization of organizational members during a merger.

Source: Berkelaar B. (2013). Joining and leaving organizations in a global information society. *Communication Yearbook* [serial online]. May 2013; 37:33–64. Available from: Communication & Mass Media Complete, Ipswich, MA. Accessed October 29, 2015.

A COMMUNICATION PERSPECTIVE ON ORGANIZATIONAL CULTURE

Reviewing the body of research on organizational culture is a tantalizing and confusing task. Just about anything is regarded as culture, and studies purporting to study culture do so in dramatically different ways. As a result, no consistent treatment of communication has emerged in the culture literature.

For this reason, we propose a perspective in which theories of organizational culture have the following five characteristics:

1. They view communication as the core process by which culture is formed and transformed and see culture as patterns of behavior and their interpretation.
2. They acknowledge the importance of everyday communication as well as more notable symbolic expressions.
3. They encompass not only words and actions but also all types of nonverbal communication (such as machinery, artifacts, and work processes).
4. They include broad patterns of interaction in society at large and examine how they are played out in the workplace. Therefore, they view each organization's culture as a cultural nexus of national, local, familial, and other forces outside of the organization (Martin, 1992).
5. They acknowledge the legitimacy of multiple motives for researching culture, from improving corporate performance to overthrowing existing power structures.

SUMMARY

Cultural approaches bring the symbolic life of organizations to the forefront. Organizational cultures are constructed through language, everyday practices, and members' sense making. Several cultural elements combine to create an organization's unique sense of place, including metaphors, rituals, stories, artifacts, heroes and heroines, performances, and values.

The focus on culture and its constitutive elements developed in response to three trends. First, Japanese companies that were thought to have mastered the process of building robust and responsive organizations by developing strong and unified cultures provided a model for many American corporations. Second, the increased use and acceptance of ethnographic and interpretive methods among communication scholars created a critical mass of research that sought to better understand members' cultural experiences. Third, the social climate that was beginning to value participation and diversity and recasting work as a more meaningful experience looked to culture as a vehicle for such change.

Three broad approaches characterize the study and practice of organizational culture. The practical view treats cultural elements as tools that managers leverage to build more effective organizations or "cultlike" cultures. Using ethnographic methods, the goal of the interpretive view is to develop richer understandings of how cultures emerge through the everyday interactions of all organizational members, not just managers or leaders. Finally, critical and postmodern approaches unpack the power and politics that underlie organizational cultures and recognize that cultures are not always integrated, but can be differentiated and fragmented.

Recent scholarship in organizational culture highlights the importance of socializing new members into ongoing cultures through face-to-face and, increasingly, computer-mediated communication. Effective socialization, as a cultural practice, has been found to be particularly important for high-reliability organizations that operate in dangerous environments. And recent research on socializing reveals that a broader number of factors are now entering into employee decisions to join or leave an organization.

While several different and sometimes competing approaches to organizational culture exist, we suggest that a communication perspective on organizational culture provides a useful, but complicated and dynamic, framework for understanding, participating in, and transforming organizational culture. In conclusion, then, we offer the following thoughts on organizational culture and research:

A culture—any culture—is like an ocean. There are many wonderful things and creatures in it that we may never understand; they change and so do we, regardless of the depth or perspective of our study. But the ocean is also made up of waves that are as regular as the cycles of the moon, and just as mysteriously musical, powerful, and enchanting. The top millimeter of the ocean is a world unto itself, and a vital one, in which the broader secrets of biological and evolutionary life . . . are contained. But even their meanings must be read in a vocabulary that is separate and distant. . . . So it is that within that millimeter, among those waves, we find clear and recurring themes. Like the great questions about culture that we pursue, those themes are always with us and not yet fully understood. (Goodall, 1991, p. 108)

QUESTIONS FOR REVIEW AND DISCUSSION

1. What is organizational culture? What makes studying an organization's culture different from studying a national culture like Norwegian or French?

2. Why are symbolic action and metaphor central to the study of organizational cultures?

3. What historical, political, and social trends contributed to the development of cultural studies of organizations?

4. What major questions are posed by viewing organizations as cultures?

5. Compare and contrast the major characteristics of the three approaches to organizational culture (practical, interpretive, and critical and postmodern).

6. Describe the process of organizational socialization. Describe the various tactics that a new employee might use to learn more about an organization's culture. What are the macro-, meso-, and micro-level factors that may impact organizational socialization into organizational culture(s)?

7. What are the advantages and limitations of studying organizations as cultures?

8. What are the characteristics of a communication perspective on organizational culture?

KEY TERMS

Anticipatory socialization, p. 146

Artifacts, p. 125

Critical and postmodern views, p. 141

Differentiation perspective, p. 142

Ethnography, p. 130

Fragmentation perspective, p. 143

Heroes and heroines, p. 127

High-reliability organization (HRO), p. 148

Integration perspective, p. 141

Interpretive view, p. 137

Metaphor, p. 126

Organizational assimilation, p. 146

Organizational culture, p. 125

Performance, p. 127

Practical view, p. 133

Ritual, p. 127

Socialization, p. 144

Theory Z, p. 128

Value, p. 127

Studying the Culture of Meetings

Helen Schwartzman writes in *Ethnography in Organizations* (1993) that "nothing could be more commonplace than meetings in organizations," yet most studies of organizational cultures fail to look closely at the exchanges of talk at those meetings (p. 38). Schwartzman argues that close readings of those exchanges can tell us much about various aspects of a company's culture, including power; domination; resistance to domination; gender, race, and class divisions; concepts of time and money; and regional differences. Her argument is compelling and still holds true today according to contemporary communication scholars (Scott, Shanock, & Rogelberg, 2012).

ASSIGNMENT

As a student of organizational communication and a member of an organization (your class, college, sorority or fraternity, or place of employment), you may be intrigued by the idea that meetings hold important clues to organizational cultures. For this case study, you will immerse yourself in a culture to understand, analyze, and write about it in the form of an ethnography. You will collect the data to be analyzed and then write about it using what you have learned in this and other chapters. Here are some guidelines for conducting your cultural study:

1. Record and transcribe the exchanges between members of the group, team, or organization at one or more of its meetings. Use the following questions and illustrations to guide your work:

    a. Who opens the meeting? Who takes notes? Answering these questions should tell you something about the leadership of the meeting, as well as the role of one or more of the group members.

    b. In general, who says what to whom and with what effect? Answering this question may help you isolate particular relationships and power structures.

    c. Pay close attention to exchanges of conversation—both on-topic and off-topic—that occur during the meeting. What are the exchanges about? What do they say about the role and relative power of the group members? What is the role of silence in the group? Is anyone excluded from the talk?

    d. What is the function of humor in the group, if any?

    e. What clothing do the group members wear to the meeting? Is there a relationship between their clothing and the tone of the meeting (e.g., formal, informal)?

(continued, Studying the Culture of Meetings)

    f. Does the group use a particular style of language? For example, is it highly technical? Does it contain a lot of jargon or slang? Can you tell "who is in the know" just by listening? Can you tell who isn't? Is there any attempt to mentor newer group members? Are there any metaphors that recur in the group and seem to suggest a common understanding?

    g. What other affiliations or associations can you assume characterize group members' lives outside of this meeting? How are those affiliations and associations brought into the culture of the meeting?

    h. How does the meeting end? Are assignments made? Are they equitably apportioned? How much does expertise play a role in the assignments? How about friendship?

2. Decide how you will analyze the data based on your reading in this and other chapters. For example:

    a. What management or communication approach (e.g., scientific management, human relations, human resources, systems, cultures, etc.) best characterizes the meeting?

    b. Does the group operate like a system? If so, how? If not, why not?

    c. What is the role of leadership in the group?

    d. How are power relations established and maintained? How are they challenged?

    e. What is the role of gender, race, class, or sexual orientation in the group? How do you know?

3. Perform your analysis.

    a. Write a narrative account (i.e., a story) about the group meeting. Include as much detail about the conversations and your impressions as you can. Make sure your story has an identifiable beginning, middle, and ending.

    b. Where possible, apply material from the chapters you have read to the story. When you are finished with a draft, add an introduction that theoretically frames the story and a conclusion that attempts to "sum up" what you have learned about this culture from the study.

4. Share your ethnography with your class.

CASE STUDY II

Cultural Constructions of Gender and Sexuality in College Fraternities and Sororities

Alan DeSantis and Audrey Hane (2004) provide a detailed and shocking ethnographic analysis of the cultural constructions of gender and sexuality in college fraternities and sororities. In their study, they highlight the terminology used by both sexes to differentiate the sexual proclivities of undergraduate students. They show how labels develop based on perceptions of bodies and the frequency of supposed (or real) sexual activities. They further describe the influences these labels have on the meanings of gender and sexuality among men and women in fraternities and sororities. More recent ethnographic studies of Greek life on campus have explored the variations in the construction of gender and sexuality along social class and racial/ethnic lines (see, for example, Sweeney, 2014).

ASSIGNMENT

If you are a member of a sorority or fraternity on your campus, write a brief account of the language used to describe gender and sexuality. If you are not a member of one of these social organizations, select a group that interests you or in which you are a member, and write a brief account of the language used in that group to describe gender and sexuality. In either case, allow your writing to be guided by the following questions:

1. What specific terms (and definitions for those terms) derived from gender and sexuality are used to differentiate among members of the organization? How are those terms used to socialize new members? How are they used to control perceptions? How do they organize hierarchies within the organization?
2. What is the relationship of body size, shape, and habits of dress to perceived value and meaning within the organization? How do those values transfer into other aspects of academic life?
3. What activities are used in stories about group members to construct their gendered identities? Do the activities need to be true to be used?
4. How do rumors and gossip about sexual activities figure into the social and cultural construction of identities within the organization?
5. Who benefits from these constructions? Who suffers? What are the communication mechanisms for countering a negative construction?
6. How much of the everyday "work" of identity management in the organization is associated with management of gender, sexuality, and reputation?

CHAPTER 6

Critical Approaches to Organizations and Communication

The perspectives considered in this chapter examine, challenge, and offer alternatives to the assumptions of the dominant frameworks discussed in earlier chapters. **Critical organizational theory** reveals the sometimes hidden but pervasive power that organizations can have over individuals and over our society. It questions the assumption that free-market capitalism is the best way to organize for all stakeholders. Critical approaches, as we will see, pose difficult and important questions about the nature of power and control.

CRITICAL THEORY

While all communication scholars are "critical" in their approach to research, there is a particular brand of scholarship—sometimes called critical approaches or critical organizational theory—that has a very particular way of viewing organizational life. These critical approaches—theory and research that focuses squarely on the role of overt and covert power in organizational life—have emerged as one of the most vital areas of scholarship in organizational communication studies. The questions these scholars pose in their explorations of the workings of power address broad concerns about the relationship between communication in organizational contexts and issues of justice, democracy, equity, and freedom. Next, we explore the origin of this brand of theory and research.

☐ Historical and Cultural Background

When we think of people as being "critical," we imagine them challenging some action or decision that they consider inappropriate or unfair. This is what critical theory and critical approaches to organizations do—they challenge the unfair exercise of power. Critical theory first emerged in response to the growing power that a small but elite segment of society held over the rest of the public during the Victorian period (1837–1901). This era was marked by a brutally abusive system of low wages, squalid working conditions, and wealthy, isolated business owners (Mead, 1991). Child labor was common, particularism (or the ability to hire and promote people due to their relation with the leader or social rank) was the rule, and employees had little protection from the cruel whims of their employers. Women, children, and minorities were paid far less than adult white men for performing the same work, and their opinions about how work should be done or how workplaces could be improved were ignored (Banta, 1993).

For too many working people across the globe today, unjust and unsafe conditions remain a reality. For example, the coal mines in Duki, Pakistan, have been the source of repeated deadly accidents. In Bangladesh, a 2012 factory fire killed more than one hundred workers, many of whom were destitute women. Their supervisors refused to let them leave their sewing machines and, in some cases, locked the doors so they could not escape. In 2015, eight workers were killed and fourteen injured when a mine collapsed in Duki. In January 2016, three workers died from inhaling poisonous gas.

Lest we think this is a problem that affects only citizens of other countries, we must remember that the factory workers killed in the Bangladesh blaze were producing garments for Western corporations and their consumers, including Walmart and Sears. Workplace hazards are not uncommon in the United States. According to the U.S. Department of Labor, in 2014, nearly five thousand American workers died on the job as a result of acts of violence, transportation incidents, fires, falls, and exposure to harmful substances. American workers also report increasingly high levels of work-related stress that materially impacts their mental and physical health and the productivity of organizations (Boren & Veksler, 2015; Ganster & Rosen, 2013).

The roots of critical theory can be traced to Karl Marx (1818–1883). Marx viewed the division between business owners and paid laborers as inherently unfair, and he predicted that it would lead inevitably to a violent overthrow of the owners as workers seized the means of production. The world has since witnessed many practical adaptations of Marx's ideas (e.g., in China, Cuba, and the former Soviet Union), none of which proved to be very successful as well-intentioned egalitarian ideals were quickly usurped by autocratic dictators who, while ideologically committed to equality, nonetheless centralized power and wealth.

☐ The Rise of Critical Theorizing in the United States

Critical theory gained popularity in the United States during the 1980s (Strine, 1991). Today, given the rapid and sustained development of critically oriented scholarship, it no longer makes sense to refer to critical theory as a unified and singular approach. Scholars and activists use a variety of theoretical and conceptual tools to help transform the way we think about and enact organizational life. Both practical and intellectual reasons account for the current interest in critical theory in the United States, and we discuss these next.

At the turn of the twentieth century, U.S. industrialists broke from traditional capitalism, which funneled the lion's share of wealth and responsibility to the elite owners. For the first time, a connection was made between the wages paid to employees and the employees' ability to be active consumers. At Ford Motor Company in the 1920s, for example, workers were paid $5 a day—a high wage at the time. Henry Ford reasoned that to sell his cars to the masses, workers had to earn enough to buy them.

This strategy, known as **progressive capitalism**, dominated U.S. industry from the Industrial Revolution until the early 1970s, when the average, inflation-corrected weekly wage of Americans reached its peak. Throughout this period, both individuals and corporations experienced significant increases in economic well-being (Mead, 1991). In addition, for the first time in human history, a majority of individuals worked for someone other than themselves.

Decades of progressive capitalism eventually gave way to revolutionary changes in the world of work. With the globalization of labor and markets—"a phenomenon that has remade the economy of virtually every nation, reshaped almost every industry, and touched billions of lives"—employers had the option of hiring low-wage workers overseas (Rosenberg, 2002, p. 28). Although this practice led to human-rights abuses reminiscent of early capitalism, they occurred far enough away from home that most Americans ignored them until recently, when high-profile revelations about the employment practices of large companies like Apple and Nike caused people to take notice. Critical scholars from a variety of academic disciplines have called for organizational leaders, policymakers, and consumers to pay closer attention to the ways unchecked globalization can lead to the exploitation of vulnerable groups, including children (Aaronson & Zimmerman, 2007) and those who occupy positions with little or no job security, particularly during economic downturns (Schwartz, 2009).

Pulitzer Prize–winning journalist and National Book Award winner Tina Rosenberg (2002) investigated the impact of globalization around the world. She found that although globalization has indeed produced additional jobs in Latin America, it has also led to dramatic increases in crime, the rise of new dictatorships, the economic collapse of Argentina, the financial panic that continues to haunt Brazil, and the economic woes of Uruguay and Venezuela. Rosenberg found that in India, the influx of new money to support high-technology investments by American firms has led to further economic and social division between the literate and illiterate populations, rekindling cultural and religious tensions over the importation of Western capitalist values. The same story has generally been true throughout Southeast Asia, where the widespread use of child sweatshop labor by large American firms (e.g., Nike, Walmart, The Gap, Disney) created a public outcry and has led to some reforms. For example, in 2014 the U.S. State Department awarded $7 million to Winrock International to implement a global project known as Country Level Engagement and Assistance to Reduce Child Labor, or CLEARII. CLEARII provides assistance to governments, including Nepal and Burkina Faso, that want to reduce child labor.

Beginning in the 1980s, elected leaders of both the United States and Britain adopted an economic philosophy that departed from decades of progressive capitalism (du Gay, 1995). With this approach, more resources and support were given to big business (e.g., tax exemptions and reduced regulatory fines and controls) than to individuals, with the expectation that increased profits would "trickle down" to the needy population (this approach has also been labeled "supply-side economics"). Instead of promoting a more equitable sharing of wealth, however, the result has been a steady decline in the average employee's real wages, benefits, and standard of living. Today, many Americans work at one or more low-paying service jobs and struggle to make ends meet. And since the global economic downturn, many people who are employed bring home smaller paychecks while facing increased health- and child-care costs (Lim, 2008). A 2014 study sponsored by the Brookings Institution found that nearly a third of all Americans live hand to mouth or paycheck to paycheck.

The gap between people who *own* things (homes, cars, stocks, and stock options) and those who do not is big and getting even larger (Aguir & Bils, 2011; Bivens & Mishel, 2011). Over the past several years, the rich have been getting significantly richer, the middle class is shrinking and their wages have remained relatively stagnant, the poor have actually become poorer (Motif Investing, 2016), and while there are opportunities for income and wage growth, they are becoming limited to those employees who are highly skilled (Ernst, 2015). In addition, those who do have access to the trappings of a middle-class life are finding it increasingly difficult to maintain that lifestyle. Not since the Great Depression has it been this hard for families, even those with two working adults, to secure health insurance, job stability, and affordable housing—the three basic elements of progressive capitalism and the so-called American dream (Kamp, 2009; Shipler, 2004; Warren & Tyagi, 2003). As the divide between rich and poor has widened, new information technologies exacerbate the problem by offering companies unprecedented opportunities to send jobs overseas. By outsourcing to poorer nations and increasing their reliance on temporary workers, these firms maximize profits for shareholders while at the same time contribute to the widening income gap worldwide (Townsley & Stohl, 2003). These trends have squeezed the middle class by generating fewer jobs that support a living wage, while the ranks of the working class have swelled. And that is true around the world; in fact, the global economy began shrinking in 2009 for the first time since World War II (Andrews, 2009).

Together, these changes have had a revolutionary impact on all of our lives. The critical approach to organizational communication seeks to advocate for the interests of working people rather than the interests of corporate leaders and shareholders, who are typically favored by management theory and practice. Critical approaches seem at first glance to pit people against profits. Particularly in a growing economy, critical approaches are often criticized for not taking a pro-profit stance and for underestimating the need for companies to remain profitable in an increasingly competitive global market.

One way the tension between people and profits plays out in real life is between similar companies that take differing positions on the matter. Some describe Walmart, the nation's largest retailer, as the epitome of the pro-profit position, while describing Costco as reflecting the pro-people position (Friedman). Many consumers value Walmart's "flattening" process, which takes all the "fat" (including labor costs, of course) out of its business model. Yet as employees we may prefer to have some of the "fat left on the bone," particularly when it affects health-care coverage or wages (Friedman, 2005, p. 220). According to one website, Walmart's starting wages fall 3 percent below market averages and Costco's wages start 15 percent above market averages (payscale.com). Costco pays its hourly workers nearly $21.00 while Walmart's average pay per hour is $12.67 (Cardenal, 2014). Walmart has historically discouraged labor organizing and unions, but some workers are beginning to advocate for better wages and working conditions. (See *What Would You Do?* on page 163.) There is some evidence that Walmart has been listening to these concerns and the company has increased entry-level wages (Hirsch, 2015), though they are unlikely to match Costco's entry-level wages any time soon.

Rather than framing the debate as an either-or choice between profits and people, we find it more productive to ask how the varied needs of all organizational stakeholders—including managers, workers, workers' families, host communities, the environment, and shareholders—can be adequately addressed. Profitability is essential to the success of nearly all organizations, but it should not be maximized at the expense of other equally important social needs, including living wages, sustainable development, quality of work life, and self-determination. In this chapter, we examine ideology, manufactured consent, concertive control, and the power of discourse as conceptual tools to better understand how what we take for granted about work may inhibit our individual and collective abilities to balance the needs of people with the needs of profit. Central to this tension are notions of power.

The (Im)possibilities of a Living Wage

Wage and labor disputes can pose a significant challenge to an organization's communication practices. In this chapter, for example, we discussed how Costco and Walmart take different approaches to employee wages. While Walmart opts to "cut the fat," Costco prefers to pay its employees a higher wage that some scholars and economists refer to as closer to a "living wage." The Economic Policy Institute defines a living wage as a salary or hourly rate of pay that allows workers to meet their basic needs like a safe home and healthy food. Living wages are often calculated based on regional, state, and county costs of living, as well as marital status and the number of dependents (e.g., children, elderly parents) in a household.

For most managers, economists, and politicians, the possibility of achieving a living wage is a bit of a myth. The complexities of improving corporate profits make it far too easy for managers and CEOs to cut employee wages as a way to increase their bottom lines. At the same time, Costco CEO Craig Jelinek has repeatedly shown how paying employees a living wage can lead to increased profits. In early 2013, Jelinek encouraged lawmakers to increase the federal minimum wage from $7.25 to $10.10 per hour. Less than a week later, Jelinek reported an increase in his corporation's profits from $394 million in the first quarter of 2012 to $537 million in the first quarter of 2013. In addition, the average employee spends $10,000 per year at Costco, whereas the average Walmart employee spends only $7,400 at that store. Jelinek's strategy appears to be paying off, demonstrating that the myth of a living wage might have some potential in reality (Cardenal, 2014). Just as this edition of this book was going to press, voters in California and New York opted to increase the minimum wage in those states to $15 per hour, and other states are likely to follow (*USA Today*, 2016).

DISCUSSION QUESTIONS

1. What are the potential benefits and drawbacks of advocating for a living wage at the federal level? What kinds of risks is someone like Costco CEO Craig Jelinek assuming by speaking out for a living wage? What potential benefits could Costco earn? What ethical obligations does Jelinek have to promote the well-being of his employees? What ethical obligations does he have to his stockholders?

(continued, The (Im)possibilities of a Living Wage)

2. Imagine that you are an upper-level executive or CEO of a national corporation. How would you respond if the board of directors pressures you to oppose an increase in the federal minimum wage, even though you know that your company could afford it? Likewise, how would you respond if the board of directors pressures you to support an increase in the federal minimum wage, even though you know such a move would dip significantly into corporate profits?

3. As a consumer, where would you prefer to spend your money? Would you rather support a business that pays its employees a more livable wage, even if that means you might have to pay a bit more? Or do you think it's more important to maximize corporate profits as a way to provide the cheapest goods possible? Are we ethically obligated to support one organization over the other, or should we just be able to spend our money without thinking too much about it?

☐ The Centrality of Power

Early scholarly attempts to define **power** were based on the assumption that it is something a person or group possesses and can exercise through actions. In a classic paper on the subject, Robert French and Bertram Raven (1968) described five types of social power, following the assumption that person A has power over person B when A has control over some outcome B wants:

1. *Reward power.* Person A has reward power over person B when A can give some formal or informal reward, such as a bonus or an award, in exchange for B's compliance.

2. *Coercive power.* Person A has coercive power over person B when B perceives that certain behaviors on his or her part will lead to punishments from A, such as poor work assignments, relocation, or demotion.

3. *Referent power.* Person A has referent power over person B when B is willing to do what A asks in order to be like A. Mentors and charismatic leaders, for example, often have referent power.

4. *Expert power.* Person A has expert power over person B when B is willing to do what A says because B respects A's expert knowledge.

5. *Legitimate power.* Person A has legitimate power over person B when B complies with A's wishes because A holds a high-level position, such as division head, in the hierarchy.

French and Raven's approach to power is further reflected in some research on compliance-gaining (Kipnis, Schmidt, & Wilkinson, 1980) and behavior-altering techniques (Richmond, Davis, Saylor, & McCroskey, 1984). Examples include research on how supervisors can persuade subordinates to do undesirable tasks, how employees can persuade supervisors and coworkers to give them desired resources, and even how teachers can encourage students to complete assignments.

This traditional approach to understanding power, however, is incomplete. By focusing on the overt or superficial exercise of power by individuals, we learn little about the more covert or deep structures of power (Conrad, 1983). Unlike overt power, which is easy to observe in what people publicly say and do and can in principle be resisted (though often at great cost), covert or hidden power is more insidious. Critical approaches focus on the control of employers over employees (Clegg, 1989) where power "resembles a loose coalition of interests more than a unified front. Critical theory is committed to unveiling the political stakes that anchor cultural practices" (Conquergood, 1991, p. 179). In short, critical theorizing seeks to expose the dark side of organizational life by actively questioning the status quo—how it came to exist, whose interests it serves, and how it marginalizes and devalues some people while privileging others.

Consider, for example, all of the hidden or unconscious factors that can influence your choice of major in college or, for that matter, your even being in school. Since the Industrial Revolution, nations have funded "public schools" mainly to prepare society's youth for a lifetime of work in organizations. The Industrial Revolution inspired an educational system that was responsive to the manufacturing organizations that defined the era. Like factories, schools were designed to demand compliance with rules and standards. Educational processes were designed as a linear series of steps that were the same for all students. And, like factories, the majority of schools were organized around a specific academic division of labor with tasks (classes) divided into specific units of space (classrooms) and times indicated by the bell. "While these principles may work well in manufacturing products, they can cause all kinds of problems educating people" (Robinson & Aronica, 2015). Dissatisfaction with a factorylike approach to education has been challenged somewhat at every level, by private grade schools (e.g., Montessori and Waldorf), public charter schools, and private liberal arts colleges. Nevertheless, the overwhelming majority of schools at all levels have historically followed the traditional model.

But things may at last be changing. In today's environment, the kinds of organizations, careers, and skills that higher education was designed to respond to have changed dramatically. The question educators face today is how to best prepare students for the new world of work. Critical approaches maintain that our system of education—and our outmoded assumption of lifetime employment with a single company—are long overdue for reformation, or perhaps, transformation. Ken Robinson, an internationally recognized leader in education, suggests that education should enable students to become:

1. economically responsible and independent;
2. understanding and appreciative of their own cultures and to respect the diversity of others;
3. active and compassionate citizens; and
4. able to engage with the world within them as well as the world around them (Robinson & Aronica, 2015, pp 45–51).

Achieving these four basic principles invites us to think not about specific disciplines but around broad competencies that would enable students to thrive socially and economically. Those competencies might include the following:

- Curiosity—The ability to ask questions and explore how the world works
- Creativity—The ability to generate new ideas and apply them in practice
- Criticism—The ability to analyze information and ideas and to form reasoned arguments and judgments
- Communication—The ability to express thoughts and feelings clearly and confidently in a range of media and forms
- Collaboration—The ability to work constructively with others
- Compassion—The ability to empathize with others and to act accordingly
- Composure—The ability to connect with the inner life of feeling and develop a sense of personal harmony and balance; and
- Citizenship—The ability to engage constructively with society and participate in the processes that sustain it (Robinson & Aronica, 2015).

These competencies encourage thinking about problem solving, innovation, entrepreneurialism, and flexible organizations for teaching and learning, and to move away from a system designed to perpetuate the factory assembly-line model and outmoded assumptions about the world of work.

POWER AND IDEOLOGY

An **ideology** is a system of ideas that serves as the basis of a political or economic theory, as in a Marxist or capitalist or feminist ideology. In our use, the term *ideology* refers to basic, often unexamined, assumptions about how things are or ought to be. During the era of classical management, for example, the dominant ideology about work was based on various assumptions: that men (especially white men) were better suited to assembly lines than were women; that white men could learn faster than women and minorities and therefore should hold supervisory positions; that the U.S. system of work was second to none in the world; that Americans had a right to use the world's natural resources to build their cities, roads, and systems of commerce and industry; and that the American form of government was superior to all other forms (Banta, 1993).

Ideology touches every aspect of life and shows up in our words, actions, and practices. The existence of ideology helps us to understand that power is not confined to government or politics, nor is it always overt or easy to spot. Because ideology structures our thoughts and interpretations of reality, it typically operates beneath our conscious awareness. Ideology is the medium through which social reality is constructed—it shapes what seems "natural," and it makes what we think and do seem "right" (Deetz & Kersten, 1983). Ideology informs us what exists, what is good, and what is possible in organizational life (Therborn, 1980). In so doing, it limits our imaginations regarding how our work and life could be different.

One of the first efforts to investigate the relationship between ideology and everyday organizational culture was undertaken by Dennis Mumby, an organizational communication scholar at the University of North Carolina at Chapel Hill. In his analysis, Mumby (1987) critiqued an often-told cultural narrative from IBM. The story, about a new employee's encounter with IBM's then CEO Thomas Watson Jr. (namesake of IBM's "Watson," a computer whose artificial intelligence system enables it to answer questions in real time), goes as follows:

> The supervisor was a twenty-two-year-old bride weighing ninety pounds whose husband had been sent overseas and who, in consequence, had been given a job until his return. . . . The young woman, Lucille Berger, was obliged to make certain that people entering security areas wore the correct identification. Surrounded by his usual entourage of white-shirted men, Watson approached the doorway to an area where she was on guard, wearing an orange badge acceptable elsewhere in the plant, but not a green badge, which alone permitted entrance at her door. "I was trembling in my uniform, which was far too big," she recalled. "It hid my shakes, but not my voice. 'I'm sorry,' I said to him. I knew who he was alright. 'You cannot enter. Your admittance is not recognized.' That's what we were supposed to say." The men accompanying Watson were stricken; the moment held unpredictable possibilities. "Don't you know who he is?" someone hissed. Watson raised his hand for silence, while one of the party strode off and returned with the appropriate badge. (pp. 117–118)

Organizational culture scholars interpret this story as providing two important messages to IBM members. For higher-status members, the story says, "Even Watson obeys the rules, so you certainly should." To lower-status members, the story's message is "Uphold the rules, no matter who is disobeying" (Martin, Feldman, Hatch, & Sitkin, 1983, p. 440). In his analysis, Mumby moves beyond showing how shared meanings are produced to expose how ideology functions through seemingly benign organizational stories to reinforce the power of some dominant organizational members and marginalize others. He argues that ideology functions in four different ways to support the power of organizational elites:

1. *Ideology represents sectional interests to be universal.* In other words, ideology works to make the interests or concerns of the managerial elite appear to be the interests of all organizational members. The story seems to suggest that all "IBMers" should be concerned with upholding the rules. What is obscured, however, is that the rule system was created by the corporate elite

to protect both core technologies and their own interests. After all, managerial elites are much better served by security rules than are line workers.

2. *Ideology denies system contradictions.* Mumby claims that system contradictions are inherent in capitalistic organizational life. Primary among those contradictions is the fact that we live in a democracy where one of our highest decision-making values is "one person, one vote," but at work we often willingly leave our democratic ideals at the door and operate under the assumption that "a few vote for everyone else." Mumby explains that the IBM story itself is contradictory because it suggests that at IBM "no one is above the law," but if Watson really were subject to the same rules as other employees, this story would have little significance. The story is only interesting and worth retelling because Watson chose to obey the rules he clearly could have decided to break.

3. *Ideology naturalizes the present through reification.* **Reification** refers to the process whereby socially constructed meanings come to be perceived and experienced as real, objective, and fixed, such that members "forget" their participation in the construction of those meanings. In the IBM story, the rules, the organizational hierarchy, and traditional gender roles are reified such that they appear "just the way things are." (See *Everyday Organizational Communication* on page 169.)

4. *Ideology functions as a form of control.* By creating an unquestioned agreement regarding the way the world "really" is, ideology furthers the control of dominant groups. Power and control are not explicitly exercised as much as embedded in routine thoughts, actions, and organizational processes. Ideological control is subtle and indirect, but highly effective. Known also as **hegemony**, ideological control "works most effectively when the world-view articulated by the ruling elite is actively taken up and pursued by subordinate groups" (Mumby, 1988, p. 123). By enforcing a rule, Lucille Berger actively perpetuates the rule system that is created by and for the organizational elites. We see hegemony operating when the organization's interests and rules are maintained from the bottom up rather than having to be imposed from the top down.

The four functions of ideology—representing sectional interests as universal, denying contradictions, naturalizing the present through reification, and serving as a form of control—are often most evident in organizational narratives. Critical scholars recognize that organizational stories are literally "power-full" because they provide members with a "vision of the organization which is relatively complete, stable, and removed from scrutiny" (Mumby, 1988, p. 125). Mumby's analysis provides a model for understanding how other cultural elements, such as jokes, rituals, or mission statements, can be critiqued to reveal the underlying ideology that privileges the interests of dominant organizational groups over those of others. Organizational communication scholars have successfully applied Mumby's work to explain how

- violent extremists use ideological narratives to recruit new members, justify their actions, divide audiences, and further their causes (Corman, Trethewey, & Goodall, 2008);

EVERYDAY ORGANIZATIONAL COMMUNICATION

Gender, Ideology, and Power in Career Paths

Ideologies are pervasive in nearly every aspect of daily life, though they often remain implicit and unquestioned. Consider, for example, how ideologies about gender may affect the very activity in which you are currently engaged: studying and preparing for a career. Ideological constructions can encourage us to consider particular kinds of work, whether in a professional organization or in a major course of study in college, as appropriate for men or women. Have you ever considered the ways in which your own choice of major or professional aspirations might have been influenced by gendered ideology?

Critical scholars remind us that assumptions about gender, college majors, and career paths are often grounded in ideologies that support the interests of those in power. If our ideologies prompt us to associate men and masculinity with power, then we also come to associate "masculine" majors and professions with power, influence, and prestige. Is it more prestigious to be a third-grade teacher or a cardiologist? Whose starting salary is higher: the social worker's or the engineer's?

The power associated with masculine professions is further evidenced in examples of men and women making career choices that run counter to ideological assumptions about gender. Even if women are not thought to be a "natural" fit for careers in science and engineering, they are often considered "trendsetters" and "role models" for pursuing careers in these prestigious fields. Dozens of organizations, from the Women's International Science Collaboration Program to the Committee on Women in Science, Engineering, and Medicine, aim to support women in overcoming ideological boundaries that keep them from entering such fields in larger numbers.

But is the same true for men who wish to enter less-powerful, less-prestigious feminine professions? Consider the example of Steve France, a college graduate who chose to leave behind a powerful "masculine" career to work hours as a personal secretary. The ideological assumptions of his colleagues and supervisors posed substantial challenges for Steve. He had to grovel for his first secretarial job and prove himself capable by working for free while learning PowerPoint and Excel. The other secretaries—all women—frequently questioned him about his career choice: Why would he want to be a secretary (Pendele, 1999, para. 12)? Male nurses often face similar obstacles and are asked, "Why would you become a nurse when you could be a doctor?"

(continued, Gender, Ideology, and Power in Career Paths)

Discussion Questions

1. Consider the four functions of ideology described in this chapter. How does ideology operate in the examples of male secretaries and male nurses? Of females in traditionally male-dominated fields like manufacturing or engineering?

2. Ideologies are often difficult to recognize and articulate because they come to be seen as natural, normal, and just "the way things are." It is when we encounter an exception to the ideological "rule" that we are forced to think critically about power. How are female pilots and firefighters the "exception," and more important from a critical perspective, and why are their stories exceptional?

3. Now consider your daily life. What experiences have you had or heard of that have caused you to think critically about power and how it operates, especially in organizational contexts? Have you confronted exceptions to the rule that have given you pause? What do your responses to those exceptions tell you about our taken-for-granted assumptions of organizational life? Why do those ideologies persist?

4. Finally, consider your choices. Is it possible that your own choices about your major and your career goals have been influenced by gendered ideologies? How? Have your choices supported and reinforced gendered assumptions that maintain the power of dominant groups in organizational life? Alternatively, in what ways might your choices resist or transform those ideologies?

- faith-based nonprofit organizations navigate the seemingly contradictory ideologies of spirituality and secularism, of discourses of faith and business (Molloy & Heath, 2014);

- corporations frame work-life balance by articulating work as the most important aspect of the equation, equating life with family, and positioning individuals, not organizations, as responsible for balancing work-life demands (Hoffman & Cowan, 2008);

- male professors who have been victims of sexual harassment often reproduce the ideology of dominant masculinity in their own accounts, thereby perpetuating the notion that "real men" cannot be victims (Scarduzio & Geist-Martin, 2010);

- black women are often positioned by the intersecting ideologies of racism and sexism at work, which they both resist and accommodate in their everyday organizational lives (Davis, 2016); and

- feminist organizations dedicated to promoting gender equality must manage the tensions between the competing ideologies of advocacy for women's issues and financial viability (D'Enbeau & Buzzanell, 2011).

Ideology has provided scholars with a useful conceptual tool to uncover how power operates in everyday organizational communication practices. In the next section, we explore how common aspects of organizational cultures create and maintain organizational power.

☐ The Hidden Power of Culture: Myths, Stories, and Metaphors

As Mumby's analysis of organizational ideology indicates, organizational culture, including the myths, stories, and metaphors that reproduce it, can be viewed as expressions of ideology. **Myths, stories, and metaphors** are the day-to-day, commonplace surface-level forms of communication that contain implicit, hidden, and taken-for-granted ideological assumptions which reside at a deep-structure level of power. Because ideology is ingrained and therefore hard to see, we must closely examine the details and discourse of everyday life to see how and where it operates.

Myths contribute to the strength of a culture's ideology and its sources of power. These specialized narratives often reveal the beliefs and values of a culture as they tell the stories of legendary heroes, of good and evil, and of origins and exits. In myths, we find evidence of basic metaphors that structure "our" view of things. For instance, in American culture, the myth of Horatio Alger is one that infuses our shared understanding of organizational life. Specifically, the myth suggests that anyone—no matter his or her personal identity or circumstances—can through luck and pluck "make it." The popularity of the entrepreneurial showcase *Shark Tank* reinforces this perception. Another pervasive myth in American culture is the idea of what constitutes (and fails to constitute) a "real job" (Clair, 1996). Although the phrase has the effect of naturalizing the idea that some jobs are more "real" (important, fulfilling, worthy) than others, it can also be seen as a way of privileging certain kinds of work. Specifically, most people think of a real job as one that involves collecting good wages from an organization. This relegates all kinds of important work—artistic, nonorganizational, unpaid, home-based, odd-hours, service-oriented work—to the margins.

Similarly, our culture has supported the idea of a career being tied to societal norms or to a social contract. As Purdue University professor and communication scholar Patrice Buzzanell (2000) points out, when the old social contract was replaced with the new social contract, the career aspirations of many "marginalized workforce members (people of color, white women, poor and lower-class persons, and the less educated)" were sacrificed (p. 211). The old social contract that idealized individual commitment, hard work, and loyalty to a company in exchange for lifetime employment and a good retirement program is dead (Beaton, 2015). And the new social contract promises only a series of work contracts over a lifetime to those able to keep abreast of technological change.

Critical approaches seek to understand why organizational practices that maintain strong controls over employees are considered legitimate and not resisted (McPhee, 1985). This kind of legitimation is maintained, as we saw earlier, through such symbolic forms as cultural myths. Specific organizational stories also legitimate and naturalize organizational power. Southwest Airlines, for instance, has been able to offer lower fares to its customers while consistently maintaining profitability in an industry that has been plagued by bankruptcy, labor strife, and other problems. A cornerstone of Southwest's success is its employees, who accept the company "LUV story" (a play on the company's New York Stock Exchange symbol "LUV"). Part of that story can be read in its mission statement (Southwest.com, 2016):

> We are committed to providing our Employees a stable work environment with equal opportunity for learning and personal growth. Creativity and innovation are encouraged for improving the effectiveness of Southwest Airlines. Above all, Employees will be provided the same concern, respect, and caring attitude within the organization that they are expected to share externally with every Southwest Customer.

Evidence of the everyday practice of this mission statement is found in a story, which made national news, about a Southwest pilot's actions on behalf of one of its customers. The pilot held a full plane to wait for a passenger who was on his way to see his dying two-year-old grandson before the child was taken off life support. According to aviation consultant John Nance, the pilot's "gesture is especially unusual in an age of more airline fees, diminished service and customer complaints. The difference, Nance says, is that the corporate culture at Southwest allows employees more freedom to make snap decisions without fear of being suspended or fired."

Organizational stories are regularly employed to justify managerial decisions regarding hiring, firing, promotions, and raises. In Southwest's case, these stories are largely empowering. In other organizations, where employees' interests are less likely to be supported, employees generally accept these controls as part of the "story" that distinguishes the organization and its culture. Over time, such myths, metaphors, and stories can come to define appropriate behavior and may suspend employees' critical thinking. Once again, a critical perspective helps us to see how our taken-for-granted ways of thinking and speaking can mask important power relationships (Clair, 1996; Mumby, 2000). The case study on page 192 asks you to explore how metaphors can interfere with or suspend our ability to think critically.

☐ The Hidden Power of Legitimation: Manufactured Consent and Concertive Control

The hidden power of organizational systems and structures has been a central focus of critical theory. German philosopher and social theorist Jürgen Habermas (1972) argues that social legitimation plays a major role in holding contemporary organizations together. According to Habermas, capitalist societies are characterized by **manufactured consent**, in which employees at all levels willingly adopt and enforce the legitimate power of the organization, society, or system of capitalism.

It is only when this perceived legitimate power is challenged that the basic order might face a crisis.

The fact that this kind of power is hard to perceive only increases its strength. Westerners are immersed in capitalism and are trained to be consumers first and citizens second, if at all. Most activities are structured around either consuming or finding ways to "add value" to ourselves and our families (Carlone & Taylor, 1998; Nadesan & Trethewey, 2000). Employees have, for some time now, accepted the odd label of "human resources," which suggests an objectification of people that in turn makes it easier to either mold or get rid of them. The magic of hegemonic consent is that the people themselves buy into this vocabulary and, despite how it casts them as disposable objects, have difficulty imagining an alternative reality.

Manufactured consent is evident when an employee or manager justifies a decision or action by saying, "I was just doing my job" or "I had no other options." As Dennis Mumby (1987) points out, domination involves leading people to organize their behavior around a rule system. The system, not individual managers or actors, can then be blamed—but not held accountable—for actions taken in its name. A law aimed at correcting this situation makes the senior managers of large corporations personally responsible for any criminal actions taken on behalf of the company. As a result, in the wake of the 2010 BP Deepwater Horizon oil spill that killed eleven people, three individuals were indicted on criminal charges of manslaughter and obstruction. BP ultimately pleaded guilty to fourteen criminal charges and paid a fine of more than $20 billion in a settlement with the U.S. Justice Department.

Manufactured consent has become unmoored from its bureaucratic heritage. Even in flatter organizations with ostensibly "democratic" aims, power and control feature prominently. Jim Barker is a professor of management and strategy at Dalhousie University in Canada. His research on self-managing teams (1993, 1999) reveals the power of "concertive control" in seemingly more humane and democratic organizational forms. **Concertive control** occurs when employees police themselves, developing the means for their own control. "Workers achieve concertive control by reaching a negotiated consensus on how to shape their behavior according to a core set of values, such as the values found in a corporate vision statement" (Barker, 1993, p. 411). Workers in these systems do not need supervisors to create and maintain rules; rather, rules are created collaboratively among all members. Barker's ethnographic study of one communications company indicates that concertive control systems can become even more stringent and less forgiving than their traditional, bureaucratic predecessors. Their self-generated system of rational rules constrains them even further as the power of their value consensus compels their staunch obedience. Several recent studies have explored how young architects, engineers (Sturges, 2013), and video game developers (Peticca-Harris, Weststar, & McKenna, 2015) are not just ambivalent but tolerant and even supportive of "work intensification," which entails long hours and an intense, driving work culture characterized by concertive control, because they love their work, are eager to join the workplace culture, or advance in a field that goes "hard and fast" (Peticca-Harris et al., 2015, p. 572).

Concertive control can also be experienced in playful, fun, and even humorous ways, according to one study. Southern Methodist University professor, and former chef, Owen Lynch (2009) studied the functions of humor in the hotel restaurant kitchen. He found that teasing and "in-group" jokes were used to ensure that "kitchen activity conforms to in-group members' standards and norms. . . . Humor, therefore, makes the chef conform to what is considered a good chef rather than allowing each chef to perform as an individual" (p. 454).

Concertive control makes it difficult to hold on to the idea that organizational elites, namely managers, shape organizational meanings, rules, and structures to support their own interests at the expense of labor. A study by organizational communication professor Greg Larson at the University of Montana and University of Colorado, Boulder, and professor emeritus Phil Tompkins revealed that "managers who implement a concertive-control system for employees may themselves come to be controlled by that same system" (2005, p. 15).

▧ DISCOURSE AND DISCIPLINE

Critical approaches that focus on ideology are mainly interested in how dominant groups influence subordinate groups, treating power as a repressive force that is somehow held by these powerful groups or individuals. This view of power has been revised through a turn toward postmodern understandings of power (Ashcraft & Mumby, 2004). Borrowing heavily from French philosopher Michel Foucault (1978, 1979), many critical scholars now view power as a widespread, intangible network of invisible forces that weaves itself into subtle, everyday behavior. As such, power does not reside in things or in people but "in a network of relationships which are systematically connected" (Burrell, 1988, p. 227). In this view, power operates primarily in and through discourse.

For Foucault, **discourse** is more than simply a shared system of meanings. Instead, discourse—the interactions which occur between people—is itself always a site of struggle over competing meanings, varying ideas of what is true or real. What we understand to be true about ourselves and the world is produced through discourse: "Discourses are more than ways of thinking and producing meaning. They constitute the 'nature' of the body, unconscious and conscious mind and emotional life of subjects which they seek to govern. Neither the body nor thoughts and feelings have meaning outside their discursive articulation" (Weedon, 1997, p. 105). Seen this way, power works in a subtle fashion, not to actively "repress" individuals or deny their "real" interests, but to literally "produce" them in a way that aligns with a preferred ideology. In organizational contexts, a focus on discourse encourages questions like these: How is "truth" or knowledge produced through organizational discourse? Whose "truth" counts? And with what effect?

☐ The Hidden Power of Knowledge: Surveillance, the Panopticon, and Disciplinary Power

Foucault's (1979) work on the history of prison systems reveals how contemporary penal discourses articulate and create the "subject" of punishment—namely, the prisoner. The prisoner becomes defined and controlled through communication about, and practices related to, punishment. At the same time, discourse establishes the prisoner's relationship to society. Foucault's analysis suggests that a central feature of current modes of power is **surveillance**, or constant supervision. Such supervision is a structural feature of modern power systems, epitomized by the **panopticon**, a type of institutional building designed by the English philosopher and social theorist Jeremy Bentham in the late eighteenth century. The panopticon, which incorporated surveillance into the design of an ideal prison, consisted of a central core that housed the guards and was surrounded by individual cells such that the inmates were constantly visible. But because the inmates could not see the guards in the central core, they never knew if they were in fact being watched, only that the possibility existed.

Bentham's design assumed that power should be visible and unverifiable. "Visible: the inmate will constantly have before his eyes the tall outline of the central tower from which he is spied upon. Unverifiable: the inmate must never know whether he is being looked at at any one moment; but he must be sure that he may always be so" (Foucault, 1979, p. 201). This created a system of disciplinary power in which inmates internalized the "gaze" of the guard by keeping a watchful eye on their own behavior.

Foucault offers the panopticon as a useful metaphor to explain modern-day systems of power, including those found in most workplaces. Organizational members are increasingly subject to systems in which a real and present possibility of surveillance exists, whether it is in the form of "secret shoppers" who monitor customer service or recording devices that monitor telephone calls for "quality-assurance purposes." As a result, employees often behave as if they are being monitored, even when they are not. They correct, modify, and discipline themselves in the name of the organization. The primary effect of the panopticon is that the members are "caught up in a power situation of which they are themselves the bearers" (Foucault, 1979, p. 201). Critical scholars have examined the communicative dimensions of disciplinary power, the impact of discipline on the creation of scientific knowledge in a research laboratory, and the reinforcing effects of technology and disciplinary power among workers in a call center, among other topics (Barker & Cheney, 1994; Brannan, 2005; Kinsella, 1999). Yet it is the expanding potential of technology to survey and discipline organizational members that has received the most attention from critical scholars and activists alike.

☐ The Technological Panopticon

Certainly, critical scholars recognize the benefits that technology affords individuals and organizations in their everyday lives. Who among us has not conducted our banking online or on our mobile phones, downloaded music or movies from the Web, or Googled someone or something? Critics warn that the ideology that glorifies technology in general, and knowledge-management systems in particular, frames technology as "universally desirable" (Chan & Garrick, 2003).

Critical scholars encourage a more complex understanding of technology that reveals both its benefits and its burdens (Iedema, Rhodes, & Scheeres, 2006; Sewell & Barker, 2006, 2012). Several features or by-products of technology have garnered attention from critical scholars. For example, for all their advantages, new communication technologies keep employees more tightly tethered than ever before. The proliferation of smartphones, laptops, and tablet computers means that many workers have difficulty creating boundaries between work and the other spheres of their lives (Edley, 2001). Likewise, employers face the challenge of maintaining boundaries between employees' need for privacy and the organization's desire for surveillance and monitoring (Allen, Coopman, Hart, & Walker, 2007; Snyder, 2010).

One recent variation of this technological panopticon is the organizational practice of **cybervetting**—"the process whereby employers seek information about job candidates online." Typically the information that potential employers collect about potential employees is "informal, non-institutional, other-sourced, and/or aggregated" (Berkelaar & Buzzanell, 2015, p. 87). As more information about individuals is made available online, employers may be turning to those sources to corroborate, extend, or challenge information traditionally supplied by job candidates through cover letters, résumés, and interviews. Table 6.1 summarizes the types of information gleaned through cybervetting and how that information may be used. There is evidence that some employers find the information gathered through cybervetting to be more credible than that provided by the candidate (Berkelaar & Buzzanell, 2014, 2015; Brown & Vaughn, 2011). The assumption is that information gathered from "non-work contexts, unobtrusive observations, and people other than job candidates promise insight into a person's true identity, character, and work ethic" (Berkalaar & Buzzanell, 2015, p. 87). Employers also indicate that cybervetting helps to mitigate the "risks" associated with hiring decisions (Berkelaar & Buzzanell, 2014) by identifying "red flags" that might have gone unnoticed in more traditional screening processes.

The degree to which online postings are assumed to be a window into a job applicant's "real" self is evidenced by a recent study that explored how the "Big Five personality traits" could be inferred from online posts. Stoughton, Thompson, and Meade (2013) believe that online behavior "mimics the behavior expected by one's offline disposition" and so they explored how two types of online posts—namely, posts that "badmouthed" superiors, and posts related to consuming alcohol and drugs—correlated with the various personality traits. For example, they found that

TABLE 6.1

Online Information Employers Report Using for Personnel Selection

WHAT TYPE OF INFORMATION	HOW INFORMATION IS USED
Present or Visible Online Information	
Visual	
• "Definitely Pictures"	• To disqualify because of "red flags"
• Illustrations	○ Red flags are not limited to salacious
• Avatars	information, vices or illegal activity; they
• Site design	may simply be "unprofessional" actions
	○ Employers rarely validate accuracy
Textual	
What, how, and amount written, including:	
• Spelling and grammar	• To qualify or disqualify candidates in terms of
• "Textspeak"	character, professionalism, written communication
• Online content (e.g., blogs, forum postings,	skills
pins, status updates, tweets, websites)	• To assess whether people have a singular passion
• E-mail addresses	aligned with the position
Relational	
• Connection to same people	• To assess and/or verify reputation and
• Industry and roles of connections	trustworthiness
• Number of connections	• To evaluate relevant social capital
• Demographics of connections	
Technological	
• Ways people use technologies	• To qualify candidates who participated in "relevant
• Technologies used	projects," received high rankings, and/or aligned
• Time stamps	with professional expectations
• Settings	• To disqualify candidates who visibly engaged in "a
• Participation indicators (e.g., counts of postings,	lot" of leisure activities, who did not use adequate
response, community ranking)	privacy settings, or who did not appear fully
	committed to work
Absent or Invisible Online Information	
• Lack of professional or work-related	• Primarily to disqualify candidates during later
information online	stages, especially when compared to otherwise
• Lack of regular participation in forums	equally qualified candidates
related to occupation or job	• Not limited to social media positions
• De facto or functional invisibility from having	• It might not apply to people considering covert
popular name or sharing name with celebrity	occupations

Source: Adapted from "Online employment screening and digital career capital: Exploring employers' use of online information for personnel selection," by B. L. Berkelaar and P. M. Buzzanell, 2015, *Management Communication Quarterly*, *29*(1).

self-reported substance use postings correlate with extraversion, while badmouthing negatively correlated with agreeableness. In a similar vein, another group of psychology researchers amassed the written language from over 65,000 Facebook users and their questionnaire-based self-reported Big Five personality traits to build a predictive model of personality based on the user's online language. They then used the model to predict the five personality factors in a separate sample of over 4,000 Facebook users. The researchers found that individuals who used words such as "love," "party," and "amazing" tended to score high on extraversion, while individuals who used obscenities, and words like "hate," "weird," and "stupid" tended to score low on conscientiousness. The researchers suggest that these methods could be used to measure and assess not only Big Five personality traits, but mood, emotional well-being, attitudes, and even psychological trends which could identify individuals who may be at risk for suicide or committing violent crimes. Finally, these methods that rely on computerized linguistic analysis can "quickly and cheaply assess large groups of participants with minimal burden" (Parks et al., 2015, p. 934). Indeed, there is now an app for that. Five Labs developed an app based on the aforementioned study that will analyze your Facebook posts to assess your personality using the Big Five framework.

What has yet to be fully explored by researchers are the communicative implications of cybervetting on employees and employers. There is little support to indicate that cybervetting actually helps employers make better hiring decisions. Additionally, we know that the "amount, source, order, context, type and/or channel of information is different in cybervetting relative to traditional hiring processes and how both potential employees and employers make sense of that information (Berkelaar & Buzzanell, 2015, p. 85). Importantly, cybervetting is fraught with potential legal challenges and ethical quandaries. For example, the information that employers can gather about each potential applicant may be quite varied and unstandardized and may impact equitable treatment. Potential employees may not have an opportunity to respond to information that is viewed as negative, and online information may enable discrimination based on publicly available pictures, videos, or posts (Brown & Vaughn, 2011). As we will discuss next, opaque processes are potentially unethical and reinforce the technological panopticon. For the practice of cybervetting to "progress in a positive direction, evidence for the validity and job-relevance of information obtained" from online sources as well transparent processes that create safeguards against potential misuses of cybervetted data need to be established (Brown & Vaughn, 2011, p. 219).

Knowledge-management (KM) systems such as searchable databases, interactive expert systems, apps like the one described above, discussion forums, and computer-supported cooperative work forums have been similarly critiqued. These systems are designed to "enhance and increase the value of the generation, sharing, and application of knowledge." From a critical perspective, the role that knowledge-management systems can play in increasing the invasiveness and constancy of organizational oversight is a concern. It has always been the case that the control of employees has hinged on oversight and observation, but advances in technology, including KM systems, has created conditions for heightened, continuous, and more insidious forms of control. Indeed, one study indicates that over 80 percent of workplaces employ some form of employee surveillance (Ciocchetti, 2011; D'Urso, 2006). Technology is now in place that can monitor employees' speech, their every keystroke, their geospatial locations, and even their hygiene habits in the company washroom. The challenge organizations face is to build surveillance systems that are both productive and ethical (Iedema & Rhodes, 2010). Critical organizational communication scholars are advancing precisely those sorts of models. For example, Angela Trethewey and Steve Corman (2001) have proposed a model that articulates two ethical dimensions that can be used to assess any particular KM system: the inclusivity-exclusivity dimension and the transparency-opacity dimension (see Table 6.2).

The first dimension centers on the degree of participation that KM systems enable and encourage. Systems that are inclusive or designed with input from a variety of stakeholders toward a collective good are more ethical than those that are exclusive. Exclusive systems are designed for and by a certain segment of the organization. The second dimension focuses on the degree to which KM systems

TABLE 6.2

Ethical Dimensions of Knowledge-Management Applications

A Model for Knowledge Management	Transparency	Opacity
Inclusivity	Active consent. Example: technical support forums that use threaded discussion to share/collect problems, reports, and solutions	Passive consent. Example: data-mining forums that scour sources for discussion to share/collect information on relevant problems, reports, and solutions
Exclusivity	Technical/behavioral control. Example: notification of employees of possible monitoring of their systems and phone calls for training and quality-assurance purposes	Panoptic control. Example: computer monitoring systems that are installed and used without employees' knowledge

Source: Adapted from "Anticipating k-commerce: e-commerce, knowledge management and organizational communication," by A. Trethewey and S. Corman, 2001, *Management Communication Quarterly, 14,* p. 624.

and their uses are transparent or visible versus opaque or hidden from members who are affected by them. In transparent systems, employees know when and how information is being collected and/or generated about them and their work, how those data are being used, and the consequences of such monitoring. The least ethical systems are those that most closely mirror the panopticon and are both opaque and exclusive. The most ethical are those systems that are inclusive and transparent.

Trethewey and Corman warn that the trend toward the commodification of knowledge, efficiency, and managerial control will lead to KM systems that are located at the opaque/exclusive ends of the continua unless participatory decision making is enacted at all levels of organizations. Such decision making ensures that those who are most immediately affected by both the opportunities and the challenges of technological systems are represented in dialogue about what "counts" as organizational knowledge and how such knowledge can and should be used (see *What Would You Do?* on page 181).

RESISTANCE: CHALLENGING ORGANIZATIONAL POWER AND CONTROL

The emphasis in critical organizational communication studies on organizational power, control, and domination foregrounds the many ways in which individuals are controlled by modern-day organizational forms and practices. Critical scholars call attention to the ways corporate ideology and managerial discourse have seeped into and shaped our daily lives, not just at work, but at school, at home, and through the media (Dahlberg, 2005). University of Colorado professor Stanley Deetz (1992), a pioneer of critical studies in the communication discipline, calls this form of control the "corporate colonization of the life world" and believes it leads to the eventual breakdown of families, schools, and other social institutions. Issues like childbirth, education, and even morality have been removed from the domain of the family and turned into externally purchased goods and services (Lukes, 1986). People's decisions about where to live, when to have children, and how to spend their leisure time are increasingly based on career-related concerns. Alienation and loss of identity result when people can no longer turn to the social institutions (e.g., school, church, neighborhood) that once fostered a sense of belonging to a family or community and turn instead to their work.

As noted, schools and the media also play a role in normalizing corporate colonization. For example, education reinforces the notion that corporate domination is both practical and acceptable as schools are increasingly concerned with training students for occupations. The media, too, sponsor a corporate vision of success through both literal representation (e.g., product placements in films and television programs) and figurative representation of the "good life," grounded in material

Unintentional Surveillance?

Allyson Murdock, a district sales manager for Pyramid Printing, was recently promoted to regional manager. Allyson has worked for Pyramid for several years, moving up the ranks from local sales representative to her current position as a middle manager. She is eager to make her mark on the company, to make a favorable impression on her superiors, and to advance even further into organizational leadership positions. However, she also wants to maintain a positive relationship with former colleagues in her sales district and keep abreast of what is happening in her old haunts. As is common for many midlevel managers, Allyson feels divided loyalties between her former colleagues and her current colleagues. This feeling is often exacerbated by the ongoing conflict that has characterized Pyramid's culture.

Those at the very top levels of the organization increasingly believe that there should be uniform policies and procedures in both regional and district offices. Such policies would ensure that each unit is accountable and would make it easier for the corporate office to evaluate how effectively and efficiently resources are being used across units. Those at the regional level have been tasked with ensuring that the district offices are in compliance with the new policies. As a result, one of Allyson's new roles is to enforce the new policies among her old colleagues. It is a role that she is not particularly comfortable with, but one she is willing to perform in order to impress her bosses. She feels she is uniquely able to keep an eye on her subordinates, particularly in her old district office, because she is still on the office's e-mail list. When she sees a potential issue emerge — as it is discussed online — she can intervene before the issue becomes a problem, thus saving her former colleagues any "heat" from the corporate office.

However, members of the sales force at Pyramid Printing believe that it would be much more effective if the corporate office would simply "get out of the way" and not allow bureaucratic rules to hamstring what they see as their creative and innovative efforts. Sijai, one of Allyson's former colleagues and one of the district's top sales reps, claims:

> Every time I try to do something creative for one of our clients, corporate comes down on me. Just last week, I sent an e-mail message to my colleagues to let them know that I scored a huge sale after I offered one of my clients playoff tickets for Pyramid's corporate suite if he would sign on the dotted line. I was thrilled with my results and wanted to share the good news with my team. But just an hour later, I had a note from Allyson telling me that corporate needs to approve all

(continued, Unintentional Surveillance?)

requests to offer "swag" to clients before a salesperson makes an offer to a client. Failing to do so, she said, was a violation of corporate policy. Ever since she moved up to the regional office, it almost feels as if Murdock's spying on us.

While Allyson enjoys her connection to her former colleagues via the e-mail list, her former coworkers find her presence oppressive. The sales team at the district level has a long history of using e-mail as a vehicle to connect with one another—to share success stories, their gripes about corporate, job-related information and news, and even occasional jokes. With their former peer now viewing their exchanges from a new vantage point, the sales team is becoming increasingly wary of using e-mail. They are not sure how to proceed. One solution would be to remove Allyson from their e-mail list, given that she is no longer a peer. However, Sijai warns, "It's not a good idea to offend the new boss and make her feel like she's not wanted." Another solution might be to find another channel for group communication, though the group likes the convenience of e-mail. Allyson, too, could help by simply removing herself from the conversations so as not to, even unwittingly, exploit her new, more powerful role. What should this team do?

DISCUSSION QUESTIONS

1. How would you characterize this situation using Trethewey and Corman's (2001) ethical dimensions of knowledge management applications? What might be done to move the situation described above toward inclusivity and transparency?
2. Does Allyson have the right to use the e-mail list as a window into her former district when she does not have the same access to other district sales teams in her region?
3. What might be gained by moving sensitive discussions offline? What might be lost?

wealth and consumption (Deetz, 1995). And corporations influence schools in myriad ways through a growing and pervasive "school improvement industry" (Meyer, 2010). In sum, we consider again Deetz's words:

> With such institutional domination in place, every other institution subsidizes or pays its dues for the integration given by the corporate structure, and by so doing reduces its own institutional role. The state developed for public good interprets that as the need for order and economic growth. The family that provided values and identity transforms that to emotional support and standard of living. The educational institution fostering autonomy and critical thought trains for occupational success. (1992, p. 17)

Under the enormous and ubiquitous weight of market-driven, corporate colonization of our everyday lives it is hard to imagine a way to push back.

Yet what often remains "hidden" but is always present is resistance to organizational and increasingly corporatized power and control (Scott, 1990). Despite the best efforts of organizations to control their members fully, those members often engage in **resistance**—distancing and defending themselves from organizational power (Fleming, 2005). Resistance to organizational domination can take a variety of forms, ranging from large-scale social movements, including boycotts and strikes, to individual tactics designed to carve out a small but satisfying space of agency, action, and autonomy (Holmer-Nadesan, 1996).

Shiv Ganesh, Heather Zoller, and George Cheney (2005) are critics who urge organizational scholars to devote increased attention to **global transformation** (see also Pal & Dutta, 2008). The term *transformation* highlights how local social movements attempt to "effect large-scale, collective changes in the domains of state policy, corporate practice, social structure, cultural norms, and daily lived experience" (p. 177). These social movements often begin as locally based and loosely organized groups of people who are working toward change. The Internet has become a valuable tool in mobilizing grassroots campaigns against corporate domination. These resistance movements have real and material effects, as witnessed in several successful examples:

- The Occupy movement, which began in September 2011 in New York City and spread across the country, was originally organized and promoted by the anti-consumerist Adbusters Media Foundation to protest "the erosion of our physical and cultural environments by commercial forces" (McDermott, 2012). The lasting effects of that nationwide movement are, at this point, still difficult to define. Some argue that the movement has managed to change the national conversation to reflect the concerns of the "99 percent" rather than the nation's superrich (Tangel, 2012).
- The protesters involved in the "Battle of Seattle" claimed a significant role in halting the Multilateral Agreement on Investment during the World Trade Organization meeting in 1999 (Ganesh et al., 2005).
- In 2000, poor Bolivians took to the streets in Cochabamba to resist Bechtel's purchase of their national water system (Ganesh et al., 2005).
- In November 2005, thousands of individuals in Argentina gathered in Mar del Plata, site of the Summit of the Americas, to protest free trade agreements that are thought by many to "enslave" Latin American workers (Bash, Mirian, & Newman, 2005).
- In February 2008, millions of protesters took to the streets of Bogotá, Colombia, in an anti-FARC (Revolutionary Armed Forces of Colombia) demonstration that was started by one man's plea, "No more kidnapping, no more lies, no more deaths, no more FARC," on his Facebook page only one month earlier (Markey, 2008).

Organized activist movements like these that center on issues like fair trade, social justice, and corporate responsibility are one means through which individuals can effect change. Many organizational members, however, find themselves hard-pressed for the time and energy it takes to participate in organized activism. Moreover, as forms of workplace control and surveillance have increased in both "strength and ubiquity," the possibility for collective, confrontational forms of worker resistance has waned (Mumby, 2005, p. 38). Instead, many members now turn to more subtle, covert, and hidden tactics to create momentary, but potentially transformative, "resistant spaces" (Gabriel, 1999). Critical scholars have documented how members have used humor, irony, "bitching," "hidden transcripts," and cynicism in pursuit of some measure of autonomy (Bell & Forbes, 1994; Collinson, 2002; Fleming & Spicer, 2003; Martin, 2004; Mulholland, 2004; Murphy, 1998; Sotirin, 2000; Trethewey, 1997, 1999b). Consider the following examples:

- The former employee who posts on a public "counterinstitutional website" or "suck" site to complain about an organization and its policies and practices (Gossett & Kilker, 2006)
- The Enron employee who uses e-mail to share messages to encourage company leaders to return to their ethics and values during the company's fall from grace (Turnage, 2013)
- The McDonald's employee who wears a shirt with the phrase "Mc[expletive]" emblazoned across his chest under his official uniform (Fleming & Spicer, 2003)
- The flight attendant who wears her high heels only in the concourse where she knows supervisors are looking, then quickly changes into comfortable loafers once she's in an unsupervised zone (Murphy, 1998)
- The client who "performs" an appropriately subservient role in order to receive material assistance from a social service agency (Trethewey, 1997)
- The worker who privately relates a representative story about an alienated, displaced, anxious, or angry worker—a story that functions as a therapeutic tool for relieving job pressure, assessing work-related situations, and regaining control over emotions (Goodall, 1995)

What these organizational members share is the desire to assert control in an oppressive context. Of course, what is notable about all these forms of resistance is that they operate under the managerial radar screen. These tactics make clear that resistance is never enacted outside dominant forms of power; rather, resistance is always performed in direct response to power. Resistance emerges in the ever-changing and contestable space between accepting and revolting. A Malaysian proverb illustrates this dialectical relationship between control and resistance: "When the great lord passes, the wise peasant bows deeply and silently farts" (quoted in Mumby, 2005, p. 21). Critical organizational scholars, then, should not focus only on the bow ("an ostensible act of obeisance to power"), nor should they focus exclusively on the fart ("a covert act of resistance to power"), but rather on the "complex ways in which these intersect in the moment to moment to produce complex and often contradictory dynamics of control and resistance" (Mumby, 2005, p. 21).

Another way employee resistance has been explored is through organizational dissent. Jeffrey Kassing (1997, 2008, 2009, 2011), an organizational communication professor at Arizona State University West, has developed a rich research program exploring the contours and consequences of employee dissent. **Employee dissent** refers to "the verbal expression of disagreement or contradictory opinions" from that of management or the organization (Kassing, 2008, p. 343). Before employees decide to make their displeasure known, they must consider personal, relational, and organizational factors. Personal factors include an employee's personality and standing within the organization. Relational factors include the type and the quality of relationships the employee has with superiors and coworkers. Finally, organizational factors refer to the unique organizational culture within which the potential dissenter operates. Does the organization respond to employee voices? Have dissenters historically been rewarded, ignored, or punished? These factors influence whether an employee might dissent. But, says Kassing (2008), the decision to dissent "actually originates with a specific issue" or "dissent-triggering event" (p. 345). Kassing's earlier work (Kassing & Armstrong, 2002) suggests that workers are more likely to express dissent in response to issues that affect their coworkers, such as decision making or change efforts, than they are in response to unethical organizational practices. Kassing (2011) recently turned his attention to the coping strategies employees use when they engage in dissent. Interestingly, employees who express upward dissent report little need for coping strategies as they already feel empowered, engaged, and in control in the context of their organizations. Those who are less engaged, however, tend to direct their dissent outward, to friends and family.

Despite their rather dire descriptions about the largely oppressive state of organizational life, critical scholars hold out hope of change at the individual, organizational, and cultural levels. Resistance to organizational oppression is necessary if we hope to reclaim and retain the democratic potential of our contemporary lives. According to Deetz, the basic problem is not a lack of awareness about what to do; much help is available there. After all, communication scholars and students, in particular, are armed with communication tools (e.g., listening, decision making, persuasion, leadership) that can enable them to be active change agents through resistance. Rather, the problem is *wanting* to do it, seeing the necessity of change, and taking the risks that accompany change (Deetz, 1995). This chapter may challenge you to consider the ways you might resist organizational power and control to create more empowering and enabling opportunities for yourself and others. In so doing, you may decide that you are interested in taking on the role of the critical theorist/activist.

☐ The Role of the Critical Theorist

In many respects, research from a critical perspective is similar to that of the cultural approach (see Chapter 5). To discover the deep structures of power, the investigator must look for details about not only what happens in the organization and why it happens, but also how it is shaped by economic, political, and social forces worldwide. From a critical perspective, the cultural approach moves in a useful direction by focusing on meaning and sense making, but it neglects to ask in whose interest certain meanings and interpretations lie. A critical theorist, then, gathers interpretive cultural data about race, class, gender, age, language, motives, and actions and makes judgments about the power relationships that exist in all aspects of organizing. This is a very subjective enterprise; not only can critical theorists be criticized for all of the same faults as cultural researchers (e.g., narrow samples and bias in selecting participants and events), they can also be criticized as elitists.

Critical theorists have been classified as elitists because, in practice, they must be willing to argue that certain individuals or groups are oppressed but are unaware of their oppression. This is the most serious problem with asserting the existence of hegemony. In a marked departure from the cultural approach, critical theorists may maintain that people do not know their own minds (Clegg, 1989). Perhaps this is one reason why more recent critical studies of organizations openly embrace an advocacy role and political agenda (Cheney, 2007) and why critical and cultural studies theorists often rely on passionate, highly personal experiences and arguments to make their cases.

As champions of organizational "underdogs," critical scholars have often conceived of their task as one more closely aligned with social activism than with traditional objective science. The role of the critical scholar has been described in terms of critiquing dominant discourses; educating organizational members, leaders, and the larger culture on the inequities of contemporary organizations; and emancipating organizational members from oppression through the articulation of positive and transformative alternatives to present structures and processes. Deetz (2005) claims that critical theory means more than adopting a particular role; rather, it is a way of life characterized by three tension-filled, **critical modes of being**:

1. *Being filled with care.* Caring for and directing attention to others characterizes this way of being. At its root, it involves efforts to understand others on "their own terms," and in so doing, the self's "values become exposed as partial and incomplete" (pp. 101–102). Of course, when we begin to take seriously the "other," our understanding of our own self and our world becomes much more complicated, complex, and sometimes problematic. Barbara Ehrenreich embodies this ethic of care in *Nickel and Dimed: On (Not) Getting By in America* (2011). In it she tells the story of the working poor from the perspective of the diverse individuals who make up the largest cadre of employees in our country. Her story is grounded in the lives, meanings, and everyday experiences of the working poor in our country. Hearing the stories of these individuals' lives, told from the perspective of their complex and difficult lived experience, makes it hard for the reader to do anything but care about their plight. Being empathetic is only one aspect of living life as a critical scholar.

2. *Being filled with thought.* Moving from caring about or empathizing with individuals to considering and acting on the larger social and political ramifications of seemingly "individual" stories is a hallmark of being filled with thought. For example, Ehrenreich's text moves beyond revealing personal stories to address the systematic and structural causes and consequences of class divisions in our country. Additionally, her book invites middle-class readers to recognize their often-unwitting complicity in systems that perpetuate the deep class divisions in our country and to work toward changing those systems.

3. *Being filled with good humor.* While care and thought require seriousness, a critical way of being also requires a willingness to recognize the ironic and contradictory aspects of life. Good humor means accepting uncertainty and embracing a willingness to "make it up as we go" (Deetz, 2005, p. 103). It means realizing that we can never "fix" social problems with a singular or final response, but we must act anyway to provide solutions (which are inherently partial, partisan, and problematic). Although some may feel that despair is the most appropriate response to this ontological insecurity or fundamental openness, we believe that good humor, even laughter, is a more appropriate response. The critique of organizational inequities and laughter can go hand in hand (Trethewey, 2004). Critical scholars have explored the ways marginalized organizational members, including women, middle managers, secretaries, female clients in social service agencies, and male shop floor workers, have used humor to resist oppression and to create spaces of empowerment at work (Bell & Forbes, 1994; Collinson, 1992; Lynch, 2009; Martin, 2004; Trethewey, 1997).

These three modes of being can be harnessed in service of organizational empowerment and justice.

SUMMARY

Critical theories emerged when scholars recognized a lack of attention in previous scholarship to the pervasiveness of power and control in shaping members' experiences of organizational life. The principal observation is that power in organizations is important because it is often exercised inequitably, resulting in the reproduction of organizational haves and have-nots. Critical approaches have moved away from economic explanations of power inequities to address the myriad ways that power operates through everyday communication practices like storytelling, language use, and the establishment of routine. With the collapse of progressive capitalism, critical approaches have become an ever-more-necessary counterbalance to organizational theorizing that privileges those who already possess some form of power (e.g., reward, coercive, referent, expert, or legitimate power), including managers, leaders, white-collar employees, and professionals.

Critical approaches remind us, however, that power is more than simply the ability to get someone else to do one's bidding. Power and its attendant inequities are also reproduced through ideology. Ideology both shapes and limits our social constructions of reality by providing a sense of what is good, right, and possible. Critical theorists point out that ideologies are never neutral; rather, ideologies serve some organizational groups and interests better than others. The functions of ideology include (1) representing sectional interests to be universal, (2) denying system contradictions, (3) naturalizing the present through reification, and (4) serving as a form of control. Ideologies rarely announce themselves, so critical scholars often tease out ideologies as they are manifest in organizational myths, metaphors, stories, and other cultural practices. Moreover, critical theorizing suggests that ideology is not only imposed on members from those in power; rather, through processes of manufactured consent and concertive control, employees often willingly participate in power systems that are not necessarily in their best interests.

Recent trends in organizational communication research have focused attention on the power of organizational discourses and on the knowledge they enable and create. Borrowing from French social philosopher Michel Foucault, scholars have revealed how knowledge gathering and knowledge-management practices have increased the opportunity for organizational surveillance and discipline. Such heightened surveillance strategies find their most problematic expression in the technological panopticon. Critical scholars warn that we must find ways to use technology ethically if we are to avoid the most dangerous features of the technological panopticon, including the ethics of cybervetting employees. In addition to technology, critical scholarship has also emerged in the area of health communication to better understand, challenge, and transform how ideology and consent shape health-care encounters and employee wellness programs.

While critical theorists are quick to point to the many problems and power imbalances in organizational life, they are also interested in how members of society and members of organizations can bring about positive change. The study of organizational resistance centers on challenges to power and control in contexts ranging from global social movements to individualized "micropractices." Within organizational resistance research, employee dissent is an emerging area of study with the potential to contribute to positive change. Both remind us that the role of the critical researcher is one that embraces care, thought, and good humor in service of organizational empowerment and justice.

QUESTIONS FOR REVIEW AND DISCUSSION

1. What are the advantages and disadvantages of viewing organizational communication in terms of power?

2. Trace the historical roots of critical approaches. Do you think critical theorizing is still relevant today? Why or why not?

3. Describe the different views of the nature of power in organizations.

4. What is ideology, and how does it both enable and constrain communication in organizations?

5. What roles do metaphors, myths, and stories play in maintaining and transforming existing power relations?

6. What is concertive control? What are some examples of concertive control that you have experienced as an employee or a consumer?

7. What is discourse? How are discourse and organizational knowledge related to one another?

8. What elements, if any, of the panopticon still exist in contemporary institutions?

9. What role does electronic surveillance play in the exercise of power at work?

10. Discuss the benefits and burdens of cybervetting from the perspective of an employer. What about from a potential employee's perspective? Does the practice of cybervetting change how you might engage social media? In what ways?

11. Of the forms of resistance discussed in the chapter, which ones have the greatest potential to effect change? Given what you have read in this chapter, why isn't organizational dissent more common? Why aren't resistance movements widespread?

12. What modes of being are encouraged by critical approaches to organizations? As a critical student of organizational life, what is the one issue or problem you are most concerned about? How is that issue or problem an outgrowth of ideology, hegemony, or concertive control? What can you do to transform that issue or problem?

KEY TERMS

Concertive control, p. 173

Critical mode of being, p. 186

Critical organizational theory, p. 158

Cybervetting, p. 176

Discourse, p. 174

Employee dissent, p. 185

Global transformation, p. 183

Hegemony, p. 168

Ideology, p. 166

Knowledge-management (KM) system, p. 178

Manufactured consent, p. 172

Myth, story, and metaphor, p. 171

Panopticon, p. 175

Power, p. 164

Progressive capitalism, p. 160

Reification, p. 168

Resistance, p. 183

Surveillance, p. 175

CASE STUDY I

Risky Business:
Consent, Safety, and Firefighter Culture

The Bay City Fire Department (BCFD) provides fire and emergency medical service to a major U.S. city and is widely regarded in the fire service community as one of the most advanced in the country. However, department leaders have become increasingly concerned about safety issues. For example, a firefighter was killed in a fire at a hardware store, two clients were killed in ambulance accidents, and several firefighters were injured when two fire engines collided. What most disturbs administrators is that these injuries and deaths could easily have been prevented if members had followed the standard operating procedures in which they were trained. For example, the firefighter who died did so when he and his peers were still trying to put out the fire from the inside even though they knew that everyone had been rescued and that the building was already a total loss. The two fire engines collided because the drivers were racing each other for the chance to arrive first on the scene of the fire and enter the blaze at its peak, a common scenario.

It's not as if BCFD has failed to be "safety minded." Many of the safety reforms implemented in fire departments nationally and internationally were first developed at BCFD, and members regularly participate in a variety of safety training exercises. However, there has been some resistance to the increased dialogue about safety. Some members actually believe that the department is too conservative in the way it manages fires. They want to stay in fires longer, fighting "the beast" and "getting it on" from the inside rather than using the "surround and drown" approach from outside. The union chief complained, "Don't they call 911 because they want us to put out the fire?"

Newer firefighters who have received the most safety training, and claim to be more safety-conscious than senior members, seem to be the biggest violators. Both of the ambulance deaths occurred while a second-year firefighter was driving, and in another incident, two novice firefighters were nearly killed after disobeying orders to leave a burning building for safety reasons. Internal investigations revealed that the two stayed in the fire because they had been trying to melt their helmets. In the culture of the fire service, a disfigured helmet is a sign that one is a "real" firefighter and can "take it." Investigations have also revealed that novice firefighters have broken driving regulations in an effort to prove themselves as "real" firefighters, attempting to shield themselves from the "care bear" label often applied to those who staff the department's ambulances.

The fire chief and his assistants aren't sure how to handle these problems. The fire chief recently said in a staff meeting, "We are killing our customers as we try to help them, and we are killing firefighters for empty buildings that are going to be torn down anyway. I shouldn't have to tell our guys that it's not okay to die in a fire." After years of trying to fix the problem with better training, they are beginning to think that training deficiencies are just a small part of the problem.

Assignment

1. Why do you think firefighters are violating standard operating procedures? How might your response be informed by an understanding of ideology, manufactured consent, or discipline?
2. How does organizational discourse enable and constrain the occupational behaviors of these employees?
3. If you were an organizational communication consultant hired to increase the firefighters' compliance with safety procedures, what would you do?

Source: Scott, C. (2005). *The discursive organization of risk and safety: How firefighters manage occupational hazards.* Unpublished doctoral dissertation, Arizona State University.

CASE STUDY II

Racing through the Hurricane of Airport Security: Organizational Metaphors and Standing in Line

Successfully navigating an airport security line can be an emotionally taxing event for both passengers and airport employees. Since the September 11, 2001, terrorist attacks, airports have become organizational sites full of uncertainty, emotional stress, and heightened surveillance. As a consequence, both airline passengers and airport employees are expected to act in certain ways in order to make the security screening process operate as smoothly as possible.

Organizational communication researcher Shawna Malvini Redden (2013) uses metaphors like a "race" and an "emotional weather system" to describe the process of moving through an airport security line. Airline passengers must negotiate a series of hurdles, and successfully clearing the security screening is much like crossing the finish line. Moreover, this process is complicated by daily changes in airport climate and passenger load. Some screenings are easy and calm, while others are more like being caught in a hurricane of long lines, crying children, and rolling luggage.

Individual airports and government agencies are always seeking out new and innovative ways to improve the experience of standing in line at a security checkpoint. In late 2012 and early 2013, for example, the Transportation Security Administration (TSA) started rolling out a new security screening program called TSA PreCheck and its international counterpart, Global Entry. This program allows frequent flyers to enroll in a prescreening initiative. Prescreened passengers are allowed to keep their shoes and belts on and can keep their laptops and liquids in their carry-on luggage as they move through security. They also have dedicated security lines that are designed to expedite the screening process. While programs like TSA PreCheck might alleviate some of the stressors that make air travel tedious at the airport, they also ask passengers to go through increased surveillance and risk-assessment before they arrive.

Assignment

Organizational structures like airports are particularly interesting because they involve a dense network of sites and policies that make air travel possible. From small regional airports to large international airports, from government agencies to consumer advocacy groups, many organizations are involved with getting a plane and its passengers from point A to point B. Consider how each of the following scenarios address issues related to metaphors and the security screening process:

1. You are a risk and safety communication consultant for the TSA. You travel to multiple airports every month to assess how their communication practices can improve the security screening process. As part of your current assignment, you are looking for possible organizational metaphors that can inspire new ideas about the security screening process. You are intrigued by the idea of comparing security screening to a race. You decide to play around with this metaphor, and you mock up some signs, slogans, and brochures that would help passengers "win the race" through security. The materials include cartoon graphics of hurdles and other images that support the "race" metaphor. When you test some of these new signs and brochures with different focus groups, they backfire miserably. Several passengers—most notably senior citizens and adults with children—explained that the "race" metaphor made them even more agitated and anxious when moving through the security line. These passengers already had a difficult time moving through security, and they felt as if the signs were pressuring them to move even faster. How might metaphors backfire on us when we use them to organize processes (like moving through the line at a security checkpoint)?

2. You are a TSA liaison at a small, regional airport in the southwestern United States. Your supervisor has asked you to review Redden's (2013) research, which uses metaphors like "race" and "emotional weather system" to talk about how passengers manage their feelings while standing in the security line. Because your airport is on the small side, the general climate of your security line tends to be more like a calm sea than an uncontrollable hurricane. Some passengers have actually reported that they can take their time moving through security. You begin to wonder if there are better metaphors to characterize how things are done at your particular airport in a way that makes you stand out from the "race to the finish" or the "emotional weather system" metaphors. What other metaphors could be used to characterize the process of moving through the security line? How can metaphors help us develop new stories that are counter to the dominant narrative?

3. You were hired recently by a consumer advocacy group that focuses on protecting travelers' rights. Your organization worked tirelessly to support the Airline Passenger's Bill of Rights, which was expanded in 2011 to include tarmac wait times and reimbursements for lost luggage. You have been assigned to look into the new TSA PreCheck program to identify potential problems related to prescreening initiatives. Because the program is voluntary, you do not see any immediate problems with the TSA's new program. At the same

(continued, Racing through the Hurricane of Airport Security)

time, the growing popularity of TSA PreCheck gets you thinking. Passengers seem quite willing to give up personal information and go through a risk assessment in order to avoid the "emotional weather system" that has become the security screening process at most major airports. You are curious if these passengers have reflected critically on modern-day transportation and its connections to increased security and surveillance. How might metaphors like the "emotional hurricane" of security screening short-circuit our critical-thinking processes when it comes to security and surveillance in the air travel industry?

PART III

Contexts for Organizational Communication

CHAPTER 7

Identity and Difference in Organizational Life

Our understandings of how we are both similar to and different from others shape our sense of self, and this is particularly true in the context of organizational life. In this chapter, we explore the concept of organizational identity. **Identity** is defined as how individuals position themselves in the world through language and action. We will look at four approaches to understanding identity and difference, and examine how each one shines a particular light on the organization, communication, and identity relationship. First, however, we provide an historical context for current understandings of identity.

◨ THE HISTORY OF IDENTITY IN ORGANIZATIONAL COMMUNICATION

The degree to which organizations have influenced and permeated people's personal lives has varied throughout history. Before industrialization, notions of the self were largely fixed and unified. Individuals' self-definition derived largely from their craft, locale, and family, and did not vary much throughout their life. In contrast, classical management theories regarded the individual as an inhuman cog in a complex machine, a situation that was accomplished through the bureaucratic separation of the personal and public selves. Bureaucracies sought to establish control over the public side of each employee, the side related to work. This public realm was called the individual's **zone of indifference**. Throughout the industrial era (i.e., most of the twentieth century), employees saw their "real selves" as existing

197

mainly outside the work setting and appearing only when the bureaucratic rules and roles of work life were loosened or removed.

Organizations have lost a great deal of their ability to directly control what individuals can become, thus allowing for a broader range of employee identities. At the same time, some young people are unhappy with a sharp separation between their personal life and their occupation, causing them to seek to bring more of their personality into their work, creating a greater continuity of identity across public and private contexts. This trend is propelled by a growing desire for **authenticity**, for being true, real, and honest in how we live and work with others. Earlier notions of identity referred to an individual's ability to look inside oneself (or outside one's professional work) to find one's real self, while contemporary ideas of authenticity focus much more on the ethics and consistency of one's behaviors. In other words, we must reveal our true selves not only in personal relationships and during our personal time, but also through our choices of professional and organizational affiliations. The motto for those who hold such beliefs is reflected in the now popular career guidance advice to "do what you love!"

Despite attempts to achieve consistency across contexts, as a society we are continually bombarded by media images that do not reflect social realities and, at the same time, offer inconsistent and competing images. Regarding gender, for example, a study of female characters in the top-grossing films of 2014 revealed chronic underrepresentation of women in leading roles, persistent gender stereotypes, and a lack of ethnic diversity (Indiewire, 2015). Regarding the inconsistency of media portrayals, think of the many different ways that the identity of a "working mother" is represented in the media; no single identity is represented in magazines (parenting magazines, fashion magazines), television programs (from soap operas to *The Middle*, *The Mindy Project*), films (*This Is 40*, *Life as We Know It*, *The Kids Are All Right*), and books, such as Allison Pearson's (2003) novel *I Don't Know How She Does It*, which was adapted into a film in 2011. While there may be some commonalities across these representations—namely that women bear the burden of balancing work and life—there is no clear, consistent, and consensual model. The same could be said for working fathers, organizational leaders, and successful employees. Most Westerners' identities tend to be both fluid and multiple, or what Kenneth Gergen (1991) describes as a state of "multiphrenia." In response to the condition of multiphrenia, some organizational communication researchers are asking which identities matter most in organizational contexts (Lammers, Atouba, & Carlson, 2013).

For most of us, the reality of multiple, fluid identities can be complex, stressful, and at times tenuous as we seek to establish a core set of values that we can adhere to as we perform multiple, varied roles (e.g., student, parent, citizen, employee, fan, partner). The proliferation of multiple possible identities makes it even more critical that we select some "horizons of significance" by which to orient ourselves

(Taylor, 1991). These horizons are the most critical values or beliefs about which we may be authentic.

Organizations exert a powerful influence on members' identities and help define for members the categories of difference that "make a difference" in the context of everyday organizational life. For instance, some organizations are recognizing the difference that generations make in the workplace and that leaders must work to effectively negotiate those differences (Trapp, 2015). Baby boomers and millennials are thought to have different communication styles and priorities. Baby boomers (born between 1946 and 1964) tend to anchor their identities to their careers, believe that they sacrificed and worked long and hard to achieve success, and expect new employees to do the same. Millennials (born between 1981 and 1995) report that their identities are more closely aligned with their personal relationships and lifestyles than with their careers. They are more interested in work-life balance than their older counterparts, they value meaningful work over high pay, and they are more comfortable using technology than previous generations (Myers & Sadaghiani, 2010).

These differences can cause problems when expectations clash, or they can serve as openings for change. Baby boomers, who often hold leadership positions, may interpret millennials as having a weaker work ethic when they seek flexible schedules, the opportunity to work from home, or other ways to manage work-life balance, making it difficult for millennials to gain credibility in the workplace. On the other hand, millennials may prompt boomers to consider reconnecting with their own families, to challenge their willingness to sacrifice personal happiness for workplace success, or to reframe "face time" as equivalent to productivity. As a result of these generational differences, many workplaces are creating programs and practices to facilitate better relationships and more productive organizational interactions across generations.

Over the past several decades, scholars have attempted to explain how we make sense of difference and understand and practice our own identities in a variety of ways. Specifically, identity and difference can be understood in four ways: (1) as organizational practices and performances; (2) as essential or fixed aspects of the self; (3) as features of the organization that influence members; and (4) as products of social and popular narratives.

IDENTITY AND DIFFERENCE AS ORGANIZATIONAL PRACTICES AND PERFORMANCES

The most prominent approach to understanding identity and difference in recent years is as products of two interrelated organizational performances: identity regulation and identity work.

☐ Identity Regulation

A significant goal of many organizations is to regulate and control their members' identities. Mats Alvesson and Hugh Willmott (2002), two European critical management scholars, describe several specific practices that organizations use to "make" members' identities. This practice is described as **identity regulation**, and it works to articulate how and in what ways differences among members will be valued:

1. *Defining a person directly.* Those who are described as midlevel managers, as opposed to senior-level managers, have their leadership capacities curtailed, by definition.
2. *Defining a person by defining others.* Many organizations encourage members to create positive identities by contrasting their positions with the positions of others. For example, low-level hospice care providers who have little organizational status or authority often describe themselves as providing real, hands-on care, while describing registered nurses as paper pushers.
3. *Providing a specific vocabulary of motives.* Organizations often explicitly describe the motivations that drive their ideal employees. An elementary school that recruits and retains only those employees who care passionately about children and education provides employees with a road map for successful identities. For example, a "successful" teacher is one who does not request a higher salary or a stipend to buy items for the classroom. A successful teacher is "in it for the kids."
4. Promoting *specific morals and values.* As discussed in Chapter 5, organizational cultures routinely offer employees an explicit set of guiding values, such as innovation, customer service, and efficiency, that they may use to craft or regulate their identities at work.
5. *Providing specific knowledge and skills.* Organizations provide some members with specific knowledge (of the law or of medicine, for example) or provide the skills necessary to execute a specific process or practice, which then serves to define members in particular ways.
6. *Fostering group categorization and affiliation.* When organizations foster feelings of "us" and, often less explicitly, "them," they generate feelings of community, belonging, and loyalty. Students, for example, who are integrated into the fabric of the university are more likely to retain spirited connections to their alma maters.
7. *Reinforcing hierarchical dynamics.* One of the central ways that we answer the question "Who am I?" is by figuring out the superiority/subordination dynamics between ourselves and others. Those relations are often both symbolically and materially reinforced in organizations.
8. *Establishing and clarifying a distinct set of "rules of the game."* Organizational communication creates and naturalizes rules and taken-for-granted ways of doing and being. For example, specific ways of being a "team player" (e.g., working without complaint, not outdoing a superior, protecting teammates from mistakes) often serve to regulate employees' behavior.

9. *Defining the environment.* Organizational leaders often define the environment in which employees operate. When globalization, excessive competition, and rapid and unpredictable change are said to mark the environment, organizations tend to value those who are adaptable, aggressive, and entrepreneurial.

Taken together, these organizational strategies help build particular member identities, privilege some differences, and define the self in the context of work.

☐ Identity Work

There are a variety of ways that members actively respond to their organizational positioning by forming, maintaining, strengthening, revising, or resisting the identities that have been (largely) defined for them by organizational discourse. Alvesson and Willmott (2002) refer to this process as **identity work.** After all, organizational members are not necessarily willing to become exactly the person the organization wishes or privileges. In his research, Mats Alvesson (2010) has identified seven sense-making devices or "images" that help articulate how members respond to their organization's efforts (as well as to efforts by the broader culture, the media, family, and friends) to influence or regulate their identities. These seven images, presented in Table 7.1, provide a useful set of tools for thinking about the complexities involved in building a successful and satisfying organizational self.

Self-Doubter

The defining features of the **self-doubter's** experience are uncertainty and insecurity. David Collinson (2003), a British critical management and leadership scholar, argues that over time our identities have shifted from being "assigned" to us by our location in the social hierarchy, to becoming increasingly dependent on our ability to "achieve" a particular identity that is always subject to further insecurity. Two types of insecurity are a common result of everyday organizational life, according to Collinson. First, symbolic insecurity arises from status and social anxieties, a lack of self-respect, esteem, autonomy, and well-being. Second, material insecurity is born of concerns about one's job and the economy more generally. Not surprisingly, these two forms are often mutually influencing in practice.

Canadian management development scholar Suzanne Gagnon (2008) explored how organizational discourse in a multinational insurance company created heightened insecurities for high-potential middle and senior managers participating in a leadership-development program. The managers who were selected for the program by the organization's leadership felt they had no choice but to participate. The program emphasized a very specific identity for its leaders: They were to have "edge, energy, decisiveness and speed." The organization then tied the achievement of this leader identity to performance. The participants described the "panic zone" they entered early in the program when their projects began to require as much effort as their regular jobs, not the 25 percent commitment indicated by

TABLE 7.1

Seven Images of Identity

Image	Key Characteristics	Driver or Challenge	Empirical Examples
Self-Doubter	Trying to cope with insecurity and uncertainty	Multiple social relationships, ontological insecurity	Potential corporate leaders (Gagnon, 2008)
Struggler	Dealing with contradictions and conflicts between views of the self and external demands	Conflicting demands and challenges	Dignified miners (Lucas, 2011); Aboriginal leader (Sinclair, 2005)
Surfer	Responding to a complex world of multiple discourses by creating fragmented and fluid identities	Multiple discourses (of work, family, culture, etc.) pushing individuals between different identities	Gay-straight friendships at work (Rumens, 2010); female leaders in technology groups (Anderson & Buzzanell, 2007)
Storyteller	Crafting a relatively coherent personal narrative of the self	Attempting to create order and direction in life	Caribbean immigrants (Bridgewater & Buzzanell, 2010); narrating "cancerland" (Goodall, 2011)
Strategist	Producing a synthesis between individual "authenticity" and organizational adaptation	Being true to self vs. wholeheartedly adopting an organizational image	Jamaican leaders (Hall, 2010); gay men working in religious, intercultural contexts (Murphy, 2013);
Stencil	Being shaped or "drawn" by powerful, dominant, and disciplining discourses	Exposure to disciplinary forms of power (e.g., concertive control, hegemony)	Aging, unemployed workers (Ainsworth & Hardy, 2009)
Soldier	Embracing attractive social categories for social and organizational identification	Pressure and the desire to subordinate oneself to a greater whole; affiliation with a group	Firefighters (Myers, 2005); sorority members (Reno & McNamee, 2015)

Source: Adapted from "Self-doubters, strugglers, storytellers, surfers and others: Images of self-identities in organization studies," by M. Alvesson, 2010, *Human Relations, 63,* p. 199.

the program organizers. The organizers made clear that this enabled them to find out which would-be leaders could withstand the most "work-related pressure." In another test of "decisiveness," participants were asked to publicly rank their peers from the best leader to the worst leader in just thirty minutes (p. 382). Not long into the program, four of the initial twenty-five participants dropped out and one was fired; later four more were fired. Participants realized, "over time, that the program was a test rather than an opportunity for learning, or a game that you either 'got the hang of' or did not" (p. 383).

This rather cutthroat culture is not uncommon. An exposé by *Vanity Fair*'s Kurt Eichenwald (2011) describes a similar environment at Microsoft. The company implemented a management system defined by "stack ranking—a program that forces every unit to declare a certain percentage of employees as top performers, good performers, average and poor" (para. 2). This system led to employees competing with one another rather than with the company's market competitors, an inability to innovate, and turnover.

When organizations attempt to manage employees' "insides" using these anxiety-producing methods, employees can respond in a variety of ways. The most common strategy is to conform to expectations, however unrealistic, and to try to become exactly what the organization wants. Many participants in Gagnon's (2008) study explicitly tried to change themselves, to tamp down their seemingly natural responses, and to become "better" or at least closer to what managers wanted. While most members conformed, a few resisted the program, including the ranking exercise. However, there were negative consequences for these participants, including being labeled as "arrogant" and "bad listeners," further fueling their sense of instability and insecurity at work (p. 388).

Struggler

The **struggler** is characterized by "a basic conflict, a dilemma, or contradictory forces" (Alvesson, 2010, p. 201). The central task of the struggler, then, is to draw on a variety of resources to produce, perhaps heroically, an identity that is both coherent and distinct. The struggler works actively to "produce and sustain a self-image, neither independent of, nor totally victimized by" organizational discourses (p. 201).

Socioeconomic status also makes a difference in our culture and in organizations. The value that society ascribes to white-collar workers differs from that typically assigned to blue-collar manual laborers, or "dirty workers" (Ashforth & Kreiner, 1999; Tracy & Scott, 2006). University of Nebraska organizational communication scholar Kristin Lucas (2011) studied the struggles of thirty-seven miners who worked diligently to construct positive identities by highlighting the inherent dignity of their work. The miners recognized that most people value corporate executive positions (and the people who occupy them) more than they do miners. The miners, in contrast, argued that all jobs are necessary and therefore valuable. Moreover, dignity and a positive image are products of a job done well and "the way people are treated and treat others," not the products of any specific job or position.

Lucas argues that miners can valorize and appreciate the social rewards of high-status positions and perhaps aspire to those jobs, while at the same time recognizing the value of blue-collar workers who earn and deserve dignity. This identity work, Lucas points out, is a complex and ongoing challenge or struggle for employees of this type.

Charles Sarra, an Australian Aboriginal leader, provides another example of how the meanings people may project on others' bodies can cause significant struggle. Management professor Amanda Sinclair (2005) studied the embodied performances of leaders like Sarra who are able to bring about change in stagnant systems. Sarra, the youngest of nine children born to an Aboriginal mother, was never encouraged by his teachers to attend university, and none of his siblings attended. Sarra, a talented "footballer," was recognized for his physical prowess. Yet he realized that his racialized physicality often encouraged others to see him as limited, as so many "young Aboriginals are stereotyped as bodies without brains" (p. 393). He resolved to do something about the problem, putting himself through university, and becoming the principal of a small, underperforming school in an Aboriginal settlement in Queensland.

His leadership style focuses on physical well-being, and creates an inviting environment in the school. His vision for the school, "Strong and Smart," highlights how Aboriginal children can be simultaneously physical, intelligent, and as capable as their white counterparts.

Sarra's identity work is a struggle, but he strives to create a largely unified cultural identity in the face of perpetually competing demands. His "Aboriginal way of doing things presents itself as an indivisible leadership package—head, heart, body, spirit, family, race and culture. . . . It is not a leadership that is bifurcated by home-work dichotomies or massaged into different identities for different constituencies" (p. 396). The image of the struggler suggests that there is hope for crafting identities that, although influenced by organizational and other discourses, are not entirely determined by them.

Surfer

Catching waves, being open to experience, and at times being tossed about by shifting tides and currents are apt metaphors for the surfer. The surfer image is grounded largely in postmodernist theories which suggest that "social, economic, and technological changes have stripped away the traditional structures shaping individual identities, placing increased pressure on individuals to construct employable and flexible selves" (Kuhn, 2006, p. 1339). The **surfer** identity is almost entirely dependent on existing, though shifting and unstable, discourses located in the media, organizations, and cultures "out there," rather than on any essential, fixed, authentic, or internal core. If the struggler is characterized by an ability to craft a unified self in the face of conflicts, the surfer simply adopts multiple identities to fit multiple situations, with the same flexible attitude that a surfer might take in the search for the perfect wave. Here "'identity' is put in motion without much friction; it flows with the various forces and contingencies acting on it. Pain and resistance are less salient elements here, as the self . . . is adaptable and implicated by the discourses and varieties of social identities to which it is compliant" (Alvesson, 2010, p. 203).

British critical management scholar Nick Rumens (2010) studied how gay men negotiate friendships in the workplace and revealed that they often surf between and across discourses of gender, sexuality, and friendship in ways that create new possibilities for identity. His poststructuralist approach frames friendship as a product of discourse. Discourses of contemporary masculinity, for example, may enable male-male friendships as action-oriented and nonsexual, but they constrain the possibilities for emotional or sexual connections. Discourses of (homo)sexuality have emphasized the struggle of gay men to create meaningful bonds amid conditions of oppression in which homosexuality has been conceived of as deviant or diseased, even when organizations explicitly attempt to create the veneer of "asexuality" (Rich, Schutten, & Rogers, 2012). Against this backdrop, gay men have developed friendships with other gay men to build support, acceptance, and solidarity. The workplace offers yet another discursive resource that may constrain and enable men's friendships, as several studies have demonstrated that organizations are largely heteronormative spaces in which heterosexuality is the presumed norm (Rich et al., 2012; Spradlin, 1998).

Rumens's (2010) study, in which he conducted in-depth interviews with twenty-eight gay men ranging in age from the midtwenties to midfifties, across various organizations, makes clear that while the friendships that gay men form with other men sometimes reinforce binary understandings of gender and sexuality, they can also complicate both. For example, some gay men describe themselves as the "feminine" partner in a friendship with a "masculine" other, reinforcing stereotypical norms that position heterosexual men as masculine. Others, however, have formed friendships that challenge those binary, either-or positions. Jack and Martin, for example, developed a friendship that has a "sexual edge," involves some flirting, and is playful and erotic. Both men, one of whom is gay, the other straight, acknowledge that the friendship has encouraged them to make sense of sexuality in more fluid and ambiguous ways. Their relationship also challenges the idea that the only authentic form of friendship between men is entirely platonic. Thus, these men strategically surf across discourses as a means of developing meaningful workplace relationships and identities. In a separate study, Rumens (2011) found that gay men and lesbian women often value and sometimes prefer friendships with heterosexual colleagues at work because those friendships serve as resources "for mentoring, climbing managerial career ladders, fitting into existing work cultures and developing gay and lesbian managerial identities" (p. 444).

Female leaders employ similar surfer strategies as they negotiate shifting identity positions in a technology group, according to a study by communication scholars Wendy Anderson and Patrice Buzzanell (2007). In one university group, female participants negotiated the discourses of technology (moving between a utilitarian approach to an aesthetic one) and discourses of gender (a concern and attention to appearance more aligned with traditional notions of femininity to participation in "one-liners" and other forms of humor more aligned with masculine speech patterns). The women moved fluidly across identity discourses as situations and context demanded, changing their identities to match the needs of the moment.

Storyteller

The **storyteller** seeks to build an integrated and meaningful identity by crafting a story of the self that is coherent across time and space. This image gives individuals lots of freedom to craft their own stories, and the power of discourses recedes into the background. Here the self assembles a narrative, using resources drawn from "cultural raw material," including language, symbols, meanings, interactions with others, and experiences. These communicative materials are combined into "a coherent and vivifying life story [that has] . . . the capacity to integrate the individual's reconstructed past, perceived present, and anticipated future, rendering a life-in-time sensible in terms of beginnings, middles, and endings" (Dan McAdams, cited in Alvesson, 2010, p. 203). In this rendering, the self narrates a coherent story that brings a successful and positive identity to fruition.

While many critical communication scholars are reluctant to fully discount the power of discourses to influence identity, some interpretive studies highlight how individuals "story" themselves into being. In one study, organizational communication professors Melissa Bridgewater and Patrice Buzzanell (2010) examined how Caribbean immigrant workers made sense of their cultural and organizational experiences and differences through stories. The authors argued that the "dynamic nature" of storytelling provides immigrant employees with "opportunities to revise, create, and reposition themselves and their workplace communication" (p. 236). These workers all recognize the idealized American dream in which anyone, with luck and pluck, can "make it" in America and live the lifestyle of abundance and limitless opportunity that is so popular in globally mediated stories. However, they create a more realistic version of that narrative for themselves, one that also features hard work, educational and professional opportunities on a larger scale than in their countries of origin, and participation in and adaptation to the fast-paced lifestyle that defines their new home while maintaining their cultural values of humility, care, compassion, and resourcefulness. These stories, in turn, influence how they respond to both positive and negative cross-cultural interactions in the workplace. For instance, when one participant was unfairly singled out for questioning when office cash went missing, she responded with a story that emphasized her hard work, her qualifications, her character, and a resolution that validated her view of herself in the context of the broader culture, the organization, and her immediate experience.

Situated at the intersections of health discourses, ethnographic scholarship, and organizational communication tradition, H. L. "Bud" Goodall was a narrative scholar who, while the seventh edition of this textbook was being written, was invoking a storytelling self in the face of an advanced pancreatic cancer diagnosis. For most of his career, Dr. Goodall championed storytelling as a legitimate form of scholarship because he believed in the power of narrative to shape our experiences, our lives, and our selves on cultural, organizational, and individual levels. When diagnosed with terminal cancer, he chose to write himself into being as a man who lived with cancer and who embraced each day. His scholarly blog, where he chronicled his life in "cancerland," offers a hopeful story of his past, present, and an uncertain, likely truncated, but joyful future. His story did not change his diagnosis, nor could he erase his pancreatic tumor through the writing process, but he did offer a compelling narrative in response to his terminal illness and in doing so offered his storyline to others who could do the same.

Strategist

The strategist is perhaps the most utilitarian and goal-directed in his or her self-making efforts. As a new employee, a strategist might develop a variety of possible selves to try by "observing role models, experimenting with provisional selves and evaluating results against internal and external standards" (Alvesson, 2010, p. 205). The **strategist** often moves between a self that feels true and authentic and one that is more closely aligned with a preferred organizational or occupational self, revising and refining an identity as an active and ongoing process.

The strategist helps explain both individual and collective identities as works in progress. On an individual level, organizational members draw on various discourses to craft strategic identities that enable professional and personal success. Organizational communication scholar Alexandra Murphy (2013), describes the strategic efforts of a group of American educators working with local partners to promote HIV/AIDS education in Nairobi. Murphy points to the "discursive frictions" that emerge in international contexts where individual group members do not share cultural, religious, or sexual orientation and identities. Two members of the American group were gay men who are deeply invested in stemming the HIV epidemic in Africa. Yet, in order to do so, the gay, secular men had to "pass" or perform a strategic identity that "read" as both heterosexual and religiously affiliated to be accepted in the Kenyan context. In Kenya, homosexuality is explicitly forbidden, gay men are routinely beaten and killed, and subject to jail terms if "discovered." To maintain the partnership, then, the men strategically hid their "primary identifications" (Murphy, 2013, p. 14).

Collectively, the strategist image recognizes how groups may come together by developing shifting alliances and allegiances in response to contextual and local conditions. Maurice Hall (2011), a communication professor at Villanova University, investigated how Jamaican leaders act strategically to develop organizations and identities for themselves and other members. The national context is a complex and interesting one for leaders of Jamaican organizations. Jamaica, like many countries around the world, was colonized by the British Empire from the mid-seventeenth century until 1962, when it became independent. The colonial past still exerts a significant influence on Jamaican culture, particularly organizational cultures that have been steeped in Western managerial traditions. Moreover, many organization leaders in Jamaica have studied management in the United States or in Britain and have returned home to manage companies and to translate what they have learned into a local context.

For example, Jamaican leaders at a bank owned by a North American parent company consciously and strategically took the mandates from their Western headquarters and appropriated them to better reflect more "authentic" Jamaican culture. When the corporate headquarters mandated a daily staff meeting, the Jamaican leaders quickly adapted the practice to better suit their local environment and to build an organizational identity that reflected Jamaican values in the context of a Western structure and value set. The daily "huddle," as it was described by the Western headquarters, was quickly transformed into "the Combo." Says one manager: "It's everything from acting, singing, to morning devotions . . . something we require as part of the culture we want to build" (Hall, 2011, p. 635). The manager explains that they took the Western practice of the huddle and made it something new. This sort of conscious, directed, and goal-oriented use of discourse to create a collective identity is at work in the strategic image.

Stencil

The **stencil** foregrounds the power of organizational communication to generate a template or standard identity position. Members are understood as copies, outlines, or stencils of an organizationally preferred or dominant discourse. Unlike the surfer whose identity is fluid, shifting, and light, the stencil's identity is "fixed" and "heavy," "held in place by a single, dominant Discourse that essentially sets up an ideal self for subjects to replicate, mainly as an effect of the forces operating on them" (Alvesson, 2010, p. 206). As discussed in the previous chapter, the concept of discipline and its impact on creating normalized and docile bodies is at play in this image (Deetz, 1992; Tracy & Trethewey, 2005; Trethewey, 1999a, 2001). Individuals are seen as having very little agency to create their own identity. Instead, they are an effect or a product of discourse (Foucault, 1979).

A study by Susan Ainsworth and Cynthia Hardy (2009), management scholars at the University of Melbourne, demonstrates how discourses of aging cause older workers to create stencil identities. Specifically, the talk and practices surrounding the physical aspects of aging combine to produce a narrative of aging as "inevitable decline" and loss (p. 1201). As individuals' waistlines expand, faces wrinkle and sag, and hairlines recede and turn gray, Western culture begins to devalue them because negative meanings are attached to the aging process. Some have argued that aging has become a process and a feature of identity that individuals should "manage," such that successful aging is judged by our ability to stave off and minimize the aging process.

It is in the context of these broad discourses that aging workers must create a valued identity, to get both their minds and their bodies in shape as they age. Ainsworth and Hardy's (2009) study reveals that these two discourses regulate aging workers' identities in a fairly muscular fashion with little resistance from aging workers themselves. Workers often participate in the discourse of decline even while they simultaneously try to describe themselves as *atypical* older people who work diligently to avoid the long slide into decline and disuse. Alternately, when older workers attempt to point to the broader social or organizational reasons, like discrimination, for older workers' underemployment or unemployment, their conversational partners often disallow and deny those claims, thereby further entrenching the regulating power of aging discourses.

The stencil image of identity helps explain why individual differences—gender, sexuality, religion, ability, race, ethnicity—are sometimes regulated and erased in organizational contexts rather than celebrated. Even discourses that purport to celebrate difference and diversity may have the effect of minimizing those individual differences. Management scholar Linda Perriton (2009) argues that the use of the "business case" for diversity actually has the effect of regulating individual women, particularly their ability to complain about mistreatment at work (p. 230). The net effect of this discourse is to encourage women to keep from going outside the organizationally drawn lines, to not complain, and to serve the company well by being good women who contribute to the company's bottom line.

Soldier

Unlike the stencil, whose identity is stamped by the organization, the soldier willingly embraces the organization's preferred identity. The **soldier** emphasizes the process of identifying with a social unit and the drive to belong to something larger than one's self. Alvesson (2010) suggests that the soldier demands "a fairly low degree of insistence on personal uniqueness. Instead, the unit that one belongs to provides the source of identity" (p. 207). The slogan that declares, "There is no I in Team," celebrates the soldier image. The individual is "depersonalized" and instead is seen as an embodiment of the "in-group" prototype (Alvesson, 2010, p. 207).

Occupations that require uniforms encourage employees to identify with the organization and to downplay their individuality, and many employees embrace that opportunity. Military personnel, firefighters, police officers, theme park employees, chain restaurant servers, and others often celebrate their ability to look, act, and feel their organizational role. For some management scholars, this form of identification can be very positive in that it creates harmony between the self and the organization (e.g., Dutton, Dukerich, & Harquail, 1994). Other research suggests that individuals whose sociopolitical attitudes are less egalitarian may be more drawn to occupations that reinforce hierarchy and minimize individuality (Ho et al., 2012).

Firefighters' socialization into their occupational and organizational culture may encourage strong identification even before they join a particular firehouse. Research by Karen Myers (2005), an organizational communication professor at the University of California, Santa Barbara, reveals that firefighters are required to identify with their organizations long before they enter as newcomers. Many of the firefighters in Myers's study indicated that firefighting was the only thing they ever wanted to do and that they had to endure physical trials and training, participate in ride-alongs, spend time at firehouses, and compete with 4,500 applicants for only forty positions, sometimes for several years running, before being hired (p. 358). In short, would-be firefighters must "soldier on" by demonstrating and embodying identification in order to even be considered. Further, Myers's study indicates that the new firefighters do not engage in role negotiation. They do not work to put their individual "stamp" on the role of firefighter or to individualize their role. Instead, they spend considerable time and effort working to establish their trustworthiness to their peers and leaders.

Health and organizational communication scholars Jeanna Reno and Lucy MacNamee (2015) studied how sorority members' embodied identities were impacted through organizational socialization, identification and, specifically, memorable messages. The researchers surveyed over two hundred sorority members to learn about the memorable messages they had received regarding their body image and weight and/or appearance-related behaviors. The results indicated that sorority women received positive and affirmative messages about their bodies and appearance from their sisters and that those messages were internalized and important to the sorority members. But while the messages were overtly positive, they may have the effect of emphasizing the importance of physical appearance for members identities over and above overall health and well-being. One young woman reported that "when members of my sorority tell me it looks like I've lost weight, it makes me more focused on making sure I continue to lose weight and not gain it back" (Reno & MacNamee, 2015, p. 393). However unintentionally, sorority socialization may encourage women at a crucial state in their development, to view "soldiering on" toward thinness as a critical identity performance.

The seven images of identity we have just outlined treat identity and difference as products of organizational efforts to regulate how identities are manifest and members' corresponding responses to those efforts. (See *Everyday Organizational Communication* on page 211 to consider the identity work that you do as a college student.) While this is the most common approach to explaining identity and difference in recent years, we turn now to three other approaches that help round out our understanding.

IDENTITY AND DIFFERENCE AS FIXED ASPECTS OF THE SELF

If you have ever assumed that people are just "born different," then you might be operating from a position that some features of our identity are inherent and natural outcomes of *either* our biology *or* our socialization. In other words, our identities are in many ways determined for us, whether by "nature" or by the ways we have been "nurtured." This approach to identity has deep historical roots, as we suggested earlier, and still occupies a prominent position in our culture.

EVERYDAY ORGANIZATIONAL COMMUNICATION

Images of Identity: Making Sense of Yourself in College

Are you a storyteller or a surfer? A strategist or a self-doubter? In this chapter, we suggest that many of us share certain images of identity when it comes to our relationships with organizations. College is one of those organizations in which individuals do a lot of identity work. The college years can be a time of great transition for many students as they learn different perspectives and develop new interests and friendships. Some may experience adult responsibilities for the first time; others learn how to balance work, family, and classes. Students often use their time in college to try out different images of identity (Alvesson, 2010) to see which ones make the most sense and are the best fit.

Given the changes that students go through during their college years, it is not surprising that college is also a time when many students begin to develop new facets of their identities and shed others. A resource guide to the first-year experience at Minnesota State University at Mankato puts it best:

> As students ask themselves, "Who am I and who do I want to become?" they may also try out new values and experiment with different roles. They may seek out challenges or take risks, small and large, that they have not tackled before. For some students, this means adopting a new image—unique clothes, different friends; for others it may mean testing out new behaviors. Still others will be confronted with new views on politics, morality or religion and may consider adopting an alternate view for a short time or for longer. ("The College Transition," 2006)

DISCUSSION QUESTIONS

Think back to your first few days on campus. How are you a different person today? How are you similar to the person you were that first day on campus? The following discussion questions ask you to look more closely at the images of identity outlined by Alvesson (2010). Think about whether his images ring true in your own experiences.

1. Do any of Alvesson's images of identity resonate with the identity work that you have done as a college student? Which image fits with your understanding of how communication works? Which one would you like to try on for size to see if it improves your organizational success and satisfaction?
2. Can you think of a situation in which the self-doubter identity might be useful? What about the surfer? What are the drawbacks of each of the images outlined by Alvesson?

(continued, Images of Identity)

3. Do you feel as if you have a "core" sense of self? Or do you feel as if you enact and embody different aspects of identity in different situations? For example, are you a storyteller with your friends, but a soldier with your family? Now think about this question in an organizational sense. Do you enact one image of identity, like a soldier or a surfer, when you think about your overarching relationship with your college or university? Do you enact another image of identity, like a storyteller or a stencil, when it comes to your relationship with specific student organizations and classes?

The popularity of certified family therapist John Gray's (2002) book *Men Are from Mars, Women Are from Venus* attests to the cultural belief that men and women communicate in fundamentally different ways. This best-selling book and follow-up texts (Gray, 2011) treat gender differences as "a socialized but relatively fixed identity . . . organized around biological sex . . . which fosters fairly predictable communication habits" (Ashcraft, 2004, p. 276). Men's and women's communication styles, therefore, are outgrowths of gendered socialization and are made manifest in organizational contexts. Scholarship on gender communication differences supports this frame. Deborah Tannen's (1990) book *You Just Don't Understand: Women and Men in Conversation* provides a comprehensive view of how gendered identities, learned in childhood, drive men's and women's conversational styles. Men treat conversations as a hierarchically ordered space in which they can demonstrate and vie for status; women treat conversations as a weblike space in which they can demonstrate and vie for connections. According to this literature, these different conversational orientations can lead to misunderstandings between men and women, who often experience the same conversation in very different ways. Tannen suggests that the trick to conversational success is for men and women to learn to interpret one another's speech styles in new ways and to develop a larger conversational repertoire so that it becomes easier to be heard by those who occupy different gendered speech communities.

Early research on gender in organizational contexts sought to document men's and women's different communication styles and their effects on organizational processes and outcomes. In such studies, women's seemingly tentative, self-deprecating, and inclusive speech was initially assumed to be ill-suited to the hard-driving demands of organizational life, and management in particular. Women's communication style was perceived as preventing them from forming networks and moving up the career ladder (see, for example, Reardon, 1997).

More recent research suggests that women do not ask for things (e.g., raises and promotions) or negotiate on their own behalf as often or as forcefully as their male counterparts. The lack of this specific communication behavior can lead to fairly dramatic and troublesome outcomes. Carnegie Mellon University economics professor Linda Babcock and journalist Sara Laschever (2003) argue that women need to follow the assertive man's lead and ask for what they deserve. Failure to do so results in "molehills" (a one-time missed negotiation) becoming "mountains" (lack of a comfortable retirement). For example, if a man and a woman are both offered the same initial salary for a job at age twenty-two and the man negotiates a $5,000 salary increase while the woman simply accepts the salary offered to her, at the end of their careers, the man will likely have accumulated at least $500,000 more than the woman (Babcock & Laschever, 2003).

While much of the early research treated women's communication style as a deficit or a liability at work, some scholars have attempted to demonstrate the utility, perhaps even the superiority, of "women's ways" of knowing, being, and leading (Helgesen & Johnson, 2010). Yet even when men and women engage in similar behaviors, it is often made meaningful or interpreted in very different ways. What persists is a well-entrenched ideology of "gender differences" that continues to hold sway in the popular imagination.

The assumption that men's and women's communication styles are fundamentally different has implications for the ways that men and women negotiate their work and personal lives. Because women are assumed to be more nurturing and relationally focused, women's caregiving at home has been viewed as a "natural" outgrowth of women's love for their partners and children. As a result, women have often assumed greater responsibility for domestic labor, even when they work as many hours outside the home as their partners (Alberts, Tracy, & Trethewey, 2011; Chesley, 2011; Coltrane, 2000; Denker, 2013; Erickson, 2005). Sociologist Arlie Hochschild (1989) labeled this phenomenon the **second shift**. The term captures the significant labor that women perform in the private sphere for which they receive little compensation or gratitude (Hochschild, 2003).

Current research suggests that women who work outside the home typically still do significantly more routine housework as their male partners, despite a slight increase in men's participation in household labor over the past several years (Coltrane, 2000; Nomaguchi & Bianchi, 2004; Sifferlin, 2014). These assumptions about difference and identity prevent many working women and men from creating the flexibility that is desired by much of the current workforce (O'Driscoll et al., 2013).

This approach to identity as "fixed" also provides a useful base for a discussion of race and difference in organizations. For example, over the past two decades, scholars have explored communication differences between African Americans and European Americans. Intercultural communication scholar Judith Martin and her colleagues (2001) outline seven issues derived from previous research on African Americans' and Mexican Americans' accounts of satisfying and dissatisfying features of interethnic conversations. Those communication issues are presented in Table 7.2. They found that African American men and women routinely faced these issues in their organizational interactions and adopted a variety of conversational strategies to make their workplace interactions more productive and satisfying.

TABLE 7.2

Communication Issues in Interethnic Conversations

1. *Acceptance* is described as a perception that the other accepts, confirms, and respects opinions and self.
2. *Understanding* is described as a mutual perception that meaning is successfully conveyed.
3. *Expressiveness* refers to the communication of feelings by both partners, reflected verbally and nonverbally.
4. *Stereotyping* involves communication in which the communication partner racially categorizes, rather than treating the other as an individual.
5. *Powerlessness* is described as feelings of being controlled, manipulated, and trapped as a result of the other taking charge and interrupting.
6. *Authenticity* refers to a feeling of genuineness and truthfulness communicated by meaningful exchange of messages on the part of both the interactants.
7. *Goal attainment* is the mutual realization of objectives through learning or listening, or obtaining desired ends from the communication.

Source: Adapted from "An African American perspective on conversational improvement strategies," by J. N. Martin, S. Moore, M. L. Hect, & L. Larkey, 2001, *Howard Journal of Communications, 12,* 1–27.

For example, all the respondents said they had experienced the issue of stereotyping in the workplace. Their European American colleagues "assumed they could dance, were athletic, were from rough neighborhoods, or had experience with guns" (p. 15). In response, participants reported using conversational strategies to educate their coworkers and to enlighten them about stereotypical and potentially racist assumptions. Most African American participants indicated that because they were seen as "different" in organizational contexts, their communication strategies were often designed to help them succeed in workplaces that are based on European American expectations and communication norms.

Other studies suggest that there are significant differences between the communication behaviors of white women and African American women (Shuter & Turner, 2004) and between African American women and Asian American women (Lee, Soto, Swim, & Bernstein, 2012). A report from the Executive Leadership Council and the Executive Leadership Foundation entitled, *Black Women Executives Research Initiative Findings* (2008), summarizes some of the challenges black women face in the workplace, saying "because both their race and gender are beyond the norm in corporate America, black women, like other women of color, face the burden of being 'double outsiders'" (p. 9). Black women are still understood as "different" in organizational contexts, but that "difference" may be a vitally important resource for organizations. The report suggests that black women's inclusion at senior levels can "help heighten the chance for broader and more innovative approaches throughout the organization" because they "champion new viewpoints to companies mired in status quo thinking" (p. 9).

◩ IDENTITY AND DIFFERENCE AS ORGANIZATIONAL FEATURES THAT INFLUENCE MEMBERS

A third way of understanding identity and difference in organizational life starts from the assumption that organizations, themselves, have identities. This approach to identity is grounded in feminist theorizing. The organization's identity works to "guide interaction, predisposing and rewarding members to practice in particular ways" (Ashcraft, 2004, p. 281). Feminist scholars have suggested, in particular, that organizations themselves are gendered. The organization acts like an agent or a character that both produces and is a product of gendered scripts or discourse. Here, gender is a fundamental feature of organizations that affects identities in a variety of taken-for-granted ways.

In a foundational essay, sociologist Joan Acker (1990) argues that far from being "neutral" backdrops, organizations are themselves gendered structures that reflect and reproduce patriarchy or the systemic privileging of masculinity. A **gendered organization** is one in which "advantage and disadvantage, exploitation and control, action and emotion, meaning and identity, are patterned through and in terms of a distinction between male and female, masculine and feminine" (p. 146). The gendered organization emerges out of at least four processes:

1. **The social construction of divisions of labor, positions, and types of work along gendered lines.** The types of work that women and men do are often differentiated in organizations such that women assume support roles and men assume leadership roles.
2. **The social construction of symbols and images that reinforce gender divisions.** Images of leadership often rest on a masculine model.
3. **The mundane communication interactions between men and women, men and men, and women and women.** These interactions often reproduce gender divisions in ways that reinforce men's (relatively) powerful position. Women's speech is often presumed to be ill-suited to organizational life.
4. **The ways in which individual actors often take up identities that reinforce the three processes described above.** Career choices, style of dress, interaction patterns, and everyday performances result in gendered identities.

Gender is a fundamental element in "organizational logic" or a "gendered substructure that is reproduced daily in practical work activities" (Acker, 1990).

Through these processes, organizational structures, jobs, and even bodies are gendered in specific ways. For example, Acker argues that the dominant organizational logic creates a preference for a "male worker whose life centers on his full-time, life-long job, while his wife or another woman takes care of his personal needs and children" (p. 151). While the expectation of a linear career path has gone away in practice, management theory continues to contain traces of the idea that careers unfold smoothly and without disruption. Feminist scholars suggest that, as such, the very notion of career has been biased in ways that have favored men (Ashcraft, 1999; Marshall, 1989). For women, embodying the "ideal" worker is difficult, as that which is associated with the private sphere and domesticity is excluded from organizational logic. Thus, "women's bodies—female sexuality, their ability to procreate and their pregnancy, breast-feeding, and child care, menstruation, and mythic 'emotionality'—are suspect, stigmatized and used as grounds for control and exclusion" (p. 152).

Feminist organizational communication scholars Paaige Turner and Kristen Norwood (2013) take up this theme in their study of nursing mothers who are employed. Their study explores how working mothers are routinely asked or demanded to separate the "maternal" and the "professional" in the context of work such that women must negotiate being "good mothers" or "good workers." This separation becomes particularly challenging for working mothers who are breast-feeding. While most women worked to accommodate their need to breast-feed to suit the organizational norms, some used the material practice of breast-feeding to challenge our taken-for-granted assumptions about the divide between "good mothers" and "good workers" to carve out a space for "good working mothers," who were unapologetic about their need to breast-feed at work and were eager to serve as role models for others.

Professors Patrice Buzzanell and Meina Liu (2005) examined the experience of several women during their maternity leaves and found that many, much like many of the breast-feeding working mothers in Turner and Norwood's (2013) study, had difficulty maintaining an identity that was valued, recognized, and rewarded in gendered organizations. The authors suggest that organizations could develop more gender-equitable policies by, for example, establishing an advocate in the human resources department who would assist women in their negotiations with their supervisors for leave, special accommodations, and career opportunities or by making parental leave policies unambiguous, automatic, and streamlined (Buzzanell & Liu, 2005).

Fortunately, some organizations are making system-wide changes to better accommodate and serve the diverse needs of their working men and women. Deloitte, an international Big Four accounting and consulting firm, recognized that the gendered character of their organization was resulting in a high turnover rate among its most highly qualified women and dissatisfaction among many of its employees, who felt they could not effectively balance work and life responsibilities. In response, the organization made large-scale changes in eight areas: child care, organizational culture, flexible schedules, generous parental leave policies, women's advancement programs, total compensation, work-life culture, and family-friendly programs, including paid leave for new fathers. As a result, the company has won numerous awards, including being named to *Working Mother* magazine's "100 Best Companies for Working Mothers" for over twenty consecutive years (2015). These instrumental changes have nearly eliminated the gender gap in turnover and serve as a model for other organizations hoping to reduce gender inequality.

Acker's model of the gendered organization has influenced many communication scholars who have studied its consequences. Patricia Parker's research (1997, 2003; Grimes & Parker, 2009) extends Acker's model by suggesting that, in addition to being gendered, organizations are also "raced" and "classed" in ways that reflect and reproduce inequitable divisions in everyday organizational life (see also Ajnesh, 2012; Allen, 2003, 2007; Ashcraft & Allen, 2003; Ashcraft & Allen, 2009; Ashcraft, Muhr, Rennstam, & Sullivan, 2012; Sobre-Denton, 2012). Recruiting and promoting practices, for example, contribute, however unintentionally, to job segregation along gendered, raced, and classed lines. While racial discrimination may have decreased somewhat over the past two decades, African American men are still disadvantaged compared to similarly skilled white men. One recent report indicates that African American male millennials must have two or more levels of education to have the same employment prospects as their white male millenial counterparts (O'Sullivan, Mugglestone, & Allison, 2014). According to an analysis of U.S. Census Bureau Annual Social and Economic data, "an African American male has to have taken some college classes to have the same employment prospects as a white male without a college degree" (O'Sullivan et al., 2014, p. 9). The organizational logic that defines "whiteness" as the unspoken but pervasive norm also requires that African Americans prove to potential employers that they do not conform to racial stereotypes by adopting a "middle-class" persona, including appearance, style of dress, and manner of speech (Kim & Tamborini, 2006). Organizations are a race game that African American men must learn how to play, and "victory is constantly negotiated and never definitive" (Hopson & Orbe, 2007, p. 83).

The gendered, raced, sexualized, and classed character of organizations sometimes enables and often constrains the identities that employees and employers perform in their daily organizational activities (Forbes, 2009; Fox, 2013; Hall, 2011; Nuru, 2014). This approach reminds us that identities usually cannot be changed simply through individual choices or performances; rather, the organizational systems, structures, and policies that reflect and reproduce gendered, raced, or classed inequities must change.

IDENTITY AND DIFFERENCE AS POPULAR CULTURE NARRATIVES

The final approach to identity and difference directs our attention outside the organizational context to the broad social discourses that shape both individual identities and organizational forms. This approach "shifts attention from communication *in* organizations to communication *about* organization, or how a larger society portrays and debates its institutions and the very notion of work" and workers (Ashcraft & Mumby, 2004, p. 19). The assumption is that social texts which exist outside the organization, such as those found in popular culture, both reveal and reproduce cultural understandings about the nature of work, life, and identity. In other words, the meanings we assign to ourselves, our work, and our organizations are significantly influenced by the texts—films, books, television shows, news reports, magazines, fashions, and even scholarship—we consume in our everyday lives. Social texts like these provide us with discursive fragments that serve as raw materials for constructing our own gendered identities in everyday life. Think, for example, about how television programs like *Celebrity Apprentice* or *Shark Tank* might influence a young viewer's ideas about superior-subordinate relationships, the seemingly competitive character of work life, and the general nature of leadership.

Of the approaches we have addressed so far, this approach is the most recent in organizational communication theorizing and research. The few studies using this method have traced representations of executive women and white-collar masculinity in film and representations of working women in magazines (Ashcraft & Flores, 2003; Eikhof, Summers, & Carter, 2013; Schuler, 2000). The most comprehensive study to date that adopts this approach is Karen Ashcraft and Dennis Mumby's (2004) project, which explored the historical emergence of contemporary understandings of airline pilots as (largely) white, male, middle-class professionals. Through a critical reading of diverse texts, including historical texts and images, museum displays, poetry, films, government documents, and personal interviews, the authors track the shifting identity position of pilots from the end of World War I to the beginning of the twenty-first century.

After the war, popular images portrayed pilots as "hard-living, hard-drinking playboys" who "embodied distinctively masculine themes of physical and sexual prowess, individualism, debonair courage and rugged adventure, peppered with a dash of science" (Ashcraft & Mumby, 2004, p. 135). While romantic, appealing, and fascinating, the images did little to alleviate the public's fear of flying, which was shaping up to be a new mode of public transportation. Perhaps not surprisingly, a new discourse emerged to ease the public's concern. This discourse featured "lady-fliers," "ladybirds," or "lipstick pilots" who took up flying as a "graceful sport" and managed to fly airplanes while maintaining their physical grace and beauty. During the late 1920s and early 1930s, this discourse, which was reproduced in advertisements for beauty products and cigarettes, reassured the public that flying was easy (since women could do it!) and that planes were trustworthy. However, this discourse also proved risky and threatening to prevailing gendered assumptions. The lady-flier raised the possibility that, at least in the air, men and women could be equals. Rather than questioning the assumption that there really were few differences between male and female pilots, the public perception was that flying was simply easy or that it was not real work.

The move to reestablish flying as a masculine activity emerged in the late 1930s and early 1940s. At that time, the airline industry was struggling to become profitable and was looking for ways to ensure long-term viability. The lipstick pilot heightened interest in flight, but not necessarily as a safe and reliable form of transportation. So the airline industry created a public relations campaign designed to give pilots a "makeover" (Ashcraft & Mumby, 2004, p. 147). The body of the pilot was remade in the image of the authoritative sea captain, complete with uniform. The new bureaucratized pilot was explicitly white, male, professional, and disciplined. Indeed, fearing that nonwhite pilots would damage the image of the "clean-cut Anglo-American type" pilot that the airlines were trying to create, the Air Line Pilots Association adopted a "formal whites-only clause until 1942, retaining a tacit prohibition against pilots of color for sometime thereafter" (p. 147). This new image commanded professional privilege that is, in many ways, still unmatched. The heroic and inspiring story of Captain Chesley Burnett "Sully" Sullenberger who safely landed a disabled commercial jetliner, with 155 passengers and crew members on board, on the Hudson River in 2009 has perhaps reinforced the public narrative of the airline pilot as an authoritative masculine hero (Sullenberger & Zaslow, 2009).

While the professionalized, racialized, and masculinized pilot garnered public and federal support, secured a professional monopoly, and institutionalized high salaries, the lady-flier did not disappear entirely from view. She simply was moved from the aptly named cockpit to the cabin, where she was transformed into a domesticated and feminized stewardess. It is that model that frames current understandings of gendered relations, identities, and the division of labor in the aviation industry, as evidenced by the fact that less than 6 percent of commercial airline pilots are women (Mireille, 2011). Ashcraft and Mumby's analysis using this approach productively moves between historical and contemporary texts and between micro- and macro-discourses as they affect, in material and symbolic ways, individual and collective identities.

In an increasingly media-saturated world, workers and organizational members of all types, not just organizational heroes and leaders, are routinely bombarded with cultural texts that offer myriad representations of work, workers, and work lives. This approach to identity explores how popular texts shape identities in the larger culture and how those culturally conditioned identities affect work life. For example, many scholars suggest that a growing force in popular culture is consumption (Schor, 1998, 2010). **Consumption** is a cultural practice through which individuals craft a self. Our consumptive choices regarding work (e.g., smartphones, tablet computers, laptops, vehicles, dress) speak volumes about how we wish to show ourselves to family, friends, and colleagues.

Through a variety of popular self-help texts, employees are increasingly encouraged to treat the self as an enterprise, an ongoing project, and even a brand that can be managed (Ashcraft et al., 2012; Carlone, 2001; Gill & Ganesh, 2007; Lair, Sullivan, & Cheney, 2005; Molyneux, 2015; Nolan, 2015). According to organizational communication scholar Rebecca Gill (2013), the entrepreneurial self, or what she terms "the entrepreneurial man," is fast becoming the archetypal organizational ideal. The entrepreneurial self, so pervasive in popular culture, "relies upon the image of an independent, resourceful, creative, and aggressive professional.

This person is expected to be agile in a fluctuating job market, responsive to any opportunities, self-motivating and self-promoting" (Lair et al., 2005, p. 318). And the best way to do this is to turn one's self into a value-added commodity, or a **personal brand**. Even stay-at-home mothers are adopting this strategy by defining themselves as "family CEOs," developing family "mission statements," and treating the family as an enterprise (Medved & Kirby, 2005). While this model may, in fact, increase the likelihood of workplace success, it has rather problematic implications for success in other spheres. First, the entrepreneurial self, in a constant bid to enhance one's personal brand, often sacrifices family and relationships to work. Second, while the popular texts that espouse personal branding imply that everyone is equally able to create a successful "brand," they also imply that women should aspire to do it all. Personal branding encourages women to get ahead at work, work as hard or harder than their male counterparts, and reach for the top but also to look womanly, take care of their external appearance, be there for their children and husbands (if a woman has them—but recognize that if she does, she may not be viewed as a 100 percent company woman), and routinely act in the caretaker role at work (Lair et al., 2005, p. 328). This is a tall order that few can achieve, and yet the popular narrative places the blame squarely on the woman's shoulders if she fails to achieve the entrepreneurial ideal.

These texts rarely address the ways that culture, organizations, and families make many unrealistic demands on working women. The personal branding texts similarly ignore the difficulties that aging, disabled, minority, or working-class individuals face in creating a "winning" personal brand that is based on a white, middle-class, male model (Hasinoff, 2008). Indeed, successful entrepreneurs often rely on working-class, Third World individuals to take on the burdens of the domestic sphere—including child care, housework, and yard maintenance—so that they can focus on success in the public sphere (Flanagan, 2004). Backstage, others often make significant, though undervalued and unrecognized, contributions to what appears to be an individual's success at work.

Finally, this approach to identity and difference assumes that although popular culture affects individual identities by offering resources through which individuals can craft identities, those narratives are rarely adopted wholesale. Moreover, this frame develops a historic and holistic understanding of gendered discourse as it encourages scholars to trace the emergence of particular identities in popular culture. Such analyses of popular culture may encourage individuals to be more critical consumers of cultural identity narratives. In short, individuals have the power to adopt, reject, and even transform the social narratives that guide them. Or, as H. L. Goodall (2004) asked, Are you a character in someone else's story, or are you the author of your own?

The *What Would You Do?* box on page 221 invites you to reflect on the different approaches to identity that we have covered in this chapter and to think about how individuals enact, transform, and reject identities in complex and sometimes contradictory ways.

The Secret Identity of an English Professor

By outlining multiple and different approaches to defining organizational identity, our intent is not to suggest that identity exists in discrete categories. On the contrary, most individuals enact multiple and sometimes conflicting identities at any given moment, and the identity work that we do is rarely easy to categorize. Consider the following example of an English professor who must navigate some unexpected changes in his identity.

It's Thursday morning, and Michael Carter, an assistant professor of English at a large research university in the Midwest, sits at his desk and looks at the mountain of student papers that he needs to grade. But Michael is not resentful. He loves his work and was overjoyed at landing a tenure-track position in a competitive, overcrowded field. Even though he has two Ivy League degrees, numerous teaching awards, and several prestigious publications, Michael knows that he is lucky to have any job at all—let alone one at a solid school located only two hours from his wife's family. Michael vows that he will never again face the exhausting academic job search and interviewing process. He must work hard to earn tenure. It is the only way to secure a permanent academic position.

Fortunately, Michael is well on his way to making himself an invaluable member of the English department. He is well respected by his colleagues and his students, and he has earned a reputation for being dedicated and hardworking. Michael frequently volunteers for academic committees and departmental projects while teaching three courses a semester (one of which he designed himself) and working on a book project that he hopes will end in a prestigious publication with a university press. He works long hours grading papers, advising students, and socializing with department faculty.

But Michael has a secret. Three years ago, while he was finishing his dissertation, he began to experience occasional trembling, dizziness, and blurred vision. He attributed these episodes to stress and long hours of work at the computer, but gradually the bizarre symptoms began to increase—and new ones appeared. Fearing that his job was destroying his health, Michael sought professional help to learn to control the symptoms. His doctors, however, gave him an extremely shocking and upsetting diagnosis: multiple sclerosis (MS), a disease of the central nervous system that can, in some cases, lead to paralysis, difficulty communicating, and cognitive challenges.

Michael's doctors told him that he should continue to work and try to lead a normal life. But they warned him that he may suffer from fatigue (particularly as MS treatments can sometimes cause flu-like symptoms) and that he may need

(continued, The Secret Identity of an English Professor)

to cut back on a few of his time-consuming commitments. Thinking about the possible progression of the disease, Michael knows that he may eventually need special accommodations from his employer, as guaranteed by the Americans with Disabilities Act.

Michael knows that the university cannot legally discriminate against him for suffering from an illness. But he also knows that his job is not secure until he receives tenure, and he worries that his colleagues will view him as useless if he doesn't volunteer for committees and develop new courses. He worries that his teaching evaluations will suffer if he takes too long to return student papers—even if he has a valid, medical reason for taking time. He considers keeping his news a secret from his colleagues and supervisor until after he is tenured or until the time comes that he must tell them. What should he do? What would you do if you were in his position?

Discussion Questions

1. Consider the positions of power that Michael has enjoyed. He is a young, white, heterosexual man with a prestigious education and job. How might his sense of power change when his privileged position intersects with his illness?
2. Should Michael tell his supervisor and his colleagues about his condition? Should he tell his students? Why or why not? If you were Michael's friend, what would you advise him to do?
3. If Michael shares his condition at work, what types of struggles might he face in negotiating multiple identities? If he keeps his news a secret, will he encounter similar struggles?

◨ COMMUNICATING IDENTITY AND DIFFERENCE

As symbol users (and abusers), human beings use communication to construct their own and others' identities. In this chapter, we have shown how interpersonal interactions, organizational structures and policies, and larger social discourses of power shape, privilege, and disadvantage different social identities as they are enacted at work and in life. As Brenda Allen (2003) says, difference matters. How difference matters is up to us. Thoughtful and responsive communicators will make conscientious decisions about communicating in ways that value difference, resist stereotyped assumptions about particular social identities, acknowledge the power of communication, and foster agency (Allen, 2003). Allen offers three specific strategies that enable individuals and groups to better communicate multiple identities:

1. *Be mindful.* When you communicate with others, be conscious about your own responses. It is helpful, though often difficult, to note your own privilege. What are the ways in which your social identity is privileged or valued in the communication context? How might your own privilege influence the responses you have to others? Are your attitudinal and behavioral responses based on stereotypes or other socially constructed assumptions? If so, consider the ways you might reframe your approach.

2. *Be proactive.* When you communicate with others, take the initiative to create positive changes or be "response-able" (p. 193). For example, once you are mindful of the ways you are privileged, you can use your privilege to mentor, network with, or support those who are less so. Alternately, you might put the person as a unique and complex individual first rather than foregrounding and responding to a noticeable identity category (like gender, race, or ability). If you are in a position of power, you might try to be more flexible in your role. Being proactive means responding to behavior that is discriminatory or inappropriate (e.g., not laughing at racist or sexist jokes). There are many ways to be proactive; your challenge is to become more "response-able" each and every day.

3. *Fill your communication toolbox.* The most "response-able" communicators are those with the widest array of tools or the broadest communicative repertoire. Utilizing effective listening and critical thinking, building persuasive arguments, using theories in applied contexts, creating the space for real dialogue, and balancing the constraints of any given situation with the needs, or the creativity, of the parties involved are all potentially useful skills for bridging differences at work and in life.

We encourage you to be mindful, be proactive, and use your tools well in the service of creating richer and more fulfilling identities for yourself and for others.

Summary

Difference is created, reinforced, rewarded, and transformed in organizational life. While early theories of identity assumed that the self was fixed, unitary, and essential, more recent theories define identity as a dynamic product of ongoing communication processes. Even though identities and differences are now viewed as more fluid, some identities are still more valued in organizational contexts than others. And organizations engage in a variety of strategies to encourage members to align their identities with the organizational ideal. We presented four approaches to understanding identity and difference as (1) organizational practices and performances, (2) essential or fixed aspects of the self, (3) organizational features that influence members, and (4) products of social and popular narratives.

The first approach argues that identity and difference are products of *identity regulation*, in which organizations attempt to "make" members' identities, and of *identity work*, in which individuals respond to organizations' attempts to define their identities. Organizations use a variety of strategies to perform identity regulation: defining a person directly, defining a person by defining others, providing a specific vocabulary of motives, offering specific morals and values, providing specific knowledge and skills, fostering group categorization and affiliation, reinforcing hierarchical dynamics, establishing rules of the game, and defining the environment in which employees operate. Individuals may perform identity work by using one or several self-images: self-doubter, struggler, surfer, storyteller, strategist, stencil, and soldier.

While the first approach is the most prominent today, we explored three more approaches that help us understand identity and difference in organizational life. The second approach suggests that identity and difference are fixed and determined by our nature or how we were nurtured. The third approach proposes that organizations themselves have identities which influence their members' identities. The fourth approach argues that social narratives, such as those found in popular culture, significantly influence our individual identities and organizational forms.

Finally, we rounded out the chapter by offering three strategies for communicating identity and difference thoughtfully and responsibly by being mindful, being proactive, and filling your communication toolbox.

Questions for Review and Discussion

1. How do organizations routinely seek to regulate and control members' identities? Is identity regulation a legitimate organizational concern? Why or why not?

2. Which of the seven images of identity "fits" with your understanding of how organizational communication works? Which one would you like to try on for size to see if it improves your organizational success? Which might improve your organizational satisfaction?

3. In what situation might the self-doubter identity be useful? What about the surfer? What are the drawbacks of each of the images outlined in Table 7.1?

4. Do you believe that identity and difference are fixed and determined either by our biology or our socialization, as the second approach argues? Explain.

5. How does an organization become gendered? How can organizations address inequitable divisions in everyday organizational activities?

6. What are the popular cultural images that have had the greatest impact on your understanding of identity at work and in life?

7. As a "response-able" communicator, how might you communicate in ways that value difference in the workplace?

KEY TERMS

Authenticity, p. 198
Consumption, p. 219
Gendered organization, p. 215
Identity, p. 197
Identity regulation, p. 200
Identity work, p. 201
Personal brand, p. 220
Second shift, p. 213

Self-doubter, p. 201
Soldier, p. 209
Stencil, p. 208
Storyteller, p. 206
Strategist, p. 207
Struggler, p. 203
Surfer, p. 204
Zone of indifference, p. 197

CASE STUDY

Valuing Identities across Five Generations

For the first time in history, the U.S. workforce is composed of five generations—each with different values, goals, and definitions of work.

- **Traditionalists** (born before 1945) are known for their work ethic. They expect a certain formality and professionalism in their communication practices, especially precise grammar and spelling, and they tend to prioritize long-term goals. When it comes to their communication styles, traditionalists prefer letters, memos, personal notes, and individual interactions.
- **Baby boomers** (born from 1946 to 1964) are often well educated and have excellent teamwork skills. They are strongly influenced by the Vietnam War, which sometimes leads them to question authority. Baby boomers prefer face-to-face interaction, phone calls, and formal networking.
- **Generation X** (born from 1965 to 1980) grew up in an era of increasing divorce rates, and they are sometimes referred to as the "Latchkey Generation." They are both independent and family focused. They tend to resist bureaucracy, and they are known for their critical-thinking skills and social responsibility. Generation Xers appreciate direct communication through voice mail and e-mail that gets to the point, lets them know what you need, and clarifies when you need it.
- **Millennials** (born from 1981 to 1995) are often critiqued as being an entitled generation. They are also heavily influenced by technological developments, and they demand a healthier approach to work-life balance. Millennials often require a more positive approach to communication, and they prefer text messages and other digital media.
- **Linksters** (born after 1995) are in the early stages of their working years. They are sometimes referred to as the "Facebook Crowd," and they are technologically dependent when it comes to their communication practices. They are family focused, with strong ties to their parents. Like the millennials, they tend to prefer digital media and text messaging as their primary forms of communication.

Managing the goals, needs, and identities of workers across these five generations can pose a significant challenge to even the most skilled organizational members. The following discussion questions ask you to think critically about how you would manage multigenerational identities in the workplace.

Assignment

1. You consider yourself a "late-model Generation Xer." You were born in 1978, but you're also fascinated by technology like some of your millennial counterparts. You are a middle-level manager at a small, community-based bank. In one month, you are scheduled to be promoted to vice president and head cashier when Mary, the current VP, retires. Mary has worked at the bank for sixty-two years, starting at age eighteen as a teller and working her way up to her current position. She comes from the traditionalist generation, and she places a high value on a strong work ethic and impeccable writing skills. To prepare for her retirement, Mary has been asked to share some of her expertise with you, as the incoming VP, as well as with the current crop of bank tellers. The bank tellers are mostly women and represent a wide range of ages, from eighteen to fifty-seven. One morning, Mary calls you into her office and asks for your help. She is frustrated because she is having trouble communicating with two of the newest bank tellers, who are eighteen and twenty-two. Mary explains that both tellers seem to lack a solid work ethic, and she is particularly annoyed that their e-mail exchanges have multiple spelling and grammar errors. "Now, I might be eighty years old," she says, "but I'm still pretty savvy when it comes to e-mail. Do they realize just how poorly these mistakes reflect on their work? You're going to have to start managing them in a month. What would you say to them?" How would you respond to Mary's request for advice?

2. You consider yourself to be a fairly typical individual from the millennial generation. You are working for a nationwide newsmagazine in your first managerial position. Recently, your editor asked you to brainstorm with your staff about personalizing the magazine. He wants you to develop a more direct connection between the magazine's readership and the staff writers, sales associates, and account managers who bring the magazine to life. He is particularly interested in the magazine's online presence and wants to use social media to build a stronger relationship between readers, writers, and other staff.

   You decide to hold a staff meeting to start the brainstorming process. You currently manage a group of fifteen, and your staff is very diverse—especially in terms of age. On one end, you have a few staff writers and account representatives who have been with the magazine for more than thirty years and identify strongly with the baby boomer generation. On the other end, you have two interns who are eighteen years old, are enrolled in their first semester of college, and are classic linksters. During the brainstorming session, Lily,

(continued, Valuing Identities across Five Generations)

one of your millennial sales associates, has an idea. She suggests that every member of the staff develop a personal Web page where they can post important stories from the magazine and can link to their personal social media accounts like Facebook and Twitter. Most of your staff is fairly comfortable with social media, and they immediately like the idea. You agree to get feedback from individual staff members before moving forward with any ideas.

After the meeting, Bob, one of your baby boomer staff writers, asks to speak with you. He says that he didn't want to mention it in the staff meeting, because he didn't want to look like the "old guy who is out of touch with technology," but he's not comfortable with Lily's idea. He's fine with creating personal Web pages where each staffer can post stories, but he doesn't like the idea of linking his personal Facebook and Twitter accounts to his workplace page. "Frankly, I don't even have my own Facebook page," he says. "My wife has one to keep up with all of our kids, so I just look at hers. I just feel like we're sacrificing privacy in the name of personal connections, and I think we're overstepping our bounds." You acknowledge that he has a point. How would you respond to Bob's concerns without devaluing Lily's idea?

Source: Material adapted from "Engaging a multi-generational workforce: Practical advice for government managers," by S. Hannam and B. Yordi, 2011, IBM Center for the Business of Government. Retrieved from businessofgovernment.org/report/engaging-multi-generational-workforce-practical-advice-government-managers.

CHAPTER 8

Teams and Networks: Communication and Collaborative Work

As advances in communication technology fueled a global economy in the late twentieth century, the nature of organizing underwent five key changes. We have already discussed two of them: (1) the development of flatter organizational structures and (2) the birth of the "customer-supplier" revolution, propelled by the demand for organizations of all kinds to work together to provide ever-improving quality in products and services to a demanding global marketplace. This chapter addresses the final three changes: (1) the new global demand for increased participation in decision making; (2) new models of collaboration between and among managers and workers; and (3) a change from traditional top-down bureaucratic models of communication and management to team-, group-, and network-based models.

   Central to all of these new ways of working together is the need for new forms of organizational communication. This chapter will explore how teams and networks can encourage new approaches to collaboration within and across organizations. We begin by situating the chapter in the conversation about workplace democracy and employee engagement. The chapter then turns to the specifics of teams and networks, by outlining types of teams and ways of analyzing networks. Finally, we consider the importance of technology when it comes to empowering teams and networks, as well as the creative potential of those new forms of organizing.

◳ DEMOCRACY IN THE WORKPLACE

Increased participation and collaboration in organizations places less emphasis on top-down decision making and relies more on engaging multiple stakeholders both in setting direction and in developing operational tactics and plans. Organizational scholar Stan Deetz's (1995) multiple-stakeholder model provides a useful way to think about the value of increased participation and democracy in the workplace. The **multiple-stakeholder model** asserts that organizations ought to be concerned with the interests of many different individuals and groups, not just shareholders or stockholders (see Figure 8.1). It seeks to balance the demands of global economic competition with a respect for the health and well-being of people and the environment. As such, the model raises critical questions about the potential and (generally negative) consequences of centralized decision making in the hands of multinational corporate and governmental leaders. In place of this decision-making style, the Deetz model promotes a greater voice and broader involvement in decision making by multiple stakeholders and stakeholder groups, in the service of a more democratic work environment. But how can this admittedly political model be applied to participation at the local organizational level? Deetz outlines four

FIGURE 8.1

Multiple-Stakeholder Model of the Corporation in Society

STAKEHOLDER GROUPS	MANAGING PROCESS	OUTCOME INTERESTS
Consumers		Goods and services
Workers		Income distribution
Investors	Coordination →	Use of resources
Suppliers		Environmental effects
Host communities		Economic stability
General society		Labor force development
World ecological community		Lifestyles
		Profits
		Personal identities
		Child-rearing practices

Source: From *Transforming communication, transforming business,* by S. Deetz, 1995, p. 50.

steps for increasing workplace democracy and shared decision making among a broad range of stakeholders:

1. *Create a workplace in which every member thinks and acts like an owner.* The point of business is to be of service; this is best accomplished when every stakeholder becomes responsible for decision making and is accountable for the outcomes of those decisions both to the business and to society.

2. *Reintegrate the management of work with the doing of work.* The cost of people watching other people work for the purpose of controlling what gets done and how it is done can no longer be seen as economically efficient. Moreover, it often leads to bad decisions (i.e., decisions about how to do work are best made by those who actually perform it and will be rewarded by its outcomes) and to less accountability (i.e., "watched" people tend to resist domination by finding ways to slow down work processes or to goof off on the job).

3. *Widely distribute quality information.* To fully empower workers and the people they serve, the current system of filling up the day with mostly meaningless memos, e-mails, and newsletters that only encourage control and domination should be replaced by the distribution of "real" information about the business and how it is affecting society and the planet.

4. *Allow social structure to grow from the bottom rather than be reinforced from the top.* If the basic idea of a participative democratic workplace values the consent of the governed in the governance of everyday affairs, everything from routine office policies to limiting the terms of managers should be accomplished through ongoing negotiations among the multiple stakeholders. (Deetz, 1995, pp. 170–171)

Although practically challenging, implementing Deetz's suggestions can help move us toward a more democratic dialogue, or what he calls "constitutive codetermination" (1995, p. 174). Similar strategies have been implemented in newer manufacturing plants, such as BMW of North America. Indeed, Deetz's model may be easier to implement in newly formed companies than in existing corporate and government institutions because existing institutions may face logistical difficulties when incorporating more diverse voices into their decision-making processes.

The Gallup Organization has established a global research and consulting practice, similar to the multiple-stakeholder model, that is focused on helping employers see the value of what they call "employee engagement" as a primary driver of organizational effectiveness. A descendent of earlier concepts like job satisfaction, participative management, and empowerment, **employee engagement** is reflected in employees who are fully involved in and enthusiastic about their work. Leaders can increase employee engagement by communicating in ways that demonstrate caring, valuing of employees' contributions, and a clear connection between employees' work and the success of the company.

Gallup researchers report significant increases in productivity for companies in which a majority of employees are actively engaged in their jobs (Harter & Adkins,

2015). There is also a hidden cost of disengagement: Businesses with a surplus of disengaged workers suffer 31 percent more turnover than those with a critical mass of engaged employees. When it comes to losses in productivity, disengaged employees cost organizations 85 percent more than their engaged counterparts due to absenteeism and health problems.

More specifically, in Gallup research involving more than one million employee interviews over decades, twelve elements of management that make a difference emerged, as shown in Table 8.1. Many organizations across a wide range of industries and agencies now measure their performance against these twelve dimensions, tracking their engagement scores, comparing them with industry norms, and developing managers and leaders who behave in ways that foster these perceptions, resulting in improved performance.

Considered more generally, the idea of sharing information and authority through the development of more democratic structures often involves creating collaborative teams and networks. For example, a 2016 report from *Forbes* states that newer companies are experimenting with structures that allow them to build engagement into the fabric of the organization (Hansen, 2016). Companies like Zappos and Medium are implementing management systems that enable them to replace traditional hierarchical power with power that is distributed to employees. One example comes from Valve Software in Seattle, which allows employees to select the projects they want to work on and to design their own workspaces to more easily collaborate with their peers.

The desire to organize in ways that foster employee engagement comes from the realization that no single individual (or, for that matter, no small group) is sufficient to achieve complex organizational goals. In the following sections, we build

TABLE 8.1

Twelve Dimensions of Employee Engagement (often called the Q12)

1. I know what is expected of me at work.
2. I have the materials and equipment I need to do my work well.
3. I have the opportunity to do what I do best every day.
4. In the past seven days, I have received recognition for doing good work.
5. My supervisor or someone at work seems to care about me as a person.
6. There is someone who encourages my development.
7. My opinions seem to count.
8. The company's mission makes me feel that my job is important.
9. My fellow employees are committed to doing quality work.
10. I have a best friend at work.
11. In the past six months, someone has talked to me about my progress.
12. This past year, I had opportunities at work to learn and grow.

Source: 12: The elements of great managing, by R. Wagner and J. Harter, 2006, pp. xi–xii.

on the previous discussion of participation and democracy by addressing communication that occurs in teams and networks. Today, most work that goes on inside organizations utilizes a team approach, whereas work that takes place outside organizations (e.g., entrepreneurship, outsourcing, or consulting) relies more heavily on networks and networking. If knowledge is power, it is a kind of power that is inevitably exercised in webs of relationships and in the creation of robust and resilient communication networks.

◩ COMMUNICATING IN TEAMS

Most U.S. employees now work in some form of *team-based organization* where, in addition to their individual responsibilities, they also serve as members of one or more working groups. The importance of teamwork has long been appreciated in business. Filene's, a Boston-based department store (bought by Macy's), introduced the concept of teamwork in the United States in 1898. However, today's emphasis on teams goes far beyond the original meaning of teamwork, which is simply working together. A **team-based organization** is one that has restructured itself around interdependent decision-making groups, not individuals, as a means to improve work processes and provide better products and services to customers.

Team-based organizing differs sharply from bureaucratic forms of organizing. First, consistent with the human resources approach, in team-based companies every employee is seen as possessing valuable knowledge that must be widely shared for the benefit of the whole. **Teams** are groups of employees with representation from a variety of functional areas within the organization (e.g., sales, manufacturing, engineering) to maximize the cross-functional exchange of information. In a bureaucracy, a hierarchical chain of command distinguishes managers (as "thinkers") and workers (as "nonthinkers"), emphasizing the need for division of labor and close supervision. Team-based organizations, in contrast, encourage informal communication and view all employees as capable of making decisions about how to manage work tasks. In the most progressive team-based organizations, supervisory work is conducted by *self-managed* work teams. In these settings, employees are "knowledge workers" dedicated to self-improvement, positive results, and productive collaboration:

> In the conversion to post-bureaucratic organizations, teams form the basic unit of empowerment, small enough for efficient high involvement and large enough for the collective strength and the synergy generated by diverse talents. Within teams, people can take wide responsibility for one another, for the organization, and for the quality of their products and services. (Pinchot & Pinchot, 1993, p. 194)

The hiring philosophy at Google exemplifies this trend. On their website, they say that they are seeking "smart, team-oriented people who can get things done." More specifically, they go on to say that they are looking to see "how you've flexed different muscles in different situations in order to mobilize a team. This might be by asserting a leadership role at work or with an organization, or by helping a team succeed when you weren't officially appointed as the leader."

In the sections that follow, we'll examine several important dimensions of teams, including basic and advanced types of teams, communicative dimensions of teamwork, and a possible retreat from teams in everyday practice.

☐ Basic Types of Teams

Despite widespread enthusiasm for team-based organizing, definitions of what constitutes a team remain varied and ambiguous. Not every identifiable group in an organization is sufficiently interdependent to warrant classification as a team. A simple collection of people working together in some capacity might be dubbed a committee, task force, or ad hoc group without qualifying as a team. Teams, in contrast, generally fall into three categories: project teams, work teams, and quality-improvement teams.

Project Teams

Project teams, which help coordinate the successful completion of a particular project, have long been used by organizations in the design and development of new products or services. For example, a project team at a computer company might include software and hardware engineers, programmers, and other technical specialists who design, program, and test prototype computers. A project team might also be assigned to address a specific issue or problem.

Project teams may struggle because people lack the communication skills needed to collaborate across different specialty areas and the divides between them. Collaborative behaviors are hard to learn; while many project teams are formed with great optimism, they face considerable challenges, and few succeed (Jassawalla & Sashittal, 1999; Love, Fong, & Irani, 2005). Management must expend great effort to foster real collaboration, which can result in an increased commitment to team decisions and a deeper level of caring about team outcomes and accomplishments. A new model of how to create positive collaboration is described later in this chapter.

Work Teams

A **work team** is a group of employees responsible for the entire work process that delivers a product or service to a customer. One such work team at a California aerospace company is responsible for all metallizing of components. The team resides together, outlines its own work flow (e.g., the steps for applying metal coatings to parts), and is engaged in making ongoing improvements in the work process (e.g., making the metal coating as thin and light as possible).

Such teams have been found to improve an organization's efficiency. FedEx, General Electric, Corning, General Mills, and AT&T have all recorded significant productivity improvements after incorporating work teams (Van Tien, Moseley, & Dessinger, 2012; Wellins, Byham, & Wilson, 1991). Texas Instruments Malaysia managed to boost employee output by 100 percent and cut production time by

50 percent after moving to a team-based approach. Teams have an especially positive history in manufacturing. The president of Toyota explained his company's relative success compared to some based in the United States by saying, "Detroit people are far more talented than people at Toyota. . . . But we take averagely talented people and make them work in spectacular teams" (cited in Evans & Wolf, 2005, p. 104). Teamwork is the basis of Toyota's high-performance organization.

Successful work teams are supported by a commitment to employee engagement and empowerment. Because they are given the discretion and autonomy to make decisions and solve problems, empowered teams are not frustrated by a lack of authority to implement their ideas and solutions. A group can also do a better job of managing its resources when it understands the big picture, has the authority to adapt to changing work conditions, and feels that its work is meaningful and has an impact (Kirkman & Rosen, 1999). Unfortunately, these conditions are not yet the norm.

Work teams differ in degree of empowerment, as indicated in Figure 8.2. As empowerment increases, the team assumes responsibility for the continuous improvement of work processes, the selection of new members, the election of a team leader, and capital expenditures. At the highest level of empowerment, the self-directed work team is also responsible for performance appraisals, disciplinary measures, and compensation (Wellins et al., 1991).

Effective managers of work teams create a climate for honest and supportive dialogue and possess the necessary communication skills to do so. The considerable challenges involved in such an undertaking are reflected in *What Would You Do?* on page 237.

Quality-Improvement Teams

Back in the 1980s, informal problem-solving groups called *quality circles* were popular in various organizations, meeting voluntarily each week to address work-related issues (Kreps, 1991). Quality circles have since been replaced by **quality-improvement teams**, whose goals are to improve customer satisfaction, evaluate and improve team performance, and reduce costs. Such teams are typically cross-functional, drawing their members from a variety of areas to bring different perspectives to the problem or issue under study. In theory, a quality-improvement team uses its diverse talents to generate innovative ideas.

Monsanto formed such a team several years ago in response to a problem with their product Saflex, which was used to make laminated windshields. The Ford Motor Company told Monsanto that the dimensions of the Saflex materials changed between the time the products left Monsanto's plants and when they arrived at Ford's facilities. Monsanto immediately assembled a quality-control group. Within two months, the team traced the problem to packaging, designed a new prototype, tested it, and implemented a new packaging process. Monsanto's response satisfied Ford.

Another example of a quality-improvement team is a program called Work-Outs at General Electric, which was initiated by CEO Jack Welch in 1989.

FIGURE 8.2

The Empowerment Continuum of Work Teams

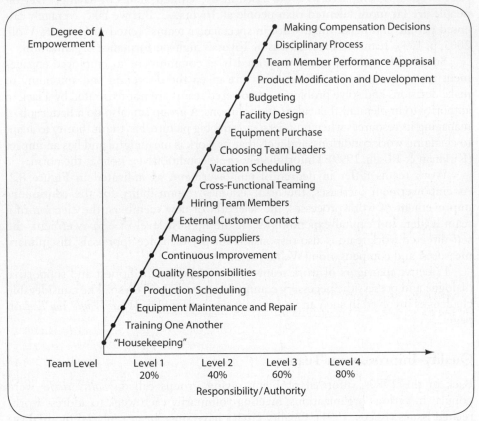

Source: From *Empowered teams*, by R. Wellins, W. Byham, and J. Wilson, 1991, p. 26.

At General Electric, management selects up to one hundred employees to attend a three-day conference (Stewart, 1991). A facilitator divides the employees into five or six smaller groups, and each group works independently for two days to identify problems with the company and to prepare a presentation to senior management proposing changes. On the third day, the panel of senior managers views the presentations, and the managers must agree or disagree with each proposal or ask for more information (in which case, the group agrees to supply it by a specified date). This is a dramatic example of how organizations are using teams to encourage creativity and to open the dialogue between managers and employees.

The Dilemmas of Participative Management at a University

Joan Brittle is the new president of a large public university in the Midwest. Recently, she attended a workshop where she learned that most successful educational institutions today have adopted participative, team-based structures. While she has little formal education in management (she is a physicist by training), the team approach makes sense to her and fits with her personality and management style, which is all about cultivating strong relationships.

Following the workshop, she returns to her campus and enthusiastically charges a team of her top faculty to design a series of strategic initiatives for the school that both capitalize on the existing strengths of the institution and are responsive to emerging social trends. To ensure that she does not impede their dialogue, she does not join the team but asks one of the more senior faculty members whom she trusts to lead the team and provide her with periodic updates. She is confident that "many heads are better than one" and anxiously awaits the team's report, which she believes will affirm and extend her ambitious vision for the future of the institution. She feels that both the opportunity and the optimal path to greatness for the university are fairly clear.

The strategic initiatives team attacks the new challenge with enormous energy and enthusiasm. In three short months, they develop a comprehensive plan featuring five initiatives for the school to pursue over the next ten to twenty years. When President Brittle receives their report, she is both stunned and disoriented. Based on her beliefs and perspectives, she assumed that the team would come back with a plan that was responsive to changing environmental conditions and apparent opportunities in the state. Instead, their proposal is mostly an ambitious extension of current faculty interests and offerings that fails to suggest any kind of new direction or breakthrough. She wonders: How could this superb group be so far off base? From her perspective, the initiatives are too internally focused, reflecting faculty interest and expertise, and are out of touch with the needs and desires of the board of trustees, the legislature, and the community. In addition, they do not represent any of her personal and professional interests in health and the life sciences.

Discussion Questions

1. How did the group wind up with initiatives that differed so much from President Brittle's expectations? What steps could President Brittle have taken to avoid the polarity of this outcome?

(continued, The Dilemmas of Participative Management at a University)

2. What does this situation tell you about the risks and pitfalls of encouraging employee participation in decision making?
3. Based on your reading about teams, what would you advise the president to do now? Why?

☐ Advanced Types of Teams

Depending on the location of and general relationships between team members, any of these basic types of teams might also develop into an advanced category of team. At their core, these advanced teams are still work, project, and/or quality-improvement teams; however, they also serve additional, unique functions that deserve attention. These more advanced categories of teams include virtual teams and community-engaged teams.

Virtual Teams

In response to a dynamic global economy, most large organizations and many smaller ones have found it advantageous to maximize their geographic reach and become immersed in a wide range of local cultures. Companies ignore cultural differences at their own peril. Unfortunately, the geographic distribution of employees creates predictable communication difficulties associated with time and space, often resulting in serious misunderstandings. Fortunately, a range of technologies (think Skype, Google Drive, Dropbox, and more) have evolved to support groups of people who work together around the world in what are called **virtual teams**.

A surface analysis of virtual teams can identify likely problems such as language barriers and differences in cultures, religions, and work customs and habits. But deeper consideration reveals that all virtual teams engage in a developmental process that builds a negotiated order—a shared set of practices or "micro-cultures" that emerge among members (Gluesing, 1998). Some of the items that are typically up for negotiation include division of labor, activity sequencing, and the nature and regularity of outcome assessment. In addition, virtual teams must work out more mundane but still vexing issues surrounding the use of e-mail lists, intranets, and telepresence. This team-development process is highly social (though largely through electronic media) and involves the development of mutual respect and trust (Baba, 1999). The development of virtual teams has increased exponentially with the development of more realistic telepresence technology and the entrance of younger, digital-native workers into the workforce. On the technology side, Cisco and others have developed extraordinary high-definition cameras and monitors to simulate face-to-face interactions. From an employee perspective, members of the millennial generation are much more comfortable than their predecessors with multitasking and multiple, mediated forms of communication.

Pamela Shockley-Zalabak (2002), an organizational communication scholar and chancellor of the University of Colorado at Colorado Springs, conducted an important study of an international, self-managing, virtual team created by a technology company seeking to do a better job of meeting customer needs. She describes the functioning of this team over a two-year period as "protean," constantly changing in structure and form. Her research revealed some of the challenges associated with these kinds of structures. Two years into the company's experiment, the members of this team did not want to return to a hierarchy. They did, however, express a strong desire for more structure in the form of better processes and clearer work rules. While the idea of geographic boundaries was no longer relevant, a new kind of boundary was important to the team. Specifically, they wished for "boundary as guide, sense of place, commitment, relationship, and shared meaning [amidst continuous change]" (p. 249). Future studies of virtual teams will no doubt shed more light on the pragmatics of succeeding with this new organizational form. One important factor that team members must consider in a global world is how cultural influences may affect communication among virtual team members. Some of these cultural influences are described in Table 8.2.

Community-Engaged Teams

In order to fully realize concepts like the multiple-stakeholder model and employee engagement, many organizational scholars have begun to rethink what qualifies as a team (e.g., LeGreco, Ferrier, & Leonard, 2015). **Community-engaged teams** are a specific type of team that involves a bona fide working relationship between employees in an organization and the community members who care about and are impacted by that organization. Although community-engaged teams can manifest as project, work, or quality-improvement teams, they typically emerge as project teams, assembled for a specific goal (e.g., open a restaurant, evaluate public housing efforts). For example, celebrity food truck owner Roy Choi and celebrity chef Daniel Patterson recently teamed up to open LocoL in the Watts neighborhood of Los Angeles. The restaurant features healthy fast-food options at an affordable price and is the result of an eighteen-month collaboration between Choi, Patterson, members of the Watts neighborhood, fellow chefs, and community organizers. This neighborhood is in the midst of significant revitalization and economic development, and Choi, in particular, has formed a meaningful working relationship with his neighbors to create menus, provide jobs, and develop a sense of ownership among the people who live and work in Watts.

TABLE 8.2

Cultural Influences on Global Virtual Teams

Variable	Implication for Multicultural Teams
Individualism vs. Collectivism	• Individualistic team members will voice their opinions more readily, challenging the direction of the team. The opposite is true of collectivists. Collectivists will want to consult colleagues more than individualists before making decisions. • Collectivists don't need specific job descriptions or roles but will do what is needed for the team, ideally together with other team members. Individualists will take responsibility for tasks and may need to be reminded that they're part of the team. • Individual-oriented team members will want direct, constructive feedback on their performance and rewards that are closely tied to their individual performance. Collectivists, however, might feel embarrassed if singled out for particular praise or incentives. • Collectivists prefer face-to-face meetings over virtual ones.
Power Distance	• Team members from cultures that value equality (i.e., low power distance) expect to use consultation to make key decisions. From the viewpoint of a team member from a higher power distance culture, however, a team leader exercising a more collaborative style might be seen as weak and indecisive. • Members from high power distance cultures will be very uncomfortable communicating directly with people higher in the organization.
Uncertainty Avoidance	• In a culture where risk taking is the norm or valued, team members tend to be comfortable taking action or holding meetings without much structure or formality. Members who are more risk averse need a clearer, prepared meeting structure, perhaps with formal presentations by all members of the team. They're unlikely to take an active part in brainstorming sessions. • Members from lower uncertainty avoidance cultures will not respond well to "micromanagement." They may also be more willing to use new technologies.
Task/Relationship Orientation	• Team members from relationship-oriented cultures want to spend extra social time together, building trust, and may have problems interacting smoothly with short-term members.

Source: From "Critical success factors for global virtual teams," by J. Goodbody, 2005, *Strategic Communication Management*, *9*, p. 20.

Community-engaged teams are more than ad hoc groups or task forces inasmuch as they reflect a shared commitment between the company and the community. They are also different from cooperatives; the term *cooperative* usually refers to the structure of the organization, whereas community-engaged teams are often composed to carry out a specific work function that bridges community, corporate, and governmental interests. When teams are truly engaged with their communities, ensuring that community voices matter just as much as a traditional shareholder or employee, they represent not only a new form of organizing but also a truer representation of what Deetz argues for with his multiple-stakeholder model.

Although community-engaged teams give organizations the opportunity to explore the depths of a multiple-stakeholder approach, they are not without their challenges (Dempsey, 2009; McDermott, Oetzel, & White, 2008). The mix of members of many community-engaged teams can include people who are paid to be there as part of their jobs, and others who are participating because they are personally committed to the work being done. With this composition, organizations often run the risk of exploiting the "free labor" of community members and taking advantage of neighborhoods without offering some sense of reciprocity. As a consequence, community-engaged teams face their fair share of paradoxes of participation (McDermott et al., 2008), especially when community members are asked to participate on teams with people of varying skill sets, education levels, and economic status. Community-engaged teamwork requires a delicate balance of reflexivity, social support, and reciprocity to ensure that both communities and organizations are acting in the best interests of the entire team.

☐ Communicative Dimensions of Teamwork

Simply calling a group a "team" does not make it one. A group becomes a team through the kinds of communication it displays over time and the resulting feelings (if it works!) of trust and interdependence. More specifically, there are five communicative elements of team interaction that are essential to consider: roles, norms, decision-making processes, management of conflict and consensus, and cultural diversity. The following sections address each of these elements.

Roles

Effective teamwork requires a balance between the goals of individual members and those of the team. While individual behavior can vary significantly, team members tend to adopt predictable **communication roles**, which are consistent patterns of interaction within the team (Goodall, 1990). According to the classic typology, the three broad types of communication roles are task, maintenance, and self-centered (Benne & Sheats, 1948).

In performing the **task role**, the team member summarizes and evaluates the team's ideas and progress or initiates the idea-generating process by offering new ideas or suggestions. In the **maintenance role**, the team member's communication seeks to relieve group tension or pressure (e.g., by telling jokes or by changing the subject of a conversation) or to create harmony in the group (e.g., by helping to reconcile conflict or disagreements; Shockley-Zalabak, 1991). A role with far less positive effects is the **self-centered role**—a team member who seeks to dominate the group's discussions and work or to divert the group's attention from serious issues by making them seem unimportant. The self-centered role is always considered inappropriate and unproductive.

H. L. Goodall (1990) has identified two other roles: the prince and the facilitator. The **prince role** is exhibited by group members who fancy themselves to be brilliant political strategists and see the world as a political entity. In the **facilitator role**, a team member focuses exclusively on group process (e.g., following an agenda and maintaining consensus in decision making) for the benefit of the team, while refraining from substantive comments on issues.

Some people both serve on teams and seek to facilitate team communication, playing different roles at various moments. A training manager, for example, may act as a facilitator if, during a team meeting, the conversation drifts off topic. At the same time, the manager may suspend the facilitator role by offering information or opinions relevant to the discussion.

Norms

Norms are the informal rules that "designate the boundaries of acceptable behavior in the group" (Kreps, 1991, p. 170). For example, team members may be expected to attend meetings on time, prepare for meetings in advance, and distribute the meeting's agenda by an agreed-on deadline. Norms about conflict may express varying degrees of tolerance for disagreement. For a number of years, Intel encouraged employees to engage in "constructive confrontation" when they perceived a colleague to be advocating something that ran afoul of the company's core values (although it appears that it may no longer be working).

Taking a different tack, one software company CEO insists that no one should ever kill a new idea. He instead encourages "idea angels" who are charged with saying *something* positive about every new idea that is introduced. Team norms, which are shaped by the national and organizational culture as well as by personal agendas, strongly affect member roles. For example, a large U.S. insurance company emphasizes positive employee relations to such a degree that the organizational culture is largely intolerant of conflict. As a consequence, work teams tend to avoid conflict at all costs and hence fail to deal with key performance issues.

Decision-Making Processes

As a general rule, teams make better decisions than individuals. The classical management approach separates decision making from implementation; the use of teams permits a departure from this approach by getting more people involved in the decision-making process. The additional people can, in turn, generate more information and ideas. In addition, the simple act of participating in decision making makes team members more aware of important issues, more likely to reach a consensus, and better able to communicate about the issues.

Team decision making also poses a number of problems. Strong-willed or verbose team members may dominate conversations, intimidate others, or manipulate team decisions to benefit themselves in an effort to gain power or to improve their image. **Groupthink**, a well-known problem associated with team decision making that was initially identified by psychologist Irving Janis (1971), occurs when team members go along with, rather than critically evaluate, the group's proposals or ideas.

A number of strategies for dealing with groupthink are consistent with our ideal of promoting organizational dialogue and greater employee engagement:

- Encourage team members to voice their objections and to critically evaluate others' ideas.
- Use more than one group to work on a problem to generate a variety of proposed solutions.
- Encourage team members to discuss the team's deliberations with people outside of the group to obtain feedback.
- Invite outside experts into the group to obtain their input and feedback.
- Make one team member responsible for ensuring that the team explores all sides of an issue.
- Divide the team into subgroups that work independently on a problem and then report back to the team.
- Arrange a special meeting after a consensus has been reached to give team members the opportunity to discuss any remaining doubts or concerns (Gibson & Hodgetts, 1986).

Decision making by teams also requires team members to sort through multiple interpretations of an issue to find the single best course of action. This is a significant challenge, especially for members who are intolerant of others' perspectives. For this reason, extensive research has been conducted on identifying effective decision-making strategies.

Small-group communication scholar Aubrey Fisher's (1980) model of group decision making sees decisions as the product of four stages:

1. *Orientation*: Teams get to know and trust one another.
2. *Conflict*: Members express and debate different ideas.
3. *Emergence*: Teams develop consensus and move toward action.
4. *Reinforcement*: Teams experience a spirit of cooperation and accomplishment.

Teams that skip the orientation phase may never truly feel comfortable as a group; members may only know one another as roles, not as people. They may also lack direction. Teams that avoid the conflict stage—mainly through cowardice in the face of difficult conversations—run a risk of groupthink (i.e., of agreeing on a course of action before exploring all the available information or alternatives). Teams lacking in communication skills often fall apart at the emergence stage, as group members find it impossible to work together and agree on a common direction. Many teams don't even survive to experience the reinforcement stage.

Other studies of team decision making challenge the stage models proposed by Fisher and others by suggesting that most teams follow a less defined path toward decision making. These writers believe that group decision making is more varied and complicated (e.g., Poole, 1983; Poole & Roth, 1989). From their perspective, teams experience periods of order and disorganization that are unpredictable; they tend to go through cycles and to repeat stages multiple times, and they may engage in activities (e.g., managing tasks and establishing work relationships) in a haphazard rather than coordinated fashion. In many cases, stages do not occur in an orderly or predictable pattern.

Management of Conflict and Consensus

Conflict occurs among members of organizations and teams because people pursue different interests. **Conflict** is defined by organizational communication scholars Linda Putnam and Marshall Scott Poole as "the interaction of interdependent people who perceive opposition of goals, aims, and values, and who see the other parties as potentially interfering with the realization of these goals" (1987, p. 552). In organizations, conflict most often arises from the acquisition and use of resources. Like other types of communication, conflict changes or evolves over time and is unpredictable. It also takes place in the interdependent relationships among people who rely on one another to some extent for resources.

Attitudes toward conflict in U.S. organizations have changed significantly since the 1950s, when overt conflict was viewed as counterproductive and always to be avoided. By the 1970s, some recognition of the benefits of conflict had emerged, such as its role in generating different ideas and perspectives (and thereby helping avoid groupthink) as well as in facilitating a greater sharing of information. Studies have found that some degree of team conflict is essential to achieving high levels of productivity and effective communication (Franz & Jin, 1995). An absence of conflict over an extended period of time is more likely a sign of group stagnation or fear than of effectiveness. The constructive role of conflict is mostly understood today, although it remains difficult to realize in practice.

Because team conflict is inevitable, we are concerned with how team members handle it. Broadly distinguished as emphasizing either a "concern for self" or a "concern for others," conflict style is also marked by degrees of assertiveness and cooperation (Kilmann & Thomas, 1975). Collaboration, which is generally seen as the most effective conflict style, emphasizes high assertiveness combined with high levels of cooperation. In contrast, compromise is considered less effective in resolving conflicts because neither party's preferred solution is adopted. Collaboration is more likely to lead to a novel solution that satisfies both parties.

Unfortunately, there is often a significant gap between individuals' expressed or preferred conflict style and how they behave across a variety of conflict situations. For example, while supervisors' strategies for dealing with problem employees reflect their styles when the conflict first surfaces, over time they tend to use more coercive strategies regardless of their *expressed* conflict style (Fairhurst, Green, & Snavely, 1984).

Finally, effective conflict management through consensus means accepting the inevitability of differences and remaining committed to alternative perspectives, creative decision making, and the ongoing dialogue that can lead to these results—and the creation of a consensus. **Consensus** reflects an overarching belief that in the long haul, "all of us are smarter than any one of us." Notably, consensus does *not* mean that all team members agree with a decision, but instead that they feel the team has adequately considered their views. "If there is a clear alternative which most members subscribe to, and if those who oppose it feel they have had their chance to influence, then a consensus exists" (Schein, 1969, p. 56). Naturally, people agree to a group consensus with the understanding that their point of view will be accepted at least some of the time; otherwise they would most likely leave the group.

Cultural Diversity in Teams

As corporations make greater use of intercultural teams in response to global competition, researchers are increasingly concerned with the effects of cultural differences on team member communication. Scholars have established key dimensions of cultural diversity, including power distance, uncertainty avoidance, and belonging or "fit" within organizations (Glenn & Jackson, 2010). In one study, communication scholar Charles Bantz (1993) reports on his experiences as a member of a ten-person intercultural research team. Though he notes a wide range of tactics that cross-cultural teams use to manage their differences, he highlights four common ones: (1) gather information; (2) adapt to differing situations, issues, and needs; (3) build social as well as task cohesion; and (4) identify clear, mutual long-term goals (p. 19). Bantz also points out that "awareness of cultural differences is necessary, but not sufficient for the accomplishment of cross-cultural team research" (p. 19).

Negotiation is another key to managing intercultural team differences. The following four phases in the negotiation process occur in all cultures (Varner & Beamer, 1995), but the amount of time devoted to each phase and its relative importance may differ:

1. *Developing relationships with others.* Members of a newly formed intercultural team need sufficient time to explore long-term team goals, build trust, and adapt to cultural differences. In most cultures, candid answers to questions mark the beginning of a productive relationship, even when the required answers may be perceived as self-disclosing. However, face saving is just as important to members of Asian, African, and Middle Eastern cultures as candidness is to other cultures. Therefore, it is wise to avoid insensitive remarks, to express tolerance of others' goals and values, and to respect the status that others enjoy in their native culture.

2. *Exchanging information about topics under negotiation.* Honest or frank disclosures are one way to generate trust, but information exchange may also be enhanced by responding to questions with other questions that open up the team dialogue. Questions can be used not only to access information and to clarify ideas, but also to call bluffs or show interest in another's ideas. Team

members also become more aware of how culture plays a role in the answers generated by questions; for example, why-questions are answered with explanations of cause and effect in Western cultures, but they are answered more generally through stories, personal narratives, and cultural myths in non-Western cultures.

3. *Recognizing multicultural techniques of persuasion.* Rational arguments are considered persuasive by members of many cultures, but different perspectives on what is considered rational, and different ways of communicating rational arguments, can pose difficulties for intercultural teams. Teams can focus more on gaining information than on persuading, and team members can also respect cultural differences when persuasion is necessary. For example, using *I* is less persuasive than the more inclusive *we*, and using such words as *must*, *should*, and *ought* may be viewed as arrogant by members of non-Western cultures.

4. *Emphasizing the role of concession in achieving agreement.* Most cultures appreciate the value of fair exchange, including the value of concession in gaining agreement. In general, concessions are best expressed as if-statements (e.g., "We can deliver those services if your suppliers can meet this schedule"), rather than as directives (e.g., "We can deliver those services but your suppliers must meet this schedule"). Additionally, American culture usually relies on a formal contract to ensure that concessions are properly carried out, but in most Asian cultures, a contract may be superseded by informal relationships. Similarly, an American conducting business in Finland may be surprised to learn that formal written agreements are often considered unnecessary because verbal agreements are executed with trust.

This research on teams shows an increasing emphasis on interacting with, learning from, and giving credit to people who are different from us. More diverse teams can also face new challenges, especially in the early stages of building the team. Using his intercultural workgroup communication theory, John Oetzel and colleagues (Oetzel, 2005; Oetzel, McDermott, Torres, & Sanchez, 2012) argue that cultural diversity in workgroups must include both task and relational outcomes. In other words, teams need to be productive and make good decisions, but must also develop positive working relationships—like the desire to work with each other again. Much of the existing research reinforces the idea that diverse teams tend to struggle more at the beginning of their work process; however, those struggles can be mitigated over time as the team develops a history and learns how everyone fits together.

In order to reach these task and relational goals, the intercultural workgroup communication theory emphasizes the importance of *situational features*, which are deeper-level elements of diversity that stand in contrast to surface-level categories like race and gender. In one test of their theory, Oetzel and his colleagues note a wide range of conflicting research conclusions that show positive, negative, neutral, *and* curvilinear relationships between ethnic diversity and group interaction (Oetzel et al., 2012). To explain this, they turn to situational features. For example, their study found a positive relationship between diversity and group interaction—while focusing primarily on work teams in largely metropolitan regions, where many employees were already accustomed to working on diverse teams. Other research has reached different conclusions, studying work teams residing in more homogenous communities with more similar backgrounds. A major takeaway from this theory is that diversity is often *locally situated*, meaning that "our interpretation of, and reaction to, diversity may be more determined by local composition and everyday expectations rather than the macro demographics of a nation" (Oetzel et al., 2012, p. 162).

Team Learning

Successful team-based organizations foster an environment that values and rewards team learning (Pinchot & Pinchot, 1993; Senge, Ross, Smith, & Roberts, 1994). MIT management and systems experts Peter Senge and colleagues (1994) define **team learning** as "alignment" or the "functioning of the whole":

> Building alignment is about enhancing a team's capacity to think and act in new, synergistic ways, with full coordination and a sense of unity [among] team members. . . . As alignment develops, [members do not] have to *overlook or hide* their disagreements to make their collective understanding richer. (p. 352)

Senge and colleagues go on to suggest that team learning transforms the skills of "reflection and inquiry" into "vehicles for building shared understanding" (p. 352). More specifically, they identify the following three guidelines for team communication:

1. *Balance inquiry and advocacy.* Teams need to balance inquiry (i.e., asking questions that challenge the existing assumptions and beliefs about work) with advocacy (i.e., stating opinions and taking action). Neither inquiry nor advocacy should control the team's learning process. Figure 8.3 identifies various types of inquiry and advocacy commonly used by teams.
2. *Bring tacit assumptions to the surface of team dialogue.* Senge and colleagues suggest that because "we live in a world of self-generating beliefs which remain largely untested" (1994, p. 242), our beliefs appear to be the truth, the truth seems obvious to us, and the evidence for our beliefs is limited to the data we select from our experience. A team that learns to question these assumptions moves down the "ladder of inference," revealing the motivations behind our beliefs (Figure 8.4). As the team brings tacit assumptions to the surface of its dialogue, it discovers the role of those assumptions in the development of beliefs and conclusions.
3. *Become aware of the assumptions that inform conclusions.* Once assumptions have surfaced, it is beneficial for teams to reflect on how these particular beliefs give rise to interpretations of events that support specific conclusions about

work processes, employees, or customers. Making these connections explicit makes them easier to change. Conclusions, then, are filtered through members' assumptions and beliefs, which are unobservable and highly personalized. This is what makes the generation of new ideas challenging. However, by counteracting these abstract influences on the thought process, teams can promote creative thinking.

FIGURE 8.3

Balancing Inquiry and Advocacy

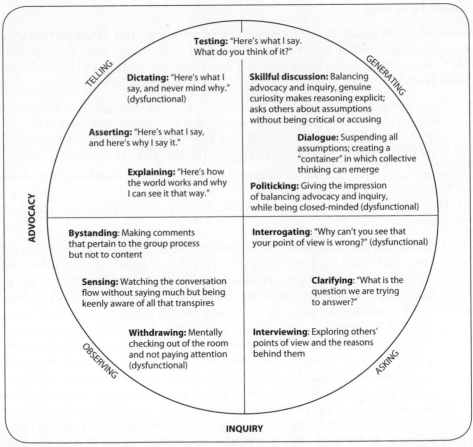

Source: From *The fifth discipline fieldbook*, by P. Senge, C. Roberts, R. Ross, B. Smith, and A. Kleiner, 1994, p. 254.

FIGURE 8.4

The Ladder of Inference

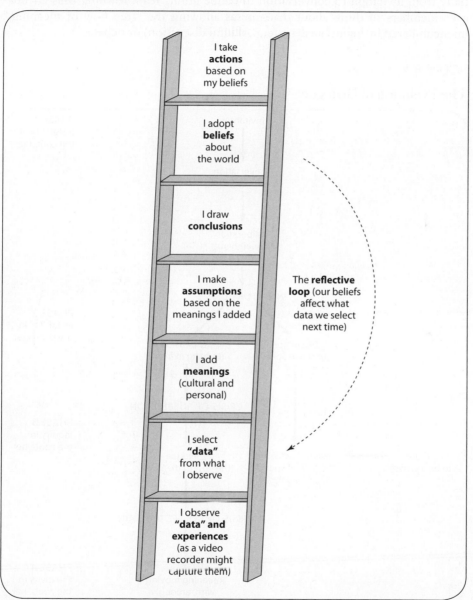

Source: From *The fifth discipline fieldbook*, by P. Senge, C. Roberts, R. Ross, B. Smith, and A. Kleiner, 1994, p. 361.

Dialogue is important to team learning. According to Senge and colleagues' (1994) model of the "evolution of dialogue" (Figure 8.5), team dialogue moves initially from invitation to conversation to deliberation. Team learning thus encourages members to think about dialogue as allowing the "free flow of meaning," unencumbered by logical analysis (e.g., skillful discussion) or debate.

FIGURE 8.5

The Evolution of Dialogue

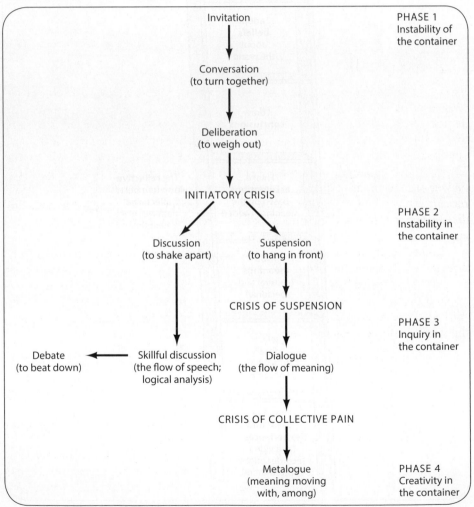

Source: From *The fifth discipline fieldbook,* by P. Senge, C. Roberts, R. Ross, B. Smith, and A. Kleiner, 1994, p. 361.

People from Western cultures may find it difficult to learn the speaking and listening skills associated with this type of dialogue because they may be accustomed to placing an advocacy and rational argument. In addition, a freer-flowing dialogue challenges many of the assumptions of traditional communication in organizations. In dialogue, the objective is not to argue a point effectively but to balance inquiry with advocacy in ways that contribute to the knowledge of the team as a whole. In the transition to a team-based approach, then, the organization's responsibilities extend beyond helping employees cope with the structural change. The organization must also help them learn new ways of communicating. This is a formidable challenge that requires a constant commitment to training and team learning.

☐ A Retreat from Teams?

Ideally, self-directed work teams help contemporary organizations deal with the pressures of global competition and help promote autonomy, responsibility, democracy, and empowerment in the workforce. In practice, however, the ideals of the team-based approach are not always realized by organizations. Employee engagement has remained stagnant in the United States since 2000, with about 32 percent of employees reporting that they feel engaged at work (Adkins, 2016). Newer organizations tend to fare better on this front, but many larger corporations remain reluctant to embrace new forms of organizing, horizontal structures, and diverse collaborations. For as much fanfare as team-based organizations receive, we appear to be retreating from teams in our everyday practices.

Indeed, managers sometimes resist the move to empower autonomous, self-directed work teams (Tjosvold & Tjosvold, 1991). For managers and supervisors, team-based organizing requires a fundamental change in their role, from operational expert or overseer to coach or facilitator. The ability to oversee an empowered work team has become an increasingly important leadership skill. It requires the supervisor overseeing a team to:

- act as a facilitator to keep the group on track while respecting a free exchange of ideas;
- be hard on rules, agendas, goals, and accountability but soft on the means by which the team chooses to organize itself and do its work;
- communicate extensively with others to keep the team informed of the work of other teams and of the organization as a whole; and
- be willing to admit that the team's ideas may be better than your own. For example, a nurse manager we know recalls her initial skepticism about a decision her team made, only to discover later that it was much better than what she had planned to do before receiving their input.

In one notable case, a small airline tried to implement self-directed work teams but found that the decision-making process was hindered by disagreements among team members. For example, the mechanics were frustrated by the unwillingness of other groups to defer to them on all safety issues. This company's experience reveals the importance of the following four factors in successful team formation:

1. Teams are only as good as their members; the careful selection of members is thus essential.
2. Teams must be trained in group decision making and communication.
3. Only decisions involving a significant challenge and an outcome that affects many people should be assigned to teams. Simple tasks with limited impact are best assigned to individuals.
4. Some members of a team have more expertise and experience than do other members; therefore, all members do not contribute equally.

At various times in the past, companies like Ford, Procter & Gamble, and Honda have found that teams take too long to make decisions and tend to shield their members from responsibility (Chandler & Ingrassia, 1991). Because team-based organizing really does represent a different, often foreign way of working, traditionally minded employees tend to view them with skepticism, at least initially. Their attitudes can change; if employees feel empowered by the team approach, they often become strong advocates. More often, however, management does not follow through on its promise of empowerment, and teams fail. Teams also fail when they believe that they haven't reached their goals or that their productivity hasn't been enhanced by teamwork (Coopman, 2001). Finally, teams fail when management neglects to define the types and functions of the teams it seeks to establish (Drucker, 1992). As a result, teams do not have a clear understanding of their function in the organization. A highly empowered, cross-functional team that does not receive strong leadership support is almost certain to fail.

COMMUNICATING IN NETWORKS

We observed earlier that contemporary organizational communication has shifted from an emphasis on face-to-face teams to virtual networks of people, across multiple locales, organized for a common purpose. Although networking has always been key to business success, specific **communication networks**—groups of individuals who communicate regularly—are a primary mode of organizing in the new economy. Networks are emergent, informal, and somewhat less interdependent than teams. Networks matter because regular contact between identifiable groups of people, whether scientists or political action groups, can play an important role in establishing access to information and in the quality and direction of decision making.

Within organizations, the concept of a network has emerged as a result of researchers' enduring interest in the structure of organizational groups. Human relations theorists recognized that small groups do much of the important work in organizations. Many factors affect the pattern of communication among members of these groups; these factors form the group's *communication structure*. For example, management may design a group in a way that hinders its communication, or employees with low status in a group (e.g., newcomers) may be less willing to communicate freely than those with high status. Formal lines of authority and rules about communication may also restrict the flow of information in a group. These investigations into communication structures have led to the idea of communication networks.

In this section, we examine communication networks in more detail, focusing on basic types of communication networks—including emergent communication networks and interorganizational communication networks—as well as strategies for analyzing them.

☐ Basic Types of Networks

Small-Group Communication Networks

Early research on communication structure focused on examining **small-group communication networks**—groups of five people—to determine the effects of centralized versus decentralized networks on decision making. Four types of small-group communication networks were typically studied: circle, wheel, chain, and all-channel (Figure 8.6). The circle and all-channel networks are highly decentralized, whereas the chain and wheel are centralized. It was found that centralized networks are more efficient than decentralized networks, as reflected in the speed with which they can complete a task (Leavitt, 1951). Further investigations, however, reveal that centralized networks are not necessarily superior to decentralized networks. Hierarchies can often impede the social support that is necessary for groups to enable participation and propose solutions (Scott, 1981).

However, many critics argued that the experimental small-group networks studied had little in common with actual groups in organizations (Farace et al., 1977). In fact, research interest has recently turned toward what have been dubbed "bona fide groups" in organizations, groups that really function "in the wild." Bona fide groups have real histories and come together to solve real organizational and

FIGURE 8.6

Small-Group Communication Networks

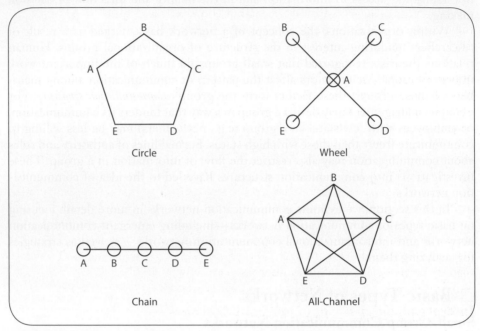

Source: From *Organizations: Rational, natural, and open systems,* by W. R. Scott, 1981, p. 8.

social problems. Early research suggests that these real embedded groups act in more contradictory and disorderly ways than were anticipated by laboratory studies (Sunwolf & Seibold, 1998).

Emergent Communication Networks

The most powerful groups within organizations are those that emerge from formal and informal communication among people who work together. These groups are referred to as **emergent communication networks**.

To study communication networks, researchers examine the relationships that emerge naturally within organizations as well as the groups and member roles associated with them (Rogers & Kincaid, 1981). Formal networks and emergent networks coexist in organizations, and each is best understood in the context of the other (Monge & Contractor, 2001; Monge & Eisenberg, 1987). For example, although new employees may rely on a copy of the formal organizational chart to understand reporting relationships and the structure of departments, over time they realize that the actual communication relationships among employees do not mirror the organizational chart. Departments with no formal connections may nonetheless communicate in order to manage the work flow, and salespeople working on different product lines may share common experiences at lunchtime. Identifying the discrepancies between informal emergent networks and the formal organizational chart can demonstrate a lot about an organization's culture.

Early research on emergent communication networks investigated the so-called organizational grapevine. The term *grapevine* dates to the Civil War, when telegraph wires strung through trees resembled grapevines (Daniels & Spiker, 1991). This term has since come to mean the persistent informal network in an organization, sometimes referred to disparagingly by management as the "rumor mill." In reality, the rumors are usually true, and important information travels quickest through informal channels. Building on American business executive and public administrator Chester Barnard's (1968) observations about the value of informal communication, Keith Davis (1953) argued against the standard party line, which encouraged managers to suppress the rumor mill. He instead supported the importance of such communication to the health of an organization, both as a source of information and for bolstering a sense of belonging. Subsequent research has shown that informal communication through the grapevine is as a rule more efficient and accurate than the formal dissemination of information (Hellweg, 1987).

Interorganizational Communication Networks

Employees communicate with coworkers within the organization as well as with customers, suppliers, and others in different organizations or institutions. In an advertising agency, for example, account managers interact with people from various newspapers and television stations, and in a university, the gifts and development staff communicates with alumni, accountants, attorneys, and local officials. In this way, communication networks cross organizational boundaries.

Interorganizational communication networks are the enduring transactions, flows, and linkages that occur among or between organizations. Such networks vary in terms of their openness, density, and interdependence. Tightly coupled or highly interdependent interorganizational networks are sensitive to environmental jolts that affect whole industries (e.g., in the deregulated airline industry, a minor change introduced by one carrier, such as reduced fares, significantly affects all others). At the other end of the spectrum, until recently physician's offices operated relatively independently in terms of their systems, schedules, and practices—health care more generally has been a loosely coupled system. But the advent of pervasive electronic medical records and greater financial transparency about billing practices may over time make everyone more closely connected.

Organizations participate in interorganizational communication networks in various ways. When one organization builds parts or provides services that another needs for its delivery of a product or service, the two organizations are said to be vertically integrated. For example, Pratt & Whitney manufactures aircraft engines for sale to Boeing. In contrast, when two companies' customers are passed from one to the other in the service cycle, they are said to be horizontally integrated. An example of this is the connections between a cancer-screening clinic, a hospital, and a hospice center. One of the reasons why Ashley Furniture is the world's leading furniture company is their complete vertical integration; their company performs all of the subprocesses required to design, build, and market their products.

Eisenberg and colleagues (1985) developed a typology of interorganizational communication that is useful in sorting out different kinds of linkages for the exchange of materials and information. There are three types of these linkages: institutional, representative, and personal. An institutional linkage occurs without human communication, as in the automatic transfer of data between companies. A representative linkage exists when people from various organizations meet to negotiate a contract, plan a joint venture, and the like. A personal linkage occurs when members of two organizations communicate privately.

However, it may be difficult to distinguish between personal and representative linkages when people meet informally without any intentions of discussing business but do discuss business with significant results. Types of linkages may also change over time; for example, two companies planning to engage in a joint venture may initially host luncheons or dinners intended to make people more comfortable with one another personally. Later, representatives may be identified to work out the details of the plan, part of which may include the automatic transfer of data between the organizations.

While interorganizational linkages can create significant connections between institutions, sometimes more formal alliances are worth pursuing. In the contemporary economic environment, organizations are most likely to turn to strategic alliances—such as mergers, acquisitions, and joint ventures—to enhance their financial status and political power. Most companies recognize that they need to narrow the scope of their services by coordinating their activities with those of other organizations. This need is especially pronounced in industries that are highly specialized but serve a population that seeks a range of integrated services. For example, strategic alliances are common among highly specialized health-care providers, as they respond to consumer and government pressures to better integrate care. Strategic alliances are also increasing in higher education where no single university can afford to offer a complete menu of programs. Similarly, high-technology organizations are investing in joint research and development ventures to cut costs and improve the collective work of scientists.

Interorganizational networks are pervasive in the nonprofit sector as well. Recently, in the wake of significant river flooding, researchers at the University of North Carolina cosponsored a workshop on the uses of interagency collaboration for protecting wildlife habitat and reducing flood losses in the Mississippi River basin. The participants represented a unique mix of federal, state, and local agencies and organizations, including the U.S. Department of Agriculture's Natural

Resources Conservation Service (NRCS) and the U.S. Fish and Wildlife Service (FWS), along with many local and state wetlands managers. In their report on the workshop, participants admit that while difficult, the advantages of collaboration are significant. They further emphasize the importance of "strengthening networks and opening lines of communication" in their future collaborative work.

Studies show the clear advantages for organizations of interorganizational participation. A study of 230 private colleges over a sixteen-year period showed that "well-connected" schools were better able to learn from and adapt to changing environmental conditions (Kraatz, 1998). A ten-year study of more than four hundred hospitals in California showed that hospitals were more likely to adopt service innovations when they were linked to peer institutions (Goes & Park, 1997). Finally, university scientists accustomed to working in isolation in their respective disciplines have increasingly entered into collaborative partnerships to do their work. At the University of South Florida, for example, engineers, physicists, and chemists colocated their laboratories to better support one another as they developed new materials for use in energy and health care. At the same time, they extended their collaboration to a leading research university in Saudi Arabia. The result has been the development of a new, efficient material for carbon capture (Nugent et al., 2013).

Although the potential benefits are clear, interorganizational communication networks can be difficult to manage. For example, scientists with allegiances to different organizations may be reluctant to share their best ideas with each other. Formal interorganizational alliances are risky because they require a good deal of trust, a willingness to give up autonomy, and the juxtaposition of potentially incompatible organizational cultures. Many mergers and acquisitions in recent years have been problematic because the organizational partners brought to the alliance different levels of formality and different attitudes toward employees. As such, the needs for interorganizational cooperation across organizational, industrial, and national boundaries will become greater.

☐ Analyses of Communication Networks

Analyses of communication networks examine the structure of informal, emergent communication in organizations, reflecting the tendency of individuals to forge new linkages that are separate from formal rules or boundaries. Informal communication in organizations is fluid and in a constant state of change. Whereas formal reorganizations may occur only infrequently, informal reorganizations occur continuously (Monge & Contractor, 2001). In studying emergent communication networks, we are concerned mainly with overall patterns of interaction, communication network roles, and the content of communication networks. Recent research on communication network analysis has begun to demonstrate a clear connection between understanding network patterns and organizational strategic effectiveness (Eisenberg, Johnson, & Pieterson, 2015).

Patterns of Interaction

A number of informal groups or cliques emerge as a result of communication among people in organizations, both within and across departments or functions. Communication networks vary widely in density, which is determined by dividing the number of communication links (reported communication contacts) that exist among all organizational members by the number of possible links if everyone knew everyone else. For example, a professional association is a low-density network because communication among its members is infrequent, but the kitchen crew of a restaurant is a high-density network in which most or all members communicate regularly with one another. Similarly, formal hierarchies are less dense than more progressive organizations that encourage employee participation in decision making.

Research suggests that the density of organizational networks has considerable influence over whether other employees adopt a new idea or technology. In a study of elementary schools and administrations, it was found that denser networks of personal relationships play a key role in the development and acceptance of new ideas when cliques form to focus on those ideas (Albrecht & Hall, 1991). These close connections help people overcome feelings of uncertainty and make them more likely to adapt to change.

The density of an organizational communication network can have some less obvious implications for organizational effectiveness. For example, we get less new information from people we work with every day than we do from people we know but contact less often. These infrequent contacts, called *weak ties*, can be very helpful for uncovering new perspectives and helpful people, as often happens in job hunting or recruiting (Granovetter, 1973). More recent research reveals that these same dynamics may apply globally; people in all cultures make use of their personal and professional networks in seeking new opportunities (Gao, 2006).

Some researchers use what they call a "network approach to participation" to redefine empowerment (Marshall & Stohl, 1993). According to this view, empowerment is a "process of developing key relationships in the organization in order to gain greater control over one's organizational life" (p. 141). An employee's personal communication network affects the experience of empowerment, involvement, and participation at work.

Extraorganizational networks—contacts from the industry or community—may be particularly important resources for employees in historically marginalized groups who have difficulty finding mentors and other supports in positions of power within the organizations (see *Everyday Organizational Communication* on page 259). For example, among African American women, networking and building informal coalitions and communities with other African Americans within and outside their employing organization is a key strategy for upward mobility (Bell & Nkomo, 2001; Parker, 2003). Such networks serve as a means of maintaining a "collective identity" even "as they ascend the corporation with what might otherwise become an individualistic

EVERYDAY ORGANIZATIONAL COMMUNICATION

Networking on Campus: Communication, Identity, and Empowerment

As research by communication scholars Elizabeth Bell and Stella Nkomo (2001) and Patricia Parker (2003) indicates, extraorganizational networks benefit historically marginalized groups by providing mentors and support as well as a "collective identity" in professional settings. But such networking opportunities can begin even before entering into a profession. Most colleges and universities, for example, have developed identity-based groups—from lesbian, gay, bisexual, transgendered, and queer (LGBTQ) coalitions to the Muslim Students Association—to provide students with a space in which to congregate, share resources, and network with other students, faculty members, and professionals both on and off campus.

For example, at our home campus (Arizona State University), the Hispanic Business Students Association (HBSA) defines its mission as follows: "The mission of the Hispanic Business Students Association is to prepare our members to be future leaders, serve our communities, promote diversity and create a progressive learning environment" (HBSA, 2013). To achieve its goals, HBSA sets out clear objectives, such as increasing the number of Hispanic students receiving a professional degree, developing leadership and business skills among Hispanic students regardless of college major, utilizing technology as a form of communication and education, promoting Hispanic culture, and providing interaction among all students at the university (HBSA, 2013). As such, the organization provides numerous opportunities for networking with alumni as well as corporate sponsors, allowing students to meet potential mentors and future employers and learn more about their professional options after graduation. In addition, the organization stresses volunteerism and encourages members to give back to their community.

DISCUSSION QUESTIONS

Consider what you have read about networks, as well as your own experience with networking on campus, and answer the following questions.

1. Are you a member of a student organization dedicated to the support and empowerment of a particular group, whether social, cultural, religious, or even major-based (e.g., English or business honor society)? If you are not, visit your university's website and take a look at the variety of organizations available, or speak with a friend who is an active member of such an organization.

(continued, Networking on Campus)

2. If you are a member, describe why your organization exists. In other words, what are the conditions, within the university and beyond, that encouraged your group to form?
3. What are your organization's goals? How does your organization work to achieve those goals? Do you anticipate that you will need a group like this once you leave the university? If so, why?
4. How does your group help you network and form ties with other students, faculty members, or outside professionals who support the organization's goals? How have you benefited from such opportunities? How might you benefit from such networking in the future?

quest for success" (Bell & Nkomo, 2001, p. 183). That such networks often maintain an explicit attention to empowerment is evidenced by a gathering of African American members of corporate boards of directors, a group that is still woefully small in number. At that meeting, directors were reminded of their obligation to continue to bring up issues of diversity in their board meetings; otherwise, issues of diversity, inclusion, and empowerment are not likely to be part of the boards' conversations. One member of the group commented, "This is a group of African Americans whom CEOs listen to. That's why developing this network is so important" (Cora, 2004, p. 43).

Communication Network Roles

Communication network roles—or the location individuals occupy in the flow of interaction—affect employees' experience of work and their degree of influence on others. Well-connected individuals in an organization tend to be the most influential and the least likely to leave (Brass, 1984). Four types of communication roles occur in networks: the isolate, group member, bridge, and liaison. *Isolates* have little contact with others in the organization; they work alone either by choice or because their jobs require them to be structurally or geographically isolated from other employees (e.g., salespeople or service technicians who travel constantly). *Group members* communicate mainly within an informal clique, which may at times involve communication with a departmental, professional, or demographic grouping (e.g., an accounts receivable specialist or a member of an advertising team). *Bridges* (who are also group members) have significant communication contact with at least one member of another informal group (e.g., a human resources representative dedicated to serving a particular department), and *liaisons* have connections with two or more cliques but are not exclusive members of any one group (e.g., mediators or facilitators who are not themselves part of a team; some senior managers specializing in cross-functional initiatives like quality or strategy).

Within organizations, liaisons can be the dominant interpreters of the organizational culture. As key communicators with tremendous influence on the direction of the company, they are able to transform any message into an interpretation that is consistent with their beliefs and to pass that interpretation quickly throughout the company (and at times to customers and the community). When organizational improvement efforts fail, it is very often a result of the improper mobilization of liaisons.

While we often think of networking as a means to develop and exploit one's connections for personal gain, for some these networks are necessary strategies for balancing work and family concerns. African American women have historically formed communities of "other mothers" who helped one another care for children and families. In contemporary culture, poor, working-class African American women continue to develop networks in which they often act as "border guards" who bridge boundaries between work and family, home and street. "In their roles as border guards, these women employed collective forms of empowerment that included shared resources among families trying to keep their children and homes safe in neighborhoods riddled with violence and drug use" (Parker, 2003, p. 268). Networks are clearly instrumental both within and outside organizational life.

Any attempt to analyze communication network roles in an organization may be a sensitive issue for employees, who do not always perceive their degree of communication contact with others in the same way. For example, a subordinate might report having regular contact with a superior, whereas the superior may claim to have no communication with the subordinate. Differences in status or perception may also cause employees to respond in ways that reflect not actual, but expected communication roles, reporting contact only with people they think they *ought* to communicate with at work. In addition, employees may be reluctant to participate in a network analysis because the results may reflect negatively on them. For example, in our analysis of network roles in a professional association, a department head who was identified by his subordinates as an isolate was subsequently dismissed from the organization. Consequently, it is critically important to collect and handle network analysis data with an awareness of the political implications of various findings. Network structures should not be shared with top management or the public without first considering the possible impact on employees who participated in the study.

Content of Communication Networks

Emergent communication networks develop around specific topics, or content areas, of communication (Farace et al., 1977). Each content area is regarded as defining a separate network; for example, a bank may have a social network for communication about personal matters and a task network for discussion of work duties. An isolate in one network may be a bridge or a group member in another. We all know people who are "well connected" when it comes to gossip but much less so with regard to business updates and company strategy.

Moreover, the identification of multiple types of communication content contributes to our understanding of the relationships between people in networks. For example, two people who communicate only about work are said to have a uniplex relationship, whereas people who communicate about two or more topics—say, personal issues, task issues, and new ideas—are said to have a multiplex relationship. Multiplex linkages have been identified as significant sources of social support and organizational innovation (Albrecht & Hall, 1991; Ray, 1987).

The content of communication networks takes on added significance when we consider it in terms of the sense-making process. In an attempt to extend the cultural approach to organizations, Peter Monge and Eric Eisenberg (1987) suggested that analysis of "semantic" networks (in which people hold similar interpretations of key organizational symbols or events) may be useful. The same network measures may be applied (e.g., isolate, group member, bridge, and liaison), in this case, however, they would refer not to the presence or absence of communication, but to overlapping interpretations of key cultural symbols.

Individuals who are in the mainstream with regard to employee values and beliefs would be group members; those holding radically different interpretations would be isolates. Measures of network density would also apply. In a dense semantic network, for example, there is shared meaning about major organizational issues. This approach has been successfully applied to the analysis of perceptions of organizational missions and value statements (Contractor, Eisenberg, & Monge, 1992; Peterson, 1995).

TEAMS, NETWORKS, AND NEW FORMS OF ORGANIZING

Building effective and empowered teams is a daunting task. Organizations must balance a variety of resources and needs, from clearly defined roles to technology to cultural diversity. In this final section, we look at the innovative and creative potential of teams and networks as a new form of organizing. We consider the growing importance of technology in organizations as a key communication resource for teams. Additionally, we look to new models of positive collaboration and creativity in organizations as a way to illustrate some future directions in team-based research.

☐ Technological Resources for Teams and Networks

In the 1950s and 1960s, organizational researchers emphasized the importance of face-to-face communication between supervisors and employees and among coworkers. Although face-to-face interaction is still important in today's organizations, advances in communication technology—from e-mail to texting to Skype—have overcome some of the limits of face-to-face interaction, especially those associated with speed, geographic distance, and processing capacity. As a result, contemporary organizations can no longer function effectively without the extensive use of communication technology. Furthermore, implementing a new technology significantly affects work processes, employees' productivity and work life, and the character of interpersonal and power relationships.

Learning New Technologies

In his novel *Ready Player One*, author Ernest Cline writes of a not-so-distant future where almost all human interaction takes place in a virtual world called OASIS. People log into OASIS to work, play, and even watch movies with their friends. Using specialized headgear, haptic gloves, and even smell sensors, users can simulate the material world almost seamlessly. This doesn't yet describe the world we live in, but technology has certainly become a pervasive and expansive part of organizational life. As such, classification of web-based technologies has expanded over the years; scholars and practitioners now identify four distinct categories. Initially, we had Web 1.0, which focused on the first phases of the Internet, including websites with hyperlinked materials. Web 2.0 was first coined in 1999 and brought into the mix social media sites, blogs, and other platforms that allow for user-generated content. In 2006, the category of Web 3.0 became part of our vocabulary, bringing with it a variety of apps, software, and technologies that helped users organize content and anticipate interests—almost like a personal assistant. Finally, *PC World* announced recently that Web 4.0 is upon us, and with it more communication technologies that bridge computers and humans—perhaps Cline's fictitious OASIS is not so distant, after all.

Communication technologies have become a key resource for basic teams and an absolute necessity for virtual and community-engaged teams (LeGreco, Leonard, & Ferrier, 2012). Two broad categories of communication technology for teamwork are available to organizations:

1. **Computer-assisted communication technologies** include the various methods of text, voice, and image transmission, including fax, videoconferencing, e-mail, voice mail, the Internet, and smartphones. These are widely used both within organizations and among customers and suppliers as part of the massive development of global e-commerce.
2. **Computer-assisted decision-aiding technologies** include online management information systems, group decision support systems, information-retrieval database systems, augmented reality software, and expert systems or programs that provide technical information. Traditionally used as tools internal to the organization, these technologies are now offered to customers as well.

Computer-assisted communication technologies are designed to enhance the speed of communication as well as the ability of people to communicate regardless of their geographic location. Most college students have experience with instant messaging (IM) as well as other forms of text messaging (SMS, MMS) that can be sent and received worldwide by computers, cell phones, and other devices. Text messaging has even developed its own vocabulary, an extension of the abbreviation process that began with e-mail. That vocabulary has moved into the nonverbal realm with the increased use of ideograms or emoticons, such as smiley, sad, surprised, bored, winking, or angry faces. Other popular computer-assisted communication technologies include voice mail, voice messaging, audio conferencing, and a host of smartphone applications. These technologies are so accessible and addictive that business meetings have routinely been disrupted by their overuse. In addition, health professionals report an increase in chronic hand injuries as a result of the proliferation of handheld communication devices.

Computer-assisted decision-aiding technologies are designed primarily to provide easy access to hard-to-find information needed to make decisions. For example, a company may use market data accessed via an external database to decide whether it should introduce a new product. Internally, a sales manager may access information about last quarter's sales to decide whether the company's salespeople would benefit from a proposed training program. Information on virtually any topic is available online, and augmented reality software (such as Layar) can instantly access this information. At present, systems that support decision making but leave final decisions to the user are more successful than systems that substitute computer decisions for human decisions or that significantly curtail the user's freedom of action.

An especially useful decision-aiding program is the search engine that permits computer users to direct a search for information based on their personal preferences. For instance, search engines have been developed that work off user information about vacation preferences (e.g., location, price range, and other preferences) to help users shop for and book a trip (e.g., Travelocity, Kayak, Hotwire, Orbitz). These search utility tools significantly extend consumer reach by searching obscure and hard-to-find sources of information.

Mediated Interpersonal Communication

With the widespread use of telephones, computers, and overnight delivery services, many interpersonal work relationships are routinely conducted by people who never meet face-to-face. The result is a new hybrid of social relationships that we call **mediated interpersonal communication**. At the core of mediated interpersonal communication is the need to manage knowledge, share and retrieve documents, and collaborate across a variety of local and global settings. These needs are especially important for virtual teams and interorganizational networks, many of which attempt to bring together members from multiple locations for routine interactions. One of these interactions, file sharing, has become a particularly smooth process with the growing popularity of platforms like Google Drive and Dropbox. Thanks to the proliferation of "cloud" technologies and support systems, these platforms even allow multiple people to edit a single document simultaneously from remote locations.

Similar patterns of mediated communication are found in many U.S. companies, where brick-and-mortar offices are being replaced by virtual ones (Gephart, 2002). A virtual office, with most of the usual functions of an office, can be located literally anywhere the user can gain access to a high-speed or wireless Internet connection. (Judging by our informal survey of local Starbucks coffeehouses, many people are using them as mobile offices.) The productivity of distributed workers in a virtual office can be up to 20 percent higher than that of office-based, nondistributed workers. Distributed workers also tend to experience less job-related stress (Grantham, 1999).

As workers become more distributed, more organizational members are transitioning to what has been called "nomadic" work (Bean & Eisenberg, 2006), encountering an array of challenges and opportunities along the way. For example, Dropbox users have experienced a number of data breaches and "glitches" that put information and data at risk. In 2014, computer hackers claimed to have held seven million Dropbox usernames and passwords for ransom; prior to that, Dropbox users learned that their files were being catalogued by search engines. These breaches raise serious questions for teams engaging in virtual work, particularly when it comes to protecting data, ideas, and intellectual property. At the same time, these are risks that many users are willing to take, especially because of the perceived benefits and opportunities afforded by the ability to work wherever and whenever they like.

As the logistical problems involving collaborative media and file transfer continue to be resolved, we can more productively turn our attention to the effect of such arrangements on social relationships and organizational culture. Research on e-mail use reveals the tendency of users to feel less inhibited online and to say things that they would not in a face-to-face encounter. One would expect a similar dynamic to surface in distributed work. At the same time, the potential for outrageous emotional displays may be somewhat modulated by the increase in electronic surveillance (discussed in Chapter 6). As nearly everyone who works for a living comes to appreciate that their electronic communication is open to public scrutiny, we may see norms develop that encourage less, not more, intense disclosure.

The Digital Networked Society

Within only a few years, our understanding of what constitutes a network has changed considerably, from the connections among people within a single organization—such as a hospital, manufacturing plant, or school—to the connections among people in a global society. During this short time, we have seen tremendous growth both in network marketing and in computer networks on the Internet.

Global communication networks have been transformed by instantaneous online communication. Significant changes in communication behaviors have been noted, especially in information seeking and relational development. For example, computer users post questions on Internet forums and receive responses within seconds from people around the world. In search of meaningful relationships, millions of computer users participate in virtual gathering places (currently dominated by Facebook), provide continual updates on their activities (e.g., Twitter, Reddit), and stay in touch with a vast number of contacts who may or may not be properly classified as "friends."

Some critics mourn the demise of local communities, whereas others envision an electronic global village that provides people with instantaneous access to information and other people worldwide. Even terrorist organizations have turned to online communication as a means of recruiting and staying connected with new members—with potentially disastrous consequences (Corman et al., 2008).

The explosion in online communication technology is changing every aspect of how we live, and the increasing power and capabilities of smartphones mean that we live a nearly constantly connected life. That said, the mere existence of these connections says little about their quality. Just as research on multitasking shows a general degradation in the quality of work given distributed effort, greater amounts of connectivity may not indicate greater levels of collaboration or meaningful communication. Moreover, greater connectivity greatly increases the vulnerability of systems and networks, which are only as strong as their weakest component. For example, a security breach in Java software provided a back door for hackers to attack any system on which the software was installed. Tightly connected systems are easier to defeat than loose, distributed ones, because a blow to one part can affect the whole. Similarly, dense communication networks can be sites of significant diversity of opinion but also of groupthink, as members police each other's postings and "defriend" those who feel differently. Much more research is needed for us to develop a more fine-grained understanding of the possibilities and problems associated with the unprecedented ease of instantaneous global communication.

From an organizational perspective, new communication technologies in general and social media in particular can appear to be disruptive technologies that challenge traditional business models (Christensen, 2011). For example, in the education and health-care industries, information technology is now the leading driver of change. In higher education, an explosion in access to free online education (largely through massive open online courses, or MOOCs) is both creating unprecedented educational opportunities worldwide and challenging the control that colleges and universities have over the granting of degrees and other forms of certification (Skorton & Altschuler, 2013). In health care, the evolution of sophisticated electronic health record systems could provide real coordination of care and lead to greater control for individuals over their health information. In both cases, technology with the potential to create new levels of connectivity is presenting a major threat to traditional industry models and assumptions.

In both of these examples—and in many other industries—it is instructive to remember that the mere existence of these technologies does not in and of itself result in greater transparency, collaboration, or engagement. That kind of measurable improvement can still be elusive: A number of research and consulting groups have developed recently that seek to define the conditions under which digital, social, and mobile media are most likely to be successful (e.g., the Altimeter Group). Common to all of the consultants' recommendations is the idea that the technical integration of communication media continues to get easier, while many of the cultural and interpersonal issues surrounding the uses of technology remain unresolved. There is significant research yet to be done in this area, including, for example, the effect of smartphones on intimate relationships and the influence of Skype on the effectiveness of job interviews and meetings.

☐ Creativity and Constraint in Teams and Networks

The role of technology in organizations receives a great deal of attention for its potential to facilitate new forms of organizing and working in teams and networks. At the same time, we have not exhausted the potential of face-to-face and other hybrid forms of communication when it comes to innovative organizing. Before we bring this chapter to a close, we must consider how creativity is balanced with constraint when communicating across teams and networks. We focus on both positive collaboration as well as efforts to spark creativity in team-based work.

Positive Collaboration

Much of what we have said about effective teamwork in particular also applies to collaboration in general. Regardless of whether they are formal team members, some people have trouble appreciating ideas that originate from a different worldview, while at the same time they hesitate to share their own good ideas for fear of losing credit or control. Meaningful collaboration is rooted in what many organizational and health communication scholars have begun to call positive organizational scholarship (Lutgen-Sandvik, Riforgiate, & Fletcher, 2011; Tracy & Huffman, 2014). Extending from the work of Julien Mirivel (2014), positive communication draws from both interpersonal theory and leadership techniques to inspire influence. It involves a variety of communication concepts including compassion, gratitude, and social support.

Mirivel's model highlights six interrelated strategies that can be applied to positive team collaboration:

1. Create — *greet* each other to create human contact.
2. Discover — *ask* questions to discover the unknown.
3. Affect — *complement* each other to affect our sense of self.
4. Deepen — *disclose* to build deeper relationships.
5. Give — *encourage* each other to show support.
6. Transcend — *listen* to transcend differences.

These strategies create the conditions that allow positive collaboration to emerge in team settings. But they are not strategies that are unique to organizations and teams. In extending Mirivel's model to organizational settings, some additional considerations must be made.

First, fostering collaboration begins with the articulation of a common goal, something that diverse individuals and groups can agree on as a shared aspiration (Lencioni, 2002). In large organizations, it is especially important that the senior leadership team model collaboration for the organization. Next, both training programs and incentives must be aligned to support leaders who simultaneously aspire to excel in their own area *and* seek out opportunities for successful collaborations with others outside their unit. Hansen (2009) calls this balanced approach "T-shaped management." Finally, individual leaders must engage in sustained self-reflection to identify personal barriers to collaborative leadership. Many of these barriers can be overcome by a willingness to learn by engaging others in dialogue.

Concentrated Creativity

Team-based organizations face the challenges of balancing creativity and constraint in group relationships and of productively dealing with diverse interpretations. The members of a newly formed team are typically anxious about their role, and they struggle to find a voice for themselves in the context of the group. This can be a formidable challenge during the orientation phase of a team's development.

During the conflict and emergence stages, members attempt to creatively articulate their perceptions, but their efforts are heavily weighted with constraints (e.g., "We tried that, and it didn't work" or "Management will never take our proposal seriously"). Other constraints can be useful in promoting team effectiveness, such as meeting times and places, agendas, and problem-solving procedures. In general, however, team members' ability to function as a group depends on their skill in balancing the creative contributions of individual members with the constraints imposed by the group as a whole.

The key to this balance is to harness a team's creativity in ways that allow the team to act effectively and meaningfully for each other and the larger organization (Harvey, 2014; Lee & Lee, 2015). Although many artists will tell you that one cannot rush the creative process, a common critique of teams is that they take too long to act. As such, some companies and community groups have begun experimenting with new forms of organizing that treat creativity in a more concentrated fashion.

For example, several communities have begun organizing events called hackathons. Dating back to 1999, hackathons emerged from the world of computer programming, where *hack* also means "exploratory programming," not just a computer crime. Hackathons are intense periods of collaboration, bringing together computer programmers, software and app designers, community members, graphic designers, and others to develop tech-based solutions to community-identified problems. Most hackathons follow a fairly standard format, with community members presenting problems and topics (e.g., food insecurity or lack of public transportation) to frame the "hack," followed by the formation of groups based on skill set and expertise, structured time to collaborate and receive feedback from event organizers, and final presentations where teams share their creations with their fellow hackers. Hackathons condense team-based projects into short periods of time, lasting anywhere from one day to a long weekend, with teams working around the clock to make their contributions.

There is something to be said about bringing people together, in the same room, for periods of concentrated creativity. Composer, actor, and MacArthur genius Lin-Manuel Miranda realized this when he organized the cast recording for his Tony Award–winning musical *In the Heights*. Whereas most cast albums are recorded with cast members in isolated booths in separate rooms, Miranda felt that *In the Heights* presented a unique case. The musical focuses on the Washington Heights neighborhood of New York City and has a distinct community and collaborative feel to it. Recording everyone separately would have somehow felt artificial, so Miranda set up multiple recording booths in a single room. Each booth was partitioned off by Plexiglas windows, so cast members could still see and interact with each other while their audio was captured clearly for the record. The ability to see and interact with each other allowed for a much richer experience for the *In the Heights* team, as well as a much more lively and engaged cast album that captured the spirit of the musical.

New forms of organizing teams and networks—like positive collaboration and concentrated creativity—can become notable for the speed at which they diffuse creative new ideas among large groups of people. Mostly independent of the usual constraints, such as formal positions and hierarchy, informal communication networks encourage innovation and collaboration. Nevertheless, even a concentrated creative process still requires at least some structure and set of practices that give shape and form to future interactions.

SUMMARY

Collaboration between and among employees and managers can occur in various ways and to varying degrees; employee participation in decision making is both natural and desirable. The ideal of a democratic workplace describes a situation in which organizations concern themselves with the interests of many different individuals and groups (not just the stockholders). The multiple-stakeholder model and a focus on employee engagement promote the type of participation necessary to achieve this ideal.

Teams and networks are now common organizational forms for collaborative work. The drive to organize in such a manner comes from the realization that no single individual—or pair of individuals—is sufficient to achieve complex goals. In team-based organizations, employees from a variety of organizational functions serve as members of one or more working groups. These employees might work on one of several different types of teams, such as project teams that help coordinate the successful completion of a particular project; work teams that are responsible for a "whole" work process that delivers a product or service to a customer; quality-improvement teams that meet to improve customer satisfaction, evaluate and improve team performance, and reduce costs; and virtual teams that achieve goals and complete tasks across time and space. All types of teams, however, grow through five essential communicative elements: roles, norms, decision-making processes, management of conflict and consensus, and cultural diversity. Positive collaboration can be achieved through the development of shared goals and a disciplined approach to balancing individual achievement with the need to reach out to others.

Communication networks, or groups of individuals who share regular lines of communication, have emerged as a primary mode of organizing in the new economy. Networks are emergent, informal, and somewhat less interdependent than teams. They matter because regular contact between identifiable groups of people (e.g., scientists or political action groups) can play an important role in accessing information and in the quality and direction of decision making. In organizations, types of small-group networks include circle, wheel, chain, and all-channel. The more powerful emergent types of networks (grapevines, cliques, and loosely coupled networks) emerge from formal and informal communication among people in organizations. Interorganizational types of networks include institutional, representative, and personal linkages. Network communication is affected by patterns of interaction, communication network roles, and the content of communication networks.

Thanks in large part to advances in computer networks and online technology, our understanding of what constitutes a network has changed considerably. What was once a connection among people within a single organization is now a connection among people in an entirely global society. As advances in technology continue to expand, especially the growth of mobile media and social media sites like Facebook, we will see additional significant changes in communication behaviors, particularly in the areas of information seeking and relational development.

Questions for Review and Discussion

1. What is meant by employee participation in decision making?

2. What is Stan Deetz's ideal for democracy in the workplace? How does the multiple-stakeholder model challenge accepted ideas about effective organizational communication?

3. What are the benefits associated with an organization's attempts to increase levels of employee engagement? What would be the main challenges to doing so?

4. List and explain the types of teams used in today's organizations. What are the advantages and disadvantages of taking a team-based approach to organizing?

5. What unique challenges are associated with virtual and community-engaged teams?

6. What is a communication role on a team? What types of roles are available to team members? Discuss the advantages and disadvantages of using a diverse array of roles in a team-based situation.

7. What are communication networks? What characteristics do communication networks share with organizational teams? How does a communication network differ from a team?

8. What are some examples of prominent interorganizational networks in your local community?

9. How do new network forms affect the way an organization thinks about growth and expansion? What effect does this new way of thinking have on the nature and challenge of competition between organizations?

10. What impact does the explosion of mobile technology and social media have on organizational communication? Does it make dialogue more or less likely?

KEY TERMS

Communication network, p. 252
Communication network role, p. 260
Communication role, p. 241
Community-engaged team, p. 239
Computer-assisted communication technologies, p. 263
Computer-assisted decision-aiding technologies, p. 263
Conflict, p. 244
Consensus, p. 245
Emergent communication network, p. 254
Employee engagement, p. 231
Extraorganizational network, p. 258
Facilitator role, p. 242
Groupthink, p. 243
Interorganizational communication network, p. 255

Maintenance role, p. 241
Mediated interpersonal communication, p. 264
Multiple-stakeholder model, p. 230
Norm, p. 242
Prince role, p. 242
Project team, p. 234
Quality-improvement team, p. 235
Self-centered role, p. 241
Small-group communication network, p. 253
Task role, p. 241
Team, p. 233
Team-based organization, p. 233
Team learning, p. 247
Virtual team, p. 238
Work team, p. 234

CASE STUDY 1

Spellman Gardens

Jean and John Spellman are former bank executives living in Seattle, Washington. Although they were employed by different banks, both banks became insolvent in the 2008 credit crisis, causing the Spellmans to reconsider their options in a hurry. In a courageous move based in part on Jean's farm background, they decided to start a small business whose mission is to provide all of the seeds and equipment needed for home vegetable gardens. Their thinking at the time was that in a down economy, people would once again be attracted to the idea of growing at least some of their own food.

Their bet paid off almost immediately. Sales of seeds and garden tools increased rapidly, fueled entirely through word of mouth and Internet advertising. It was the classic case of "the right idea at the right time."

But even overnight successes have their challenges. Orders came in so quickly that even though the couple put all of their friends and family to work filling them, they still lagged behind. Their biggest fear was that they would develop a reputation for being slow to fill orders, which they knew would be the kiss of death for today's consumer. Grudgingly, John realized that they would have to put some more organization around their labor of love if it were to succeed.

In March 2009, Spellman Gardens had twelve employees, but the Spellmans expect to need more than forty by the end of the year. Both Jean and John enjoy the informal, family feeling of their start-up company, but when they contemplate adding dozens more employees, their imaginations quickly go to their bank experiences, complete with reporting levels and defined departments. They have a gut feeling that it won't work to recreate a bank structure in their small business, but they are less sure about the alternatives. What kind of structure would be most likely to allow their fledgling but successful business to grow?

Assignment

1. What should the Spellmans do to hold on to the informality they enjoy about their new business? What should they definitely not do? Why?
2. What lessons, if any, should they take from their banking experience in developing a structure that will grow their new company?
3. What would it look like if they adopted a team-based structure for their growing company? What kinds of teams should they form, and how should they be organized and led?
4. What role, if any, should communication technology play in their growth and staffing plans? Should they try to keep all employees based in Seattle, or might there be advantages to building a broader network of employees?

CASE STUDY II

The Networked Community

BACKGROUND

Founded in 1913, Fleeberville is an average American city of 1.5 million people with typical urban problems. The city is located on a large, spring-fed lake in a mountain setting just north of Atlanta, Georgia. Industrial pollution has become a serious problem over the years. Traffic on the two major highways gets worse every year, as does the rate of violent crime. The software companies that dominate the local economy are downsizing, and the remaining jobs require extensive technical expertise. The result has been an expanding underclass, much of which has been forced to seek public assistance. People with resources have increasingly isolated themselves from the city as a whole, and gated communities and private schools grow more numerous each year. Meanwhile, basic city services and public schools are in decline.

ASSIGNMENT

Imagine that you are an activist, community organizer, and communication expert who has recently decided to make Fleeberville your permanent home. You intend to put down roots, start a career, get married, and raise children there. However, for many reasons, you feel that the city must embark on a path of self-renewal.

You observe that many citizens seem to care about the city, but isolated efforts to improve things (e.g., clean up the lake, clothe the homeless, and sponsor a school) don't appear to be very effective. Knowing what you do about systems, teams, networks, and organizing, how would you approach the problem of making Fleeberville a better place to live?

1. What actions would you begin with, and whom would you contact for help?
2. What patterns of communication would you encourage, and how should they change over time?
3. How would you deal with existing groups of people who feel uniquely responsible for determining the future direction of the city?
4. What teams and networks would you build to promote such a massive effort, and how would you prepare these groups for the challenges?
5. How would you evaluate the success of your efforts?

CHAPTER 9

Communicating
Leadership

In an essay for the international journal *Leadership*, organizational scholars David Collinson and Keith Grint (2005) write,

> Since the 1940s there has been an enormous outpouring of writing on leadership. Yet, there is little consensus on what counts as leadership, whether it can be taught, or even how effective it might be. . . . Leadership "research" has frequently been at best fragmented and at worst trivial, too often informed by the rather superficial ideas of management and academic consultants keen to peddle the latest, pre-packaged list of essential qualities deemed necessary for individual leaders and as the prescribed solution to all leadership dilemmas. (p. 5)

Despite this pessimistic assessment of the history of leadership research as well as the "best practices" models offered by leadership consultants, interest in articulating new ways of thinking about leadership continues to grow, and the stakes for finding and training effective leaders worldwide have never been higher. Failures in leadership span the globe and punctuate our present era. They include the various financial debacles of the late twentieth and early twenty-first centuries and the failures of political leaders in the United States and in some European countries to address fiscal and environmental challenges in a deliberate and planful fashion.

In this chapter, we will provide some ideas about leadership drawn from both traditional and more contemporary sources. Newer thinking in particular provides opportunities to demonstrate that in essence leadership *is* communication. To guide us in our examination, we will honor the advances made in leadership research over the last century. We do so because without understanding this history, we risk abandoning some useful insights that continue to serve us well. From that traditional foundation we move on to more innovative ways of thinking about leadership as communication and sense making, featuring the powerful role of narrative in shaping individual and collective identity and propelling organized action.

◨ LAYING THE FOUNDATION: USEFUL INSIGHTS FROM PRIOR LEADERSHIP THEORIES

In this section, we detail trait leadership, leadership style, situational leadership, transformational leadership, and discursive leadership. We explore the implications of each approach for communication, along with its limitations.

☐ Trait Leadership

Trait theory is one of the earliest attempts to fashion a theory of leadership. It focused entirely on an individual's physical and social attributes. From the oral histories of the Peloponnesian Wars (circa fifth century BCE) that chronicled the feats of warriors and goddesses to the profiling of more contemporary political leaders, religious leaders, and sports heroes, we remain fascinated by the physical and behavioral characteristics of those who attain greatness or infamy. What makes them unique?

Management researchers and theorists from the 1930s through the mid-1950s drew heavily on trait models to formulate the first profiles of great business leaders. Rather uncritically, these efforts reflected the biases of the European cultures that generated them, so the traits of recognized leaders tended to be those of tall, blond, white males from upper-class or upper-middle-class families. In the aftermath of Hitler's rise to power in pre–World War II Germany (which emphasized the purported superiority of the white Aryan nation), the trait approach lost much of its appeal. Nonetheless, traits associated with great leaders (and great sports heroes) still capture the public imagination and influence decision making. Candidates for the U.S. presidency, for example, are still expected to "look like leaders," which, at a minimum, means being fit, tall, well groomed, and physically attractive.

For scholars who understand the appeal of visual culture and its reliance on a commodity-based form of capitalism, the appeal of trait theories of leadership transfers easily to traits associated with celebrity and popular culture stardom. In a striking critique, *New York Times* columnist Maureen Dowd (2005)—exasperated by the fact that so many of the younger women she comes in contact with look alike, have the same hairstyles, wear the same fashions, and express themselves in a very similar celebrity-speak manner—commented that the triumph of feminine sameness is also the death of the feminist ideal. But this one-size-fits-all "picture of perfection" doesn't stop with fashion or even with plastic surgery. In a study of flight attendants, organizational scholar Alexandra Murphy (1998) points out that physical traits are still used in the selection, promotion, and retention of workers in the airline industry, particularly with regard to female employees. Drew Whitelegg (2005) further develops the argument that flight attendant work is simultaneously liberating and constraining, affording a wide range of experiences but at the cost of tiring, disorienting work and constant self-monitoring. In a related study, Angela Trethewey (1999a) discusses the "disciplining" of the female body in the workplace more generally and provides an analysis of how appearances at work are signs of power, authority, and privilege. Disciplining refers to the often-unspoken expectation that women will go to great lengths to monitor their appearance to meet what they perceive to be expected standards of employment.

One insight we can gain from the trait approach to leadership is that physical attractiveness is a key component—and an enduring one—of effective leadership. This reality was dramatically revealed decades ago when those who listened to the Kennedy-Nixon presidential debates on the radio rated Nixon much more highly than those who saw the debate on television; much was written about Nixon's "five o'clock shadow" and "shifty eyes," which were contrasted with JFK's "boyish good looks." The most recent U.S. presidential campaign is rife with references to the candidates' appearances, from body weight (Christie) to sweatiness (Rubio) to hairstyle (Clinton) and even hand size (Trump). Despite the democratically dubious and clearly flawed logic that underscores it, ours is a world that more often than not gives a competitive edge to those who most closely resemble whatever physical and behavioral model of cultural attractiveness happens to be current.

☐ Leadership Style

Theories of leadership have long been associated with issues of power and authority. Many years ago, social scientists Ralph White and Ronald Lippitt (1960) proposed that **leadership style** should be conceived of as a continuum from autocratic (boss-centered power and authority) to democratic (managers and subordinates sharing power and authority) to laissez-faire (subordinate-centered power and authority with little to no guidance from managers).

This leadership taxonomy reflected the world political climate during the time of its formation (post–World War II period), right down to the language used to associate the purportedly "weak" French style (e.g., the term *laissez-faire*) of leadership that failed to defeat the Nazis in 1940. At the other end of the leadership continuum, the term *autocratic* is equally suspect, as dictators capable of bending nations to their will were well known—and, for good reason, often feared—throughout the world. It should be no surprise that the middle ground occupied by democratic leaders was the favored approach among postwar North American and European researchers. Democracy had triumphed over dictatorship, and democratically elected leaders had also saved those countries whose own leaders had failed them. Why shouldn't this political approach apply equally well to the workplace?

From the outset, one problem associated with the "styles" approach to leadership was its rigidity. What appeared as three distinct styles emerged as overlapping sets of behavior in practice. Effective leaders often displayed a dominant style but were usually capable of behaving in other ways when the situation warranted. Moreover, the effectiveness of any given style depended on the consent of followers, who varied in their tolerance for different leadership styles. This remains true today, where the styles appropriate to manufacturing work don't play as well with, for example, physicians or professors. Just as political leaders seldom remain in office if they violate the trust or expectations of the electorate, so too do other leaders rise and fall with the success and relative satisfaction of their subordinates and other stakeholders.

Despite these problems, the styles approach to leadership continued to attract academic supporters and benefited from various theoretical refinements. For example, Robert Blake and Jane Mouton created the Blake and Mouton Managerial Grid (1964, 1985) as a by-product of the human relations and human resources movements (see Chapter 3). According to the grid, two primary dimensions define appropriate choices of leadership style: concern for relationships (people) and concern for tasks (production). Figure 9.1 illustrates how those two key dimensions allow for five style-based options.

As with trait theory and the styles approach, this model closely fits the prevailing cultural and political climate of its time. Management is portrayed as a simple matter of balancing competing goals through rational decisions about people and tasks. Complicating factors like race, class, gender, and ethnicity are all absent from this model. At the center of the grid is a clear display of 1950s' middle-class suburban values, a preoccupation with avoiding conflict, and no clear role for communication processes in either creating productive relationships or completing tasks.

The five categories that inform the grid say as much about prevailing preferences for a class-based system for organizing as they do any enduring organizational reality. The top of the pecking order is divided into "Country Club Management" (for leaders more oriented toward "satisfying relationships") and "Team Management" (for those whose leadership role is defined by a group accomplishment of tasks because of "trust and respect"). At the bottom of the pecking order we find two choices as well: "Impoverished Management," with language seemingly drawn from a critical and simplistic view of the welfare state, pitted against a fascistic "Authority-Obedience" leader, with little or no concern for the value of human life.

Between these extremes we have the aptly named "Organization Man Management," a concept of leadership that balances a concern for others with a concern for the completion of tasks. The "Organization Man" reference is to a best-selling book by William H. Whyte Jr. that offered a highly pessimistic description of a developing North American culture of complacency in large organizations promoted by leaders who are more concerned with being liked than with being regarded for their good business sense. In Whyte's (1956) classic study, "good communication" (read: compliance and complacency) was the ticket to a rewarding career because "the social ethic" (with its emphasis on fitting in, not standing out, and on being

FIGURE 9.1

The Blake and Mouton Managerial Grid

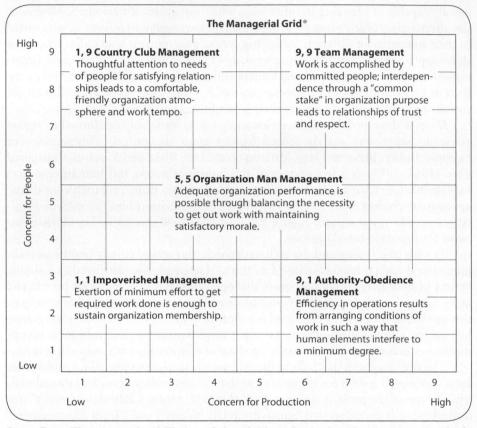

Source: From *The managerial grid III: A new look at the classic that has boosted productivity and profits for thousands of corporations worldwide,* by R. Blake and J. S. Mouton, 1985, p. 18.

well liked) had displaced the Protestant work ethic of rugged individualism capable of independent judgment and a singular attention to the value of hard work and its positive effects on character. Whyte lamented these developments but had little hope for an alternative future.

☐ Situational Leadership

Situational Leadership suggests that effective leadership emerges from behavior that is responsive to varied situations. The literature on leadership became more nuanced as systems theories began to suggest that appropriate behavior in any situation was more a matter of reading and responding to contingencies than it was a fixed condition of traits and styles. For example, in 1977 management theorists Paul Hersey and Kenneth Blanchard determined that the effectiveness of a leader had to do with the maturity of the group. They categorized four distinct styles of Situational Leadership based on a group's maturity: telling, selling, participating, and delegating. Over time, the Situational Leadership® model evolved away from the concept of maturity and the notion of reaching a fully developed state to one related to an individual's or group's *readiness* to perform a specific task. Readiness, in this context, is less a function of time than it is of ability and willingness.

A group's knowledge, experience, and skill determine its ability to perform a task. Do the group members know how to do what is being asked of them? Have they done the task before? Are they already doing it? The answers to these questions are good indicators of ability, but they answer only half of the readiness question. Things like confidence, commitment, and motivation affect a group's willingness to perform a task. "I can. I will. I want to." Statements like these indicate a willingness to perform a task. Considering both ability and willingness, then, helps indicate the readiness of others to complete a specific task. Figure 9.2 displays the concept. The higher the level of "Performance Readiness"® of the group for a specific task, the less direct authority (telling) or persuasion (selling) is required to successfully and effectively complete the task. Less direct supervision is also necessary.

As groups change in their readiness level for a specific task, effective leaders match their leadership style to the groups' needs. For instance, if a group isn't performing the task yet, doesn't know how to do it, and lacks confidence in its ability, it is low in readiness. Group members need their leader to provide structure, to tell them the next steps. A group that is beginning to perform and is excited about the job at hand needs both structure and relationship behavior. Group members don't know what they don't know, so they need their leader to reassure and guide them while explaining the why behind the task (selling). A group that is doing the work well but feels a little insecure because the leader isn't quite so involved anymore needs reassurance and support, not direction in how to do the job. A group that is doing the job well and is confident, committed, and motivated to continue doing so needs little from its leader. An effective leader in this instance can delegate decision-making responsibilities to group members and empower them to create alternative ways and means to carry out tasks and evaluate performance.

☐ Transformational Leadership

Transformational leadership emphasizes organizational change as the essential task of effective leaders. Warren Bennis (1998), an organizational scholar and pioneer in the area of leadership studies, identified characteristics of such effective leaders for the global marketplace. This "new type of leader" is a positive **change agent**, one who seeks to lead an organization through an increasingly turbulent global business environment through the strategic use of communication.

FIGURE 9.2

Situational Leadership Model®

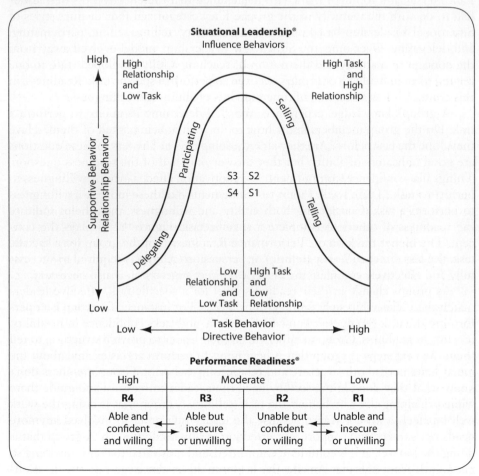

The world experienced a great deal of political, social, and economic change in the late 1980s and early 1990s. The Cold War, which had dominated the global political stage since the end of World War II, ended with the tearing down of the Berlin Wall in 1989 and the resignation of Soviet premier Mikhail Gorbachev on Christmas Day 1991. The U.S. economy was in flux, so much so that presidential candidate Bill Clinton's chief strategist, James Carville, made the mantra "It's the economy, stupid" the basis for Clinton's electoral vision for change, a vision that led to his surprising victory in 1992. Organizations still rebounding from the massive restructuring that took place after the first Arab oil crisis and the sudden and unpredicted dominance of Japan in world manufacturing markets in the 1970s and 1980s were learning how powerful the new information technologies—specifically the desktop computer—could be, as well as how quickly the Internet was changing the way business was done. And after years of creating campaigns for ecological awareness, the Green movement in Europe and environmental advocates in North America finally witnessed progress as world governments began to take seriously the negative consequences of carbon emissions, pollution, the demise of the rain forests, and the ominous potential for global warming. The time, the culture, and the economy all seemed ripe for change.

Today, more instability—such as in North Africa and the Middle East resulting from the so-called Arab Spring—has again revealed a desire on the part of people to be led in ways that embrace change. Transformational political leadership is daunting, and its track record in these regions has been mixed at best. People who had become accustomed to generations of autocratic rule have had to develop from scratch rules for shared governance. While progress has taken hold in some areas (e.g., Tunisia), many countries continue to struggle violently with the changes (e.g., Egypt, Syria).

Bennis was not the only writer espousing the need for transformational leadership in the early 1990s. Popular authors like Tom Peters (1994a, 1994b) lectured to packed audiences about the power of transforming businesses through inspired leadership, the empowerment of employees, and the strategic uses of new technologies. In the academy, researchers and theorists from a variety of fields were making a case for a new way of thinking about organizing. One such theorist, Margaret Wheatley (1992), used developments in theoretical physics to define some intriguing parameters for what she termed "the new science of leadership." In a bold extension of the democratic impulse, Wheatley's parameters encouraged leaders to think of themselves as stewards and encouraged employees at all levels to see themselves as stakeholders. She emphasized the importance of thinking relationally rather than hierarchically and of focusing on tangible human relationships over abstract notions of organizational structure. Her work inspired leaders to look beyond traits, styles, and situations to fully acknowledge and embrace their enduring connection to their employees, their society, and the world.

One leadership competency that all writers can agree on is the importance of a leader's vision. Whether in politics, religion, social activism, education, or global business management, it is important for leaders to craft a credible and compelling view of the future, or **vision**, as well as cultivate an ability to communicate that future clearly and creatively to disparate others. Moreover, inspiring a vision for change requires creating a language for that vision. Changing how we think requires changing how we speak because, as we learned from our discussion of Max Weber in Chapter 3, human beings are "suspended in webs of significance that we ourselves have spun" (cited in Geertz, 1973, p. 434). Those webs are constructed out of language, and the organizing practices we build are spun within them. Transformational leadership requires leaders to have a singular ability to communicate vision in a way that inspires others—what Noel Tichy (2012) called a "teachable point of view." For this reason, the new way of thinking about leadership began with a new way of valuing communication as the essential component of inspiration and change. Seen this way, communication is the essence of all leadership.

☐ Discursive Leadership

Recent research on leadership communication looks directly at people's ability to influence the ebb and flow of work conversations and the meanings that emerge from this discourse. These scholars (Cooren, 2010; Cooren, Taylor, & Van Every, 2006; Fairhurst, 2010; Putnam & Fairhurst, 2015; Robichaud & Cooren, 2013) focus on what they call **discursive leadership**, or the social, linguistic, and cultural aspects of leadership as reflected in concrete interactional processes. They draw on theories of the social construction of reality and resonate with our view of organizational communication as the moment-to-moment balancing of creativity and constraint.

Gail Fairhurst (2010) identifies two notions of "discourse" that can be applied to the analysis of leadership. The first, which she calls "little d discourse," refers to the moment-to-moment choices people make in everyday conversations. The second, "big D discourse," examines how broader cultural narratives of knowledge and power come to be reflected in everyday talk. The difference between these approaches has more to do with level of analysis than subject: Both aim to expose how meaning gets constructed in conversations between leaders and potential followers. Little d discourse, for example, might examine conversational turn taking, interruptions, and the strategic use of pronouns, whereas big D discourse might focus on how common cultural concepts like customer satisfaction or work-life balance are used in specific settings to foster certain meanings and actions. From a practical perspective, discursive leadership highlights the image of leaders as storytellers and speakers. It reaffirms the value in leaders sharpening their ability to use communication strategically to guide employee sense making and interpretation of organizational realities.

One feature of discursive leadership theory is unique enough to warrant mention. Students of this approach do not limit their understanding of discourse to language alone, or even to human beings. Instead, they are equally interested in the ways in which objects (e.g., corner offices, articles of incorporation, computer systems, and office cubicles) have built-in properties that reflect past organizing. If you examine leadership discourse from this angle, you can see immediately how these nonhuman entities seem to have a life of their own as they are invoked in conversation. Meaning-laden objects, like founding organizational texts (e.g., vision, mission, constitution, credo), play a significant part in shaping organizational talk and action. Seen this way, people are both "passers" and "actors" in social situations (Cooren & Sandler, 2014). They are passers because multiple aspects of their social context find expression in their communication, but also actors because they are selective in picking and choosing what counts out of the context.

Finally, a central point in discursive theories of leadership is that effective leaders somehow manage to transcend simple and misleading dualities (i.e., stability versus change, centralized-decentralized, the individual versus the institution) to embrace these tensions simultaneously. Using what some call dialectics and others have dubbed a "polarity lens," effective leaders must focus both on what needs transformation and what must be preserved from the past (Jacobs, Brinkerhoff, & Johnson, 2003; Putnam & Fairhurst, 2015).

But understanding the role of communication in effective leadership is not the same as knowing how to do it or doing it consistently over time in a range of challenging settings. The next phase in leadership studies moved from an emphasis on articulating a compelling vision to establishing behavioral habits that enact and reinforce that vision—in other words, "walking the talk." Many of these habits are also communicative in nature.

LEADERSHIP RECONSIDERED: EFFECTIVE LEADERSHIP HABITS

Recent work in psychology and neurology finds that habits can explain much of why we act as we do (Duhigg, 2012). Contemporary authors who write on leadership suggest that great leaders possess a unique combination of habits: habits of mind, habits of character, and habits of authentic and compelling communicative performance. Understanding each of these sets of behavior helps inform our contemporary notion of leadership.

☐ Habits of Mind

Habits of mind are patterned ways of thinking that define how a person approaches issues and conceives of alternative ways of resolving or dealing with them. Management scholar Robert E. Quinn, writing in the *Harvard Business Review* (2005), echoes the problems associated with leadership training when he observes:

> Nearly all corporate training programs and books on leadership are grounded in the assumption that we should study the behaviors of those who have been successful and teach people to emulate them. . . . But my colleagues and I have found that when

leaders do their best work, they don't copy anyone. Instead, they draw on their own fundamental values and capabilities—operating in a frame of mind that is true to them yet, paradoxically, not their normal state of being. I call it the fundamental state of leadership. (pp. 75–76)

Quinn goes on to elaborate the differences between a leader's "normal state of being" and the state of mind required to perform and communicate as a leader. He offers these four guidelines for leaders:

1. *Move from being comfort-centered to being results-centered.* Ask yourself: What results do you want to create? For example, establishing benchmarks or timetables for the accomplishment of tasks and then using those metrics to evaluate your own performance is one way to move from comfort-oriented to results-oriented thinking.

2. *Move from being externally directed to being more internally directed.* For example, stop complying with others' expectations and clarify your core values. Increase your integrity, confidence, and authenticity.

3. *Become less focused on yourself and more focused on others.* Put the needs of the organization above your own. By thinking this way, you contribute to the greater success of the whole organization, which, in turn, usually means that your own success will be enhanced.

4. *Become more open to outside signals or stimuli, including those that require you to do things you are not comfortable doing.* For example, scanning the environment for new information—including the global information environment afforded by the Internet—is one concrete way to expand your perspective and become more aware of trends in the making. Additionally, stop relying as heavily on rote patterns of thinking and being; call into question your taken-for-granted assumptions about "the ways things are" as well as your usual responses to the behavior of others. (p. 75)

Quinn's main point is that leadership is less a prescribed set of behaviors than it is a uniquely expansive mind-set, one that is focused on the creation of possibility (see also Zander & Zander, 2002). This theme is echoed in the work of Peter Senge and his colleagues at the Society for Organizational Learning in Cambridge, Massachusetts (Senge, Scharmer, Jaworski, & Flowers, 2005).

☐ Habits of Character

Jim Collins, who is known for the idea of the "high-performance organization" and is widely recognized for his studies of "visionary companies" that endure through turbulent times, echoes Quinn's views of the importance of internal states associated with what he terms "Level 5 leadership," or the highest quality of leadership (Collins, 2005, p. 136). Yet for Collins, the essential component is only one part state of mind; it is also composed of ways of being in the world, or what we call **habits of character**. Within those habits, we find that almost without fail the essence of a leader's character is not shameless self-promotion or iconic bombast or personal flamboyance, but simple modesty.

Collins's studies of eleven great companies helped him construct a hierarchy of learning experiences that prepare great leaders for modesty. These experiences begin with the identification of a *highly capable individual* who then advances to *contributing team member*; from success at the level of teamwork (which includes some leadership), the highly capable person evolves into a position where she or he can demonstrate skills as a *competent manager*. *Effective leaders* emerge from successful managerial experiences, in which success is also combined with lessons learned from failure. Collins labels Level 5 leaders as *executives*, and this is the only level where he found that rarest of human combinations: personal humility alongside professional will.

Professional will (drive) is widely understood as a key characteristic of success in the business world. Unfortunately, it is often confused with a "take no prisoners" mentality and a desire to succeed at all costs. But those traits, while they may be found in leaders, are not what define success as a leader. Instead, professional will is generally made up of a strong drive to succeed based on a clear and compelling vision for the company that includes a close connection between one's self-image and one's professional identity. Ironically, individuals who rise to prominence through unrelenting personal ambition and a drive to succeed seldom achieve Level 5 leadership because they lack the corresponding essential quality of character: modesty. **Modesty**—personal humility about one's accomplishments and a profound commitment to the good of the company—is vital to leadership because it both inspires others and leaves oneself open to learning and to personal improvement.

The unique blend of professional will with personal humility is also found in the idea of "servant leadership" (Greenleaf, 1998). Leadership researchers Beverly Alimo-Metcalfe and John Alban-Metcalfe (2005) provide an empirically field-tested definition of the *servant leader* that is composed of the following six qualities:

1. Valuing individuals (having genuine concern for others' well-being and development)
2. Networking and achieving (being an inspirational communicator)
3. Enabling (empowering, delegating, developing potential)
4. Acting with integrity (being consistent, honest, open)
5. Being accessible (being approachable, in touch with others)
6. Being decisive (being a risk taker)

These habits of character are less learned or taught than they are cultivated through everyday disciplined thinking about the "work of the self" in a world of others. This principle is similar to what Warren Bennis and Burt Nanus (2003) call "management of self" and Peter Senge (1994) calls "personal mastery"—the capacity for acquiring a critical appreciation of one's accomplishments in the context of a lifelong journey toward selfhood and the challenge of working with others to achieve a vision or create an imagined community. Such disciplined thinking views the evolving, questing, relating self as part of a much larger human project. For this reason, it carries with it an active commitment to the success of others as well as an appreciation for the privileges of education, race, class, gender, age, or simply being in the right place at the right time to succeed. Humility about one's accomplishments—regardless of what they are or how grandiose they may appear to be—is the inevitable result of habits of mind and habits of character that are then realized fully in authentic communicative performance.

☐ Habits of Authentic Communicative Performance

From the outset, most leadership research has advanced the idea that effective leaders are skilled at **authentic communication**, or relating to others in a way that reflects their own deeply held values and beliefs. They are excellent communicators who have the ability to use language to influence and motivate others. This core idea has been key to every new approach to leadership since the ancient Greeks passed along this saying: "When Aeschines speaks, the people say, 'How well he speaks,' but when Demosthenes speaks, the people say, 'Let's march against Philip!'" The ability to get others to do willingly what you ask of them is the singular mark of a great leader.

When we consider the power of the spoken word to inspire change, we may recall images from political and religious figures like Martin Luther King Jr., speaking the famous words "I have a dream," or John F. Kennedy, who during his inaugural address said, "Ask not what your country can do for you—ask what you can do for your country." We may also think of Ronald Reagan, who combined a natural storytelling style with clear and compelling messages and who was known during his presidency as "the Great Communicator." We may think of Mary Kay Ash, visionary founder of Mary Kay Cosmetics, who was able to combine traditional femininity, personal storytelling, and an entrepreneurial vision. Or we may think of Oprah Winfrey, who for twenty-five years provided a forum for talk about previously uncomfortable or publicly unspeakable topics, such as child abuse and molestation, racial inequality, obesity, and the importance of literacy worldwide. As an informal opinion leader in the public sphere, Winfrey uses her speaking platform to be a change agent for issues of social justice. In all of these examples of leadership—as diverse in vision as they are in kind—the one common denominator is effective and authentic communication.

However, the term *communication* applied to organizational settings can mean — and has meant — a lot of different things, as we have shown throughout this book. For example, during the scientific management era, effective communication meant top-down clarity and the cultivation of an authoritative style. The measure of communicative success was the strict adherence of employees to orders given by the boss. This definition of good communication changed with the advent of the human relations and human resources eras, as researchers and managers learned that how employees felt they were being treated mattered to them. One lasting change from this era was a gradual new appreciation and behavioral focus on the importance of listening and responding skills, something that was unthinkable to authoritative, top-down managers engaged in what they believed were effective communication practices only a few years earlier.

Today, the concept of leadership communication includes far more than success in the sender-receiver relationship. Giving clear instructions and listening to employees' opinions are just the beginning for leaders. As in the past, communication in the early twenty-first century reflects what has surfaced in our time as important indicators of cultural, social, economic, and political success. Because we live in a highly mediated world in a highly uncertain time, and because we have constructed a commodity-based capitalist system of economy that values the material as well as the symbolic dimensions of what is said or done, leadership today is increasingly dependent on the following:

- the ability to create, in straightforward if sometimes strategically ambiguous language, a clear and compelling *vision for the future* (Collins & Porras, 1994);
- the development of a *credible life story* that emphasizes the naturalness of the path you've taken to leadership, despite having to overcome hardships and endure emotional pain while maintaining a core set of commonly held values (Benoit, 1997; Shamir, Dayan-Horesh, & Adler, 2005); and
- the ability to *use language performatively* to inspire others to choose those desirable future actions and to work hard to help you obtain them (Deal & Kennedy, 1982; Pacanowsky & O'Donnell-Trujillo, 1983; Robbins, 1997).

Good leaders not only are visionary, but lead by example. This means more than being up to the daily challenges of organizing and decision making: Good leaders must also show others how much they enjoy being in charge of the ongoing action, and they must demonstrate that they are worthy of trust and confidence. Good leaders today are, therefore, communicatively adept. They inspire others to work with them and for them through their humility and the power of their personal example.

The *Everyday Organizational Communication* box on page 288 asks you to think about how these different habits of effective leaders are represented in some of your own college experiences.

EVERYDAY ORGANIZATIONAL COMMUNICATION

Grooming Servant Leaders through Service Learning and Community Engagement

In this section, we introduce various styles of leadership, as well as traits and habits that different leaders embody. One of the most provocative habits that we discuss is the idea that leaders should be *modest*. Striking the balance between professionalism and personal humility can be a daunting task, and the concepts associated with servant leadership can be a useful framework for developing your skills as a modest leader.

Increasingly, colleges and universities are making the connection between leadership and service through models of service learning and community engagement. Communication scholar Lori Britt argues that service learning is "a form of pedagogy that engages students in community service and regular guided reflection on the service in order to deepen learning and enrich communities" (2012, pp. 80–81) and that instructors and students are drawn to service learning and community engagement because of the practical reality that they lend to the educational experience. Formal offices of leadership and service learning have been established at colleges and universities like Purdue, Concordia, and the University of North Carolina at Greensboro. Moreover, the American Association of Colleges and Universities has identified service learning and community-based learning as high-impact practices because of their focus on analyzing and solving problems in the community.

When students take advantage of service-learning opportunities, they might develop specific skills, like designing posters, videos, and other communication materials while working with a nonprofit organization. Or they might have opportunities to examine democratic practices and what it means to be a "critical citizen" while working on topics like voter registration or participatory budgeting. They might focus on social justice issues while working with community-based organizations that increase access to resources for people who are hungry, poor, or otherwise in need of help. Service-learning opportunities also allow students the chance to develop habits of modesty in their own leadership styles.

DISCUSSION QUESTIONS

1. Does your college or university offer opportunities for service learning or community engagement? If so, have you taken advantage of any of these opportunities? If not, can you think of any classes that you have taken that would benefit from a service-learning or community-engagement approach?

2. How could a service-learning or community-engagement approach help you develop your skills when it comes to servant leadership? How might community service give you firsthand experience in valuing individuals? Acting with integrity? Being accessible and decisive?
3. How would you characterize your leadership style? If you currently hold a leadership position in a campus organization, how could you use some of the points addressed in this section in your leadership role?

▧ LEADING THE ORGANIZATION: COMMUNICATING WITH EMPLOYEES

We can easily get lost in the vastness and complexity of leadership theory and research, so it is helpful to remember some constant realities. All leadership is at its essence communication and involves the purposeful exercise of influence over others. Moreover, this influence is largely independent of formal titles and reporting relationships and may extend in multiple directions both within and between organizations. In this section, we discuss how leaders influence their employees.

As we have seen throughout this book, organizational theories propose different approaches for leaders to communicate with their employees. In classical management theory, downward communication is emphasized; it is formal, precise, and work-related. Human relations theory stresses supportive communication, while human resources theory emphasizes the need for supervisors to involve employees in decision making. The systems and cultural approaches make no specific prescriptions about communicating with employees, whereas critical theorists call for a radical leveling of power and authority among superiors and subordinates in which both are regarded as equally important to the organization. No matter what their perspective, however, contemporary observers agree that leaders' effective communication with employees has at least four essential characteristics: It is open, supportive, motivating, and empowering.

☐ Openness

As a general rule, openness is a desirable goal in most supervisor-employee relationships (Redding, 1972). The parties in an **open communication** relationship "perceive the other interactant as a willing and receptive listener and refrain from responses that might be perceived as providing negative relational or disconfirming feedback" (Jablin, 1979, p. 1204). Openness has both verbal and nonverbal dimensions. Nonverbally, facial expression, eye gaze, tone, and the like contribute to degrees of open communication (Tjosvold, 1984).

Studies conducted by W. Charles Redding (1972) and his students at Purdue University reveal a positive correlation between a supervisor's open communication and employees' satisfaction with the relationship. The researchers identify five key components of an open communication relationship:

1. The most effective supervisors tend to emphasize the importance of communication in their relationships with employees. For example, they enjoy talking at meetings and conversing with subordinates, and they are skilled at explaining instructions and policies.
2. Effective supervisors are empathic listeners. They respond positively to employees' questions, listen to suggestions and complaints, and express a willingness to take fair and appropriate action when necessary.
3. Effective supervisors ask or persuade, rather than tell or demand.
4. Effective supervisors are sensitive to others' feelings. For instance, reprimands are made in private rather than in public work settings.
5. Effective supervisors share information with employees, including advance notice of impending changes and explanation about why the changes will be made.

In the 2004 book *Apollo, Challenger, and Columbia: The Decline of the Space Program*, organizational communication scholars Phillip Tompkins and Emily Tompkins examine the *Challenger* and *Columbia* disasters and find their cause to be in part due to the erosion of a culture of open communication and the loss of specific practices that ensured the exchange of ideas and information. Specifically, they describe the value of eminent scientist Wernher Von Braun's "Monday Notes" as a mechanism for both soliciting and responding to ideas. Von Braun required all of his lead engineers to submit written summaries of the progress and problems in their areas every Monday. He would read through the reports and make comments, then redistribute the entire package of notes (with his comments) to all of the submitters. In this way, he ensured regular communication across levels and departments. As Monday Notes were dropped and elements of shuttle design and manufacture were increasingly outsourced, communication was diminished and the safety of the program was put at risk (Tompkins & Tompkins, 2004). The authors' telling research on the history of NASA (and, specifically, the space shuttle program) underscores the value of open communication.

The child abuse case involving Jerry Sandusky at Pennsylvania State University appears likely to yield some important insights about leadership's role in creating a culture of openness and honesty. The report on the situation by independent investigator Louis Freeh observes that senior leaders of the university did little to disrupt a closed football culture wherein people were discouraged from reporting anything negative that could potentially hurt the program (Freeh Sporkin & Sullivan, LLP, 2012). In this sense, leadership can also be seen as a collective act by leaders to communicate in ways that promote and reinforce ethical and humane cultural practices. As Freeh makes clear in his statement, however, the "tone" or context for what constitutes appropriate behavior is set from the top of the organization:

> From 1998–2011, Penn State's "Tone at the Top" for transparency, compliance, police reporting and child protection was completely wrong, as shown by the inaction and concealment on the part of its most senior leaders, and followed by those at the bottom of the University's pyramid of power. This is best reflected by the janitors' decision not to report Sandusky's horrific 2000 sexual assault of a young boy in the Lasch Building shower. The janitors were afraid of being fired for reporting a powerful football coach.

While the Penn State case is especially grievous in the harm it caused, other situations reveal that a simple endorsement of open communication may not be realistic or desirable. Some researchers suggest that openness plays a more complex role in the superior-subordinate relationship and that its effects are not always so easy to predict. Eric Eisenberg argues that, depending on the context, openness can have dramatically different outcomes (Eisenberg & Witten, 1987). For example, a supervisor may use openness in indiscreet or insincere ways or as a way to intimidate employees. Although supervisors should strive for open communication with employees in appropriate contexts, openness should not override other concerns, such as confidentiality and ethics. For example, it would be highly inappropriate for a supervisor to disclose reservations he or she may have about the performance of a colleague. Instead, the supervisor ought to share this information with the proper audience and in the proper context—that is, with his or her boss. Problems can arise when open communication is viewed ideologically and indiscriminately as a moral mandate for full and honest disclosure, without sensitivity to the communicative context of any given situation (Bochner, 1982; Eisenberg, 1984).

☐ Supportiveness

Research suggests that **supportive communication**—which emphasizes active listening and taking a real interest in employees—is even more useful to organizational leaders than openness. According to the **theory of leader-member exchange**, or LMX (Graen, 1976), individual supervisors typically divide their employees into two types and form very different relationships with members of each group. The two types of relationships are (1) in-group relationships, which are "characterized by high trust, mutual influence, support, and formal/informal rewards," and (2) out-group relationships, which are "characterized by . . . formal authority [and] low trust, support, and rewards" (Fairhurst & Chandler, 1989, pp. 215–216). In-group relationships develop over time, tend to be more trusting, and are characterized by a greater willingness on the part of supervisors to delegate important tasks (Bauer & Green, 1996). In general, in-group relationships are associated with greater employee satisfaction, performance, agreement, and decision-making involvement as well as lower turnover rates than out-group relationships (Graen, Liden, & Hoel, 1982; Liden & Graen, 1980; Scandura, Graen, & Novak, 1986).

There is also evidence to suggest that having a positive in-group relationship with one's supervisor leads to better integration into important social networks (Sparrowe & Liden, 1997) as well as enhanced feelings of perceived organizational support, which in turn strengthen commitment and performance (Sparrowe & Liden, 1997; Wayne, Shore, & Liden, 1997). Communication researchers Gail Fairhurst and Theresa Chandler (1989) extended LMX theory in an examination of actual in-group and out-group conversations involving a warehouse supervisor and three subordinates. Their analysis reveals some consistency in the communication resources deployed by those in each type of relationship. The in-group relationship is characterized by influence and by mutual persuasion (in which both parties challenge and disagree with each other frequently) and greater freedom of choice for subordinates. In contrast, the out-group relationship is marked by the supervisor's authority, a traditional chain of command, little freedom of choice for subordinates, and a disregard for subordinates' suggestions.

Another application of the leader-member exchange model to coworker communication reveals how an employee's privileged relationship with a supervisor affected that employee's relationship with peers. In most cases, the employee's coworkers engaged in communication aimed at making sense of the preferential treatment, made judgments about the unfairness of the in-group relationship, and experienced a general erosion of trust in management (Sias & Jablin, 1995).

Although the leader-member exchange distinction focuses on broad issues of trust and support, it does not prescribe open communication as the sole means for attaining supportive relationships. Instead, supervisory communication is viewed as an ongoing attempt to achieve balance among multiple and competing relational, identity, and task goals (Dillard & Segrin, 1987; Eisenberg, 1984). Moreover, certain types of communication may ensure employee compliance but may also be demoralizing to employees. For example, a supervisor who insists on managing "by the book" despite an employee's extenuating circumstances (e.g., a personal or medical emergency) can create a negative work climate. Effective supervisors, in contrast, strive to communicate in ways that simultaneously show concern for the relationship, demonstrate respect for the individual, and promote task accomplishment.

Recent research conducted by Google further supports the importance of a supportive environment for effective leadership. In a long-term study called *Project Aristotle*, Google scientists analyzed hundreds of company work teams to determine what made them more or less effective (Duhigg, 2016). Their overarching conclusion is that teams function best when employees feel both a sense of psychological safety (i.e., that the climate is welcoming of their perspective, even if unpopular) and a sense of emotional support for them as whole human beings (i.e., no one wants to "put on a mask" when they come to work). Next to creating a compelling vision, fostering a supportive communication environment may be the most important and impactful thing a leader can do.

☐ Motivation

Motivation can be defined as "the degree to which an individual is personally committed to expending effort in the accomplishment of a specified activity or goal" (Kreps, 1991, p. 154). Although various other factors contribute to employee motivation, our focus here is on how leaders encourage or discourage employee motivation through their communication. Their communication can function in two ways to motivate employees: Leaders can (1) provide information and feedback about employees' tasks, goals, performance, and future directions and (2) communicate encouragement, empathy, and concern. In both cases, however, the motivating effect comes from the manager's ability to endorse particular interpretations of organizational issues through communication (Sullivan, 1988). The four best-known practices associated with employee motivation involve setting reasonable but challenging goals (Locke & Latham, 1984); meeting employees' expectations (Steers, 1981); treating everyone fairly and with a sense of equity in assignments, duties, and performance evaluations (Altman, Valenzi, & Hodgetts, 1985); and successfully gaining compliance with directives and goals (Keys & Case, 1990).

What is most interesting about the decades of research on human motivation is that it cannot be boiled down to either material incentives or emotional goodwill. Instead, the likelihood that an employee will achieve or even exceed a stated goal always begins with the clarity of the target—how well the leader has articulated the desired end-state. Once the goal is clear—and a mechanism is put in place to ensure the employee gets timely feedback about his or her progress toward the goal—the employee's willingness and ability to achieve it depends on a rich mixture of related factors. Meaningful financial incentives can get people moving, but they are particularly effective when combined with supportive communication that encourages employee creativity and initiative and offers interpersonal as well as financial rewards (e.g., public recognition of an employee's achievement). Finally, all of the rewards and recognition in the world cannot motivate employees to perform well if they lack the needed skills to do so. Successful employee motivation is always the result of multiple factors: communication, incentives, rewards, and skill.

In a popular TED talk, Simon Sinek introduced a related way of thinking about motivation that he calls the *Golden Circle*. In this model, he seeks to distill the motivation process into a simple but profound difference in how leaders think and speak about their work. For Sinek, followers are motivated by "why" an organization does something—the beliefs that underlie its products and services—not by "what" or "how" it is done. He gives multiple examples of competing companies (e.g., Apple versus Motorola; Kmart versus Zappos) that essentially provide the "same" products and services but with wildly different results. In each case, the successful company leader has sold employees and customers on "why" they exist—for example, to make life easier, to create a healthy natural environment, to make people happy—and this has made all the difference.

☐ Empowerment

Definitions of **empowerment** vary considerably from the willingness to share power and decision making with employees, to delegation that enables and motivates employees by building feelings of self-efficacy. The empowerment process enhances feelings of self-efficacy by identifying and removing conditions that foster employee powerlessness (Conger & Kanungo, 1988; see Figure 9.3). Furthermore, to feel empowered, an employee must also feel capable of performing the job and must possess the authority to decide how to do the job well (Chiles & Zorn, 1995).

Empowerment requires a manager to act more like a coach than a boss by listening to employees' concerns, avoiding close supervision, trusting employees to work within a framework of clear direction, and being responsive to employee

FIGURE 9.3

The Five Stages of the Empowerment Process

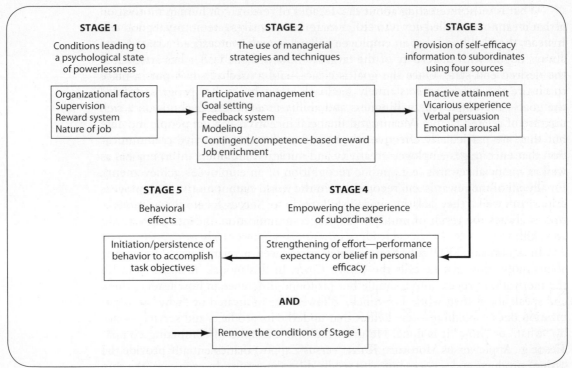

Source: Adapted from "The empowerment process: Integrating theory and practice," by J. Conger and R. Kanugo, 1988, *Academy of management review, 13,* p. 475.

feedback. An organization committed to empowerment encourages employees to take on ever-increasing responsibilities that utilize their knowledge and skills. A study of W. L. Gore and Associates, the company that invented Gore-Tex fabric, identifies six rules for empowering employees (Pacanowsky, 1988):

1. Distribute power and opportunity widely.
2. Maintain an open and decentralized communication system.
3. Use integrative problem solving to involve diverse groups and individuals.
4. Practice meeting challenges in an environment of trust.
5. Reward and recognize employees to encourage a high-performance ethic and self-responsibility.
6. Learn from organizational ambiguity, inconsistency, contradiction, and paradox.

Notice that these rules focus on providing the resources and opportunities for creating an environment in which subordinates become empowered by taking greater responsibility for their work.

Organizations, and even departments within organizations, can vary with regard to the degree of employee empowerment (Ford & Fottler, 1995). Degree of empowerment is a direct result of how decision-making authority is defined. A distinction exists between an employee's control of job content (how the job gets done) versus job context (the conditions under which the job gets done, including goals, strategies, and standards). For example, it is increasingly common for line employees to have considerable say in the scheduling and tools they use to accomplish their work (job content) but still quite rare for them to have input into things like mission, strategy, and organizational structure (job context). What is of greatest importance is for managers and employees to maintain clear agreements about the expected degree of empowerment to avoid misunderstandings that can foster resentment and mistrust.

This section has provided some practical ideas, many of them long established, about how to positively influence employees through openness, supportiveness, motivation, and empowerment. The next section considers the negative consequences of organizational leaders who use their power to berate, belittle, and demean employees and subordinates.

◫ THE DARK SIDE OF LEADERSHIP: BULLYING AND HARASSMENT

Theories of leadership have historically focused on the positive qualities associated with organizational advancement. However, as we look around us, we notice that some leaders who have risen to positions of high prominence in the government, the military, the academy, the arts, and the business world are not pleasant or kind people. Beyond the infamous bullies that we might think of, there are also standout cases of women and men in our everyday lives who have attained executive ranks by being emotionally and physically abusive to others or by creating an organizational culture that allows such abuses to occur.

☐ Bullying in the Workplace

Research suggests that emotionally abusive behavior in adults has its roots in childhood development. School-yard bullies who develop an abusive skill set that gives them authority and power over other children often find ways as adults to exercise their authority through incivility, abuse of power, and exertion of extreme control over their subordinates at work (Hornstein, 1996; Lutgen-Sandvik & Davenport Sypher, 2009; Tracy, Lutgen-Sandvik, & Alberts, 2006; Zellers, Tepper, & Duffy, 2002). This "dark side" of organizational leadership has not yet been well documented, but the best estimate is that one in six people complain of experiencing consistent mistreatment in the workplace (Meares, Oetzel, Torres, Derkacs, & Ginossar, 2004). Mistreatment is costly, not only to the individuals on the receiving end but also to the organization, because people who are bullied are neither happy nor productive workers. They often become depressed and anxious, and many choose to leave their jobs rather than put up with it.

What constitutes bullying behavior in the workplace? The Washington State Department of Labor and Industries (2011), provides the following definition for **bullying**: "Workplace bullying refers to repeated, unreasonable actions of individuals (or a group) directed towards an employee (or a group of employees), which are intended to intimidate, degrade, humiliate, or undermine; or which create a risk to the health or safety of the employee(s)" (para. 1). The Workplace Bullying Institute (2013) further clarifies that bullying behavior can consist of verbal abuse, offensive conduct (including nonverbal behaviors), or even sabotage (as in preventing someone from getting work done).

Bullying behavior is certainly aggressive, though Canadian Centre for Occupational Health and Safety (2013) notes that instances of bullying can be overt or subtle. Among the many examples they offer are spreading malicious rumors, gossip, or innuendo that is not true; excluding or isolating someone socially; intimidating a person; and undermining or deliberately impeding a person's work.

Why does bullying in the workplace persist when most people would agree that it is unfair or unacceptable? There are two major reasons. First, bullies who are not held accountable for their behavior learn to repeat it (Smith, 2005). Second, people who are bullied often don't know how to tell their story of abuse to someone who can help them and often fear organizational inaction or, worse, retribution from the bully (Tracy et al., 2006). Organizational communication scholar Pamela Lutgen-Sandvik (2003) suggests that bullies are both cultivated and rewarded in many organizational cultures. Some of the rewards are accrued unwittingly by managers and supervisors who perceive that results are more important than the means used to achieve them. But it is also true that aggressive organizational cultures tend to reinforce the conditions that cultivate bullying as a norm: high expectations, strict loyalty to the boss, cronyism in hiring and promotion, secrecy about "what really goes on," and extreme measures taken to silence those who disagree, express criticism, or oppose actions. It is also true that bullying persists because employees who have been bullied often believe that complaining about it makes them seem weak and ineffectual and consequently less likely to advance.

A recent study by Tye-Williams and Krone (2015) directly examined the narrative accounts of forty-eight individuals who were bullied at work. The researchers were interested in seeing the types of stories that these individuals told about their experience, and whether these narratives supported or compromised their ability to cope with the experience. They found that victim narratives fell into one of three types that the researchers call chaos, report, and quest narratives. Chaos narratives tended to be emotional, incoherent, and filled with a sense of loss; report narratives were unemotional and focused on the facts; and quest narratives found a way to convert the emotional chaos into meaningful life lessons and even personal transformation. The authors make a number of practical suggestions based on their study, including helping leaders and managers to broaden how they listen to bullying narratives when they arise.

Quite often, a bully is the boss (72 percent of the time), and most bullies act with impunity, being sanctioned only 23 percent of the time ("Bullying 'Facts' and 'Stats,'" 2007). One study revealed that approximately one-third of new teachers leave their schools within two years as a result of feeling bullied by their *principals* (Pogodzinski, Young, Frank, & Belman, 2012). The targets of mistreatment are often minorities and women (Meares et al., 2004). In one study by Gary Namie (2000), 23 percent of the targets of abusive behavior identified themselves as members of a minority group, and 77 percent were female. These data suggest rather strongly that patterns of bullying often draw on and perpetuate larger social inequities (see *What Would You Do?* on page 298).

☐ Harassment and Sexual Harassment

One of the most pervasive and problematic types of mistreatment in the workplace is **harassment**, a form of communicative behavior that degrades or humiliates people. Based on federal Equal Employment Opportunity Commission (EEOC) guidelines, harassment includes the following:

- Slurs about sex, race, religion, ethnicity, or disability
- Offensive or derogatory remarks
- Verbal or physical conduct that creates an intimidating, hostile, or offensive work environment
- Conditions that interfere with the individual's work performance

One type of harassment that sometimes occurs in the workplace is sexual harassment. **Sexual harassment** refers to any verbal or nonverbal communication of a

Effective Responses to Bullies, Harassers, and Bosses Who Mistreat Subordinates

Priscilla is a forty-year-old college senior studying communication at a large state university. She attends classes full time while helping out with her husband's business and caring for her elderly mother, who suffers from Alzheimer's disease. Despite the constraints on her personal time, her work at the university has been outstanding—she consistently receives high marks in her communication courses, and two of her professors have urged her to seriously consider graduate studies.

To see if graduate school might be a suitable path, Priscilla registered for a faculty/student research project in health communication with Professor Layne. Though she had not previously studied with this professor, several other students commented that she is a wonderful teacher and a great mentor. Priscilla eagerly began her research project, hoping to learn more about health communication and professional opportunities in the discipline. She even hoped that she might be able to secure a strong letter of recommendation from Professor Layne should she decide to pursue a graduate education.

Priscilla's experiences working with Professor Layne did not turn out as she had hoped, however. The professor was frequently unable to meet with Priscilla about her research. She failed to return e-mails and phone calls and often canceled meetings, claiming to be "too busy." It seems, however, that Priscilla was the only one having this problem. The other students on the project (mostly traditional college-age juniors and seniors with a strong interest in graduate studies) were able to establish positive relationships with the professor. Priscilla's situation worsened as the semester went on. When Professor Layne was finally able to find time in her schedule for meetings, she expected Priscilla to be available at 4:30 p.m. every Tuesday afternoon, even though Priscilla could not arrange for the home health-care worker to be with her mother during this time. Professor Layne began to suggest that Priscilla did not take her work seriously and, on occasion, made comments that called into question Priscilla's intelligence and capability as a student. Hurt and confused but bolstered by her previous academic success, Priscilla approached Professor Layne to discuss the prospect of graduate school, hoping to convince the professor of her sincere interest in academic study. Professor Layne, however, cut off the conversation, noting that graduate school is for "serious students" who can make a "full-time commitment to study" without the influence of "outside concerns" (which Priscilla took to mean her mother). The final blow, however, was Professor Layne's closing comment: "I'm just being honest and telling you how it is out there. Graduate school is for twenty-somethings. No one will hire a new faculty member who is pushing fifty."

We know that emotional narratives, like Priscilla's, are messy. Victims of workplace bullying, harassment, and mistreatment often remain silent. Consider Priscilla's situation: She may want to tell the department chair about her experiences with Professor Layne (especially since she now fears a low grade on her research project), but will anyone take her word over that of a generally respected, tenured professor? If no one believes her, will she risk angering Professor Layne and putting her grade in further jeopardy?

In a research study to investigate the characteristics of credible versus noncredible bullying narratives, Jess Alberts, Pamela Lutgen-Sandvik, and Sarah Tracy (2005) compared two real-world accounts with seventeen subjects. They found a clear pattern between stories of abusive behavior that were believed and those that were not. They found that credible narratives are marked by the following characteristics:

- They are linear. They have a clear beginning, middle, and end.
- They clearly identify the bully, speak as much or more about the bully as they do about the target, and provide details that paint the bully as the person who is clearly out of control and irrational.
- They "tell" about emotion, but the speaker himself or herself does not embody the emotion.
- They include details of quotations, times, places, and people.
- They include metaphors or stories to which other folks (who have not been bullied) may be able to relate.
- They include references to other people who have been bullied. (This shows that the problem is that of the bully and not necessarily of a lone problem employee or target.)
- They acknowledge small but not extremely damaging points of weakness in the target, and do so in a way in which the target is not cast as blameworthy.
- They anticipate and meet potential objections (e.g., "you're just a problem employee") through perspective talking (or considering the situation from various points of view).
- They indicate how the target has proactively met, managed, and tried to deal with the situation.
- They do not vividly expound on the harm the bullying has done to the target.

(continued, Effective Responses to Bullies)

DISCUSSION QUESTIONS

1. Based on what you have read, how should Priscilla handle her situation with Professor Layne? Should she approach the department chair about the situation? Does she have an ethical obligation to do so?
2. If she does choose to bring another person into the situation, are there any steps that Priscilla should take before she initiates action?
3. How might Priscilla gain support and credibility for her case? Based on what you know of her situation and the research cited here, construct a believable narrative.

sexual nature that interferes with someone's work. According to the Civil Rights Act of 1964, additional legislation in Congress, and federal, state, and local court rulings, there are two forms of sexual harassment: quid pro quo harassment and hostile work environment harassment:

1. *Quid pro quo ("this for that") harassment* is based on the threat of retaliation or the promise of workplace favoritism or promotion in exchange for dating or sexual favors. This principle has been interpreted to include suggestions and innuendos as well as explicit quid pro quo comments.
2. *Hostile work environment harassment* is sexually explicit verbal or nonverbal communication that interferes with someone's work or is perceived as intimidating or offensive. It is important to note that the behavior doesn't have to be intentional to create or contribute to a hostile work environment. Offhand remarks and casual displays of sexually explicit materials count as harassment. So do remarks that the sender may think of as compliments.

The EEOC maintains a comprehensive website charting the number of reported incidents of sexual harassment (see U.S. Equal Employment Opportunity Commission, 2011). Despite the widespread availability of information about harassment and its consequences, more than ten thousand cases are reported to the EEOC annually. However, we believe that continuing to provide information about sexual harassment has a positive effect on reducing the number of potential cases and making women and men more aware of what constitutes sexual harassment and what may be done about it in the workplace.

Sexual harassment lawsuits occur between people of the same sex as well as those of the opposite sex. It has become so prevalent in the United States that most for-profit and nonprofit organizations, government agencies, and schools have implemented policies, mandatory seminars, and workshops to train employees in how to recognize and prevent harassment. However, while sexual harassment is clearly recognized as a problem in the United States, it is not always viewed similarly in other countries and other cultures. Latin and Mediterranean cultures, for example, do not regulate physical contact or the use of suggestive language in the workplace. As a result, cultural misunderstandings can and do take place. Once again, we see that our assumptions about the meanings of communicative acts are, in fact, culturally derived. Indeed, even the meanings of what constitutes sexual harassment vary across organizational cultures with different sense-making practices (Dougherty & Smythe, 2004).

Women are usually the targets of sexual harassment by men because "as a group [women] have less formal and informal power than men in organizations, confront more obstacles on their path to developing organizational power, and have fewer opportunities to acquire organizational power through activities and alliances" (Bingham, 1991, p. 92). Commonplace in organizations, sexual harassment is the unacceptable behavior of men who cling to outdated notions of male-dominated leadership and organizational status quo. It is crucial to understand that sexual harassment is an organizational problem, not a personal problem. It is management's responsibility to create a work climate that reinforces appropriate boundaries between employees (Cleveland & McNamara, 1996; Pina & Gannon, 2012; Townsley & Geist-Martin, 2000).

In a special issue of the *Journal of Applied Communication Research* (Wood, 1992), a rich and complex assortment of firsthand accounts of sexual harassment on the job reveals a disturbing trend. Most often experienced initially by teenagers and students working a first job, sexual harassment may thereafter be accepted as normal or ordinary behavior. This may explain why many women tend to avoid reporting instances of sexual harassment to superiors, to underestimate their importance, or to be uncertain about identifying such behaviors (Clair, 1998). As a result, sexual harassment remains outside of mainstream communication in organizations, and women participate in both their own subjugation and the perpetuation of the male ideology. For those experiencing it, knowing how best to respond to harassment is almost always a complex predicament (Dougherty & Smythe, 2004).

In fact, male ideology has been cited as a major factor in the sudden reported increase in cases of male-on-male sexual harassment (Talbott, 2002). These cases demonstrate that "macho" male cultures contribute to hostile work environments for men as well as women, even in cases where no sexual favors are involved. In one particularly vivid case, a male sales manager for a Chevrolet dealership in Denver, Colorado, routinely grabbed the genitals of male salesmen to make them flinch, addressed them as "little girls" or "whores," and simulated masturbation when male employees talked. If a male employee failed to make a sale, he was asked "if he used tampons . . . or had to squat when he urinated" (p. 54). Even within a male-dominated car sales culture where being raunchy may have been accepted practice, the dealership was found to be at fault, paid a $500,000 fine, and promised to implement sexual harassment training for all employees. The two managers who were the perpetrators of these actions were fired. In this case, the EEOC found that it was the organization's responsibility to create a positive working environment, and the existence of a dominant male ideology was not an acceptable defense.

Dealing successfully with the problem of sexual harassment requires defining its characteristic behaviors more precisely. Once defined, this information can be used to raise employees' awareness and potentially change their abusive behavior. The following specific behaviors are examples of sexual harassment:

- inappropriate verbal comments, even those defended as compliments (e.g., "I wish my wife were as pretty as you");
- inappropriate nonverbal gestures, such as outlining body parts or eyeing someone up and down;
- inappropriate visual displays or objects (e.g., posters or calendars depicting nude women or men; pornographic or suggestive e-mails);
- inappropriate terms of endearment (e.g., "sweetie," "dear," "honey");
- inappropriate physical acts, such as patting, fondling, stroking, or standing in a doorway to obstruct someone's passage through it; and
- asking for or implying that someone must submit to sexual advances as a basis for continued employment or advancement in the company.

Julie Tamaki (1991) outlines a series of strategies for dealing with sexual harassment: (1) confront the harasser, (2) report the behavior to a supervisor or to the human resources department, (3) keep a written record of the offenses, and (4) confide in supportive colleagues, family members, and friends. If the harassment continues, the employee may request a formal investigation by the state department of fair employment or by the EEOC, or the employee may file a lawsuit.

Although the 1991 confirmation hearings of Supreme Court justice Clarence Thomas made the public aware of the difficulties of proving sexual harassment, legal awards for victims of sexual harassment at work are now quite common, especially when written records and support from others in the organization are provided as evidence.

Communication scholar Shereen Bingham (1991; Bingham & Battey, 2005) offers a communicative approach to collecting narratives and managing sexual harassment in the university or workplace. She argues that direct confrontation with a harasser is complicated by multiple risks, including losing a job, receiving an unfavorable recommendation, being demoted, and losing interest in the job. Bingham suggests that various responses—assertive, nonassertive, and even aggressive—may be appropriate in certain circumstances. Most observers agree that assertiveness helps the victim confront a harasser in a direct but nonthreatening way. However, assertiveness may also be interpreted as a rejection of the other person, which practically speaking may cause the victim to "win the battle but lose the war." When responding to a sexual advance, it may be more effective to temper assertiveness with "apparent" empathy if the victim thinks that this approach will stop the behavior in the future. If that seems unlikely, it very often makes good sense to lodge a formal complaint against the offending individual.

Finally, the emergence of male-on-male sexual harassment cases has further complicated the concept of a "hostile work environment" among legal scholars (Talbott, 2002). The idea of a hostile work environment was first introduced in the 1980s under the assumption that sexual jokes, vulgarity, and macho displays of dominance offended women because women are, as legal scholar Rosa Ehrenreich puts it, "uniquely vulnerable to men" (cited in Talbott, 2002, p. 55). However, as recent male-on-male harassment cases have documented, some men are clearly vulnerable to other men and are offended by coarse behavior. Between 1992 and 2008, the percentage of sexual-harassment charges filed by men with the EEOC doubled from 8 percent to 16 percent. Another problem is that some men are victimized by male-on-male sexual harassment because they are gay, but sexual orientation is not covered by Title VII of the Civil Rights Act of 1964.

As law professor Deborah Zalesne argues, "[If] your *harasser* is gay, you stand a good chance of winning a same-sex harassment case. If *you* are gay, you lose" (cited in Talbott, 2002, p. 57). For these and other reasons, the theoretical framework of sexual harassment law is currently undergoing revisions on a case-by-case basis. A number of cases in California have caused the EEOC to state more strongly that "men as well as women are entitled under Title VII [of the federal Civil Rights Act] to protection from a sexually abusive work environment" (Norman, 2010). A more recent study found that men who engaged in feminist activism at work—advocating for equal treatment of women—were more likely to be sexually harassed (Holland, Rabelo, Gustafson, Seabrook, & Cortina, 2016). The authors conclude that sexual harassment in these instances is a form of punishment against men who deviate from the prescriptions of traditional masculinity. As the laws develop to meet this changing reality, some male victims of sexual harassment have found that they can successfully bring charges under existing tort law, civil rights laws, and other federal and state statutes.

Sexual harassment is a crime. Organizational leaders should design educational programs for employees to help them understand sexual harassment, as well as offer strategies for dealing with it in particular situations. Workshops, films, and literature may be used to make employees more aware of the types of behavior that constitute sexual harassment in the workplace. Firms that operate with public monies are especially concerned with this issue. Responding effectively to sexual harassment requires paying close attention to ways of communicating appropriately at work.

While it's difficult to end this chapter with bullying and harassment as the final thought on leadership, we would be remiss if we didn't include the "dark side" as a complement to otherwise noble, motivational, and exemplary models of leadership. We believe that it is important to offer you a full sampling of the types of experiences that you, as future employees, may encounter in the workplace. Some examples of leadership will be inspiring; others will be frustrating and ineffective. We hope that this chapter has challenged your ideas about the characteristics a great leader should have and how you might continue to evolve as a leader on your campus, in your current organizational affiliations, and in your future.

Summary

Historically, new approaches to leadership have consistently reflected our culture and times. Ideas about what constitutes leadership emerged from an early belief that the traits associated with great leaders should be modeled by emulating the appearance, habits, and behaviors of those who had attained leadership positions. This approach, which clearly favored successful white males at a time when white males were culturally dominant and rarely challenged for leadership roles by women or minorities, was augmented by studies that emphasized the style of leading, and specifically the style of communication, used by leaders. Limitations of this approach were revealed when newer studies demonstrated that the style of leadership selected depended on situations that often required creative, rather than established, ways of thinking and acting and that called for a repertoire of leadership styles rather than one consistent style. From these early attempts to find the secret of successful leadership emerged the transformational approach. This approach emphasized the communicative dimensions of effectiveness, particularly the ability to both articulate and lead with a vision that motivated others to attain closer personal identification with the company and inspired them to achieve higher performance goals as a result. Discursive leadership studies followed with an even more granular focus on how specific communicative choices affect collective action.

The story of leadership has turned the lens back on the self—on habits of mind, character, and authentic communicative performance. While there is as yet no clear consensus on the details of these newer approaches, there is a pattern to successful leadership: the recognition of lessons drawn from one's own experiences, the ability to create an empowering vision capable of inspiring others, the articulation of a credible life story that humanizes the trajectory taken to leadership, and—in our view, most important—the everyday ethics and authenticity of communication practices that demonstrate by personal example why trust and confidence in a leader are justified.

Leadership theory and practice have also been concerned with how leaders influence their employees through communication. Specific communicative strategies include open and supportive communication, in which leaders are willing and receptive listeners who are highly trustworthy and provide formal and informal rewards. Leaders also achieve effective communication through motivation—setting attainable and specific goals, meeting employees' expectations, treating everyone fairly, and gaining compliance. The success of that motivation relies on multiple factors, including effective communication, aligned incentives and rewards, and employee skill. Above all, employees and customers are perhaps best motivated by a compelling vision for why a product or service is invaluable.

Not all people who aspire to or attain leadership positions are inherently good. Bullies in the school yard often mature into bullies in the workplace, and unfortunately some of them rise to the top of the organizational chart because they intimidate and abuse others who are too frightened to speak out against them. Sexual harassment is a particularly insidious and illegal form of bullying that has significant negative consequences for individuals and organizations.

Leadership is vital to every organization. In our global economy, the diverse skills and understandings required for success have never been more demanding. While we can learn a great deal about how to meet those challenges from investigating the history of leadership research and exploring alternative approaches to leading, there will likely never be one approach that works in every situation. The central message of this book speaks directly to that challenge: Communication is how we learn to balance the ever-present and ever-shifting terrain of creativity and constraint in organizations. The more effective we learn to be as communicators, the more likely we will be viewed by others as leaders.

QUESTIONS FOR REVIEW AND DISCUSSION

1. Describe the progression of leadership thinking over the past one hundred years. What are the main changes that you observe, and how do they reflect important social and cultural changes?

2. Describe a situation in which the careful selection of leaders is essential for public safety. Based on the leadership models you have just studied, what advice would you offer about how to best screen candidates for this position?

3. Is transformational leadership critical in every type of organization? Are there any you can think of that require leaders primarily to maintain the status quo?

4. What are some of the ways in which a leader can shape organizational discourse to produce particular desired outcomes?

5. What do leaders do to empower employees? Is it critical to communicate a sense of empowerment to all employees in every organization, or are there specific types of organizational settings that are more appropriate than others for applying the empowerment principles?

6. Look on the Web for examples of organizational vision statements. What makes for a compelling vision?

7. What kinds of life events are most likely to lead to the modesty and high level of self-examination that seem to characterize the greatest leaders? By contrast, what events are likely to result in bullying or abusive leaders?

8. Evaluate the statement "All leadership IS communication." Is this an overstatement or a fair definition of the phenomenon?

KEY TERMS

Authentic communication, p. 286
Bullying, p. 296
Change agent, p. 279
Discursive leadership, p. 282
Empowerment, p. 294
Harassment, p. 297
Leadership style, p. 276
Modesty, p. 285
Motivation, p. 293

Sexual harassment, p. 297
Situational Leadership®, p. 278
Supportive communication, p. 291
Theory of leader-member exchange,
 p. 291
Trait theory, p. 275
Transformational leadership, p. 279
Vision, p. 281

CASE STUDY

When Leadership Styles Collide

Nathan Buckley is a county health agent for a public health department in a medium-sized, Midwestern town. He has worked for the county for about ten years, and he has developed several strong relationships with other agencies and organizations in his community. Recently, he has stepped forward to chair a community-based committee to focus on health disparities across the county's African American and Latino populations. The committee is made up of leaders from other county and city agencies, nonprofit organizations, and the community at large. The committee's job is to advise the county board and the city council about policies and programs addressing the health disparities in the community.

Nathan considers himself a servant leader. He has chosen his profession because he has a genuine concern for others, and he values open and honest communication, being accessible, and empowering others to develop their own potential. He also believes strongly in working with community-based partnerships to solve problems through critical reflection and dialogue. For these reasons, he stepped forward to chair the health disparities committee.

Although a lot of support exists for this project, Nathan feels as if he's struggling to make progress with the group. The other members of the committee are all strong leaders in their own organizations and communities, but they have very different leadership styles. The committee includes the president of a community coalition in one of the Latino neighborhoods, who has always been considered a transformational leader. There is also the executive director of a local nonprofit, who most often leads like a country club manager. The remaining members embody management traits that sometimes come into conflict with one another. Then there is Owen Harris, a community leader who tends to play the devil's advocate during most conversations. He is very passionate about his community, but some of his comments come across as passive-aggressive. Owen is generally good-natured; however, he has quietly started to bully Nathan behind the scenes.

Nathan feels as if he's unable to integrate the different leadership styles during committee meetings; therefore, the group has made little progress toward developing recommendations for the county board and the city council. Nathan has also started to pick up on Owen's behind-the-scenes bullying. More than anything, he wants to bring the leadership potential of this group together so they can achieve their goals; however, he's starting to feel burned out and helpless.

(continued, When Leadership Styles Collide)

Assignment

1. You are a friend of Nathan's from graduate school. You took an organizational communication class together, and you even gave a presentation together about leadership in community health contexts. Nathan trusts you when it comes to questions about leadership, and he sends you a message about his situation. What advice would you give Nathan about managing these different leadership styles?

2. Nathan remembers that effective communication with employees is open, supportive, motivating, and empowering. He feels as if most of the committee's conversations are open, motivating, and empowering, but group members aren't always supportive with their communication practices. What advice would you give Nathan about creating a more supportive environment?

3. How would you advise Nathan when it comes to communicating with Owen? If Owen's bullying is passive-aggressive and often occurs behind the scenes, it might not be as obvious to the other members of the committee. How can Nathan turn around his relationship with Owen?

CHAPTER 10

Organizational Alignment: Managing the Total Enterprise

For an organization to succeed over time, senior leaders and boards of directors must take a bird's-eye view of the total enterprise, both to see how it appears from the outside and to learn how it is regarded by various publics, partners, and competitors. Nevertheless, the temptation to avoid this activity is great. More pressing decisions tend to take precedence on agendas, and honest talk about how others see the organization can be difficult. Still, those with the discipline to engage in **strategic thinking**—the process of collecting relevant environmental data and making conscious choices about organizational values, positioning, and direction—end up ahead of the game both financially and in terms of employee engagement and morale.

Even when leaders have the insight and courage to think strategically, no strategy works all the time. Consumer tastes, market conditions, and countless other factors alter the organizational landscape on what can seem like a weekly basis. A strategy that made sense a few months ago may no longer make sense today. The only way to deal with this level of dynamism is to encourage open dialogue and continuous learning—that is, to purposefully sponsor and stage regular conversations about the appropriateness of the current strategy and the possible alternatives (e.g., "What business are we in? Is there still a customer for what we have to offer? What new developments in technology threaten to disrupt our business model?").

This chapter begins with a detailed discussion of strategic positioning as a communication issue, followed by a description of strategic alignment, which is defined as the process of bringing organizational systems in line with strategy. Central to these processes is the management of human and technological resources in all their dimensions. The next section goes into more depth about these important details. The chapter then broadens our view by looking at organizational learning more generally. Finally, we explore the relationship between organizational policymaking and communication, particularly as that relationship allows for ongoing integration and strategic alignment.

◩ POSITIONING THE ORGANIZATION

Success begins with strategy. To be successful over time, organizations must position themselves effectively in the social and economic landscape. **Strategic positioning** involves selecting a strategy or purpose that distinguishes the organization from its competitors. In addition, the strategy must be effectively communicated to employees, who will use it as a guide to decisions, and it must be clear to customers, who will use it to judge the company's image or reputation. There are two general types of strategies: lowest cost and differentiation. Moreover, different strategies may be appropriate at different times in an organization's life cycle. We will examine all of these topics in the sections that follow.

☐ Competitive Strategy

Strategy is of critical importance to the long-term success of a business. A **competitive strategy** is a clear statement of why customers should choose a company's products or services over those of competing companies. Simple descriptors such as *cheapest*, *fastest*, *most reliable*, *friendliest*, and *best quality* are typically used to express a company strategy. In addition to communicating a strategy, however, a company must ensure that all aspects of its business reflect the strategy (compare Day, Reibstein, & Gunther, 2004). Just saying that you stand for something doesn't make it so.

Despite the importance of strategy, some organizations operate without one, relying instead on their past success with a particular product or service. However, contemporary organizations that lack a strategy are at serious risk in today's highly competitive global market. Owners of brick-and-mortar movie theaters, for example, have seen their business shrink as more customers order movies on demand from their cable provider or use a mail or online service like Netflix, Apple, Hulu, or Amazon Prime. Bookstores continue to disappear in the United States with the rise of giant online retailers like Amazon. Fast-food restaurants like Checkers and Five Guys are struggling to carve out an identity in an industry dominated by McDonald's and other giant brands. And newspapers are continuing to overhaul their strategies as they work to succeed in the Internet age.

As a simple example of how a competitive strategy works in practice, let's suppose that you own a new fast-food eatery whose claim to fame is wood-fired pizza. After your first six months in business, you are concerned that business is slow because customers do not understand what makes your pizza different from that of less expensive national chains like Pizza Hut and Domino's. As a local business owner, you have been invited to attend a reception hosted by the city's chamber of commerce, providing you with a unique opportunity to promote your business. You dress appropriately for the event and bring your business cards with you. More important, you prepare what you will say about your business to others at the reception, positioning your restaurant as unique in its method of cooking, quality of ingredients, and taste. You keep in mind that it should take only about thirty seconds to explain what you do and why your business is worthy of attention (some people call this brief statement of purpose an "elevator speech" since it can be delivered in the time it takes to ride between floors in an elevator). Those you speak to will, in turn, be able to convey the same brief message to others later on, and it is your job to ensure that they will want to do so. If you succeed in making your message both memorable and distinct, your company has a competitive strategy.

As competition continues to increase and as the markets for products and services become more specialized, competitive strategies must adapt by targeting defined market niches and a narrower consumer audience (Day et al., 2004). In publishing and broadcasting, for example, both large and small companies target specific market segments with books, magazines, and news programs that cover specific topics. Small companies sell specialty products like food or dietary supplements by mail or via the Internet. Similarly, following a trend called "narrowcasting," cable television companies typically offer a number of channels that focus exclusively on sports, comedy, news, cooking, classic television shows, business, or home shopping programs. Large companies may pursue strategies to target multiple market niches. For example, to appeal to an older, more affluent audience, Honda created its Acura brand; while the Gap introduced Old Navy to appeal to very different group of consumers.

For communication specialists, crafting a competitive strategy involves close attention to message design. For instance, an effective strategy for your hypothetical pizza restaurant might focus on your unique preparation methods: "It's the only pizza place in town with a real wood-fired oven ensuring the most delicious pizza!" However, your strategy would be successful only if a niche market existed—or could be created—for your product. At times, unmet demand can be identified for a product or service so that its introduction is greeted with immediate appreciation: "We've always needed a good, authentic pizza place on this side of town." Alternatively, niches can be created for novel products and services (e.g., bottled water, minivans, or venti nonfat decaf caramel mocha Frappuccinos). The customer's reaction is "I never knew I needed that until I saw it!" A company that does not narrow its focus and attempts instead to target broad markets (e.g., "We serve pizza, burgers, fresh-squeezed juices, and deli sandwiches at the lowest prices") is unlikely to be able to serve the demands of all consumer markets or to distinguish itself as unique in any one market. Recently, the third largest retailer in the world, Tesco PLC, decided to close all two hundred of its Fresh & Easy neighborhood markets in the United States. Many analysts attribute this strategic failure to the company's decision to carry uniform assortments of products in every location rather than to adapt to regional and niche markets.

Developing a strategy for a new company often begins with the founder's personal experience or intuition about the potential demand for a product or service. For example, Starbucks CEO Howard Schultz came up with the idea for his business while frequenting a coffee bar in Italy and wondering why there weren't comparable stores in the United States. The next step is a careful analysis of the target market, the business environment (which includes potential customers, stakeholders, and community and government agencies), and the existing competition. This **competitor analysis** is especially important in identifying whether a similar product or service is offered by other companies in nearby or remote locations or if any past attempts to offer the product or service have failed. In formulating a competitive strategy, the prospective business owner must consider not only the potential demand for a product or service, but also how the company's strategy will be received by various publics. A serious objection by any one group can threaten the survival of the business.

Put another way, strategy is a compelling story, a "teachable point of view" about where a company is going and how it will get there (Barry & Elmes, 1997; Tichy, Pritchett, & Cohen, 1998). The power of a strategy to motivate employees and to attract customers is largely dependent on whether the strategy makes for a compelling narrative, and company leaders no longer have a monopoly on telling their stories. Both good and bad reviews of hotels and restaurants can be found on numerous sites such as Angie's List, TripAdvisor, and Yelp; meanwhile, bad customer experiences have led to the proliferation of highly critical blogs and even full-blown "anti-sites" (or "flaming sites") dedicated to trashing various businesses for poor quality, service, or community relations. This decreasing lack of control makes it more challenging for companies to put forth a persuasive story to the public.

☐ Types of Business Strategies

There are two basic types of business strategies: those that emphasize lowest cost and those that focus on differentiation (Porter, 1980; Walker, 2004).

Adopting a **lowest-cost strategy** involves a commitment to offering a product or service at the lowest possible price. Examples include discount appliance stores, no-frills airlines, and manufacturers of generic products. These companies emphasize their lowest-cost products or services to target consumers whose main motivation is saving money. To reach that consumer market, however, the strategy must be communicated effectively. Among the disadvantages of a lowest-cost strategy is the need to dramatically reduce operating costs. In a highly competitive global market, it can be difficult for companies choosing this strategy to manage the high costs of labor and materials.

A more popular business strategy is **differentiation**, which involves highlighting the unique or special qualities of a company's product or service. For example, a company may be the most reliable (Maytag), have the quickest delivery time (Domino's Pizza), or offer the most comprehensive warranty service in the business (Hyundai). In the automobile industry, there is a race on to see who can make the most eco-friendly car (the Toyota Prius has the lead among hybrids, but others are catching up); Volvo continues to emphasize safety, whereas BMW highlights performance. Differentiation is a highly communication-based strategy in that its success depends less on actual differences among competing products and more on the company's ability to create the perception of its product as unique in a significant way.

Developing a successful strategy can be as simple as noticing an unfilled niche in a particular market. For example, a physician may notice that a community's residents do not have access to medical care on weekends and may choose to address that need. The owner of a car rental company may respond to consumer demands for short rental periods with a strategy that incorporates both daily and hourly rates; in some cities, consumers can forgo car ownership altogether and use Zipcars for short periods of time, paying for them only when they need them. In many cases, however, developing a successful strategy is more difficult and complex because multiple businesses often compete within the same market. For example, three Los Angeles supermarkets conduct ongoing comparison studies to support their claims to offer the lowest prices in the city.

Similarly, in the battle among leaders in the overnight package-delivery business, companies use various strategies to compete within the same market. FedEx differentiates its service as being the most reliable, whereas the U.S. Postal Service touts the lowest cost. And although all of the major cell phone companies claim to offer the highest-quality service at the best price, their prices and levels of service are in reality quite similar. Finally, in most places in the United States, there is a heated battle going on among companies vying for consumers' television and broadband services, each touting the relative differentiating advantages of traditional cable, fiber-optic cable, and satellite transmission (e.g., Verizon, Bright House, DirecTV).

Strategy is critically important in highly cost-sensitive industries with low brand loyalty, such as the airline industry. Following deregulation of the industry in 1978, relatively small airlines entered the marketplace and offered fares on major routes that were significantly less than the fares charged by major carriers. A fare war ensued; airfares continued to drop, but so did profits. Many of the small lowest-cost airlines failed, taking a few major carriers with them. The survivors, scrambling for a way to encourage brand loyalty, settled on frequent-flyer programs. Airfares increased, and the carriers developed differentiation strategies to entice consumers such as claiming to offer the most on-time departures, the most leg room, and the best frequent-flyer program.

In developing a differentiation strategy, a company chooses to emphasize the most competitive aspect of its operation. This does not mean that the company is without other positive attributes, but it does mean that the company generally does not communicate them to the public as competitive advantages. Nordstrom, for instance, highlights the customer service available in its department stores even though the company is also concerned with cost, quality, and other factors. Nordstrom believes its customer service, more than any other attribute, is what separates it from its competitors.

Following is a comprehensive list of business strategies adopted by many familiar companies (Robert, 1993):

- *Product- or service-driven companies,* such as Boeing and Ritz-Carlton, strive to provide the highest-quality products or services in the business. They continually focus on how to improve their products or services as well as their work processes.
- *Market-driven companies* offer a wide range of products to a specific group of consumers. For example, Johnson & Johnson sells its products to doctors, nurses, patients, and parents. Ameriprise Financial now targets affluent individuals and sells its ability to handle all of their financial needs. Companies like these must engage in ongoing market research and cultivate consumer loyalty.
- *Production-capacity-driven companies,* such as airlines, make substantial investments in facilities and equipment and aim to have them running at full capacity at all times. They engage in market research to meet customers' needs and demands; they also offer special incentives such as reduced fares or discounted vacation packages to increase business during slack periods.
- *Technology-driven companies* like Apple, 3M, W. L. Gore & Associates, Amgen, and DuPont, own or specialize in a unique technology. For example, DuPont invented nylon; and the other companies on the list have each filed thousands of patents. Such companies invest a considerable amount of money in research and development.
- *Sales- and marketing-driven companies,* such as Mary Kay, Tupperware, Avon, and Arbonne, provide a wide range of products or services to customers in unconventional ways, including door-to-door selling, home shopping club sales, and Internet sales.
- *Distribution-driven companies* (like Walmart, UPS, Home Shopping Network, and food wholesalers) and Internet-only businesses (like Amazon, eBay, and Etsy) have unique ways of getting their products or services to the customer. Some may also push a variety of products through their distribution channels. Such companies strive to maintain a highly effective distribution system.

The overriding factor in strategy development is a keen awareness of the related industry as a whole as well as its potential for change or improvement. Before air travel was possible, people crossed the oceans on ships. With the advent of passenger air travel, however, transportation companies offering ocean passage were threatened with obsolescence. Some of them survived by redefining their strategy and, instead of focusing just on transportation, began providing entertainment on cruise lines. Similarly, McDonald's, a leader in competitive strategy, is not in the food business. People go to McDonald's for comfort, security, predictability, and safety, which are reflected in the location and cleanliness of its restaurants and in its rigid standards for food worldwide. Recently, however, the popular chain has been experiencing serious identity problems. Business analysts claim that McDonald's has lost touch with what the customer really wants, and that the proliferation of menu options is both confusing to customers and dilutes the power of the brand.

☐ Strategy and the Business Life Cycle

Strategy changes as an organization progresses through what might be called the "stages of the business life cycle" (Kimberly & Miles, 1980). Strategic and communicative challenges also differ at each stage (Maug, 2001).

At *birth*, a new company is concerned mainly with developing a strategy and finding a niche. The company secures financial backing and makes an initial foray into the marketplace.

In *childhood*, the company's major challenge is managing its growth and development. In its pursuit of multiple opportunities, the growing organization may be distracted from its basic strategy or may lack the discipline needed to maintain a focus on its competitive advantage. Effective leadership can help counteract these problems.

When the company reaches *adolescence*, it typically encounters stiff competition. As a result, the original strategy no longer functions as a competitive advantage, and the company must work to change or fine-tune it accordingly. This may require paying special attention to both internal communication (to streamline processes, cut costs, and develop new competencies) and external communication (to remind customers of why the company's product or service is superior to those of its competitors).

In the final phase of the business life cycle, *maturity*, the company faces the difficult challenge of renewal—of letting go of the old business in favor of a new one, while also maintaining a position in the marketplace. This process of renewal is often difficult to pull off. Abercrombie & Fitch attempted to redefine itself by, almost overnight, going from appealing to well-off, mature world travelers to fashion- and price-conscious teenagers. While the company initially experienced some success, A&F has struggled more recently to hold on to its new identity. One success story is Honda, which entered the world automobile market in the 1970s with the tiny Honda Civic, and is known for its strategic excellence. Since the 1970s, Honda has focused not on a particular product but on the customers who purchased the early Civics—baby boomers buying their first car. Transforming and upgrading its products to match those customers' needs, Honda introduced the Prelude and Accord as these young adults moved into their thirties, and the upscale Acura line as they moved into their forties and became more affluent. Honda's strategy is thus tied to satisfying a well-defined market segment. Finally, Toyota's introduction of the eco-friendly Prius family of cars reflects its willingness to reinvent its approach to appeal to shifting consumer demographics and tastes.

The failure rate in most industries is very high. Failure, or *death*, can occur at any point in the life cycle. In fact, few start-up companies make it past their first two years, largely because they are undercapitalized and they don't have the resources to survive the time it takes for a strategy to work, assuming that it will. In recent years, many small businesses have either gone under (e.g., Pets.com) or been sold to larger corporations (e.g., Sharper Image).

STRATEGIC ALIGNMENT

A company may communicate a strategy like "environmentally friendly" or "superior customer service," but if customers and employees do not see evidence of the company's claim, the strategy will be unconvincing and ineffective. In addition to communicating the strategy to various internal and external publics, the strategy must be reflected in various other aspects of the organization. **Strategic alignment** refers to the process of modifying organizational systems and structures to support the competitive strategy. This may affect such areas as job design, levels of authority, job training, reward systems, and staffing, among many others.

In the absence of strategic alignment, a business can neither accomplish its strategy nor create the desired image. For example, a print shop that claims to have the lowest prices in town but pays its employees above-average wages is not likely to achieve success. Similarly, a company that claims to be responsive to customers would be unable to implement that strategy if its automated phone system did not give customers the option of speaking directly with a service representative.

Successful strategic alignment is difficult because it forces a company to consider the relationship between its strategy and its internal systems. In addition, strategic alignment is complicated by employees' reluctance to see themselves as part of a system and by managers' tendency to make decisions in isolation rather than basing decisions on the company's strategy and taking the entire organizational system into account. Companies that overcome these obstacles to strategic alignment, pursuing a carefully chosen strategy, are far more likely to achieve success.

One well-established model that is particularly helpful in thinking about strategic alignment is the original 7-S model, developed by members of the consulting firm McKinsey & Company (see Figure 10.1). According to this model, strategic alignment involves consideration of the following seven factors:

1. *Strategy.* Strategy provides a common purpose for all employees and stakeholders. It differentiates the company from its competitors.
2. *Superordinate goals.* More specific than a company's mission statement, **superordinate goals** are those broad outcomes that everyone in the organization

FIGURE 10.1

The Original 7-S Model of Strategic Alignment

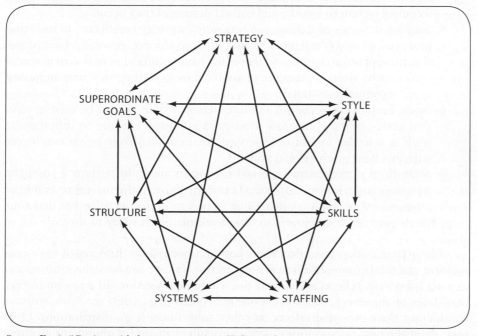

Source: From "Coping with hypercompetition: Utilizing the new 7-S model," by R. D'Aveni, 1995, *Academy of management executive*, *9*(3), p. 48.

is motivated to achieve, such as attaining a particular percentage of market share or increasing customer loyalty. To be effective, these goals must flow logically from the company's strategy. Some authors have argued that the best route to success is for firms to dream big and develop "big hairy audacious goals" (Collins & Porras, 1994).

3. *Structure.* The formal reporting relationships as prescribed by the organizational chart should reflect the company's strategy and should symbolically represent the company's values. A team-based organization or an inverted pyramid with the customer at the top are two common examples of meaningful organizational structures.

4. *Systems.* The flow of information through various media (e.g., telephones, computer systems, and meetings), the formal systems of operation (e.g., management information systems), the informal operating procedures (e.g., cultural practices), and the informal connections among people (e.g., emergent networks) should all be aligned with the company's strategy. Systems are

relevant to communication in that they deal with the distribution of information throughout a company. Certain strategies can be used only with certain types of systems. For example, a "best product quality" strategy would require a control system to identify and correct defects as they occur.

5. *Staffing.* In terms of staffing, the company's strategy is reflected in its hiring practices, in its job assignments, and in its workforce generally. Companies that promote from within and those that have technical as well as managerial career paths are two examples of approaches to staffing that may support a specific competitive strategy.

6. *Skills.* Employees' technical and interpersonal skills should be used in ways that promote the company's strategy. A company striving to differentiate itself as a leader in customer service, for example, likely needs employees with excellent interpersonal skills.

7. *Style.* Both management style and organizational culture (how a company perceives and treats its employees) can contribute to the success or failure of a business strategy. A company that strives to be competitive but that routinely permits its employees to miss deadlines is not likely to survive.

The strategic-alignment process is best approached by thinking of the organization as a total communication system. In this way, we see how the information in each subsystem reflects and affects the whole organization. In an organization that is out of alignment, decisions in one subsystem (e.g., sales) are made without considering their potential effects on other subsystems (e.g., distribution). Over time, even the best organizations' systems usually drift out of alignment as internal functions become outdated and as external developments in technology and market demographics necessitate internal change. Employees are highly sensitive to misalignment; that is, if the company claims to promote trust and empowerment, employees are likely to voice their objections if their actual decision-making participation is limited. At Disneyland, for example, employees objected to what they perceived as inconsistencies between the company's strategy—"The happiest place on Earth"—and its poor treatment and compensation of employees (Smith & Eisenberg, 1987).

The strategic-alignment process begins with the development of a strategy, preferably one that is derived from a comprehensive analysis of the present and future external environment and aims to focus and invigorate the company. Once a strategy has been developed, it must be translated into superordinate goals so that it can be communicated to all employees. Next, structure is examined to determine whether it supports the strategy. For example, in the process of transitioning from a government business to a commercial supplier, a major electronics company sought to become a customer-driven firm, unlike its competitors. However, the company's existing structure, characterized by vertical lines of expertise and authority and minimal cross-functional communication, would not support its new focus on customer relations. The company modified its structure by creating a centralized customer service office to act as an interface for customer communication, a repair center designed to meet customers' needs, and cross-functional teams to promote effective communication.

An analysis of systems typically occurs at this point in the strategic-alignment process. In our example, the electronics firm found that its existing voice-mail system kept customers on hold for too long, so it made changes to ensure that customers could reach a service representative within a reasonable amount of time. In addition, the company's past experience with military projects and lax schedules meant that group meetings would need to focus on addressing work issues more expediently. With the help of the human resources department, the company's chief decision-making groups worked together on creating a greater sense of urgency in its informal systems.

Staffing, skills, and style are the final considerations in strategic alignment. The electronics firm recruited employees with the technical and communication skills needed to enact the proposed strategy. Managers and employees in the customer service offices were trained in how to cultivate new customer-oriented styles of working and communication with openness and empathy. Employees who were less open to this change were reassigned to positions that were less visible to customers.

In Florida, the Department of Motor Vehicles (DMV) has successfully reinvented itself through strategic alignment. After suffering for years with a reputation for the worst service imaginable, DMV leaders set a new strategic focus on customer service and proceeded to implement some dramatic system changes in support of that strategy. While most people continue to hold bad memories of their past DMV experiences, the current reality couldn't be more different. The DMV offices are welcoming, the employees are friendly and helpful, and perhaps most important, the systems provide the kind of information that supports excellent customer service.

In most cases, strategic alignment is accomplished gradually; a management team focuses on each stage of the process before proceeding to the next stage. Sometimes, however, large-scale strategic alignment is attempted, as in the case of **total quality management (TQM)**, a company-wide, comprehensive effort to create a culture of quality. In pursuing the strategy of total quality, a company may simultaneously redefine its objectives (superordinate goals), overhaul its organization (structure), train or let go of managers from the "old school" (style), recruit new managers with skills better suited to the redefined structure (staffing), and train all employees in empowerment, teamwork, and other areas (skills).

As a large-scale intervention, total quality management is only occasionally successful. In addition to the difficulties associated with maintaining a focus amid rapid change in multiple areas, employees tend to react negatively to change that is radical rather than gradual. They may become suspicious of the company's intentions, worry about losing their jobs, and be less willing to commit themselves to the program's success. Another problem associated with TQM occurs when a company focuses mainly on winning external recognition for its efforts. The Malcolm

Baldrige National Quality Award, for example, is given by the U.S. government to companies for excellence in total quality management. Winning the award provides a company with excellent publicity and some powerful advertising copy. However, in the case of a Florida utility company that pursued TQM to win the award, its efforts led to internal havoc and a worse complaint record than that of several other Florida utilities (Sashkin, 1991).

Finally, strategic alignment is not just an issue for corporations and government agencies. Smaller not-for-profit companies and nongovernmental organizations (NGOs) are also challenged to define their strategies in such a way that they send a consistent message and focus their efforts through alignment (Eisenberg & Eschenfelder, 2009). A familiar example is environmental activist organizations like Greenpeace, which must be vigilant in communicating a clear and consistent focus both proactively and in response to external challenges.

The *Everyday Organizational Communication* box on page 321 takes a closer look at how TQM and other strategic-alignment practices play out at colleges and universities.

◣ ALIGNING STRATEGIES WITH RESOURCES

The shift from locally grounded industries to global knowledge work has altered the essential characteristics of most businesses. Where in the past enormous capital expenditures went into buildings and materials, today the two most critical resources for any successful business are *people* and *technology*. Increasingly, work can be done anywhere at any time, and the work of an organization may be done by people not on the regular payroll—outsourcers and subcontractors. To manage this type of work, organizations must align their strategy with the human and technological resources available to them. This section deals with the human resources that are the core of any successful enterprise, including talent and organizational development, as well as the rapidly changing landscape of technological resources that organizations must navigate.

☐ Human Resources

When manufacturing was dominant and the "machine" model of organizing was at its peak in America, hiring was done unsystematically, and nepotism (favoring one's relations) and other forms of favoritism were common. With the rise of bureaucracy in the mid-twentieth century, companies began to understand the importance of attracting and keeping good workers. They established personnel departments to provide a consistent focus on policies affecting employees. Shifting emphases toward employee participation and innovation resulted in further transformation from personnel departments to human resources departments. As discussed in Chapter 3, the term *human resources* itself reflects

EVERYDAY ORGANIZATIONAL COMMUNICATION

Helping Colleges and Universities Do What They Do Best

Every ten years, colleges and universities must go through a reaccreditation process. For schools that are part of the Southern Association of Colleges and Schools, that process includes developing and implementing a quality enhancement plan (QEP). The purpose of the QEP is not to create a new program for the college or university, but to identify common strengths across the institution and develop mechanisms to promote those strengths. In other words, a QEP is designed to help a specific college or university do what it does best.

For example, Kennesaw State University (KSU) in Georgia has implemented a QEP concentrated on "global learning for engaged citizenship." This program reflects the internationalization of the curriculum at KSU, as well as its focus on global learning leadership. Similarly, Wake Forest University in Winston-Salem, North Carolina, used its QEP to focus on "preparing students to be global citizens." Other schools, such as the University of Southern Mississippi in Hattiesburg, Mississippi, have taken a different approach with their QEPs. Southern Mississippi's program, titled *Finding a Voice: Improving Oral and Written Competencies*, highlights its Speaking and Writing Centers as core resources. These programs allow colleges and universities to specify their niche in an increasingly competitive academic environment and differentiate themselves from other schools.

DISCUSSION QUESTIONS

1. What does your college or university do best? If your school were to design and implement a QEP, what strengths do you think the program would highlight?
2. How are QEPs similar to total quality management practices? What are the strengths of implementing QEPs as a form of strategic alignment? Is there reason to be suspicious of the QEPs implemented at colleges and universities?
3. How can colleges and universities make the most of their QEPs? For example, how could the Department of Communication at Wake Forest University make the most of the focus on "preparing students to be global citizens"? How could the Speaking and Writing Centers at Southern Mississippi leverage the university's emphasis on oral and written competencies into more resources and support?

a willingness to see employees as having valuable knowledge that can serve as a resource for organizational success—the acquisition of talent and ongoing organizational development.

Talent

Many chief executive officers are quick to minimize their role in their company's achievements and are anxious to celebrate the accomplishments of their people. This makes good sense. An essential role for senior leadership is to develop robust organizational systems, including recruiting, reward, development, and communication systems, that support the acquisition and retention of talent.

Over the past few decades, human resource management has grown into a highly sophisticated discipline. In the past, salaries, benefits, and training were treated as an afterthought and were shaped by the opinions of line managers with little or no knowledge of research on attracting and developing talent. Today, most large companies have a senior vice president of human resources who reports to the president or CEO and has input into strategic decisions. Recent developments have made the wisdom of this shift even more apparent. At a conference of the five hundred fastest-growing companies, a large percentage of entrepreneur-founders were looking for people to buy their companies. The most common reason they gave for wanting to cash out was their inability to attract and retain sufficient talent.

Research shows that companies that treat people as their most important asset are also the most profitable. In one award-winning study of 968 companies across all industries, it was revealed that "a one standard deviation increase in the use of [high-performance practices] was associated with a 7.05 percent decrease in turnover and, on a per employee basis, $27,044 more in sales and $18,641 and $3,814 more in market value and profits, respectively" (Huselid, 1995). Follow-up studies have continued to provide compelling evidence that progressive human resources practices like self-managed teams, employee empowerment, pay for performance, and extensive training, are significantly and positively related to organizational performance (Syed & Jamal, 2012; Tregaskis, Daniel, Glover, Butler, & Meyer, 2012). Companies in highly competitive industries are always seeking skilled employees at all levels. Those that can afford to do so are trying new approaches, such as recruiting abroad, building employee housing, providing huge incentives to current employees who refer a new hire, and even hiring groups of friends.

Progressive human resources management has many aspects, but the following three key components have everything to do with communication:

1. *Targeted Selection.* When jobs are created in a conscious way, each job comprises critical dimensions, such as word-processing skills, strategic thinking, oral communication, or tolerance for ambiguity. **Targeted selection** is a systematic job-interview process through which selected company experts assess job candidates on the key dimensions of each job. At the end of a search process, the interviewers meet to pool their data and make an informed choice.

Employees hired through targeted selection are, with few exceptions, immediately capable of making a contribution to the company's performance.

2. *Performance Management.* Every leader should have an ongoing conversation with employees during which strategy is reinforced, objectives are reviewed, results are revealed, and gaps are examined. **Performance management** is any system that tracks and gives feedback to employees about how well they are accomplishing objectives tied to each of their key job dimensions. These systems should be thoughtful, timely, and use both face-to-face interactions and written documentation to keep managers and employees accountable to each other.

3. *Training and Development.* Businesspeople have long recognized that there are benefits to identifying the best practices in performing any given job and then communicating these practices systematically to employees. **Training and development** refers to the formal and informal efforts to develop those employee skills. What is challenging today is that the knowledge and skills to be taught are evolving at blinding speed, making even last year's training potentially obsolete.

There is further recognition that targeted selection, performance management, and training and development efforts cannot be "one size fits all." The process of attracting and retaining talent has become increasingly tailored to fit the interests, learning styles, locations, and even schedules of targeted employees. Like customers, employees want feedback and education that is "just-in-time, just-for-me." For this reason, companies are designing highly flexible and modular development centers or "corporate universities" that offer a dazzling array of learning opportunities through a range of media. The underlying idea is that the best time to teach something like Microsoft Excel or supervisory skills is when employees need to learn it for their work. Progressive companies tie these training and development efforts to their performance-management systems. In doing so, senior leaders can use summary performance data to target entire departments or regions for certain kinds of development, such as customer service or time-management training.

The best employees will get frustrated and leave if they lack appropriate tools to perform their jobs effectively. Interestingly, this problem is compounded in companies with performance-management systems because employees are acutely aware of their accountabilities and are given incentives for meeting their goals. Difficulties occur because most people avoid stressful communication situations and potential conflict. This is why so many employees report that their performance feedback is often late, if they get any at all. The worst-case scenario occurs when cowardly managers leave employees a copy of their review with a note that says, "Call if you have any questions." This is unacceptable and defeats the purpose of performance reviews.

There is one last piece of the puzzle that, when applied, can turbocharge the whole human resources function. Tying employee performance to clearly defined rewards—compensation, benefits, advancement, recognition—rationalizes the system for employees. Rather than being busy work that has little to do with the employee's "real job," the business of filling out tracking forms and meeting with managers to discuss performance becomes central to the employee's work life. Targeted selection ensures that people are hired who have a fighting chance of performing the needed functions; performance management tracks their success and provides specific feedback on where they must improve; training and development provide opportunities for continuous learning in those areas; and employees are rewarded for consistently doing the things that, by design, support the company's strategy.

Organizational Development

Any progressive human resources practitioner will tell you that no amount of training can substitute for enterprise-wide efforts to transform and sustain a new type of organizational culture. For this reason, many HR professionals have over the years been drawn to the subfield of **organizational development (OD)**, which deals with the purposeful facilitation of strategic systems change. In practice, this usually amounted to senior management enlisting the help of their internal human resources staff—or hiring an external HR consultant—to assist in promoting a particularly challenging organizational change. The occasion for such an initiative varied from mergers to reorganization to downsizing.

In every instance, the decision to involve an OD professional—many of whom have backgrounds in communication—reveals some important realities about the nature of strategic change in organizations and institutions. Having been involved in many of these initiatives ourselves, we have learned four core "lessons" in approaching the strategic-change process with a communication lens:

1. *People want to be engaged and inspired.* Particularly in the wake of the old social contract, it is important to remember that people still look to work as a potential source of meaning in their lives. A compelling vision or strategy can provide this. The flip side of this lesson is that you can't force people to change to meet a schedule; people adopt change when they are ready.
2. *People are more likely to support something they have helped to create.* Another key principle of change management is that employees must be given sufficient information and opportunities for dialogue if one expects them to support the new direction. Much of what OD practitioners actually do is facilitate these conversations.
3. *Clear line of sight is a reliable indicator of success.* A good test of the degree to which a company has successfully aligned its practices with its strategy is the degree to which employees can articulate a clear connection between the strategy and what they do every day on the job. When employees make this connection, they have a clear line of sight from their work to the goal.
4. *Actions still speak louder than words.* The competitive strategy can be inspiring and the dialogues far-reaching, but if the nonverbal behaviors of management

conflict with the espoused direction, the change effort is dead in the water. This is the hardest part of alignment for an OD professional to address, since it implicates the judgment of senior management.

☐ Technological Resources

The potential effects of communication technology are multiple and varied. Contemporary observers usually support one of four major views on the subject: utopian, dystopian, neutral, and contingent.

From the **utopian view**, information technology serves to equalize power relationships at work by bridging time and space, thereby improving both productivity and work life. Proponents of this highly optimistic view see technology as both encouraging employee voice and freeing employees to work anywhere, anytime.

In contrast, the more pessimistic **dystopian view** sees communication technology as primarily benefiting an economic elite and—through the corporate colonization of the life world (Deetz, 1992)—progressively limiting our freedoms by bringing more of our personal lives under corporate surveillance and scrutiny. Proponents of the dystopian view range from extremists, sometimes called "Luddites," who advocate a return to simpler times, to moderates, who suggest that a technology's consequences be considered. For example, many people today are frustrated with the overwhelming amount of information that has come with easier access to technology. In a survey of employees across a wide range of industries, respondents reported significant levels of overload due to the proliferation of electronic media. Indeed, the average Fortune 100 worker sends and receives hundreds of e-mail messages each day. In contrast, there are those with little or no access to technology who, in the dystopian view, are fast becoming the have-nots in a growing "digital divide" (Dunham, 1999).

The **neutral view** of communication technology holds that it has no significant effects on human behavior and that people can be expected to behave in predictable ways whether they use a traditional telephone or a computer to communicate. Proponents of this view believe that the potential effects of technology on communication and behavior are exaggerated by utopians, dystopians, and others.

The **contingent view** of communication technology is best supported by research. From this view, the effect of a given innovation depends on the context or situation in which it is adopted. For example, while smartphones may enable group members to communicate remotely or to access relevant information immediately, the overuse of such devices can also lead to organizational problems, including decreased productivity due to employee distraction. In one recent study, medical residents on patient rounds were observed missing important clinical information 34 percent of the time because they were distracted by their smartphones (Katz-Sidlow, Ludwig, Miller, & Sidlow, 2012).

The successful implementation of any communication technology takes into account the social and political aspects of the organizational environment in which it will be used. The "rational" use of communication technology is "subjective, retrospective, and influenced by information provided by others" (Fulk, Schmitz, & Steinfeld, 1990, p. 143). The authors of one study conclude:

> There is no such thing as pure technology. To understand technology, one must first understand social relationships.... Everything about the adoption and uses of media is social.... Logical expectations for the adoption and use of the new media are rarely met. The pragmatics of technological communication must always be understood in the context of motives, paradoxes, and contradictions of everyday life. (Contractor & Eisenberg, 1990, p. 143)

A good example of the relationship between technology and social context is the decision by some organizations to broadcast board meetings or senior executive updates to all employee computers via streaming video. If management-employee relationships are already strong, and if the broadcast is framed in such a way that it makes employees curious about new and relevant information which might be shared, the technology can be a smashing success. Alternatively, dropping such a broadcast into a secretive environment with no history of candid communication across levels will most likely lead at best to apathy, and at worst to resentment and suspicion. It is important to keep in mind that the same technology may have radically different effects depending on the prevailing social context. Table 10.1 identifies six important considerations in the analysis of communication technology.

Regardless of scholars' view of the effects of communication technology, there are currently three areas dominating communication and technology research with application to managing the total enterprise: synchronicity and media richness; social media, app culture, and the urgent organization; and privacy.

Synchronicity and Media Richness

When it comes to tapping in to technological resources, organizations must consider key questions regarding their choice of media—how much simultaneous or "real-time" communication does the technology allow, and how rich is the interaction. **Synchronicity** refers to the capacity of a technology to allow for simultaneous two-way (or multi-way) communication. For example, a telephone is synchronous, but an answering machine allows the telephone to become asynchronous. Similarly, while most e-mail is asynchronous, the proliferation of Internet chat rooms and text/instant messaging has created more possibilities for synchronicity. Both synchronous and asynchronous modes of communication have their advantages. For instance, certain requests and work tasks are best approached via two-way communication, whereas other tasks may be well communicated and performed through asynchronous channels (e.g., when busy people leave messages for one another across time zones). However, asynchronous communication can lead people to make more contacts than they can reasonably handle (Gergen, 1991). This is why many people in high-status or

TABLE 10.1

Six Concerns in the Analysis of Communication Technology

1. *Humans are agents.* Accept the fact that "humans are reflexively monitoring what goes on in a particular social system, that they are motivated by wants and aspirations, and that they have the power not to perform the prescription laid down by systems designers" (p. 312).

2. *Tacit knowledge should be respected.* "People know more about their lives than they can put into words. People do know how to handle practical affairs without being able to explain fully what they are really doing" (p. 312).

3. *Understanding is partial.* "There are always unacknowledged conditions for and unintended consequences of people's behavior" (p. 313).

4. *Technology is politically ambiguous.* Although a technology can be used to promote dialogue and to improve individual quality of life, the same technology can also be used to constrain, limit, and control.

5. *Informal communication must be acknowledged.* "Informal informing is an organizational fact. . . . It is necessary to understand how formal information is mediated through various more or less structured patterns of informing" (p. 313).

6. *Counterrational decision making should be acknowledged.* "The rational model is not a viable way of understanding the intricacies of modern business management. On the one hand it is questionable that decision-makers cognitively are able to cope with the complexity and amount of information needed to make rational decisions, and on the other hand, it is probable that all sorts of political and social pressures are called upon in everyday management" (pp. 313–314).

Source: From "Understanding third-wave information systems," by J. Mouritsen and N. Bjorn-Andersen, 1991, in C. Dunlop and R. Kling (Eds.), *Computerization and controversy: Value conflicts and social choices.*

high-visibility jobs sometimes limit others' access to their voice-mail and e-mail systems.

Media richness refers to the number of multiple channels of contact afforded by a communication medium (Daft & Lengel, 1984). Each channel roughly corresponds to one of our senses. Face-to-face communication is classified as most rich because it simultaneously allows for speech, nonverbal communication, vision, smell, and touch. Using this definition, a letter would fall at the low end of the media richness scale, as it only allows for verbal exchange. Videoconferencing is a richer medium than telephone conferencing, but it still falls short of face-to-face interaction. People are selective when deciding how rich a medium to use, selecting the one best suited to their personality and goals. All of us have likely sent a text message to someone because we couldn't "face" their response in person.

Social Media

The explosion of social media use both by individuals and within organizations has created an environment where one can have instant access to others' opinions, activities, and whereabouts. Most large organizations have hired employees dedicated to monitoring Facebook, Twitter, and Instagram postings to identify customer complaints and to respond directly when possible. Some less-than-ethical companies have instructed employees to pose as customers and post positive reviews on sites such as Yelp or TripAdvisor. And many schools and universities now use social media to stay in touch with students.

The positive side of social media technology is that it enables immediate feedback about organizational products and services and consequently creates the possibility of a nimble response. The negative side is that it creates an urgent "update culture" where organizational members are tempted to overemphasize "breaking news" over a longer-term, more systematic analysis of trends and reactions. This potential bias may cause some organizations to give up on good ideas too soon or to overreact to what could turn out to be a minority opinion.

Although social media can constrain the ways in which organizations rely on technological resources, having a social media presence is no longer just a good idea but an expectation for most organizations. When recruitment media firm ERE (Kutsmode, 2014) identified the top future trends in talent acquisition, the majority featured some element of a social media presence. Recommendations included identifying "passive candidates" through sites like LinkedIn, asking hiring managers to promote jobs on their personal social media sites, and using social engagement tools like QUEsocial and talentREEF to narrow in on potential talent. And this reliance on social media is not limited to recruiting and retaining talent. A variety of business news leaders—including *Fast Company*, *Business Insider*, and *Forbes*—regularly report on the best times to post on social media to promote a brand, manage public relations, and reinforce the strategic positioning of the organization.

App Culture and the Urgent Organization

The growing dependence on social media also points to another technological resource that organizations and individuals must manage. An increasing number of organizations now rely on apps, or mobile device applications, as a way to keep connected with customers, employees, and members. For most of us, the use of apps is fairly routine. These smartphone software programs help manage everything from playlists, shopping lists, credit card purchases, personal security systems, and the indoor temperature of our homes. The same holds true for organizations.

The development of mobile apps represents another resource that organizations can use to strategically position themselves. Similar to creating a social media presence, developing a content-specific mobile app has become commonplace and almost expected for contemporary organizations. Because of the relative ease and user-friendly nature of app design, national chains like Pizza Hut or Domino's can have a smartphone app that lets you create and order your own pizza, and so can your local pizza joint.

The growing popularity of this app culture allows for an increasing number of businesses, nonprofits, and groups to operate as urgent organizations. As we mentioned in Chapter 1, urgent organizations seek to shorten the time it takes to respond to customers, and mobile apps often help facilitate that process. Companies like Uber have built their entire business model around the idea that a mobile app can connect a driver to a person who needs a ride, often at a faster, and sometimes more affordable, rate than a conventional taxicab. Organizations can use mobile apps to construct that "just-in-time, just-for-me" feeling for their customers. Indeed, our own National Communication Association and International Communication Association regularly develop mobile apps for our national and international conferences.

This type of innovation can come at a price, however, as many Uber customers learned on New Year's Eve in 2015. Part of Uber's business model allows for price surges during peak times and heavy traffic, meaning that riders are subject to rates that are two, three, even nine times the regular fare. Although riders must agree to the price before accepting the ride, some customers took this for granted on New Year's Eve, with some disgruntled riders paying upwards of $300 for what was normally a $20 trip. Nevertheless, mobile apps are an incredibly popular technological resource for organizations, and virtually anyone can learn how to develop one. As such, aligning smartphone app technology across an organization's strategy will continue to be an important component of managing the total enterprise.

Privacy   The primary benefit of communication technology—the radical expansion of connections between people and institutions—is also its main liability. Every connection leaves traces that can be followed and exploited by others for personal gain. Issues of privacy, secrecy, and copyright in computer-aided interaction are currently being debated in courts around the world. In most companies, for example, managers have access to employees' e-mail messages. Major credit card companies follow consumer spending patterns very closely, including where clients make transactions. Critics of Facebook are quick to focus on the company's repeated attempts to make use of personal data in ways that some find uncomfortable or unethical. The effect of electronic surveillance on people's right to privacy is already a major issue throughout the world.

As discussed in Chapter 6, we have witnessed an enormous increase in the computerized monitoring of employee productivity, in which the frequency and speed of work are measured and stored by the computer and are reviewed by management. Most employers monitor their employees as a means of protecting themselves against possible litigation. A survey by the American Management Association (2008) and the ePolicy Institute found that two-thirds of employers monitor their employees' website visits in order to prevent inappropriate surfing, and 65 percent use software to block connections to websites deemed off-limits for employees. This is a 27 percent increase since 2001, when the survey was first conducted. The survey also found that more than one-quarter of employers have fired workers for e-mail misuse.

These types of practices are only compounded with the growth of social media sites and mobile apps. Now, not only can corporations peruse your e-mail and credit card purchases, they can monitor your Twitter and Instagram posts and track when you've "checked in" to various locations. Many individuals and organizations have become painfully aware of the implications of online activities. For example, the University of Illinois chose to revoke a job offer to Dr. Steven Salaita after the professor posted comments about the conflict between Israel and Palestine on his Twitter feed. The university eventually paid an $875,000 settlement to Dr. Salaita when he sued the institution for breach of contract and violating his freedom of speech. As another example, Justine Sacco virtually ruined her public relations career when she tweeted a racially insensitive comment before boarding an eleven-hour flight to South Africa. When she departed the flight, she learned that a post she thought was private had quickly gone viral. The *What Would You Do?* box on page 331 relates her story and asks you to consider the public and private content of your own online comments.

Anecdotally, many human resource administrators report that they routinely conduct Google searches and locate applicants' Facebook pages as part of the job interview process. Most college students today have been told repeatedly to be careful about what they post online and are becoming more cautious and sophisticated about the privacy settings on their social media accounts. Future research will likely show further shifts in employer surveillance of employee communication (D'Urso, 2006; Riedy & Wen, 2010). In the meantime, lawyers across the globe are introducing cases that seek to better define what might constitute "private" communication in the online environment (e.g., Connolly & McParland, 2012).

◪ ONGOING INTEGRATION

At the beginning of this chapter, we mentioned how organizations often do not take the time to critically reflect on their organizational practices or look at their practices from a bird's-eye view. At the same time, organizations that do carve out time to consider the positive and negative consequences of their activities have a distinct and strategic advantage toward achieving their goals. This need for reflection means that strategic positioning and organizational alignment are not one-time activities that an organization and its members need not revisit. Rather, aligning the organization's systems and structures involves ongoing activities like

When a Tweet Costs You a Career

Justine Sacco was a thirty-year-old director of corporate communications at IAC. On December 20, 2013, she boarded a plane from New York to South Africa for the holidays. Before she departed, Justine tweeted, "Going to Africa. Hope I don't get AIDS. Just kidding. I'm white!" She thought her comments were fairly innocuous—she considered it "just a joke," and she shared the comment privately with her 170 Twitter followers.

During the eleven-hour flight to Cape Town, Justine's comment went viral. The Twittersphere was quick to point out the racial insensitivity of the tweet, especially coming from a communications executive who was supposed to think before she tweets. Comments were swift and severe, calling for her termination and eventually generating the hashtag #HasJustineLandedYet. Meanwhile, at 35,000 feet, Justine remained completely oblivious to the fact that her career was unraveling on the ground. When she finally did land in Cape Town, she was flooded with text messages from friends and family telling her what had happened. The damage had been done. Justine's "joke" was the number one trending topic on Twitter, and her corporate communications career was effectively over.

Discussion Questions

1. What kind of online presence do you have? How often do you post? What devices or platforms do you use to post? If you don't have much of an online presence, do you regularly read others' Facebook pages, Instagram posts, or Twitter feeds? Why or why not?
2. How public or private do you consider your online presence? What kinds of settings do you use to ensure that publicity or privacy?
3. How would you have handled yourself if you made a questionable online post, which you thought was private, but was shared publicly and eventually went viral? What advice would you give someone in Justine's case, especially as she attempts to salvage her career?
4. What sort of line should we draw, or standards should we develop, when it comes to creating an online presence? Should the Twittersphere have enough power and influence to call for someone's termination from their job? At what point do we hold someone to the highest level of accountability or forgive someone for a mistake?
5. Are individuals who work in the fields of communication or media held to a higher standard for their public and private comments, simply because of the nature of their work? Should they be?

learning and policymaking. In this final section, we consider how strategic positioning and managing the total enterprise is an ongoing process.

☐ Organizational Learning

In our rapidly changing world, learning organizations have a distinct advantage. Composed of people who not only profit from past mistakes but also are willing to question the assumptions that led to those mistakes, learning organizations are well equipped to deal with continuous change (Marquardt, 2002; Senge, 2006; Steier, 1989). Organizational learning can include a range of activities, and here we focus on learning basic skills and collecting data for tracking and monitoring.

An essential element of organizational learning of interest to scholars and practitioners are the learning of basic skills. Most organizational practitioners, educators, and politicians agree that the U.S. educational system does a mediocre job of providing students with even the most basic job skills. The U.S. Department of Labor Secretary's Commission on Achieving Necessary Skills identifies three foundational abilities and five learning areas as essential to success in the workplace (see Table 10.2). One foundational ability is the capacity to think, reason, and make

TABLE 10.2

Necessary Workplace Skills

THE FOUNDATIONAL ABILITIES

Basic: Reading, writing, mathematics, speaking, and listening

Thinking: Creativity, making decisions, solving problems, seeing things in the mind's eye, knowing how to learn, and reasoning

Personal qualities: Responsibility, self-esteem, sociability, self-management, and integrity

LEARNING AREAS

Resources: How to allocate time, money, materials, space, and staff

Interpersonal: How to work on teams, teach, serve customers, lead negotiations, and work well with people from culturally diverse backgrounds

Information: How to acquire and evaluate data, organize and maintain files, interpret and communicate, and use computers to acquire and process information

Systems: How to understand social, organizational, and technological systems; monitor and correct performance; and design improved systems

Technology: How to select equipment and tools, apply technology to specific tasks, and maintain and troubleshoot technologies

Source: From U.S. Department of Labor Secretary's Commission on Achieving Necessary Skills, 1991. Retrieved from http://wdr.doleta.gov/scans/whatwork/whatwork.pdf

decisions. This ability in turn supports each of the learning areas, such as the ability to troubleshoot and to work with advanced technologies. Other examples of specific details discussed in the commission's categories are creativity and learning how to learn; sociability; and skills in teamwork, negotiation, and giving and receiving feedback. In addition to negatively affecting people's quality of life, widespread deficits of basic skills pose a threat to the business world. Quality and customer service suffer in any industry that depends on an inadequately skilled workforce. In an attempt to address this problem, many food outlets have resorted to equipping cash registers with pictures of food items rather than monetary figures. Similarly, a growing number of manufacturing firms are redesigning complex, good-paying positions into simple, low-paying, dead-end jobs. The result is a downward spiral of quality, service, job skills, wages, and employee self-esteem.

One proposed solution to these problems is to establish workplace literacy programs designed to teach basic skills to employees. These programs—which are offered by private companies, public agencies, and corporations themselves—vary widely in their focus and intensity. For example, some programs focus on job-related language skills, while others teach a broad array of basic skills that are useful in work and personal situations. In addition, the programs vary in length from forty to four hundred hours. Some training programs are sensitive to employees' different needs; others make no such distinctions.

The most successful programs thus far are those initiated and taught by the companies themselves. At American Honda, for instance, databases are used to match employees' level of education and skill with job opportunities and additional training and education opportunities. However, such programs are rare, and even when they do exist, they cannot adequately address the underlying problems in the U.S. educational system. A policy report written by Donna Cooper, Adam Hersh, and Ann O'Leary (2012) compared U.S. investment in education with similar efforts in India and China, concluding that these foreign governments have embarked on ambitious and extensive strategies to lift more of their citizens out of poverty and illiteracy and into the middle and upper reaches of society. Although a tremendous amount of effort will be directed at teaching basic skills to employees of the twenty-first century, without major changes in the educational system and in the nation's spending priorities, those efforts will do little to solve the problem.

Taking a broader view, however, even skills training may not be sufficient in helping the unemployed and working poor participate in an expanding economy. Social philosopher Earl Shorris (1997) has argued that it is not job skills but the ability to know about and reflect on questions central to all human existence, about life and death, right and wrong, that is the genuine portal to a better life. To test this hypothesis, Shorris assembled a team of star college teachers (including some Nobel Prize winners) and began offering a course in the humanities to economically disadvantaged adults in New York City. The twenty-eight-week project, dubbed the Clemente Course in the Humanities® (after the popular baseball player Roberto Clemente), was sponsored by Bard College and included instruction in such topics as moral philosophy, art history, and American history. The results are encouraging.

There is a big difference between teaching someone about specific business tasks and having them consider work behavior as Aristotle might have seen it. An old saying goes, "If you give someone a fish, they eat for a day, but if you teach him to fish, he will never go hungry." The Clemente Course, now being tried in many cities around the country, is one attempt to teach "fishing" to the most disenfranchised members of our society. However we address the future of work, we must be sure to factor into our thinking the "grotesque gap" that exists in income and living standards around the world. In other words, we must not think of prosperity solely in terms of financial markets (Longworth, 1998) but should instead seek to develop a kind of "ecological ethics" (Curry, 2011) that ensures globalization will work for people, not just profits.

One reason the Clemente Course was able to move from a hypothesis to a fully realized and trademarked course was its ability to track and monitor the data necessary to demonstrate the benefits and successes of its approach. They were able to communicate that information to a larger public through their website. As we mentioned at the beginning of chapter, the discipline required to collect and analyze environmental data is demanding, but the benefits of having that sort of information available for both internal and external audiences is priceless.

Many organizations will rely on simple surveys of customer and employee satisfaction as a way to track and monitor the progress toward their goals. At the same time, effective tracking and monitoring involves developing appropriate metrics that allow organizations to get at their most needed information. For example, a common practice among pharmacists is to institute a formal check-and-balance system called error audits. Pharmacists will check prescriptions during multiple stages of filling an order, and they are required to report out at each stage of the process. By making this process part of their routine, pharmacists are less tempted to rush through a prescription when they get backed up with many orders to fill. Similarly, at a 2015 conference hosted by Rural Advancement Foundation International (RAFI), a team of tracking and monitoring specialists from Farmers Market Connections discussed collecting a variety of forms of data. Farmers markets are notorious for being difficult organizations to track and monitor, often because they include a wide range of vendors, some of whom are reluctant to report financial data to anyone other than the Internal Revenue Service. The Market Connections team encouraged organizations like this to include customer counts, SNAP/EBT receipts, measures of local poundage sold, or other types of nonfinancial data that can help farmers markets show their effects on a community.

Reliable tracking and data monitoring help facilitate organizational learning. The challenge is then to communicate it to the larger public in a way that is meaningful and usable for the audience. The growing popularity of social media and mobile apps means that Western culture is becoming even more of a visual society. Simple report writing with bullet points and numbered lists is no longer sufficient. Instead, many organizations rely on data visualizations, infographics, and dashboards to capture institutional data in visually engaging ways. Dashboards, in particular, are useful for capturing tracking and monitoring data. Similar to the dashboard of a car or the Apple software application, these advanced infographics combine images like calendars, timelines, graphs, dials, and other graphics to show progress on multiple different metrics. For example, Elon University in North Carolina has developed an Elon Experiences transcript. This document tracks five extracurricular areas for students—study abroad, volunteer services, internships/co-ops, leadership, and undergraduate research. Alongside their formal academic transcript, Elon students also receive a dashboard that shows a timeline of their activities and a visual display of their progress along all five metrics. By instituting these kinds of tracking and monitoring systems, Elon helps its students engage in continual learning regarding the value of their work.

☐ Organizational Policymaking

Policies are often framed as the "documented posture" of an organization (Peterson & Albrecht, 1999). They outline the strategic position of the organization, as well as how that strategy is integrated across the people, systems, and structures that make the organization work. Organizations and individuals use policies to outline membership, job expectations, methods of performance management, tracking and monitoring procedures, and many of the topics we have outlined throughout this text. As we mentioned in Chapter 4, organizational policies get us to think about our communication from a systems perspective. In other words, policies help us document how the pieces come together.

Organizational policymaking involves the practices that organizations and individuals develop to make sense of how complex rules and resources align around the strategic position of the organization. Historically, policy research has focused on the different stages of policymaking, often framed as formulating, implementing, and evaluating policy within a workplace or other social setting. Policy is often positioned on a continuum between paternalism and participation (LeRoux, 2009). Specifically, some policies are more top-down, or paternalistic, which suggests the organization knows what is best for the member. A more classical management style might favor the paternalistic approaches to policy. On the other hand, some policies are more participatory in that they engage a broader community in their construction and enactment. A human resources style of management might adopt these kinds of policy practices.

One of the biggest questions for organizations to consider during ongoing learning and integration is how policy is used. Organizations use policies to outline norms, secure resources for members, and coordinate activities across different times, places, and contexts (Canary & McPhee, 2009; LeGreco & Tracy, 2009; LeGreco, 2012). In this way, organizational communication plays a big role in how policy texts—those documented postures of the organization—are implemented across the organization (Canary, Riforgiate, & Montoya, 2013; LeGreco & Canary, 2011). From a communication perspective, **policy implementation** is the process of translating the specifics of policy text into everyday practices for organizational members. Policies are only meaningful insofar as individuals can actually use them. A popular policy implementation cited commonly in organizational communication research is the Family and Medical Leave Act of 1993, more commonly referred to as the FMLA (Kirby & Krone, 2002). This federal workplace policy guarantees twelve weeks of unpaid leave for any worker with certain medical and family reasons—like the birth of a child or adoption placement, taking care of a newborn or adopted child, or providing primary care for an ill family member. The FMLA is an example of how policies are used to secure rights for workers. At the same time, the policy is most useful to a particular group of people—mostly those who can afford to take unpaid time off and women. Low-income workers and fathers are less likely to use these policies, often because they either can't afford to or because both men and women feel constrained by traditional gender roles.

Another way of thinking about how policy integrates practices across organizations is the Circuit of Policy Communication (LeGreco, 2012). This model brings together several concepts we have mentioned in this text to frame policymaking as a communication practice. The circuit involves five interrelated activities:

1. *Reflexive Policy Writing*. Across the life of a policy, and especially during its construction, organizational members need opportunities to talk about policy. They need to consider the consequences of their actions, as well as to make sense of the changes they enact.

2. *Navigating Policy Webs*. Policies do not exist in a vacuum, and policymakers must consider how their text is related to other policies both at the individual and organizational levels, as well as local, national, and global levels. The *Case Study* on page 339 provides an example of navigating policy webs.

3. *Addressing Ambiguity*. Related to the concept of strategic ambiguity, sometimes total clarity isn't the goal of policy. Policies help establish generalized expectations and norms; however, policies need not always be overly restrictive or detailed during their construction. This does mean that organizational members will often revisit policy texts throughout implementation and evaluation to address ambiguity as the policy is applied.

4. *Managing Paradox*. Encountering paradoxes is simply part of the policymaking and implementation process. Individuals and organizations often experience times when policy goals appear to undermine each other. Managing those paradoxes as they arise is another way that organizations engaging in ongoing learning.

5. *Attending to the Unintended*. Just as paradoxes are an expected part of policymaking, so are the unintended consequences of our policy work. Part of ongoing learning and integration means that organizations and individuals must consider how policies are applied over time, as well as the peculiar ways in which people can implement policy texts.

Taken together, the pieces of the circuit reinforce the idea that policies are documented postures of an organization. Policies give organizations a way to think about ongoing learning and integration, especially as they consider the paradoxes, ambiguities, and opportunities for reflexivity that policies afford.

Summary

Successful organizations have strategies. There are two general types of competitive strategies: lowest-cost strategy and differentiation. To succeed, a company must select its strategy carefully and then purposefully align its systems and structures to reflect that strategy. Competitive strategies are only as good as how they are communicated. When employees truly understand the big picture, they are most likely to work in ways that support the overall direction of the firm.

The management of human resources has become a highly sophisticated discipline that addresses how companies can best attract, develop, and retain talented employees. Targeted selection is the conscious selection of employees with abilities that support the company strategy. Performance management is the system by which employee accomplishments are measured and discussed. Training and development opportunities are made available to employees to support continuous learning. To be successful, a company's human resources function must be well integrated and become part of the corporate culture through its inclusion in regular conversations about results and improvement.

Technology is fundamentally changing every aspect of work and life, and scholars are mixed in their assessments of its benefits and detriments. Those who hold a utopian view believe the technology has had a positive effect on equalizing power relationships, while those with a dystopian view are more pessimistic, believing that technology will continue to widen the divide between the haves and the have-nots around the world. A neutral view of communication technology states that technology has no significant effect on human behavior: People will respond in predictable ways whether or not technology is involved. The contingent view is possibly the most realistic, noting that communication technology has advantages and disadvantages that are derived mainly from the way an individual or company chooses to utilize it. Regardless of which view one takes, it is clear that technology will continue to have a profound impact on individuals and companies, particularly in the areas of interpersonal communication and privacy.

Learning has become the watchword for organizational effectiveness in the twenty-first century. The world changes so quickly that companies must always be willing to question their assumptions about reality. Organizations and their employees must continually learn new skills and new technologies; some scholars even promote the idea of offering courses in the humanities to help promote lifelong critical-thinking skills. Organizations and individuals also rely on policies as ways to reflect on their everyday practices and consider the unintended consequences of their actions.

QUESTIONS FOR REVIEW AND DISCUSSION

1. Why is it important to take a bird's-eye view of an organization when charting its future?

2. How do competitive strategies and competitor analysis work together to effectively position an organization? What role might the specific strategies we mentioned (lowest-cost strategy and differentiation) play as well?

3. What happens to companies that do not consciously position themselves in the marketplace, or to those whose employees are unaware of their companies' positioning?

4. Which elements of strategic alignment seem the most challenging, and why?

5. In what ways does human resources management contribute to the successful implementation of company strategy? What are the roles of targeted selection, performance management, and training and development?

6. What are learning organizations, and why are they at an advantage in today's competitive market?

7. What are the pros and cons of computer-assisted communication technology and computer-assisted decision-aiding technology? What view do you take of such technology: utopian, dystopian, neutral, or contingent? Why?

8. How do organizations develop policies, and how does policymaking impact both organizational effectiveness and the employee's experience of work?

KEY TERMS

Competitive strategy, p. 310

Competitor analysis, p. 312

Contingent view, p. 325

Differentiation, p. 312

Dystopian view, p. 325

Lowest-cost strategy, p. 312

Media richness, p. 327

Neutral view, p. 325

Organizational development (OD), p. 324

Organizational policymaking, p. 335

Performance management, p. 323

Policy implementation, p. 335

Strategic alignment, p. 316

Strategic positioning, p. 310

Strategic thinking, p. 309

Superordinate goal, p. 316

Synchronicity, p. 326

Targeted selection, p. 322

Total quality management (TQM), p. 319

Training and development, p. 323

Utopian view, p. 325

CASE STUDY

Strategically Aligning School Food Policies

Policy communication is one way in which organizational members engage in the strategic-thinking practices that we mention at the beginning of this chapter. The Circuit of Policy Communication is a way to highlight the communication practices that individuals and groups use when working with policy (LeGreco, 2012). A key part of the circuit is the idea that policy texts operate within webs of other policies. As such, policy texts must align strategically with the superordinate goals of the organization.

LeGreco uses the example of school food policy to illustrate how organizational members must navigate policy webs to align their texts with the larger goals of the institution. She focused her research on the Eastland School District's Wellness Policy Council. The purpose of this council was to develop a policy that focused on food and physical activity for the Eastland School District. On several occasions, the council was limited in terms of the changes that it could enact because it had to consider other district-level, state-level, and federal-level policies that concentrated on food, physical activity, and general curriculum. Consider the following example adapted from the research:

The members of the Eastland Wellness Policy Council gathered around a large, square conference table. Fourteen members sat on the council, including the district's food service director, teachers, parents, and two members of the governing board. The goal for the day was to write the policy text about food and its relationship to curriculum for the Eastland School District. Early in the conversation, Katie, one of the veteran teachers, said to the group, "You know what I really want? I want to take a really creative approach to the way we think about curriculum. Think about math class. We have these classic examples of 'a train leaves New York traveling X miles an hour, while a train leaves Los Angeles traveling Y miles an hour. Where will they crash into each other?' Those aren't real-life examples. What if we used food examples to teach things like math and chemistry? Think about it—we could have students learn algebra by learning how to convert information on a nutrition facts label."

Many members of the Eastland council immediately liked Katie's novel approach to embedding food examples in the curriculum. At the same time, Susan, a council member who represented the district's governing board, was worried that the wellness council couldn't make these kinds of policy changes. "Will this wellness policy incorporate the multiple policies that are already written into the governing board policy?" Susan asked. "If so, maybe we need to begin by finding out what the governing board already says" (LeGreco, 2012, p. 57).

(continued, Strategically Aligning School Food Policies)

Ultimately, policies operate as a way to coordinate actions across contexts, thereby allowing organizations to align their messages strategically throughout different sites. Any attempts at policy change must consider how the new policy texts will (or won't) align with the policies that are already at play. Think about these connections between policy communication and strategic alignment as you answer the following discussion questions.

Assignment

1. How do policy texts help organizational members enact strategic thinking? How do existing policy texts, at both local and national levels, enable and constrain how organizations can strategically align their communication practices?
2. Would the 7-S model be useful to the Eastland Wellness Policy Council as it makes decisions about food policies for the school district? How?
3. How important do you think the language of the Eastland policy will be in ensuring its successful implementation? What steps would you suggest that the council members take to ensure the successful implementation of the policy?

A Field Guide to Studying Organizational Communication

Many students enrolled in an organizational communication course are required to write a term paper. Usually, the paper involves applying concepts from the course to ongoing communication processes within an organization. In most cases, when presented with the requirement to write a paper of this sort, students ask for more specific guidelines—the practical how-tos—of studying organizational communication.

For this reason, we have prepared the following practical field guide to studying organizational communication. The use of the term *field guide* is intended to evoke an *ethnographic* approach to collecting data, analyzing it, and writing the paper. (For an extended discussion, see Goodall, 2000.) An ethnographic approach uses

- *naturalistic observation* of everyday communication episodes and events as the primary source of data;
- *participant-observer interaction and interviews* to collect stories, accounts, and explanations for the events and episodes observed;
- *a critical/historical framework* for developing key questions, problems, and issues to pursue through observations of and interactions with employees; and
- *a narrative format* for describing and analyzing the data.

In short, what we describe is a way of doing field research in an organization for the purpose of finding and telling the story of one or more of its everyday communication practices.

◪ FINDING AN ORGANIZATION TO STUDY

One of the axioms of organizational ethnography is that you must "*know* where you are" (Goodall, 1994, p. 176). This means (in academic-speak) that all knowledge is *contextually derived*; it also means that it is a good idea to study an organization in your own community. Why? Because chances are pretty good that access to the organization will be easier to acquire (e.g., friends and family members work there, you had summer employment or an internship there, you know someone who knows someone). Additionally, you probably have a basic understanding of the history and role of the organization within the community, which will come in handy when you write the paper. If you are not a local and don't have personal contacts that can provide access to an organization for the purpose of conducting a communication study, ask your instructor for advice and guidance.

Approaching an organization for the purpose of doing a study is always problematic. Many for-profit companies and government agencies strictly limit access to employees and usually have no interest in allowing students from the local college or university to hang around observing people, interviewing employees and managers, and otherwise disrupting their work. Some companies even have regulations against it—and no company or agency is required to let you inside.

For these reasons, it is a good idea to develop a professional relationship with the organization you want to study before requesting permission to do a communication study. The more the people you contact trust you, the more they learn to see you as a serious person, the more likely it is that they will cooperate with your goals. To facilitate your professional relationship, we recommend the following:

- Write a one-page proposal detailing the purpose and time frame for your study, the methods of data collection that you plan to use, and the anticipated results. Your instructor can provide you with examples from prior student projects.
- Offer to provide the organization with a copy of your final paper. Agree that nothing you discover or write about will be disseminated to the public without prior written approval by the company.
- Always arrive on time, dressed in a professional manner appropriate to the standards of the organization you want to study, with a prepared list of questions to ask and a way of recording or keeping notes of interviews.
- Never directly interfere with ongoing organizational work. Make your observations as unobtrusively as possible; schedule interviews for times convenient for the interviewees.

◩ FRAMING YOUR STUDY

To write a proposal for the study, you will first need to develop a research question and ground your study in the current research literature. These writing processes are called "framing a study" because, like placing a photograph within an appropriate frame, they allow you to place *your* story within a larger academic or professional *narrative*.

There are three major resources for locating information that might help you frame a study. First, as a student, you are part of a college or university that has resident experts in just about every aspect of life. Locate an instructor with research expertise in the general area that interests you. Arrange to interview her or him to find out what the current thinking is on the general topic you have selected. Be sure to ask what the two or three best articles are on the subject, and then go to your library and check them out. For example, let's assume you want to study the specific organizational practices associated with building and maintaining a learning organization. Chances are good that someone in the communication department or the business school will be able to help you find resources to frame a study of a learning organization.

The second resource is the library. Using the references provided in this book—as well as any provided by your instructor and local university experts in the subject area—you should be able to conduct library research on most topics relevant to organizational communication. If the library research process is unclear to you, contact your library for help identifying the research librarian best able to assist you with finding information about your topic.

The third resource is the Internet. With online search engines like ProQuest, you can search a variety of databases for information. You may also join an Internet-based chat room or listserve where your topic is being discussed. Professional academic organizations typically sponsor such Internet activities and research sites. We recommend beginning your search by visiting the American Communication Association research site (http://www.americancomm.org) or the National Communication Association research site (http://www.natcom.org). You may also find relevant information by checking out the home pages of organizational communication scholars, who sometimes provide links to rich research resources relevant to their specialties.

After reading the available research on the general topic you plan to pursue, you should be able to articulate some of the questions that are of concern to scholars and professionals. Adapt these questions to the organization you plan to study and to the purpose of your paper.

Framing your study *before* you enter the organization for observations and interviews provides you with an important way to limit what you are looking at and asking questions about. You have to know what you are looking for in order to find it. However, as any ethnographer will tell you, surprises and setbacks occur.

You may find that the initial research question you posed doesn't really get at the meaning of the interactions you observe and participate in, or you may discover that you cannot complete all of the interviews you had planned. These are not necessarily problems, but they may be challenges. You may need to modify your research question. Settle for fewer interviews. Find other people to talk to. You may even need to reframe your study in light of what you find is *really* happening.

◨ TEN ASSUMPTIONS ABOUT DOING FIELD RESEARCH[1]

Organizational field researchers are interested in telling the stories that make up everyday organizational life. As such, they rarely are interested in issues typically associated with managerial notions of efficiency. For example, rather than asking how a particular routine can be streamlined or reengineered to improve the efficiency of an operation, field research asks how that particular routine came to be a routine and what it requires (mentally, morally, physically, culturally) of a person or group to accomplish it. Following are other characteristics of field research.

1. Field research is *qualitative* in nature. The quality of it is largely dependent on the insights discovered by the researcher. By contrast, many worthwhile organizational studies are *quantitative*, which means that they derive their conclusions from facts that are amenable to statistical tabulation and analysis. Field research, being qualitative, derives insights from close observation of actual, ongoing, communication processes. Conclusions are generalizable; insights are contextual.

2. Field research begins from theoretical assumptions and conceptual underpinnings but is more generally dedicated to providing documentation for the *moral and ethical* knowledge of working. For this reason, many contemporary ethnographic studies of organizations focus on issues of power and strategic control, as well as on race, age, and gender.

3. Field research assumes that every organization is as unique as an individual human fingerprint. One way to think about this is that people are not understood as "types," and activities and practices are not reducible to "behaviors."

4. What people at work *say* and *do* are the substance of who they are (at work) and what your study should be about. By comparison, think of what you are studying as an exercise in observing and documenting a television sitcom

[1]Some of the material contained in this section is adapted from Pacanowsky, M. E. (1986). *An idiosyncratic compilation of the twenty-seven do's and don'ts of organizational culture research* (Unpublished paper). University of Utah.

about work. What is the setting? Who are the characters? Where do they come from? What are their dreams? What do they think about their jobs? About each other? What do they talk about? What clothes do they wear? And so on. You might want to practice your skills by observing and analyzing just such a television show.

5. Remember that you won't be watching a television show when you enter an organization. These aren't actors performing rehearsed scripts written by someone else. You are studying ongoing life—*real* life. In real-life studies, expect a lot of empty spaces between meaningful interactions. Don't expect conflicts to be solved in thirty minutes or less. People won't be as funny as they are on television, nor are they working out a predetermined theme. The theme, the thing you are studying, the story you are trying to find and tell about, emerges gradually from disparate places and people. *You* are the scriptwriter.

6. Don't neglect the places—the *contexts*—and their influences over the interaction. As Marshall Sahlins, a famous anthropologist, once put it, "A culture is the meaningful order of persons and things." Don't forget to observe *things*. Describe them. Ask people to comment on their meanings.

7. There is no such thing as "an organization." In real life, there is only "organizing," the interactions and behaviors that create and recreate the realities we call organizations. That means that every person you observe and talk to will have a slightly different take on what "reality" is. The farther you move away from a particular group of people who interact regularly and have tacitly agreed to see reality in similar ways, the more different and complex "reality" becomes.

8. You aren't going to find any one truth. At best, you will find many copresent and conflicting truths. That is why field researchers learn to think (and write) about life as a "plural present" (Goodall, 1991, p. 320). If you doubt this statement, ask the same question three levels up the organization's ladder from where you are locating your study, and then three levels below it.

9. You are studying the *particulars* of human actions. Pay close attention to details. Nuances of speaking, of gesturing, of touching, of *not* saying something, all count. You are looking at what is said and done, what is given or foregrounded, but you are searching for what is unspoken, not done, withheld, and in the background, in the depths of shadows only the actors know.

10. Write down *everything* you observe and hear. You never know what will end up being important. Use a digital recorder if you are allowed to. Write out your notes and transcriptions the same day you take them (or else you lose 83 percent of the meaning), and write them out in story format. That is how, when, and where you will ultimately find the story line.

◩ HOW TO STUDY NATURALISTIC COMMUNICATION IN AN ORGANIZATION: A BASIC PROCESS OUTLINE WITH COMMENTARY[2]

We have found that it is very useful to instruct students to take field notes on their observations, interviews, conversations, and personal reflections on the meanings of people at work. Taking field notes is akin to keeping a diary, but instead of writing about your family and your love life, you write about your working life. In a notebook or on your computer, describe the events of your day, make theoretical and practical connections to what you are reading and thinking about, and try to use the writing process to help you figure out how to connect the dots that gradually emerge from your study.

To help you take field notes, here is a list of people and things, activities, symbols, and events that occur and have some meaning in most organizations. This list may help you isolate field note entries and organize your research.

- Begin in the parking lot. Begin early. Watch the cars file in, and note where they park. Make notes on the kinds of vehicles that individuals drive. At lunchtime, observe who drives the gang from work, and where they go. If possible, join in on their lunch conversations. Watch when they leave work in the afternoon or evening. Who leaves last? Why?
- Phone the public relations department, and ask for a company tour. Explain that you are doing research on similar types of companies in the area. Listen carefully to what the official version of the company is during the tour, and collect as much written documentation as possible. These resources will become important to you later.
- Research the financial standing of the company if it is publicly held. How is it doing? How does it compare to other companies in the industry? Do an Internet search of local newspapers to see what kinds of stories have appeared about the company and about its people in the past year or so. These details can become useful as a way of understanding the evolving context of the interaction.

---

[2]The following outline will not apply equally to all organizations or be appropriate for all classes in organizational communication. Some advisories provided here will fit the place you want to study; some won't. We recommend limiting your study to a particular work group, team, or department, but your instructor may want a larger-scale study. Depending on your instructor's preferences, you may also want to conduct a quantitative study, in which case the information in this appendix may help you create material from which you can develop hypotheses to test.

- Make a chart of the people (or the department) you plan to include in your study, and note their organizational relationships to one another. Ask yourself how your understanding of organizational hierarchies may inform what you are observing.

Using what you have read in this book about classical theories of organization and communication, what kind of organization would you say this is? Do you see Frederick Taylor or Abraham Maslow lurking about? Is this more like a Theory X or a Theory Y company? Are elements of all of the classical theories evident here? If not, why not? If so, what does this suggest to you about theories of organizing or about this place?

Now think about this group or department as a system or as part of a system. Draw or describe the group's interactions accordingly. Think about the organization of feedback among members of the group. Think about access to and distribution of information. Listen to their accounts of "how things are around here," and see if Karl Weick's "retrospective sense making" helps you understand them. Keep applying ideas from what you read to what you are seeing, hearing, and attending to.

Now do the same sort of thing with your knowledge of organizational cultures, recognizing that the people you are studying are part of a culture.

Ask questions about leadership and power. Who is in charge here—*really* in charge? How do you know that? What is it about this person's communication, manner, style, or attitude that conveys this to the people here? Perhaps there is no one leader. How is leadership shared? What does that mean, in terms of exchanges of talk, every day? In either case, how are individuals' control needs being met? How are they negotiated? What conflicts exist? How do you know this? What happens to inform your evaluations and your judgments?

- Using what you have learned about the study of power, how would you describe its uses and abuses in this organization? Is power linked to gender? To race? To age? To beauty? Are there different forms and expressions of power? Is power related to expertise? If so, how? If not, what is it related to?
- Given that all organizations exist within a global economic structure and have dealt with issues of reorganization, downsizing, team-based organizing, flattening hierarchies, information technologies, and other concepts associated with the rise of postmodernity what *stories* are told here about all of that? Are there heroes and heroines? Villains? Legendary mistakes? Bits of good fortune? What do these people talk about when they talk about the future? Are there active company training programs? What do people say about them? Are they preparing for a lifetime of employment with this company?
- You want to find as much as you can about each individual's personal experience of work. See what you can observe, discover, or otherwise find out about the organizational socialization process, about signs of organizational identification, satisfaction, and burnout. How do individuals deal with differences

that make a difference in the workplace? (See Chapter 7.) How do people negotiate the work-life balance? What stressors do people routinely deal with? How do they deal with them? Is there any difference between what they say and what you observe? What can this mean?

- How are work groups, teams, and networks organized in this organization? What systems of problem solving and decision making are employed? What is the influence of information technology on their operation and functions? What have you learned from reading about groups, teams, and networks that seems to apply directly to what happens here? What doesn't apply? For example, do you find evidence of team learning or interorganizational networks?

- You want to attune yourself to the ways in which the overall vision, mission, and core values of the organization play out in everyday discourse and interactions. Are the workers familiar enough with the organization's vision, mission, and values to talk openly about them? Do they try to consciously apply them to their everyday work habits? Where are the deviations? Why are there deviations? Are the deviations a sign of resistance or perhaps only of ignorance? How does this group or department handle crises? How do individual members' identities figure into the image of the firm?

- Trace the uses of technology in this organization. Are there stories about the introduction of new technologies? What lessons were learned about technology that are practiced today? How are the members of this department preparing themselves for continuing demands for technological skill and knowledge? How has the availability of laptops and smartphones, perhaps even fitness trackers, changed their working and personal lives? How do they feel about this?

- What is the role of communication consulting and training in this group or department? Is there an overall company plan for training and development, or is it left up to the individual workers? What kinds of issues or problems are managed by the group or department, and what kinds of issues or problems require the assistance of a professional consultant? How satisfied are the employees with past consulting interventions? What stories do they tell? How do the members describe the future of this company or agency? Do their metaphors suggest particular scenarios?

- Remember, you are studying everyday communication in this organization. How are you defining *communication* for the purposes of your study? What counts as communication? What doesn't? How valuable is our definition in your study? Can you see communication as the moment-to-moment working out of the tensions between individuals' desire for creativity and the organization's need for constraint (order)? When you examine your field notes with this definition in mind, what is accounted for? What is left out?

- If you are still having trouble deciding how to tell this story, go back over your notes and look carefully at the metaphors used by employees and managers. Many organizational scholars believe that people live and interpret their lives through the linguistic lenses of their daily metaphors. What metaphors do you find in their talk? What metaphors do you see in their actions and activities? What does the presence of these particular metaphors suggest are their binary opposites? Are the binary opposites places where you can also make sense of the unsaid, the unspoken, the covered up, or the neglected?

- When you write your account, include as many particulars—reports of conversations and observations of actions, clothes, cars, and gestures—as you can. These are your primary sources of evidence for the case that you are making. Remember that it is a case that *you* are making. You are ultimately responsible for what you say. Your views will not necessarily be the views of the people you have observed, of your instructor, or of the authors of this textbook. Write what you have lived through, what you have experienced, in the course of doing your research.

- Make sure you follow the style guide (APA, MLA, Chicago, Turabian, etc.) appropriate to your instructor's requirements.

TYPICAL ORGANIZATION OF A PAPER BASED ON FIELD STUDY METHODS

Research reports typically follow an established pattern. Here is one you can use to organize your paper:

Title page
   Title of the paper
   Your name, class, and instructor
   Date
   Academic integrity statement (optional)

Abstract
   Brief description of the purposes of the study and its conclusions

Introduction
   Narrative orientation to the company, team, or department studied
   Statement about the specific purpose of the study
   Literature review (focusing on the specific topic area)
   Research questions
   Description of method chosen to answer the questions

Body
>   Narrative account of the organization's communication organized *linearly*
>   over time, from initial observations through final conclusions, and
>   *topically* by communication issue or question raised
>   Analysis and interpretation of the field study via research questions

Conclusion
>   Review of the study, purpose, method, and major insights
>   Link or contribution of this study to current literature on the topic
>   Conclusion and suggestions for future research

References

Good luck! Studying and writing about organizations and communication can be an interesting and rewarding activity. Field study allows you to really work with concepts, apply them to ongoing processes of communicating and organizing, and find meaning in otherwise everyday occurrences. It will enrich your educational experience.

References

Aaronson, S. A., & Zimmerman, J. (2007). *Trade imbalance: The struggle to weigh human rights concerns in trade policy making*. New York, NY: Cambridge University Press.

Acker, J. (1990). Hierarchies, jobs, bodies: A theory of gendered organization. *Gender and Society, 4*, 139–148.

Adkins, A. (2016). Employee engagement stagnant in U.S. in 2015. Retrieved from http://www.gallup.com/poll/188144/employee-engagement-stagnant-2015.aspx?g_source=EMPLOYEE_ENGAGEMENT&g_medium=topic&g_campaign=tiles

AFL-CIO. (2012). CEO pay and you. Retrieved from aflcio.org/corporatewatch/paywatch/pay/index.cfm#_ftnref12

Aguir, M. & Bils., M. (2011, February). Has consumption inequality mirrored income inequality? National Bureau of Economic Research Working Paper No. 16807. Cambridge, MA. nber.org/papers/w16807.pdf?new_window=1

Ainsworth, S., & Hardy, C. (2009). Mind over body: Physical and psychotherapeutic discourses and the regulation of the older worker. *Human Relations, 62*, 1199–1229.

Ajnesh, P. (2012). Beyond analytic dichotomies. *Human Relations, 65*, 567–595.

Alberts, J., Lutgen-Sandvik, P., & Tracy, S. (2005, May). *Escalated incivility: Analyzing workplace bullying as a communication phenomenon*. Paper presented at the annual meeting of the International Communication Association, New York, NY.

Alberts, J. K., Tracy, S. J., & Trethewey, A. (2011). An integrative theory of the division of domestic labor: Threshold level, social organizing and sensemaking. *Journal of Family Communication, 11*, 21–38.

Albrecht, T., & Hall, B. (1991). Facilitating talk about new ideas: The role of personal relationships in organizational innovation. *Communication Monographs, 58*, 273–288.

Alimo-Metcalfe, B., & Alban-Metcalfe, J. (2005). Leadership: Time for a new direction? *Leadership, 1*, 51–71.

Allen, B. (2003). *Difference matters: Communicating social identity*. Long Grove, IL: Waveland.

Allen, B. J. (2007). Theorizing communication and race. *Communication Theory, 7*, 259–264.

Allen, M. Y., Coopman, S., Hart, J., & Walker, K. (2007). Workplace surveillance and managing privacy boundaries. *Management Communication Quarterly, 21*, 172–200.

Altman, S., Valenzi, E., & Hodgetts, R. (1985). *Organizational behavior: Theory and practice*. New York, NY: Academic Press.

Alvesson, M. (1993). *Cultural perspectives on organizations*. New York, NY: Cambridge University Press.

Alvesson, M. (2010). Self-doubters, strugglers, storytellers, surfers and others: Images of self-identities in organization studies. *Human Relations, 63*, 193–217.

Alvesson, M., & Willmott, H. (2002). Identity regulation as organizational control: Producing the appropriate individual. *Journal of Management Studies, 39*, 619–644.

American Management Association. (2008, February 28). 2007 electronic monitoring & surveillance survey. Retrieved from press.amanet.org/press-releases/177/2007-electronic-monitoring-surveillance-survey

Anderson, J. (1987). *Communication research: Issues and methods*. New York, NY: Hampton Press.

Anderson, W. K. Z., & Buzzanell, P. (2007). "Outcasts among outcasts": Identity, gender and leadership in a Mac users group. *Women and Language, 30*, 32–45.

Andrews, E. L. (2009, March 8). World Bank says economy will shrink in '09. *New York Times*. Retrieved from nytimes.com/2009/03/09/business/09bank.html?partner=rss&emc=rss

Arena, M., & Arrigo, B. (2005). Social psychology, terrorism, and identity: A preliminary reexamination of theory, culture, self, and society. *Behavioral Sciences and the Law, 23*, 485–506.

Argyris, C. (1957). *Personality and organization: The conflict between system and the individual*. New York, NY: Harper and Row.

Argyris, C., & Schon, D. (1978). *Organizational learning: A theory of action perspective*. Reading, MA: Addison-Wesley.

Armstrong, N. (2005, June). Resistance through risk: Women and cervical cancer screening. *Health, Risk and Society, 7*, 161–176.

Ashcraft, K. (1999). Managing maternity leave: A qualitative analysis of temporary executive succession. *Administrative Science Quarterly, 44*, 240–280.

Ashcraft, K. (2004). Gender, discourse, and organization: Framing a shifting relationship. In D. Grant, C. Hardy, C. Oswick, & L. Putnam (Eds.), *The SAGE handbook of organizational discourse* (pp. 275–291). London, England: Sage.

Ashcraft, K., & Allen, B. (2003). The racial foundation of organizational communication. *Communication Theory, 13*, 5–38.

Ashcraft, K., & Flores, L. (2003). "Slaves with white collars": Persistent performances of masculinity in crisis. *Text and Performance Quarterly, 23*, 1–29.

Ashcraft, K., & Mumby, D. (2004). *Reworking gender: A feminist communicology of organization*. Thousand Oaks, CA: Sage.

Ashcraft, K., & Trethewey, A. (2004). Developing tension: An agenda for applied research on the "organization of irrationality." *Journal of Applied Communication Research, 32*, 171–181.

Ashcraft, K. L., & Allen, B. J. (2009). Politics even closer to home: Repositioning CME from the standpoint of communication studies. *Management Learning, 40*, 11–30.

Ashcraft, K. L., Muhr, S., Rennstam, J., & Sullivan, K. (2012). Professionalization as branding activity: Occupational identity and the dialectic of inclusivity-exclusivity. *Gender, Work & Organization, 19*, 467–488.

Ashforth, B., & Kreiner, G. E. (1999). "How can you do it?" Dirty work and the challenge of constructing a positive identity. *Academy of Management Review, 24*, 413–434.

Atkouf, O. (1992). Management and theories of organizations in the 1990s: Toward a critical radical humanism? *Academy of Management Review, 17*, 407–431.

Atwood, M. (1990). *Adolescent socialization into work environments* (Unpublished master's thesis). University of Southern California, Los Angeles.

Axley, S. (1984). Managerial and organizational communication in terms of the conduit metaphor. *Academy of Management Review, 9*, 428–437.

Baba, M. (1999). Dangerous liaisons: Trust, distrust, and information technology in American work organizations. *Human Organization, 58*(3), 331–346.

Babcock, L., & Laschever, S. (2003). *Women don't ask: Negotiation and the gender divide*. Princeton, NJ: Princeton University Press.

Babcock, L., & Laschever, S. (2008). *Ask for it: How women can use the power of negotiation to get what they really want*. New York, NY: Bantam Dell.

Bakhtin, M. (1981). *The dialogic imagination* (C. Emerson & M. Holquist, Trans.). Austin: University of Texas Press.

Banta, M. (1993). *Taylored lives: Narrative productions in the age of Taylor, Veblen, and Ford*. Chicago, IL: University of Chicago Press.

Bantz, C. (1993). *Understanding organizations: Interpreting organizational communication cultures*. Columbia: University of South Carolina Press.

Baran, B. E., & Scott, C. W. (2010). Organizing ambiguity: A grounded theory of leadership and sensemaking within dangerous contexts. *Military Psychology*, *22*(S1), S42–S69.

Barker, J. (1993). Tightening the iron cage: Concertive control in self-managing teams. *Administrative Science Quarterly*, *38*, 408–437.

Barker, J. (1999). *The discipline of teamwork: Participation and concertive control*. Thousand Oaks, CA: Sage.

Barker, J., & Cheney, G. (1994). The concept and practices of discipline in contemporary organizational life. *Communication Monographs*, *61*, 19–43.

Barley, S. (1983). Semiotics and the study of occupational and organizational culture. *Administrative Science Quarterly*, *23*, 393–413.

Barnard, C. (1968). *The functions of the executive*. Cambridge, MA: Harvard University Press. (Original work published 1938)

Barry, D., & Elmes, M. (1997). Strategy retold: Toward a narrative view of strategic discourse. *Academy of Management Review*, *22*, 429–452.

Bash, D., Mirian, A., & Newman, L. (2005, November). Americas summit protest turns violent. Retrieved from latinamericanstudies.org/us-relations/protest.htm

Basu, A., & Dutta, M. J. (2008). Participatory change in a campaign led by sex workers: Connecting resistance to action-oriented agency. *Qualitative Health Research*, *18*, 106–119.

Bateson, G. (1972). *Steps to an ecology of mind*. New York, NY: Ballantine.

Bauer, T., & Green, S. (1996). Development of leader member exchange: A longitudinal test. *Academy of Management Journal*, *39*, 1538–1567.

Bean, C., & Eisenberg, E. (2006). Employee sense-making in the transition to nomadic work. *Journal of Organizational Change Management*, *19*, 210–222.

Beato, C. V. (2004, February 18). Progress review: Occupational safety and health. *Healthy People 2010*. Retrieved from healthypeople.gov/data/2010prog/focus20/default.htm

Beaton, Margaret. The social contract is dead. Retrieved from https://www.linkedin.com/pulse/social-contract-dead-margaret-beaton

Beckett, R. (2005). Communication ethics: Principle and practice. *Journal of Communication Management*, *9*, 41–52.

Bell, E., & Forbes, L. (1994). Office folklore in the academic paperwork empire: The interstitial space of gendered (con)texts. *Text and Performance Quarterly*, *38*, 181–196.

Bell, E., & Nkomo, S. (2001). *Our separate ways: Black and white women and the struggle for professional identity*. Boston, MA: Harvard Business School Press.

Belles, N. (2015). *In our backyard: Human trafficking and what we can do to stop it*. Grand Rapids, MI: Baker Books.

Bendix, R. (1956). *Work and authority in industry: Managerial ideologies in the course of industrialization*. New York, NY: Wiley.

Benne, K., & Sheats, P. (1948). Functional roles of group members. *Journal of Social Issues*, *4*, 41–49.

Bennis, W. (1998). *On becoming a leader*. London, England: Arrow.

Bennis, W., & Nanus, B. (2003). *Leaders: Strategies for taking charge*. New York, NY: HarperCollins.

Benoit, P. (1997). *Telling the success story: Acclaiming and disclaiming discourse*. Albany, NY: SUNY Press.

Berger, P., & Luckmann, T. (1967). *The social construction of reality: A treatise in the sociology of knowledge*. Garden City, NY: Anchor.

Berkelaar, B. (2013, May). Joining and leaving organizations in a global information society. In E. Cohen (Ed.), *Communication Yearbook 37* (pp. 33–64). New York, NY: Routledge.

Berkelaar, B. L. (2014). Cybervetting, online information, and personnel selection: New transparency expectations and the emergence of a digital social contract. *Management Communication Quarterly*, *28*(4), 479–506. doi:10.1177/0893318914541966

Berkelaar, B. L., & Buzzanell, P. M. (2015). Online employment screening and digital career capital: Exploring employers' use of online information for personnel selection. *Management Communication Quarterly*, *29*(1), 84–113. doi:10.1177/0893318914554657

Berkelaar, B. L., & Buzzanell, P. M. (2014). Cybervetting, person–environment fit, and personnel selection: Employers' surveillance and sensemaking of job applicants' online information. *Journal of Applied Communication Research*, *42*(4), 456–476. doi:10.1080/00909882.2014.954595

Berlo, D. (1960). *The process of communication*. New York, NY: Holt.

Bhabha, H. (1990). DissemiNation: Time, narrative, and the modern nation. In H. Bhabha (Ed.), *Nation and narration* (pp. 291–322). London, England: Routledge.

Bingham, S. (1991). Communication strategies for managing sexual harassment in organizations: Understanding message options and their effects. *Journal of Applied Communication Research*, *19*, 88–115.

Bingham, S., & Battey, K. (2005). Communication of social support to sexual harassment victims: Professors' responses to a student's narrative of unwanted sexual attention. *Communication Studies*, *56*, 131–155.

Bivens, J., & Mishel, L. (2011). *Failure by design: The story behind America's broken economy* (An Economic Policy Institute Book). Ithaca, NY: Cornell University.

Blake, R., & Mouton, J. (1964). *The managerial grid*. Houston, TX: Gulf.

Blake, R., & Mouton, J. (1985). *The managerial grid III: The key to leadership excellence*. Houston, TX: Gulf.

Blumer, H. (1969). *Symbolic interactionism: Perspective and method*. Englewood Cliffs, NJ: Prentice Hall.

Bochner, A. (1982). The functions of human communication in interpersonal bonding. In C. Arnold & J. Waite-Bowser (Eds.), *Handbook of rhetorical and communication theory* (pp. 544–621). Boston, MA: Allyn and Bacon.

Bohm, D. (1980). *Wholeness and the implicate order*. London, England: Ark.

Boje, D. (1991). The storytelling organization: A study of story performance in an office-supply firm. *Administrative Science Quarterly*, *36*, 106–126.

Boje, D. (1995). Stories of the storytelling organization: A postmodern analysis of Disney in "Tamara-Land." *Academy of Management Journal*, *38*, 997–1035.

Boren, J. P., & Veksler, A. E. (2015). Communicatively restricted organizational stress (CROS): Conceptualization and overview. *Management Communication Quarterly February*, *29*, 28–55.

Boushey, H. (2010). *Not working: Unemployment among married couples*. Washington, DC: Center for American Progress.

Brandenburger, A., & Nalebuff, B. (1996). *Co-opetition*. New York, NY: Doubleday.

Brannan, M. (2005). Effects of communication trainings on medical student performance. *Gender, Work and Organization*, *12*(5), 420–439.

Brass, D. (1984). Being in the right place: A structural analysis of individual influence in an organization. *Administrative Science Quarterly*, *29*, 518–539.

Braverman, H. (1974). *Labor and monopoly capital*. NY: Monthly Review.

Bridgewater, M. J., & Buzzanell, P. M. (2010). Caribbean immigrants' discourses: Cultural, moral, and personal stories about workplace communication in the United States. *Journal of Business Communication*, *47*, 235–265.

Britt, L. L. (2012). Why we use service-learning: A report outlining a typology to this form of communication pedagogy. *Communication Education*, *61*, 80–88.

Brown, V. R., & Vaughn, E. D. (2011). The writing on the (Facebook) wall: The use of social networking sites in hiring decisions. *Journal of Business & Psychology*, *26*(2), 219–225. doi:10.1007/s10869-011-9221-x

Browning, L. (1992 May). *Reasons for success at Motorola*. Paper presented at the applied communication preconference of the International Communication Association, Miami, FL.

Browning, L., & Shetler, J. (2000). *Sematech: Saving the U.S. semiconductor industry*. College Station: Texas A&M University Press.

Buckley, W. (1967). *Sociology and modern systems theory*. Englewood Cliffs, NJ: Prentice Hall.

Bullis, C. (1999). Forum on organizational socialization research. *Communication Monographs, 66*, 368–373.

Bullying "facts" and "stats." (2012). Retrieved from know-bull.com/factsnstats.html

Burke, K. (1966). *Language as symbolic action*. Berkeley: University of California Press.

Burke, K. (1984). *Permanence and change: An anatomy of purpose*. Berkeley: University of California Press.

Burrell, G. (1988). Modernism, postmodernism, and organizational analysis 2: The contribution of Michel Foucault. *Organization Studies, 9*, 221–235.

Buzzanell, P. (2000). The promise and practice of the new career and social contract: Illusions exposed and suggestions for reform. In P. Buzzanell (Ed.), *Rethinking organizational and managerial communication from feminist perspectives* (pp. 209–235). Thousand Oaks, CA: Sage.

Buzzanell, P., & Liu, M. (2005). Struggling with maternity leave policies and practices: A poststructuralist feminist analysis of gendered organizing. *Journal of Applied Communication Research, 33*, 1–25.

Canary, D., & Hause, K. (1993). Is there any reason to study sex differences in communication? *Communication Quarterly, 41*, 129–144.

Canary, H. E., & McPhee, R. D. (2009). The mediation of policy knowledge: An interpretive analysis of intersecting activity systems. *Management Communication Quarterly, 23*, 147–187.

Canary, H. E., Riforgiate, S. E., and Montoya, Y. J. (2013). The policy communication index: A theoretically based measure of organizational policy communication practices. *Management Communication Quarterly, 27*, 471–502.

Cardenal, A. (2014, March 12). Costco vs. Wal-Mart: Higher wages mean superior returns for investors. Retrieved from http://www.fool.com/investing/general/2014/03/12/costco-vs-wal -mart-higher-wages-mean-superior-retu.aspx

Carlone, D. (2001). Enablement, constraint, and the 7 habits of highly effective people. *Management Communication Quarterly, 14*, 491–497.

Carlone, D., & Taylor, B. (1998). Organizational communication and cultural studies. *Communication Theory, 8*, 337–367.

Cartwright, D. (1977). Risk taking by individuals and groups: An assessment of research employing choice dilemmas. *Journal of Personality and Social Psychology, 85*, 361–378.

Chan, A., & Garrick, J. (2003). The moral "technologies" of knowledge management. *Information Communication and Society, 6*, 291–306.

Chandler, C., & Ingrassia, P. (1991, April 11). Shifting gears. *Wall Street Journal*, p. 1.

Cheney, G. (2007). Organizational communication comes out. *Management Communication Quarterly, 21*, 80–91.

Chesley, N. (2011). Stay-at-home fathers and breadwinning mothers: Gender, couple dynamics, and social change. *Gender and Society, 25*, 642–664.

Chiles, A., & Zorn, T. (1995). Empowerment in organizations: Employees' perceptions of the influences on empowerment. *Journal of Applied Communication Research, 23*, 1–25.

Christensen, C. (2010). *Disrupting class: How disruptive innovation will change the way the world learns*. New York, NY: McGraw-Hill.

Christensen, C. (2011). *The innovator's dilemma*. New York, NY: HarperBusiness.

Chung, V. (2000). Men in nursing. Retrieved from minoritynurse.com/article/men-nursing-0

Ciocchetti, C. A. (2011). The eavesdropping employer: A twenty-first-century framework for employee monitoring. *American Business Law Journal, 48*, 285–369.

Clair, R. (1996). The political nature of the colloquialism "a real job": Implications for organizational socialization. *Communication Monographs, 63*, 249–267.

Clair, R. (1998). *Organizing silence: A world of possibilities*. Albany, NY: SUNY Press.

Clair, R. P. (Ed.) (2003). *Expressions of ethnography: Novel approaches to qualitative methods*. Albany, NY: State University of New York Press.

Clegg, S. (1989). *Frameworks of power*. Newbury Park, CA: Sage.

Clegg, S. (1990). *Modern organizations: Organization studies in the postmodern world*. Newbury Park, CA: Sage.

Cleveland, J., & McNamara, K. (1996). Understanding sexual harassment. In M. Stockdale (Ed.), *Sexual harassment in the workplace* (pp. 217–240). Newbury Park, CA: Sage.

Clifford, J., & Marcus, G. (1985). *Writing culture: The poetics and politics of ethnography*. Berkeley: University of California Press.

Cloud, D. (2007, May). *Routine misconduct: The myth of corporate social responsibility*. Paper presented at the annual meeting of the International Communication Association, Montreal, Quebec.

The College Transition. (2006). Retrieved from mnsu.edu/fye/parents/familyguidebook /collegetransition.html

Cohen, P. (2015). A company copes with backlash against the raise that roared. *New York Times* business P1, August 2, 2015.

Collins, J. (2001). *Good to great: Why some companies make the leap . . . and others don't*. New York, NY: Collins Business.

Collins, J. (2005). Level 5 leadership: The triumph of humility and fierce resolve. *Harvard Business Review, 83*, 136–147.

Collins, J., & Porras, J. (1994). *Built to last: Successful habits of visionary companies*. New York, NY: HarperCollins Business.

Collins, J., & Porras, J. (2004). *Built to last: Successful habits of visionary companies*. New York, NY: HarperCollins.

Collinson, D. (1992). *Managing the shop floor: Subjectivity, masculinity and workplace culture*. Berlin, Germany: Walter de Gruyter.

Collinson, D. (1999). "Surviving the rigs": Safety and surveillance on North Sea oil installations. *Organization Studies, 20*, 579–600.

Collinson, D. (2002). Managing humour. *Journal of Management Studies, 39*, 269–288.

Collinson, D. (2003). Identities and insecurities. *Organization, 10*, 527–547.

Collinson, D. (2012). Prozac leadership and the limits of positive thinking. *Leadership, 8*(2), 87–107. doi:dx.doi.org/10.1177/1742715011434738

Collinson, D., & Grint, K. (2005). Leadership. *Leadership, 1*, 1–10.

Collinson, D. L. (2003). Identities and Insecurities: Selves at Work. *Organization, 10*(3), 527.

Coltrane, S. (2000). Research on household labor: Modeling and measuring the social embeddedness of routine family work. *Journal of Marriage and Family, 62*, 1208–1233.

Conger, J., & Kanungo, R. (1988). The empowerment process: Integrating theory and practice. *Academy of Management Review, 13*, 471–482.

Connolly, R., & McParland, C. (2012). Dataveillance: Employee monitoring & information privacy concerns in the workplace. *Information Technology Research, 5*(2), 1–15.

Conquergood, D. (1991). Rethinking ethnography: Towards a critical cultural politics. *Communication Monographs, 58*, 179–194.

Conquergood, D. (1992). Ethnography, rhetoric, and performance. *Quarterly Journal of Speech, 78*, 80–97.

Conrad, C. (1983). Organizational power: Faces and symbolic forms. In L. Putnam & M. Pacanowsky (Eds.), *Communication and organizations* (pp. 173–194). Beverly Hills, CA: Sage.

Contractor, N., & Eisenberg, E. (1990). Communication networks and the new media in organizations. In J. Fulk & C. Steinfeld (Eds.), *Organizations and communication technology* (pp. 143–172). Newbury Park, CA: Sage.

Contractor, N., Eisenberg, E., & Monge, P. (1992). *Antecedents and outcomes of interpretive diversity in organizations* (Unpublished manuscript). University of Illinois, Urbana.

Contractor, N., & Seibold, D. (1992). *Theoretical frameworks for the study of structuring processes in group decision support systems* (Unpublished manuscript). University of Illinois, Urbana.

Cooke, B., Mills, A., & Kelley, E. (2005). Situating Maslow in Cold War America: A recontextualization of management theory. *Group and Organization Management, 30,* 129–152.

Cooper, D., Hersh, A., & O'Leary, A. (2012). The competition that really matters: Comparing U.S., Chinese, and Indian investments in the next-generation workforce. Retrieved from americanprogress.org/issues/economy/report/2012/08/21/11983/the-competition-that-really-matters

Coopman, S. (2001). Democracy, performance, and outcomes in interdisciplinary health care teams. *Journal of Business Communication, 38,* 261–284.

Cooren, F. (2010). *Action and agency in dialogue.* Amsterdam, The Netherlands: John Benjamins.

Cooren, F., & Sandler, S. (2014). Polyphony, ventriloquism, and constitution. *Communication Theory, 24*(3), 225–244.

Cooren, F., Taylor, J. R., & Van Every, E. J. (Eds.). (2006). *Communication as organizing: Empirical and theoretical explanations in the dynamic of text and conversation.* Mahwah, NJ: Erlbaum.

Cora, D. (2004, October 10). Finally in the director's chair. *Fortune, 150,* 42–44.

Corman, S. (2006). Using activity focus networks to pressure terrorist organizations. *Computational and Mathematical Organizational Theory, 12,* 35–49.

Corman, S. R., Trethewey, A., & Goodall, H. L., Jr. (2008). *Weapons of mass persuasion: Strategic communication to combat violent extremism.* New York, NY: Peter Lang.

Covey, S. (1990). *The 7 habits of highly effective people.* New York, NY: Simon and Schuster.

Crenshaw, D. (2008). *The myth of multitasking: How "doing it all" gets nothing done.* San Francisco, CA: Jossey-Bass.

Curry, P. (2011). *Ecological ethics.* Cambridge, England: Polity.

Curves. (2012). Retrieved from http://wwwcurves.com

Daft, R., & Lengel, R. (1984). Information richness: A new approach to managerial information and organizational design. In B. Staw & L. Cummings (Eds.), *Research in organizational behaviors* (Vol. 6, pp. 191–233). Greenwich, CT: JAI Press.

Dahlberg, L. (2005). The corporate colonization of online attention and the marginalization of critical communication. *Journal of Communication Inquiry, 29,* 160–180.

Dalton, M., Ernst, C., Deal, J., & Leslie, J. (2002). *Success for the new global manager: How to work across distances, countries and cultures.* San Francisco, CA: Jossey-Bass.

Daniels, T., & Spiker, B. (1991). *Perspectives on organizational communication.* Dubuque, IA: Brown.

Davis, D. (2016). The journey to the top: Stories on the intersection of race and gender for African American women in academia and business. *Journal of Research Initiatives, 2*(1), Article 4.

Davis, K. (1953). Management communication and the grapevine. *Harvard Business Review, 31,* 43–49.

Day, G. S., Reibstein, D. J., & Gunther, R. E. (2004). *Wharton on dynamic competitive strategy.* New York, NY: Wiley.

Deal, T., & Kennedy, A. (1982). *Corporate cultures: The rites and rituals of corporate life.* Reading, MA: Addison-Wesley.

Deetz, S. (1992). *Democracy in an age of corporate colonization: Developments in communication and the politics of everyday life.* Albany, NY: SUNY Press.

Deetz, S. (1995). *Transforming communication, transforming business: Building responsive and responsible workplaces.* Cresskill, NJ: Hampton Press.

Deetz, S. (2005). Critical theory. In S. May & D. Mumby (Eds.), *Engaging organizational communication theory and research* (pp. 85–112). Thousand Oaks, CA: Sage.

Deetz, S., & Kersten, A. (1983). Critical models of interpretive research. In L. Putnam & M. Pacanowsky (Eds.), *Communication and organizations: An interpretive approach.* Beverly Hills, CA: Sage.

Deetz, S., Tracy, S., & Simpson, J. (2000). *Leading organizations through transitions: Communication and cultural change*. Thousand Oaks, CA: Sage.

Dempsey, S. E. (2009). Critiquing community engagement. *Management Communication Quarterly*, 24, 359–390.

D'Enbeau, S., & Buzzanell, P. M. (2011). Selling (out) feminism: Sustainability of ideology-viability tensions in a competitive marketplace. *Communication Monographs*, 78(1), 27–52.

Denker, K. J. (2013). Maintaining gender during work-life negotiations: relational maintenance and the dark side of individual marginalization. *Women & Language*, 36(2), 11–34.

Derrida, J. (1972). Structure, sign, and play in the discourse of the human sciences. In R. Macksay & E. Donato (Eds.), *The structuralist controversy: The language of criticism and the science of man*. Baltimore, MD: Johns Hopkins University Press.

DeSantis, A., & Hane, A. (2004, November). *Greek sex: Understanding conceptions of gender and sexuality in fraternities and sororities*. Paper presented at the annual convention of the National Communication Association, Chicago, IL.

Dessler, G. (1982). *Organization and management*. Reston, VA: Reston.

Dillard, J., & Segrin, C. (1987, May). *Intimate relationships in organizations: Relational types, illicitness, and power*. Paper presented at the annual conference of the International Communication Association, Montreal, Canada.

Dixon, L. (2004). A case study of an intercultural health care visit: An African American woman and her white male physician. *Women and Language*, 27, 45–52.

Dixon, T. (1996). Mary Parker Follett and community. *Australian Journal of Communication*, 23, 68–83.

Donnellon, A., Gray, B., & Bougon, M. (1986). Communication, meaning, and organized action. *Administrative Science Quarterly*, 31, 43–55.

Dougherty, D., & Smythe, D. (2004). Sensemaking, organizational culture, and sexual harassment. *Journal of Applied Communication Research*, 32, 293–317.

Dowd, M. (2005, October 30). What's a modern girl to do? *New York Times*. Retrieved from nytimes.com/2005/10/30/magazine/30feminism/html

Drago, R. W. (2007). *Striking a balance: Work, family, life*. Boston, MA: Dollars and Sense, Economic Affairs Bureau.

Drucker, P. (1974). *Management: Tasks, responsibilities, practices*. New York, NY: Harper and Row.

Drucker, P. (1992, February 11). There's more than one kind of team. *Wall Street Journal*, p. 16.

du Gay, P. (1995). *Consumption and identity at work*. London, England: Sage.

Duhigg, C. (2016, February 28). Group study. *The New York Times Magazine*, pp. 20–26, 72, 75.

D'Urso, S. C. (2006). Who's watching us at work? Toward a structural–perceptual model of electronic monitoring and surveillance in organizations. *Communication Theory*, 16(3), 281–303. doi:10.1111/j.1468-2885.2006.00271.x

Duhigg. C. (2012). *The power of habit: Why we do what we do in life and business*. New York, NY: Random House.

Dunham, R. (1999, August 1). Commentary: Across America, a troubling "digital divide." *Business Week*, 40. Retrieved from http://www.bloomberg.com/news/articles/1999-08-01/commentary-across-america-a-troubling-digital-divide

D'Urso, S. (2006). Who's watching us at work? Toward a structural-perceptual model of electronic monitoring and surveillance in organizations. *Communication Theory*, 16, 281–303.

Dutta, M. J. (2007). Communicating about culture and health: Theorizing culture-centered and cultural sensitivity approaches. *Communication Theory*, 17, 304–328.

Dutton, J., Dukerich, J., & Harquail, C. (1994). Organizational images and member identification. *Administrative Science Quarterly*, 43, 293–327.

Dwyer, M. (2013, October 25) Where did the anti-globalization movement go? *New Republic*. Retrieved from https://newrepublic.com/article/115360/wto-protests-why-have-they-gotten-smaller

Edley, P. (2001). Technology, employed mothers, and corporate colonization of the lifeworld: A gendered paradox of work and family balance. *Women and Language*, 24, 27–35.

Ehrenreich, B. (2001). *Nickel and dimed: On (not) getting by in America*. New York, NY: Holt.

Ehrenreich, B. (2005). *Bait and switch: The (futile) pursuit of the American dream*. New York, NY: Metropolitan Books.

Eichenwald, K. (2011, August). Microsoft's lost decade. *Vanity Fair*. Retrieved from vanityfair.com/business/2012/08/microsoft-lost-mojo-steve-ballmer

Eikhof, D. R., Summers, J., & Carter, S. (2013). Women doing their own thing: Media representations of female entrepreneurship. *International Journal of Entrepreneurial Behaviour & Research, 19*(5), 547–564.

Eisenberg, E. (1984). Ambiguity as strategy in organizational communication. *Communication Monographs, 51*, 227–242.

Eisenberg, E. (1986). Meaning and interpretation in organizations. *Quarterly Journal of Speech, 72*, 88–98.

Eisenberg, E. (1990). Jamming: Transcendence through organizing. *Communication Research, 17*, 139–164.

Eisenberg, E. (1995). A communication perspective on interorganizational cooperation and inner-city education. In L. Rigsby, M. Reynolds, & M. Wang (Eds.), *School-community connections* (pp. 101–120). San Francisco, CA: Jossey-Bass.

Eisenberg, E. (2007). *Strategic ambiguities: Essays on communication, organization, and identity*. Thousand Oaks, CA: Sage.

Eisenberg, E., Baglia, J., & Pynes, J. (2006). Transforming emergency medicine through narrative: Qualitative action research at a community hospital. *Health Communication, 19*, 197–208.

Eisenberg, E., & Eschenfelder, B. (2009). In L. Frey & K. Cissna (Eds.), *Handbook of applied communication*. Thousand Oaks, CA: Sage.

Eisenberg, E., Farace, R., Monge, P., Bettinghaus, E., Kurchner-Hawkins, R., White, L., & Miller, K. (1985). Communication linkages in interorganizational systems: Review and synthesis. In B. Dervin & M. Voight (Eds.), *Progress in communication sciences* (Vol. 6, pp. 231–258). Norwood, NJ: Ablex.

Eisenberg, E., Johnson, Z., & Pieterson, W. (2015). Leveraging social networks for strategic success. *International Journal of Business Communication, 52*(1), 143–154.

Eisenberg, E., Murphy, A., & Andrews, L. (1998). Openness and decision-making in the search for a university provost. *Communication Monographs, 65*, 1–23.

Eisenberg, E., Murphy, A., Sutcliffe, K., Wears, R., Schenkel, S., Perry, S., & Vanderhoef, M. (2005). Communication in emergency medicine: Implications for patient safety. *Communication Monographs, 72*, 390–413.

Eisenberg, E., & Riley, P. (2001). A communication approach to organizational culture. In L. Putnam & F. Jablin (Eds.), *New handbook of organizational communication*. Newbury Park, CA: Sage.

Eisenberg, E., & Witten, M. (1987). Reconsidering openness in organizational communication. *Academy of Management Review, 12*, 418–426.

Eliot, T. S. (1949). *Notes toward the definition of culture*. New York, NY: Harcourt, Brace.

Ellingson, L. L., & Buzzanell, P. M. (1999). Listening to women's narratives of breast cancer treatment: A feminist approach to patient satisfaction with physician-patient communication. *Health Communication, 11*, 153–183.

Erickson, R. (2005). Why emotion work matters: Sex, gender, and the division of household labor. *Journal of Marriage and Family, 67*, 337–351.

Ernst, E. (2015). The shrinking middle. *Finance & Development, 21*, 20–23.

Evans, P., & Wolf, B. (2005). Collaboration rules. *Harvard Business Review, 83*, 96–104.

Evered, R., & Tannenbaum, R. (1992). A dialog on dialog. *Journal of Management Inquiry, 1*, 43–55.

Executive Leadership Council (2008). *Black women executive research initiative findings*. Executive Leadership Council, Inc. Retrieved from http://www.slideshare.net/kacarter/elc-black-women-executives-research-initiative

Fairhurst, G. T. (2010). *The power of framing: Creating the language of leadership*. San Francisco, CA: Jossey-Bass.

Fairhurst, G., & Chandler, T. (1989). Social structure in leader-member interaction. *Communication Monographs, 56*, 215–239.

Fairhurst, G., Green, S., & Snavely, B. (1984). Face support in controlling poor performance. *Human Communications Research, 11*, 272–295.

Fairhurst, G., & Putnam, L. (2004). Organizations as discursive constructions. *Communication Theory, 14*, 5–26.

Fairhurst, G., & Sarr, R. (1996). *The art of framing: Managing the language of leadership*. San Francisco, CA: Jossey-Bass.

Farace, R., Monge, P., & Russell, H. (1977). *Communicating and organizing*. Reading, MA: Addison-Wesley.

Farrell, A., & Geist-Martin, P. (2005). Communicating social health: Perceptions of wellness at work. *Management Communication Quarterly, 18*, 543–592.

Fayol, H. (1949). *General and industrial management*. London, England: Pitman.

Feldman, M., & March, J. (1981). Information in organizations as signal and symbol. *Administrative Science Quarterly, 26*, 171–186.

Fisher, A. (1980). *Small group decision making: Communication and the group process* (2nd ed.). New York, NY: McGraw-Hill.

Flamm, M. (2003). Trafficking of women and children in Southeast Asia. *United Nations Chronicle, 15*(2). Retrieved from heritage.org/Research/Economy/bg1757.cfm

Flanagan, C. (2004, March). How serfdom saved the women's movement. *Atlantic Monthly, 293*(2), 109–128.

Flanagin, A., & Waldeck, J. (2004). Technology use and organizational newcomer socialization. *Journal of Business Communication, 41*, 137–165.

Fleming, P. (2005). Metaphors of resistance. *Management Communication Quarterly, 19*, 45–66.

Fleming, P., & Spicer, A. (2003). Beyond power and resistance: New approaches to organizational politics. *Management Communication Quarterly, 21, 301–309*. doi: 10.1177/0893318907309928

Fleming, P., & Spicer, A. (2003). Working at a cynical distance: Implications for power, subjectivity and resistance. *Organization, 10*, 157–179.

Forbes, D. A. (2009). Commodification and co-modification explicating black female sexuality in organizations. *Management Communication Quarterly, 22*(4), 577–613.

Ford, R., & Fottler, M. (1995). Empowerment: A matter of degree. *Academy of Management Executive, 9*, 21–31.

Foucault, M. (1972). *The archaeology of knowledge*. London, England: Tavistock.

Foucault, M. (1978). *The history of sexuality, Vol. 1: An introduction*. (R. Hurley, Trans.). New York, NY: Pantheon.

Foucault, M. (1979). *The birth of the prison*. Harmondsworth, England: Penguin.

Fox, A. (2008, March). The brain at work: Science is shedding light on why people behave the way they do and how to better manage them. *HR Magazine*, 37–42.

Fox, R. (2013). "Homo"-work: Queering academic communication and communicating queer in academia. *Text & Performance Quarterly, 33*(1), 58–76. doi:10.1080/10462937.2012.744462

Franklin, B. (1970). *The complete Poor Richard almanacs published by Benjamin Franklin*. Barre, MA: Imprint Society.

Franz, C., & Jin, K. (1995). The structure of group conflict in a collaborative work group during information systems development. *Journal of Applied Communication Research, 23*, 108–122.

Frederick, C. (1913). *The new housekeeping: Efficiency studies in home management*. New York, NY: Doubleday.

Freeh Sporkin & Sullivan, LLP. (2012, July 12). *Report of the special investigative counsel regarding the actions of the Pennsylvania State University related to the child sexual abuse committed by Gerald A. Sandusky*. Retrieved from progress.psu.edu/assets/content/REPORT_FINAL_071212.pdf

Freire, P. (1968). *Pedagogy of the oppressed*. Berkeley: University of California Press.

French, R., & Raven, B. (1968). The bases of social power. In D. Cartwright & A. Zander (Eds.), *Group dynamics* (pp. 601–623). New York, NY: Harper and Row.

Friedman, M. (1992). *Dialogue and the human image*. Newbury Park, CA: Sage.

Friedman, T. (2005). *The world is flat: A brief history of the twenty-first century*. New York, NY: Farrar, Straus and Giroux.

Frost, P., Moore, L., Louis, M., Lundberg, C., & Martin, J. (1991). *Reframing organizational culture*. Newbury Park, CA: Sage.

Fulk, J., Schmitz, J., & Steinfeld, C. (1990). A social influence model of technology use. In J. Fulk & C. Steinfeld (Eds.), *Organizational and communication technology* (pp. 143–172). Newbury Park, CA: Sage.

Gabriel, Y. (1999). Beyond happy families: A critical reevaluation of the control-resistance-identity triangle. *Human Relations, 52*, 179–203.

Gagnon, S. (2008). Compelling identity: Selves and insecurity in global, corporate management development. *Management Learning, 39*, 375–391.

Galbraith, J. (1973). *Designing complex organizations*. Reading, MA: Addison-Wesley.

Ganesh, S., Zoller, H., & Cheney, G. (2005). Transforming resistance, broadening our boundaries: Critical organizational communication meets globalization from below. *Communication Monographs, 72*, 169–191.

Ganster, D. C., & Rosen, C. C. (2013). Work stress and employee health: A multidisciplinary review. *Journal of Management, 39*, 1085–1122. doi:10.1177/0149206313475815

Gao, J. (2006). Organized international asylum-seeker networks: Formation and utilization by Chinese students. *International Migration Review, 40*, 294–317.

Gardner, W. L., Reithel, B. J., Foley, R. T., Cogliser, C. C., & Walumbwa, F. O. (2009). Attraction to organizational culture profiles: Effects of realistic recruitment and vertical and horizontal individualism-collectivism. *Management Communication Quarterly, 22*, 437–472.

Geertz, C. (1973). *The interpretation of cultures*. New York, NY: Basic Books.

Geist, P., & Dreyer, J. (1993). The demise of dialogue: A critique of medical encounter ideology. *Western Journal of Communication, 57*, 233–246.

Gendron, G. (1999). Seizing opportunities for meaning. *Inc., 21*, 87.

Gephart, R. P. (2002). Introduction to the brave new workplace: Organizational behavior in the electronic age. *Journal of Organizational Behavior, 23*, 327–344.

Gergen, K. (1991). *The saturated self: Dilemmas of identity in contemporary life*. New York, NY: Basic Books.

Gibney, A. (Producer/Director). (2005). *Enron: The smartest guys in the room* [Motion picture]. United States: Magnolia Pictures.

Gibson, J., & Hodgetts, R. (1986). *Organizational communication: A managerial perspective*. New York, NY: Academic Press.

Gibson, M., & Papa, M. (2000). The mud, blood and beer guys: Organizational osmosis in blue-collar work groups. *Journal of Applied Communication Research, 28*, 68–88.

Giddens, A. (1984). *The constitution of society: Outline of the theory of structuration*. Berkeley: University of California Press.

Gill, R. (2013). The evolution of organizational archetypes: From the American to the entrepreneurial dream. *Communication Monographs, 80*(3), 331–353. doi:10.1080/03637751.2013.788252

Gill, R., & Ganesh, S. (2007). Empowerment, constraint, and the entrepreneurial self: A study of white women entrepreneurs. *Journal of Applied Communication Research, 35*, 268–293.

Gitlin, T. (1987). *The sixties: Years of hope, days of rage*. New York, NY: Bantam.

Gladwell, M. (2007). *Blink: The power of thinking without thinking*. New York, NY: Back Bay Books.

Gleick, J. (2000). *Faster: The acceleration of just about everything*. New York, NY: Vintage Books.

Glenn, C. L., & Jackson, R. L. II. (2010). Renegotiating identity in the field of communication. In S. Allan (Ed.). *Rethinking communication: Keywords in communication research* (pp. 137–149). New York, NY: Hampton Press.

Gluesing, J. (1998). Building connections and balancing power in global teams: Toward a reconceptualization of culture as composite. *Anthropology of Work Review, 18*(2/3), 18–30.

Goes, J., & Park, S. (1997). Interorganizational links and innovation: The case of hospital services. *Academy of Management Journal, 40,* 673–696.

Goodall, H. L. (1984). The status of communication studies in organizational contexts: One rhetorician's lament after a year-long odyssey. *Communication Quarterly, 32,* 133–147.

Goodall, H. L. (1989). *Casing a promised land.* Carbondale: Southern Illinois University Press.

Goodall, H. L. (1990). Interpretive contexts for decision-making: Toward an understanding of the physical, economic, dramatic, and hierarchical interplays of language in groups. In G. M. Phillips (Ed.), *Teaching how to work in groups* (pp. 197–224). Norwood, NJ: Ablex.

Goodall, H. L. (1991). *Living in the rock 'n' roll mystery: Reading context, self, and others as clues.* Carbondale: Southern Illinois University Press.

Goodall, H. L. (1994). *Casing a promised land: The autobiography of an organizational detective as cultural ethnographer* (Rev. ed.). Carbondale: Southern Illinois University Press.

Goodall, H. L., Jr. (1995). Work-hate narratives. In R. Whillock & D. Slayden (Eds.), *Hate speech.* Thousand Oaks, CA: Sage.

Goodall, H. L., Jr. (2000). *Writing the new ethnography.* Newbury Park, CA: Alta Mira Press.

Goodall, H. L., Jr. (2003). What is interpretive ethnography? An eclectic's tale. In R. Clair (Ed.), *Expressions of ethnography: Novel approaches to qualitative methods* (pp. 55–64). Albany, NY: SUNY Press.

Goodall, H. L., Jr. (2004). Narrative ethnography and applied communication research. *Journal of Applied Communication Research, 32,* 185–194.

Goodall, H. L., Jr. (2008). Twice betrayed by the truth: A narrative about the cultural similarities between the Cold War and the Global War on Terror. *Cultural Studies/Critical Methodologies, 8,* 353–368.

Goodall, H. L., Jr. (2012). Lucky man. hlgoodall.com/Blog/Lucky-Man.html

Goodall, H. L., Jr., & Goodall, S. (2006). *Communicating in professional contexts: Skills, ethics, and technologies* (2nd ed.). Belmont, CA: Wadsworth/Thomson Learning.

Goodier, B., & Eisenberg, E. (2006). Seeking the spirit: Communication and the (re)development of a "spiritual" organization. *Communication Studies, 57,* 47–65.

Google. (2011). Jobs. google.com/about/jobs/

Gossett, L. M., & Kilker, J. (2006). My job sucks: Examining counter-institutional Web sites as locations for organizational member voice, dissent, and resistance. *Management Communication Quarterly, 20,* 63–90.

Graen, G. (1976). Role making processes within complex organizations. In M. Dunnette (Ed.), *Handbook of industrial and organizational psychology* (pp. 1201–1245). Chicago, IL: Rand McNally.

Graen, G., Liden, R., & Hoel, W. (1982). Role of leadership in the employee withdrawal process. *Journal of Applied Psychology, 67,* 868–872.

Graham, P. (1997). *Mary Parker Follett: Prophet of management.* Cambridge, MA: Harvard Business School Press.

Granovetter, M. (1973). The strength of weak ties. *American Journal of Sociology, 78,* 1360–1380.

Grantham, C. (1999). *The future of work: The promise of the new digital work society.* New York, NY: McGraw-Hill.

Gray, J. (2002). *Men are from Mars, women are from Venus: How to get what you want in your relationships.* New York, NY: Harper Thorsons.

Gray, J. (2011). *Venus on fire, Mars on ice: Hormonal balance—The key to life, love and energy.* Coquitlam, BC, Canada: Mind Publishing.

Greenberg, C. C., Regenbogen, S. E., Studdert, D. M., Lipsitz, S. R., Rogers, S. O., Zinner, M. J., & Gawande, A. A. (2007). Patterns of communication breakdowns resulting in injury to surgical patients. *Journal of the American College of Surgeons, 204,* 533–540.

Greenblatt, S. (1990). Culture. In F. Lentricchia & T. McLaughlin (Eds.), *Critical terms for literary study* (pp. 225–232). Chicago, IL: University of Chicago Press.

Greenleaf, R. (1998). *The power of servant leadership*. San Francisco, CA: Berrett-Koehler.

Grimes, D., & Parker, P. (2009). Imagining organizational communication as a decolonizing project. *Management Communication Quarterly, 22*, 502–511.

Habermas, J. (1972). *Knowledge and human interests*. London, England: Heinemann Educational Books.

Hafner, K., & Gnatek, T. (2004, May 27). For some, the blogging never stops. *New York Times*. Retrieved from nytimes.com/2004/05/27/technology/for-some-the-blogging-never-stops.html

Hall, M. (2011). Constructions of leadership at the intersection of discourse, power and culture: Jamaican managers' narratives of leading in a postcolonial cultural context. *Management Communication Quarterly, 25*, 612–643.

Hamborg, K.-C., & Greif, S. (2003). New technologies and stress. In M. Schabracq, J. Winnubst, & C. Cooper (Eds.), *The handbook of work and health psychology* (pp. 209–235). Chichester, England: Wiley.

Hansen, M. (2009). *Collaboration: How leaders avoid the traps, build common ground, and reap big results*. Cambridge, MA: Harvard Business Review Press.

Hansen, D. (2016). Unless it changes, capitalism will starve humanity by 2050. *Forbes*. Retrieved from http://www.forbes.com/sites/drewhansen/2016/02/09/unless-it-changes-capitalism-will-starve-humanity-by-2050/2/#3ee4d9562757

Hardin, G. (1968, December 13). The tragedy of the commons. *Science, 162*, 1243–1248.

Harris, L. C., & Ogbonna, E., (2012). Motives for service sabotage: An empirical study of front-line workers. *Service Industries Journal, 32*, 2027–2046.

Harrison, T. (1994). Communication and interdependence in democratic organizations. In S. Deetz (Ed.), *Communication yearbook* (Vol. 17, pp. 247–274). Newbury Park, CA: Sage.

Harshman, E., & Harshman, C. (1999). Communicating with employees: Building on an ethical foundation. *Journal of Business Ethics, 19*, 3–19.

Harter, J. & Adkins, A. (2015). Engaged employees less likely to have health problems. Retrieved from http://www.gallup.com/poll/187865/engaged-employees-less-likely-health-problems.aspx?g_source=EMPLOYEE_ENGAGEMENT&g_medium=topic&g_campaign=tiles

Harter, L. (2004). Masculinity(s), the agrarian frontier myth, and cooperative ways of organizing: Contradictions and tensions in the experience and enactment of democracy. *Journal of Applied Communication Research, 32*, 89–118.

Harvey, S. (2014). Creative synthesis: exploring the process of extraordinary group creativity. *Academy of Management Review, 39*(3), 324–343. Published ahead of print February 14, 2014, doi:10.5465/amr.2012.0224

Hasinoff, A. A. (2008). Fashioning race for the free market on *America's Next Top Model*. *Critical Studies in Media Communication, 25*, 324–343.

Hawking, S. (1988). *A brief history of time*. New York, NY: Bantam.

Heiss, S. N., & Carmack, H. J. (2012). Knock, knock; Who's there? Making sense of organizational entrance through humor. *Management Communication Quarterly, 26*, 106–132.

Helgesen, S., & Johnson, J. (2010). *The female vision: Women's real power at work*. San Francisco, CA: Berrett-Koehler.

Hellweg, S. (1987). Organizational grapevines: A state-of-the-art review. In B. Dervin & M. Voight (Eds.), *Progress in the communication sciences* (Vol. 8). Norwood, NJ: Ablex.

Hersey, P., & Blanchard, K. (1977). *Management of organizational behavior: Utilizing human resources* (3rd ed.). Englewood Cliffs, NJ: Prentice Hall.

Hess, J. (1993). Assimilating newcomers into an organization: A cultural perspective. *Journal of Applied Communication Research, 21*, 189–210.

Hill, V., & Carley, K. M. (2011). Win friends and influence people: Relationships as conduits of organizational culture in temporary placement agencies. *Journal of Management Inquiry, 20*, 432–442. doi:10.1177/1056492611432807

Hirsch, P. B. (2015). The plebeians rehearse the uprising. *Journal of Business Strategy, 36*(5), 50–54.

Hirschman, A. (1970). *Exit, voice, and loyalty: Responses to decline in firms, organizations, and states.* Cambridge, MA: Harvard University Press.

Hispanic Business Students Association (HBSA). (2013). Retrieved from hbsaasu.org/story -mission-statement

Ho, A. K., Sidaniua, J., Pratto, F., Levin, S., Thomsen, L., Kteily, N., & Sheehy-Skeffington, J. (2012). Social dominance orientation: Revisiting the structure and function of a variable predicting social and political attitudes. *Personality and Social Psychology Bulletin, 38,* 583–60.

Hochschild, A. (1989). *Second shift: Working parents and the revolution at home.* New York, NY: Viking.

Hochschild, A. (2003). *The commercialization of intimate life: Notes from home and work.* Berkeley: University of California Press.

Hoffman, M. F., & Cowan, R. L. (2008). The meaning of work/life: A corporate ideology of work/ life balance. *Communication Quarterly, 56,* 227–246.

Hoffman, M. F., & Medlock-Klyukovski, A. (2004). "Our creator who art in heaven": Paradox, ritual, and cultural transformation. *Western Journal of Communication, 68,* 389–410.

Holland, K., Rabelo, V. C., Gustafson, A., Seabrook, R., & Cortina, L. (2016). Sexual harassment against men: Examining the roles of feminist activism, sexuality, and organizational context. *Psychology of Men & Masculinity, 17*(1), 17–29.

Holmer-Nadesan, M. (1996). Organizational identity and space of action. *Organization Studies, 17,* 49–81.

Homans, G. (1961). *Social behavior: Its elementary forms.* New York, NY: Harcourt, Brace.

Hopson, M. C., & Orbe, M. P. (2007). Playing the game: Recalling dialectic tensions for black men in oppressive organizational structures. *Howard Journal of Communications, 18,* 69–86.

Hornstein, H. A. (1996). *Brutal bosses and their prey: How to identify and overcome abuse in the workplace.* New York, NY: Riverhead Books.

Hudson, L., Iskander, A., & Kirk, M. (Eds.) (2014). Media evolution on the eve of the Arab Spring. NY: Palgrave MacMillan.

Humphreys, M., Ucbasaran, D., & Lockett, A. (2012). Sensemaking and sensegiving stories of jazz leadership. *Human Relations, 65*(1), 41–62.

Hunger, R., & Stern, L. (1976). An assessment of the functionality of subordinate goals in reducing conflict. *Academy of Management Journal, 16,* 591–605.

Hurst, D. (1992). Thoroughly modern: Mary Parker Follett. *Business Quarterly, 56,* 55–59.

Huselid, M. (1995). The impact of human resource management practices on turnover, productivity, and corporate financial performance. *Academy of Management Journal, 38,* 635–673.

Hyde, B. (1995, February). *An ontological approach to education.* Paper presented at the annual conference of the Western States Communication Association, Portland, OR.

Iedema, R., & Rhodes, C. (2010). The undecided space of ethics in organizational surveillance. *Organization Studies, 31,* 199–217.

Iedema, R., Rhodes, C., & Scheeres, H. (2006). Surveillance, resistance, observance: Exploring the teleo-affective intensity of identity (at) work. *Organization Studies, 27*(8), 1111–1130.

International Labour Organization. (2014).

Ireland, C. (2010, February 19). Slavery in 2010. Retrieved from news.harvard.edu/gazette /story/2010/02/slavery-in-2010

Isaacs, W. (1993, Fall). Taking flight: Dialogue, collaborative thinking, and organizational learning. *Organizational Dynamics, 22*(2), 24–39.

Isaacs, W. (1999). *Dialogue: The art of thinking together.* New York, NY: Doubleday/Currency.

Jablin, F. (1979). Superior-subordinate communication: The state of the art. *Psychological Bulletin, 86,* 1201–1222.

Jablin, F. (1985). Task/work relationships: A life-span perspective. In M. Knapp & G. Miller (Eds.), *Handbook of interpersonal communication* (pp. 615–654). Newbury Park, CA: Sage.

Jablin, F. (1987). Organizational entry, assimilation, and exit. In F. Jablin, L. Putnam, K. Roberts, & L. Porter (Eds.), *Handbook of organizational communication* (pp. 679–740). Newbury Park, CA: Sage.

Jackson, M. (1989). *Paths toward a clearing: Radical empiricism and ethnographic inquiry*. Bloomington: Indiana University Press.

Jacobs, R., & Brinkerhoff, L., & Johnson, B. (2013). Whole system transformation through a polarity lens. *The change champion's field guide*, Carter, L., Sullivan, R., Goldsmith, M., Ulrich, D., & Smallwood, N. (Eds.), pp. 148–177, NY: John Wiley & Sons.

Janis, I. (1971). *Victims of groupthink* (2nd ed.). Boston, MA: Houghton Mifflin.

Jassawalla, A., & Sashittal, H. (1999). Building collaborative cross-functional new product teams. *Academy of Management Executive, 13*, 50–63.

Jobs, S. (2005, June 12). Commencement address presented at Stanford University. Retrieved from news-service.stanford.edu/news/2005/june15/jobs-061505.html

Johnson, B. (1977). *Communication: The process of organizing*. Boston, MA: Allyn and Bacon.

Kamp, D. (2009, April). Rethinking the American dream. *Vanity Fair*. Retrieved from vanityfair.com/culture/features/2009/04/american-dream200904?printable=true&currentPage=all

Kassing, J. W. (1997). Articulating, antagonizing, and displacing: A model of employee dissent. *Communication Studies, 48*, 311–332.

Kassing, J. W. (2008). Consider this: A comparison of factors contributing to expressions of employee dissent. *Communication Quarterly, 56*, 342–355.

Kassing, J. W. (2009). "In case you didn't hear me the first time": An examination of repetitious upward dissent. *Management Communication Quarterly, 22*, 416–436.

Kassing, J. W. (2011). Stressing out about dissent: Examining the relationship between coping strategies and dissent expression. *Communication Research Reports, 28*, 225–234.

Kassing, J. W., & Armstrong, T. A. (2002). Someone's going to hear about this: Examining the association between dissent-triggering events and employees' dissent expression. *Management Communication Quarterly, 16*, 39–65.

Katz, D., & Kahn, R. (1966). *The social psychology of organizations*. New York, NY: Wiley.

Katz-Sidlow, R. J., Ludwig, A., Miller, S., & Sidlow, R. (2012). Smartphone use during inpatient attending rounds: Prevalence, patterns, and potential for distraction. *Journal of Hospital Medicine, 7*, 595–599.

Kauffman, R. (2008). Practical approaches to ethics for colleges and universities. *New Directions for Higher Education, 144*, 9–15.

Keeley, M. (1980). Organizational analogy: A comparison of organismic and social contract models. *Administrative Science Quarterly, 25*, 337–362.

Keys, B., & Case, T. (1990). How to become an influential manager. *Academy of Management Executive, 4*, 38–50.

Keyton, J. N. (2011). *Communication and organizational culture: A key to understanding work experiences* (2nd ed.). Thousand Oaks, CA: Sage.

Kiechel, W. (1994, April 4). A manager's career in the new economy. *Fortune*, 68–72.

Kilmann, R., & Thomas, K. (1975). Interpersonal conflict-handling behavior as a reflection of Jungian personality dimensions. *Psychological Reports, 37*, 971–980.

Kim, C., & Tamborini, T. (2006). The continuing significance of race in the occupational attainment of whites and blacks: A segmented labor market analysis. *Sociological Inquiry, 76*, 23–51.

Kimberly, J. (2010). "How BP blew crisis management 101." *CNN*. Retrieved from articles.cnn.com/2010-06-21/opinion/kimberly.bp.management.crisis_1_bp-crisis-senior-management?_s=PM:OPINION

Kimberly, J., & Miles, R. (1980). *The organizational life cycle*. San Francisco, CA: Jossey-Bass.

King, P., & Sawyer, C. (1998). Mindfulness, mindlessness, and communication instruction. *Communication Education, 47*, 326–338.

Kinsella, W. (1999). Discourse, power, and knowledge in the management of big science. *Management Communication Quarterly, 13*, 171.

Kipnis, D., Schmidt, S., & Wilkinson, I. (1980). Intraorganizational influence tactics: Explorations in getting one's way. *Journal of Applied Psychology, 65*, 440–452.

Kirby, E., & Krone, K. (2002). "The policy exists but you can't really use it": Communication and the structuration of work-family policies. *Journal of Applied Communication Research, 30*(1), 50–77.

Kirkman, B. L., & Rosen, B. (1999). Beyond self-management: Antecedents and consequences of team empowerment. *Academy of Management, 42*, 58–74.

Kovach, K. A. (1987). What motivates employees? Workers and supervisors give different answers. *Business Horizons, 30*, 58–65.

Kraatz, M. (1998). Learning by association? Interorganizational networks and adaptation to environmental change. *Academy of Management Journal, 41*, 621–643.

Kramer, M., & Miller, V. (1999). In response to criticisms of organizational socialization research. *Communication Monographs, 66*, 358–367.

Kreps, G. (1991). *Organizational communication: Theory and practice* (2nd ed.). New York, NY: Longman.

Krippendorff, K. (1985, June). *On the ethics of constructing communication*. Presidential address of the International Communication Association, Honolulu, HI.

Krizek, R. (2003). Ethnography as the excavation of personal narrative. In R. Clair (Ed.), *Expressions of ethnography: Novel approaches to qualitative methods* (pp. 141–152). Albany, NY: SUNY Press.

Kuhn, T. (2006). A "demented work ethic" and a "lifestyle firm": Discourse, identity, and workplace time commitments. *Organization Studies, 27*, 1339–1358.

Kunda, G. (1993). *Engineering culture: Control and commitment in a high-tech corporation*. Philadelphia, PA: Temple University Press.

Kutsmode, C. (2014, October 13). Top 10 future recruitment trends. Retrieved from http://www.eremedia.com/ere/top-10-future-recruitment-trends/

Lair, D., Sullivan, K., & Cheney, G. (2005). Marketization and the recasting of the professional self: The rhetoric and ethics of personal branding. *Management Communication Quarterly, 18*, 307–343.

Lammers, J. C., Atouba, Y. L., & Carlson, E. J. (2013). Which identities matter? A mixed-method study of group, organizational, and professional identities and their relationship to burnout. *Management Communication Quarterly, 27*(4), 503–536. doi:10.1177/0893318913498824

Langer, E. (1998). *The power of mindful learning*. New York, NY: Perseus.

Larson, G. S., & Pepper, G. L. (2011). Organizational identification and the symbolic shaping of information communication technology. *Qualitative Research Reports in Communication, 12*(1), 1–9.

Larson, G. S., & Tompkins, P. K. (2005). Ambivalence and Resistance: A Study of Management in a Concertive Control System. *Communication Monographs, 72*(1), 1–21. doi:10.1080/0363775052000342508

Lawler, E., III, & Finegold, D. (2000). Individualizing the organization: Past, present, and future. *Organizational Dynamics, 29*, 1–15.

Lawrence, P., & Lorsch, J. (1967). *Organization and environment: Managing differentiation and integration*. Boston, MA: Graduate School of Business Administration, Harvard University.

Leavitt, H. (1951). Some effects of certain communication patterns on group performance. *Journal of Abnormal and Social Psychology, 46*, 38–50.

Lee, E. A., Soto, J. A., Swim, J. K., & Bernstein, M. J. (2012). Bitter reproach or sweet revenge: Cultural differences in response to racism. *Personality and Social Psychology Bulletin, 38*, 920–932.

Lee, S., & Lee, C. (2015). Creative interaction and multiplexity in intraorganizational networks. *Management Communication Quarterly, 29*, 56–83.

LeGreco, M. (2012). Working with policy: Restructuring healthy eating practices and the Circuit of Policy Communication. *Journal of Applied Communication Research, 40*, 44–64.

LeGreco, M., & Canary, H. E. (2011). Enacting sustainable school-based health initiatives: A communication-centered approach to policy and practice. *American Journal of Public Health*, *101*, 431–437.

LeGreco, M., Ferrier, M., & Leonard, D. (2015). Further down the virtual vines: Managing community-based work in virtual public spaces. In M. Mervio (Ed.), *Management and Participation in the Public Sphere* (pp. 147–160). Hershey, PA: IGI Global.

LeGreco, M., Leonard, D., & Ferrier, M. (2012). Virtual vines: Using participatory methods to connect virtual work with community-based practice. In S. D. Long (Ed.), *Virtual work and human interaction* (pp. 78–98). Hershey, PA: IGI Global.

LeGreco, M., & Tracy, S. J. (2009). Discourse tracing as qualitative practice. *Qualitative Inquiry*, *15*, 1516–1543.

Lencioni, P. (2002). *The five dysfunctions of a team*. San Francisco, CA: Jossey-Bass.

LeRoux, K. (2009). Paternalistic or participatory governance? Examining opportunities for client participation in nonprofit social service organizations. *Public Administration Review*, *69*(3), 504–517.

Lester, J. (2015). Cultures of work–life balance in higher education: A case of fragmentation. *Journal of Diversity in Higher Education*, *8*(3), 139–156. doi:10.1037/a0039377

Lewin, R. (1997, November 29). Ecosystems as a metaphor for business. *New Scientist*, *156*, 30–34.

Liden, R., & Graen, G. (1980). Generalizability of the vertical dyad linkage model of leadership. *Academy of Management Journal*, *23*, 451–465.

Likert, R. (1961). *New patterns of management*. New York, NY: McGraw-Hill.

Lim, A. (2008, October 28). Economic woes mean smaller paychecks. *msnbc.com* Retrieved from msnbc.msn.com/id/27327204

Locke, E., & Latham, G. (1984). *Goal setting: A motivational technique that works!* Englewood Cliffs, NJ: Prentice Hall.

Longworth, R. C. (1998). *Global squeeze: The coming crisis for first-world nations*. New York, NY: McGraw-Hill.

Lott, A. (2009, March 9). Study: C-suite exclusion of black women due to inadequate visibility, networks. *Black Enterprise*. Retrieved from blackenterprise.com/careers/2009/03/09/study-c-suite-exclusion-of-black-women-due-to-inadequate-visibility-networks

Louis, M. (1980). Surprise and sense-making: What newcomers experience in entering unfamiliar organizational settings. *Administrative Science Quarterly*, *23*, 225–251.

Love, P., Fong, P., & Irani, Z. (2005). *Management of knowledge in project environments*. London, England: Routledge.

Lucas, K. (2011). Blue-collar discourses of workplace dignity: Using outgroup comparisons to construct positive identities. *Management Communication Quarterly*, *25*, 353–374.

Lukes, S. (1986). *Power*. New York, NY: New York University Press.

Lutgen-Sandvik, P. (2003). The communicative cycle of employee emotional abuse: Generation and regeneration of workplace mistreatment. *Management Communication Quarterly*, *16*, 471–501.

Lutgen-Sandvik, P., & Davenport Sypher, B. (Eds.). (2009). *Destructive organizational communication*. New York, NY: Routledge.

Lutgen-Sandvik, P., Riforgiate, S., & Fletcher, C. (2011). Work as a source of positive emotional experiences and the discourses informing positive assessment. *Western Journal of Communication*, *75*, 2–27.

Lutz, A. (2012, November 27). The formula that made Costco the anti-Walmart. *Daily Finance* Retrieved from dailyfinance.com/2012/11/27/how-costco-became-the-anti-walmart

Lynch, O. H. (2002). Humorous communication: Finding a place for humor in communication research. *Communication Theory*, *12*, 423–445. doi:10.1111/j.1468-2885.2002.tb00277.x

Lynch, O. H. (2009). Kitchen antics: The importance of humor and maintaining professionalism at work. *Journal of Applied Communication Research*, *37*, 444–464. doi:10.1080/00909880903233143

Lynch, O. H., & Schaefer, Z. A. (2008). Humor without interaction: A joke without a punch line. *Management Communication Quarterly, 22*, 512–520. doi:10.1177/0893318908327009

Mahar, M. (2006). *Money-driven medicine: The real reason health care costs so much*. New York, NY: HarperCollins.

Malcomson, S. L. (2008). The higher globalization. *New York Times*. Retrieved from nytimes. com/2008/12/14/magazine/14Ideas-Section2-C-t-002.html

Managing to make money. (2002). Retrieved from news.google.com/newspapers?nid=888&dat =20020618&id=_sMNAAAAIBAJ&sjid=0nMDAAAAIBAJ&pg=5140,3214512

Marcus, G., & Fischer, M. (1986). *Anthropology as cultural critique*. Chicago, IL: University of Chicago Press.

Markey, P. (2008, February 4). Colombians take to the streets in huge anti-FARC march. Retrieved from reuters.com/article/2008/02/04/us-colombia-hostages-idUSN0459656620080204

Marquardt, M. J. (2002). *Building the learning organization: Mastering the five elements for corporate learning*. Mountain View, CA: Davies-Black Publishing.

Marshall, A., & Stohl, C. (1993). Participating as participation: A network approach. *Communication Monographs, 60*, 137–157.

Marshall, J. (1989). Revisioning career concepts: A feminist invitation. In M. Arthur, D. Hall, & B. Lawrence (Eds.), *Handbook of career theory* (pp. 275–291). Cambridge, England: Cambridge University Press.

Martin, D. (2004). Humor in middle management: Women negotiating the paradoxes of organizational life. *Journal of Applied Communication Research, 32*, 147–170.

Martin, J. (1985). Can organizational culture be managed? In P. Frost, L. Moore, M. Louis, C. Lundberg, & J. Martin (Eds.), *Organizational culture* (pp. 95–98). Beverly Hills, CA: Sage.

Martin, J. (1992). *Cultures in organizations: Three perspectives*. New York, NY: Oxford University Press.

Martin, J., Feldman, M., Hatch, M., & Sitkin, S. (1983). The uniqueness paradox in organizational stories. *Administrative Science Quarterly, 28*, 438–453.

Martin, J. N., Moore, S., Hecht, M. L., & Larkey, L. (2001). An African American perspective on conversational improvement strategies. *Howard Journal of Communications, 12*, 1–27.

Maslow, A. (1965). *Eupsychian management*. Homewood, IL: Irwin.

Maug, E. (2001). Ownership structure and the life-cycle of the firm: A theory of the decision to go public. *European Finance Review, 5*, 167–200.

May, S. (1988, May). *The modernist monologue in organizational communication research: The text, the subject, and the audience*. Paper presented at the annual convention of the International Communication Association, San Francisco, CA.

Mayo, E. (1945). *The social problems of industrial civilization*. Cambridge, MA: Graduate School of Business Administration, Harvard University.

McComas, K., Besley, J. C., & Black, L. W. (2010). The rituals of public meetings. *Public Administration Review, 70*(1), 122–130. Retrieved from login.ezproxy1.lib.asu.edu/login?url =http://search.proquest.com/docview/853757624?accountid=4485

McDermott, I. (2012). Internet activism. *Searcher, 20*, 7–11.

McDermott, V. M., Oetzel, J. G., & White, K. (2008). Ethical paradoxes in community-based participatory research. In H. Zoller & M. Dutta (Eds.), *Emerging perspectives in health communication: Meaning, culture, and power* (pp. 182–202). New York: Routledge.

McDonald, J. (2015). Organizational communication meets queer theory: Theorizing relations of "difference" differently. *Communication Theory, 25*(3), 310–329. doi:10.1111/comt.12060

McDonald, P. (1988). The Los Angeles Olympic Organizing Committee: Developing organizational culture in the short run. *Public Administration Quarterly, 10*, 189–205.

McGregor, D. (1960). *The human side of enterprise*. New York, NY: McGraw-Hill.

McLarney, C., & Rhyno, S. (1999). Mary Parker Follett: Visionary leadership and strategic management. *Women in Management Review, 14*, 292–302.

McLuhan, M. (1964). *Understanding media: The extensions of man.* New York, NY: McGraw-Hill.

McPhee, R. (1985). Formal structures and organizational communication. In R. McPhee & P. Tompkins (Eds.), *Organizational communication: Traditional themes and new directions* (pp. 149–177). Beverly Hills, CA: Sage.

Mead, G. (1991, May 30). The new old capitalism: Long hours, low wages. *Rolling Stone, 27*(3).

Mead, G. H. (1934). *Mind, self, and society.* Chicago, IL: University of Chicago Press.

Meares, M., Oetzel, J., Torres, A., Derkacs, D., & Ginossar, T. (2004). Employee mistreatment and muted voices in the culturally diverse workplace. *Journal of Applied Communication Research, 32,* 4–27.

Medved, C., & Kirby, E. (2005). Family CEOs: A feminist analysis of corporate mothering discourses. *Management Communication Quarterly, 18,* 307–343.

Meyer, E. (2015, October). When culture doesn't translate. *Harvard Business Review, 93,* 66–72.

Meyer, H.-D. (2010). Local control as a mechanism of colonization of public education in the United States. *Educational Philosophy and Theory, 42,* 830–845.

Miller, D., & Form, W. (1951). *Industrial sociology: An introduction to the sociology of work relations.* New York, NY: Harper.

Miller, J. G. (1978). *Living systems.* New York, NY: McGraw-Hill.

Miller, K. (2003). *Organizational communication: Approaches and processes* (3rd ed.). Belmont, CA: Wadsworth.

Miller, K. (2012). *Organizational communication: Approaches and processes* (6th ed.). Boston, MA: Cengage.

Miller, K., & Monge, P. (1986). Participation, satisfaction, and productivity: A meta-analytic review. *Academy of Management Journal, 29,* 727–753.

Miller, V., & Jablin, F. (1991). Information seeking during organizational entry: Influences, tactics, and a model of the process. *Academy of Management Review, 16,* 92–120.

Minh-Ha, T. (1991). *When the moon waxes red: Representation, gender, and cultural politics.* New York, NY: Routledge.

Mireille. (2011, August 25). Five decades of women pilots in the U.S. How did we do? [Blog post]. Retrieved from womenofaviationweek.org/blog/tag/u-s-women-pilots-statistics

Mirivel, J. (2014). *Positive communication: Theory and practice.* New York: Peter Lang.

Mitroff, I., & Kilmann, R. (1975). Stories managers tell: A new tool for organizational problem-solving. *Management Review, 64,* 18–28.

Molinsky, A. (2013). *Global dexterity.* Cambridge, MA: Harvard Business Review Press.

Molloy, K. A., & Heath, R. G. (2014). Bridge discourses and organizational ideologies: Managing spiritual and secular communication in a faith-based, nonprofit organization. *Journal of Business Communication, 51*(4), 386–408. doi:10.1177/2329488414525451

Molyneux, L. (2015). What journalists retweet: Opinion, humor, and brand development on Twitter. *Journalism, 16*(7), 920–935. doi:10.1177/1464884914550135

Monge, P., & Contractor, N. (2001). Emergence of communication networks. In F. Jablin & L. Putnam (Eds.), *The new handbook of organizational communication* (pp. 440–502). Thousand Oaks, CA: Sage.

Monge, P., & Eisenberg, E. (1987). Emergent communication networks. In F. Jablin, L. Putnam, K. Roberts, & L. Porter (Eds.), *Handbook of organizational communication* (pp. 204–342). Beverly Hills, CA: Sage.

Morgan, G. (1986). *Images of organization.* Newbury Park, CA: Sage.

Motif Investing (2016, January 9). Is the middle class really shrinking? Retrieved from http://finance .yahoo.com/news/middle-class-really-shrinking-025451174.html;_ylt=A86 .J7_0.49WglgA70YnnIlQ;_ylu=X3oDMTEyYXAwN25lBGNvbG8DZ3ExBHBvcwMxBH Z0aWQDQjExMTVfMQRzZWMDc2M-

Motley, M. (1992). Mindfulness in solving communicators' dilemmas. *Communication Monographs, 59,* 306–317.

Mouritsen, J., & Bjorn-Andersen, N. (1991). Understanding third-wave information systems. In C. Dunlop and R. Kling (Eds.), *Computerization and controversy: Value conflicts and social choices* (pp. 308–320). San Diego, CA: Academic Press.

Mulholland, K. (2004). Workplace resistance in an Irish call centre: Slammin', scammin' smokin' an' leavin'. *Work, Employment and Society, 18*, 709–724.

Mumby, D. (1987). The political function of narratives in organizations. *Communication Monographs, 54*, 113–127.

Mumby, D. (1988). *Communication and power in the organization: Discourse, ideology, and domination.* Norwood, NJ: Ablex.

Mumby, D. (1993). *Narrative and social control: Critical perspectives.* Newbury Park, CA: Sage.

Mumby, D. (2000). Communication, organization, and the public sphere: A feminist perspective. In P. Buzzanell (Ed.), *Rethinking organizational and managerial communication from feminist perspectives* (pp. 3–23). Thousand Oaks, CA: Sage.

Mumby, D. (2005). Theorizing resistance in organization studies: A dialectical approach. *Management Communication Quarterly, 19*, 19–44.

Murphy, A. (1998). Hidden transcripts of flight attendant resistance. *Management Communication Quarterly, 11*, 499–535.

Murphy, A. G. (2013). Discursive frictions: Power, identity, and culture in an international working partnership. *Journal of International & Intercultural Communication, 6*(1), 1–20. doi:10.1080/17513057.2012.740683

Myers, K. (2005). A burning desire: Assimilation into a fire department. *Management Communication Quarterly, 18*, 344–384.

Myers, K. K., & Sadaghiani, K. (2010). Millennials in the workplace: A communication perspective on millennials' organizational relationships and performance. *Journal of Business Psychology, 25*, 225–238.

Myerson, D. E. (1991). "Normal" ambiguity? A glimpse of an organizational culture. In P. Frost, M. L. Moore, M. Louis, C. Lundberg, & J. Martin (Eds.), *Reframing organizational culture* (pp. 131–144). Newbury Park, CA: Sage.

Nadesan, M., & Trethewey, A. (2000). Enterprising subjects: Gendered strategies for success. *Text and Performance Quarterly, 20*, 1–28.

Nagpal, K., Vats, A., Lamb, B., Ashrafian, H., Sevdealis, N., Vincent, C., & Moorthy, K. (2010). Information transfer and communication in surgery. *Annals of Surgery, 252*, 225–239.

Namie, G. (2000, September). U.S. hostile workplace survey 2000. Retrieved from workplace bullying.org/multi/pdf/N-N-2000.pdf

National Communication Association. (1999, September). Credo for Ethical Communication. *Spectra*, 4.

Negrey, C. (2012). *Work time: Conflict, control, and change.* Hoboken, NJ: Polity.

Newton, J. (2011). *John Newton's Olney hymns.* Minneapolis, MN: Curiosmith.

Nolan, L. (2015). The impact of executive personal branding on non-profit perception and communications. *Public Relations Review, 41*(2), 288–292. doi:10.1016/j.pubrev.2014.11.001

Nomaguchi, K., & Bianchi, S. (2004). Exercise time: Gender differences in the effects of marriage, parenthood and employment. *Journal of Marriage and Family, 66*, 413–430.

Norman, J. (2010, October 17). Male workers can be sexually harassed too. *Orange County Register.* Retrieved from jan.blog.ocregister.com/2010/10/17/male-workers-can-be-sexually-harassed-too/47348

Nugent, P., Belmabkhout, Y., Burd, S., Cairns, A., Luebke, R., Forrest, K., . . . Zawarotko, M. (2013). Porous materials with optimal adsorption thermodynamics and kinetics for CO_2 separation. *Nature, 495*, 80–84.

Nuru, A. K. (2014). Between layers: Understanding the communicative negotiation of conflicting identities by transgender individuals. *Communication Studies, 65*(3), 281–297. doi:10.1080/10510974.2013.833527

O'Brien, S. (2012). Fired for defending her hairstyle on Facebook. *CNN*, December 12, 2012, 9:42 AM.

O'Driscoll, M., Poelmans, S., Spector, P., Kalliath, T., Allen, T., Cooper, C., & Sanchez, J. (2013). Family-responsive interventions, perceived organizational and supervisor support, work-family conflict, and psychological strain. In C. Cooper (Ed.), *From Stress to Wellbeing* (Vol. 2, pp. 229–245). London, England: Palgrave Macmillan.

Oetzel, J. G. (2005). Effective intercultural workgroup communication theory. In W. B. Gudykunst (Ed.), *Theorizing about intercultural communication* (pp. 351–371). Thousand Oaks, CA: Sage.

Oetzel, J. G., McDermott, V. M., Torres, A., & Sanchez, C. (2012). The impact of individual differences and group diversity on group interaction climate and satisfaction: A test of the effective intercultural workgroup communication theory. *Journal of International and Intercultural Communication, 5*(2), 144–167.

Oh, H. J., & Lee, B. (2011). The effect of computer-mediated social support in patient empowerment and doctor-patient communication. *Health Communication, 27*, 1–12.

O'Sullivan, R., Mugglestone, K., & Allison, T. (2014). *Closing the race gap: Alleviating young African American employment through education*. Washington, DC: Young Invincibles.

Omelaniuk, I. (2005, July 8). Trafficking in human beings. United Nations Expert Group Meeting on International Migration and Development. Retrieved from un.org/esa/population/meetings/ittmigdev2005/P15_IOmelaniuk.pdf

Ortner, S. (1980). Theory in anthropology since the sixties. *Journal for the Comparative Study of Society and History, 26*(1), 126–166.

Ouchi, W. (1981). *Theory Z*. Reading, MA: Addison-Wesley.

Ouchi, W., & Wilkins, A. (1985). Organizational culture. *Annual Review of Sociology, 11*, 457–483.

Oxfam America. (2013). Retrieved from oxfamamerica.org

Pacanowsky, M. (1988). Communication in the empowering organization. In J. Anderson (Ed.), *Communication yearbook* (Vol. 11, pp. 356–379). Newbury Park, CA: Sage.

Pacanowsky, M., & O'Donnell-Trujillo, N. (1983). Organizational communication as cultural performance. *Communication Monographs, 50*, 126–147.

Packaged Facts (2015, August 12). Global nonGMO food & beverage market reaches $550 billion, U.S. sales at $200 billion. Retrieved from http://www.packagedfacts.com/about/release.asp?id=3803

Pal, M., & Buzzanell, P. (2008). The Indian call center experience: A case study in changing discourses of identity, identification, and career in a global context. *Journal of Business Communication, 45*, 31–60.

Pal, M., & Dutta, M. J. (2008). Theorizing resistance in a global context: Processes, strategies, and tactics in communication scholarship. *Communication Yearbook, 32*, 41–87.

Parker, P. (1997). *African American women executives within dominant culture organizations: An examination of leadership socialization, communication strategies, and leadership behavior* (Unpublished doctoral dissertation). University of Texas, Austin.

Parker, P. (2003). Control, resistance, and empowerment in raced, gendered, and classed contexts: The case of the African American woman. In P. Kalbfleisch (Ed.), *Communication yearbook* (Vol. 27, pp. 257–291). London, England: Erlbaum.

Park, G., Schwartz, H. A., Eichstaedt, J. C., Kern, M. L., Kosinski, M., Stillwell, D. J., . . . Seligman, M. E. P. (2015). Automatic personality assessment through social media language. *Journal of Personality and Social Psychology, 108*, pp. 934–952.

Parks, M. (1982). Ideology in interpersonal communication: Off the couch and into the world. In M. Burgoon (Ed.), *Communication yearbook* (Vol. 5, pp. 79–108). New Brunswick, NJ: Transaction.

Parsons, T. (1951). *The social system*. New York, NY: Free Press of Glencoe.

Pearson, A. (2003). *I don't know how she does it: The life of Kate Reddy, working mother*. New York, NY: Knopf.

Pendele, G. (1999, June 9). A man in a woman's world. *The Times*. Retrieved from timesonline .co.uk

Pennsylvania State University. (2006, January 5). A brief Penn State history. Retrieved from psu .edu/ur/about/history/historyshort.html Our history. (2013). Retrieved from psu.edu/this -is-penn-state/our-history

Peppers, D., & Rogers, M. (1996). *The one to one future*. New York, NY: Doubleday/Currency.

Perriton, L. (2009). "We don't want complaining women!": A critical analysis of the business case for diversity. *Management Communication Quarterly, 23*, 218–243.

Perrow, C. (1986). *Complex organizations: A critical essay* (3rd ed.). New York, NY: Random House.

Peters, T. (1994a). *Liberation management*. New York, NY: Ballantine.

Peters, T. (1994b). *The pursuit of wow*. New York, NY: Vintage.

Peters, T., & Waterman, R. (1982). *In search of excellence: Lessons from America's best-run companies*. New York, NY: Harper and Row.

Peterson, L. (1995, November). *The influence of sharing a semantic link on social support in work relationships at a hospital*. Paper presented at the annual meeting of the Speech Communication Association, San Antonio, TX.

Peterson, L. W., & Albrecht, T. L. (1999). Where gender/power/politics collide: Deconstructing organizational maternity leave policy. *Journal of Management Inquiry, 8*(2), 168–181.

Peticca-Harris, A., Weststar, J., & McKenna, S. (2015). The perils of project-based work: Attempting resistance to extreme work practices in video game development. *Organization, 22*, 570–587, doi:10.1177/1350508415572509

Pettigrew, A. (1979). On studying organizational cultures. *Administrative Science Quarterly, 24*, 570–581.

Phillips, K. (2002). *Wealth and democracy: A political history of the American rich*. New York, NY: Broadway Books.

Pina, A., & Gannon, T. A. (2012). An overview of the literature on antecedents, perceptions, and behavioral consequences of sexual harassment. *Journal of Sexual Aggression, 18*, 209–232.

Pinchot, G., & Pinchot, E. (1993). *The end of bureaucracy and the rise of the intelligent organization*. San Francisco, CA: Berrett-Koehler.

Pogodzinski, B., Young, P., Frank, K. A., & Belman, D. (2012). Administrative climate and novices' intent to remain teaching. *Elementary School Journal, 113*, 252–275.

Poole, M. S. (1983). Decision development in small groups II: A study of multiple sequences in decision making. *Communication Monographs, 50*, 321–341.

Poole, M. S. (1996, February). *A turn of the wheel: The case for a renewal of systems inquiry in organizational communication research*. Paper presented at the Conference on Organizational Communication and Change, Austin, TX.

Poole, M. S., & DeSanctis, G. (1990). Understanding the use of group decision support systems: The theory of adaptive structuration. In J. Fulk & C. Steinfeld (Eds.), *Organizations and communication technology* (pp. 173–193). Newbury Park, CA: Sage.

Poole, M. S., & Roth, J. (1989). Decision development in small groups V: Test of a contingency model. *Human Communication Research, 15*, 549–589.

Porter, M. (1980). *Competitive strategy: Techniques for analyzing industries and competitors*. New York, NY: Free Press.

Power, D. J. (2007, March 10). *A brief history of decision support systems*. Retrieved from dssresources .com/history/dsshistory.html

Prigogine, I. (1980). *From being to becoming*. San Francisco, CA: Freeman.

Putnam, L., & Fairhurst, G. (2015). Revisiting "organizations as discursive construction" 10 years later. *Communication Theory, 25*(4), 375–392.

Putnam, L., & Pacanowsky, M. (1983). *Communication and organizations: An interpretive approach*. Beverly Hills, CA: Sage.

Putnam, L., & Poole, M. S. (1987). Conflict and negotiation. In F. Jablin, L. Putnam, K. Roberts, & L. Porter (Eds.), *Handbook of organizational communication* (pp. 549–599). Newbury Park, CA: Sage.

Quinn, R. E. (2005). Moments of greatness: Entering the fundamental state of leadership. *Harvard Business Review*, *83*, 74–83.

Raban, J. (1991). *Hunting Mister Heartbreak: A discovery of America*. San Francisco, CA: HarperCollins.

Ray, E. (1987). Supportive relationships and occupational stress in the workplace. In T. Albrecht & M. Adelman (Eds.), *Communicating social support* (pp. 172–191). Newbury Park, CA: Sage.

Reardon, K. (1997). Dysfunctional communication patterns in the workplace: Closing the gap between men and women. In D. Dunn (Ed.), *Workplace/women's place: An anthology* (pp. 165–180). Los Angeles, CA: Roxbury.

Redden, S. M. (2013). How lines organize compulsory interaction, emotion managements and "emotional taxes": The implications of passenger emotion and expression in airport security lines. *Management Communication Quarterly*, *27*, 121–149.

Redding, W. C. (1972). *Communication within the organization*. New York, NY: Industrial Communications Council.

Redding, W. C. (1985). Rocking boats, blowing whistles, and teaching speech communication. *Communication Education*, *34*, 245–258.

Reno, J. E., & McNamee, L. G. (2015). Do Sororities Promote Members' Health? A Study of Memorable Messages Regarding Weight and Appearance. *Health Communication*, *30*(4), 385–397. doi:10.1080/10410236.2013.863702

Rich, C., Schutten, J. K., & Rogers, R. A. (2012). "Don't drop the soap": Organizing sexualities in the repeal of the US military's "Don't ask, don't tell" policy. *Communication Monographs*, *79*, 269–291.

Richards, I. (1936). *The philosophy of rhetoric*. New York, NY: Oxford University Press.

Richmond, V., Davis, L., Saylor, K., & McCroskey, J. (1984). Power strategies in organizations: Communication techniques and messages. *Human Communication Research*, *11*, 85–108.

Riedy, M. K., & Wen, J. H. (2010). Electronic surveillance of Internet access in the American workplace: Implications for management. *Information & Communications Technology Law*, *19*(1), 87–99. doi:10.1080/13600831003726374

Robbins, A. (1997). *Unleash the power within*. New York, NY: Free Press.

Robert, M. (1993). *Strategy: Pure & simple*. New York, NY: McGraw-Hill.

Robichaud, D., & Cooren, F. (2013). *Organization and organizing. Materiality, agency and discourse*. London: Routledge.

Robinson, K., & Aronica, L. (2015) *Creative schools: The grassroots revolution that's transforming education*. New York, NY: Viking.

Rodin, J. (2008, July 17). The new social contract. *Time*. Retrieved from time.com/time/magazine /article/0,9171,1824100,00.html#ixzz2HRW0RTAJ

Rogers, E., & Kincaid, D. (1981). *Communication networks: Toward a new paradigm for research*. New York, NY: Free Press.

Rose, D. (1989). *Patterns of American culture*. Philadelphia, PA: University of Pennsylvania Press.

Rose, H. (1983). Hand, brain, and heart: A feminist epistemology for the natural sciences. *Signs*, *9*, 81.

Rosen, M. (1985). Breakfast at Spiro's: Dramaturgy and dominance. *Journal of Management*, *11*, 31–48.

Rosenberg, T. (2002, August 18). The free-trade fix. *New York Times Magazine*, 28–33.

Rosenfeld, L. B., Richman, J. M., & May, S. K. (2004). Information adequacy, job satisfaction and organizational culture in a dispersed-network organization. *Journal of Applied Communication Research*, *32*, 28–54.

Rumens, N. (2010). Workplace friendships between men: Gay men's perspectives and experiences. *Human Relations, 63*, 1541–1562.

Rumens, N. (2011). Minority support: Friendship and the development of gay and lesbian managerial careers and identities. *Equality, Diversity and Inclusion: An International Journal, 30*, 444–446.

SafeWork SA. (2007, July 11). Employer advice. Retrieved from safework.sa.gov.au/contentPages/ManagingSafety/ProblemsAtWork/BullyingPrevent.htm

Sahlins, M. (1976). *Culture and practical reason*. Chicago, IL: University of Chicago Press.

Said, E. (1978). *Orientalism*. New York, NY: Pantheon.

Said, E. (1984). *The world, the text, and the critic*. Cambridge, MA: Harvard University Press.

Sala, F., Drusket, V. U., & Mount, G. (2006). *Linking emotional intelligence and performance at work: Current research evidence with individuals and groups*. Mahwah, NJ: Erlbaum.

Sashkin, M. (1991). *Total Quality Management*. Germantown, TN: Ducochon.

Scandura, T., Graen, G., & Novak, M. (1986). When managers decide not to decide autocratically. *Journal of Applied Psychology, 71*, 1–6.

Scarduzio, J. A., & Geist-Martin, P. (2010). Accounting for victimization: Male professors' ideological positioning in stories of sexual harassment. *Management Communication Quarterly, 24*(3), 419–445.

Schandorf, M. (2013). Mediated gesture: Paralinguistic communication and phatic text. *Convergence: The Journal of Research into New Media Technologies, 19*, 319–344.

Scheibel, D. (1996). Appropriating bodies: Organizing ideology and cultural practice in medical school. *Journal of Applied Communication Research, 24*, 310–331.

Scheibel, D. (2003). "Reality ends here": Graffiti as an artifact. In R. Clair (Ed.), *Expressions of ethnography: Novel approaches to qualitative methods* (pp. 219–230). Albany, NY: SUNY Press.

Schein, E. (1969). *Process consultation: Its role in organizational development*. Reading, MA: Addison-Wesley.

Schein, E. (1991). The role of the founder in creating organizational culture. In P. Frost, L. Moore, & M. Louis (Eds.), *Reframing organizational culture* (pp. 14–25). Newbury Park, CA: Sage.

Schein, E. H. (1992). *Organizational culture and leadership*. San Francisco, CA: Jossey-Bass.

Schneck, D. P., & Roscoe, L. A. (2008). In search of a good death. *Journal of Medical Humanities, 30*, 61–72.

Schor, J. (1998). *The overspent American: Upscaling, downshifting, and the new consumer*. New York, NY: Basic Books.

Schor, J. (2010). *Plentitude: The new economics of true wealth*. New York, NY: Penguin.

Schuler, S. (2000, November). *Breaking through the glass ceiling without breaking a nail: Portrayal of women executives in the popular business press*. Paper presented at the annual conference of the National Communication Association, Seattle, WA.

Schwartz, M. J. (2011, December 28). Six worst data breaches of 2011. *InformationWeek*. Retrieved from informationweek.com/security/attacks/6-worst-data-breaches-of-2011/232301079

Schwartz, N. D. (2009, February 14). Job losses pose a threat to stability worldwide. *New York Times*. Retrieved from nytimes.com/2009/02/15/business/15global.html?scp=7&sq=europe%20instability%20and%20financial%20markets&st=cse

Schwartz-DuPre, R. L. (2013). *Communicating Colonialism: Readings on Postcolonial Theory(s) and Communication*. New York, NY: Peter Lang.

Schwartzman, H. (1993). *Ethnography in organizations*. Newbury Park, CA: Sage.

Scott, C. (2005). *The discursive organization of risk and safety: How firefighters manage occupational hazards* (Unpublished doctoral dissertation). Arizona State University, Tempe, AZ.

Scott, C. W., Shanock, L. R., & Rogelberg, S. G. (2012). Meetings at work: Advancing the theory and practice of meetings. *Small Group Research, 43*(2), 127–129. doi:10.1177/1046496411429023

Scott, J. (1990). *Domination and the arts of resistance: Hidden transcripts*. New Haven, CT: Yale University Press.

Scott, W. R. (1981). *Organizations: Rational, natural, and open systems*. Englewood Cliffs, NJ: Prentice Hall.

Senge, P. (1990). *The fifth discipline: The art & practice of the learning organization*. New York, NY: Doubleday/Currency.

Senge, P. (2006). *The fifith discipline: The art and practice of the learning organization*. New York: Doubleday.

Senge, P. Kleiner Roberts, Ross, & Smith. (1994). *The fifth discipline fieldbook*. New York, NY: Doubleday/Currency.

Senge, P., Scharmer, C., Jaworski, J., & Flowers, B. (2005). *Presence: An exploration of profound change in people, organizations, and society*. New York, NY: Penguin.

Senge, P. M. (1994). *The fifth discipline: The art & practice of learning organization*. New York, NY: Doubleday/Currency.

Sewell, G., & Barker, J. R. (2006). Coercion versus care: Using irony to make sense of organizational surveillance. *Academy of Management Review, 31*, 934–961.

Sewell, G., & Barker, J. R. (2012). Working under intensive surveillance: When does "measuring everything that moves" become intolerable? *Human Relations, 65*, 189–215.

Shamir, B., Dayan-Horesh, H., & Adler, D. (2005). Leading by biography: Towards a life-story approach to the study of leadership. *Leadership, 1*, 13–29.

Shenoy-Packer, S., & Buzzanell, P. (2013). Meanings of Work among Hindu Indian Women: Contextualizing Meaningfulness and Materialities of Work through Dharma and Karma. *Journal of Communication and Religion, 36*, 149–172.

Shipler, D. (2004). *The working poor: Invisible in America*. New York, NY: Vintage.

Shockley-Zalabak, P. (1991). *Fundamentals of organizational communication*. New York, NY: Longman.

Shockley-Zalabak, P. (2002). Protean places: Teams across time and space. *Journal of Applied Communication Research, 30*(3), 231–250.

Shorris, E. (1997). *New American blues: A journey through poverty to democracy*. New York, NY: Norton.

Shuter, R., & Turner, L. H. (1997). African American and European American Women in the Workplace Perceptions of Conflict Communication. *Management Communication Quarterly, 11*(1), 74–96.

Sias, P., & Jablin, F. (1995). Differential superior-subordinate relations, perceptions of fairness, and coworker communication. *Human Communication Research, 22*, 5–38.

Sifferlin, A. (June 18, 2014). Women are still doing most of the housework. *Time*. Retrieved from http://time.com/2895235/men-housework-women/

Sinclair, A. (2005). Body possibilities in leadership. *Leadership, 1*, 387–406.

Sinek, S. (2014). *Leaders eat last: Why some teams pull together and others don't*. New York, NY: Portfolio/Penguin.

Skorton, D., & Altschuler, G. (2013, January 28). MOOCs: A college education online? *Forbes*. Retrieved from forbes.com/sites/collegeprose/2013/01/28/moocs-a-college-education-online

Small, A. (1905). *General sociology*. Chicago, IL: University of Chicago Press.

Smircich, L., & Calas, M. (1987). Organizational culture: A critical assessment. In F. Jablin, L. Putnam, K. Roberts, & L. Porter (Eds.), *Handbook of Organizational Communication* (pp. 228–263). Newbury Park, CA: Sage.

Smith, F., & Keyton, J. (2001). Organizational storytelling: Metaphors for relational power and identity struggles. *Management Communication Quarterly, 15*, 149–182.

Smith, M., Cohen, B., Stammerjohn, V., & Happ, A. (1981). An investigation of health complaints and job stress in video display operations. *Human Factors, 23*, 387–400.

Smith, P. (2005, February 11). Bullies incorporated. *Sydney Morning Herald*. Retrieved from smh.com.au/news/Management-Focus/Bullies-incorporated/2005/02/14/1108229910089.html

Smith, R., & Eisenberg, E. (1987). Conflict at Disneyland: A root metaphor analysis. *Communication Monographs, 54*, 367–380.

Snyder, J. (2010). E-mail privacy in the workplace: A boundary regulation perspective. *Journal of Business Communication, 47*, 266–294.

Sobre-Denton, M. S. (2012). Stories from the cage: Autoethnographic sensemaking of workplace bullying, gender discrimination and white privilege. *Journal of Contemporary Ethnography, 41*(2), 220–250.

Society for Human Resource Management. (2011). SHRM research spotlight: Flexible work arrangements. Retrieved from shrm.org/Research/SurveyFindings/Documents/11-WorkFlex Flier_FINAL_REV.pdf

Sotirin, P. (2000). "All they do is bitch bitch bitch": Political and interactional features of women's office talk. *Women's Studies in Communication, 23*, 19–25.

Southwest Airlines. (1988, January). The mission of Southwest Airlines. Retrieved from southwest .com/about_swa/mission.html

Sparrowe, R., & Liden, E. (1997). Process and structure in leader-member exchange. *Academy of Management Review, 22*, 522–552.

Spradlin, A. (1998). The price of "passing." *Management Communication Quarterly, 11*, 598–606.

Stalk, G. (1998). Time: The next source of competitive advantage. In R. Gupta (Ed.), *Managerial excellence* (pp. 171–192). Cambridge, MA: Harvard Business School Press.

Stallybrass, P., & White, A. (1986). *The politics and poetics of transgression*. Ithaca, NY: Cornell University Press.

Steelman, J., & Klitzman, S. (1985). *The VDT: Hazardous to your health*. Ithaca, NY: Cornell University Press.

Steers, R. (1981). *Introduction to organizational behavior*. Santa Monica, CA: Goodyear.

Steier, F. (1989). Toward a radical and ecological constructivist approach to family communication. *Journal of Applied Communication Research, 17*, 1–26.

Stephens, K. K., & Dailey, S. L. (2012). Situated organizational identification in newcomers: Impacts of preentry organizational exposure. *Management Communication Quarterly, 26*(3), 404–422.

Stewart, J. (2000, April). *The practice of dialogue*. Grazier Lecture, Department of Communication, University of South Florida, Tampa.

Stewart, T. (1991, August 12). GE keeps those ideas coming. *Fortune, 40*(8).

Stiglitz, J. E. (2002). *Globalization and its discontents*. New York, NY: Norton.

Stohl, C., & Cheney, G. (2001). Participatory processes/paradoxical practices: Communication and the dilemmas of organizational democracy. *Management Communication Quarterly, 14*, 349–407.

Stoughton, J. W., Thompson, L. F., & Meade, A. W. (2013). Big five personality traits reflected in job applicants' social media postings. *Cyberpsychology, Behavior & Social Networking, 16*(11), 800–805. doi:10.1089/cyber.2012.0163

Strine, M. (1991). Critical theory and "organic" intellectuals: Reframing the work of cultural critique. *Communication Monographs, 58*, 195–201.

Sturges J. (2013). A matter of time: Young professionals' experiences of long work hours. *Work, Employment & Society* 27(2): 343–59.

Sullenberger, C. B., & Zaslow, J. (2009). *Highest duty: My search for what really matters*. New York, NY: William Morrow.

Sullivan, J. (1988). Three roles of language in motivation theory. *Academy of Management Review, 13*, 104–115.

Sunwolf, & Seibold, D. R. (1998). Jurors' intuitive rules for deliberation: A structurational approach to the study of communication in jury decision making. *Communication Monographs, 65*, 282–307.

Sweeney, B. (2014). Party animals or responsible men: social class, race, and masculinity on campus. *International Journal of Qualitative Studies in Education (QSE), 27*(6), 801–818.

Syed, Z., & Jamal, W. (2012). Universalistic perspective of HRM and organizational performance: Meta-analytical study. *International Bulletin of Business Administration, 13*, 47–57.

Talbott, M. (2002, October 13). When men taunt men, is it sexual harassment? *New York Times Magazine*, 52–57, 82, 84, 95.

Tamaki, J. (1991, October 10). Sexual harassment in the workplace. *Los Angeles Times*, p. D2.

Tangel, A. (2012, September 15). Occupy movement turns 1 year old, its effect still hard to define. *Los Angeles Times*. Retrieved from articles.latimes.com/2012/sep/15/business/la-fi-occupy-anniversary-20120915

Tannen, D. (1990). *You just don't understand: Women and men in conversation*. New York, NY: Ballantine.

Taylor, B. C. (2003). "'Our bruised arms hung up as monuments': Nuclear iconography in post–Cold War culture." *Critical Studies in Media Communication, 20*(1), 1–34.

Taylor, B. C., Irvin, L. R., & Wieland, S. M. (2006). Checking the map: Critiquing Joanne Martin's metatheory of organizational culture and its uses in communication research. *Communication Theory, 16*, 304–332.

Taylor, B. C., Kinsella, W. J., Depoe, S. P., & Metzler, M. S. (2005). Nuclear legacies: Communication, controversy and the U.S. nuclear weapons production complex. *Communication Yearbook, 29*, 363–409.

Taylor, C. (1991). *The ethics of authenticity*. Cambridge, MA: Harvard University Press.

Taylor, F. (1913). *The principles of scientific management*. New York, NY: Harper.

Taylor, F. W. (1947). *Scientific management*. New York, NY: Harper.

Therborn, G. (1980). *The ideology of power and the power of ideology*. London, England: Verso.

Thomas, L. (1975). *The lives of a cell: Notes of a biology watcher*. New York, NY: Penguin.

Thompson, J. (1967). *Organizations in action: Social science bases of administrative theory*. New York, NY: McGraw-Hill.

Tichy, N. (2012). Developing leaders. *Leadership Excellence, 29*, 5–6.

Tichy, N., Pritchett, P., & Cohen, E. (1998). *The leadership engine*. New York, NY: Pritchett.

Tjosvold, D. (1984). Effects of leader warmth and directiveness on subordinate performance on a subsequent task. *Journal of Applied Psychology, 69*, 422–427.

Tjosvold, D., & Tjosvold, M. (1991). *Leading the team organization: How to create an enduring competitive advantage*. New York, NY: Lexington.

Tompkins, P. (1984). Functions of communication in organizations. In C. Arnold & J. Bowers (Eds.), *Handbook of rhetorical and communication theory*. Boston, MA: Allyn and Bacon.

Tompkins, P., & Cheney, G. (1985). Communication and unobtrusive control in contemporary organizations. In R. McPhee & P. Tompkins (Eds.), *Organizational communication: Traditional themes and new directions* (pp. 179–210). Beverly Hills, CA: Sage.

Tompkins, P., & Tompkins, E. (2004). *Apollo, Challenger, & Columbia: The decline of the space program*. Los Angeles, CA: Roxbury.

Tourish, D., & Hargie, O. (2012). Metaphors of failure and the failures of metaphor: A critical study of root metaphors used by bankers in explaining the banking crisis. *Organization Studies, 33*, 1045–1069.

Townsley, N., & Geist-Martin, P. (2000). The discursive enactment of hegemony: Sexual harassment and academic organizing. *Western Journal of Communication, 64*, 190–217.

Townsley, N., & Stohl, C. (2003). Contracting corporate social responsibility: Swedish expansion in global temporary agency work. *Management Communication Quarterly, 16*, 599–605.

Tracy, K., & Eisenberg, E. (1991). Giving criticism: A multiple goals case study. *Research on Language and Social Interaction, 24*, 37–70.

Tracy, S. (2003). Watching the watchers: Making sense of emotional constructions behind bars. In R. Clair (Ed.), *Expressions of ethnography: Novel approaches to qualitative methods* (pp. 153–158). Albany, NY: SUNY Press.

Tracy, S., Lutgen-Sandvik, P., & Alberts, J. (2006). Nightmares, demons, and slaves: Exploring the painful metaphors of workplace bullying. *Management Communication Quarterly, 20*, 148–185.

Tracy, S., & Scott, C. (2006). Sexuality, masculinity, and taint management among firefighters and correctional officers: Getting down and dirty with "America's heroes" and the "scum of law enforcement." *Management Communication Quarterly, 20*, 6–38.

Tracy, S., & Trethewey, A. (2005). Fracturing the real-self ↔ fake-self dichotomy: Moving toward "crystallized" organizational discourses and identities. *Communication Theory, 15*, 168–195.

Tracy, S. J. (2012). *Qualitative research methods: Collecting evidence, crafting analysis*. Malden, MA: Wiley.

Tracy, S. J., & Huffman, T. P. (2014). *Compassion, presence, and hope in the face of terror: How a school bookkeeper communicatively transformed a would-be school shooting*. Presented at the annual meeting of the National Communication Association, Chicago, IL.

Trapp, R. (March 31, 2015). Leaders need to bridge the generation gap. *Forbes*. Retrieved from http://www.forbes.com/sites/rogertrapp/2015/03/31/leaders-need-to-bridge-the-generation-gap/#6b16a1732ae2

Tregaskis, O., Daniel, K., Glover, L., Butler, P., & Meyer, M. (2012). High performance work practices and firm performance: A longitudinal case study. *British Journal of Management, 24*(2), 225–244. doi:10.1111/j.1467-8551.2011.00800.x

Trethewey, A. (1997). Resistance, identity, and empowerment: A postmodern analysis of clients in a human service organization. *Communication Monographs, 64*, 281–301.

Trethewey, A. (1999a). Disciplined bodies: Women's embodied identities at work. *Organization Studies, 20*, 423–450.

Trethewey, A. (1999b). Isn't it ironic: Using irony to explore the contradictions of organizational life. *Western Journal of Communication, 63*, 140–167.

Trethewey, A. (2001). Reproducing and resisting the master narrative of decline: Midlife professional women's experience of aging. *Management Communication Quarterly, 15*, 183–226.

Trethewey, A. (2004). Sexuality, eros and pedagogy: Desiring laughter in the classroom. *Women and Language, 27*, 35–41.

Trethewey, A., & Corman, S. (2001). Anticipating K-commerce: E-commerce, knowledge management, and organizational communication. *Management Communication Quarterly, 14*, 619–628.

Trethewey, A., & Goodall, H. L., Jr. (2007). Leadership reconsidered as historical subject: Sketches from the Cold War to post-9/11. *Leadership, 3*, 457–477.

Triece, M. (1999). The practical true woman: Reconciling women and work in popular mail-order magazines. *Critical Studies in Mass Communication, 16*, 42–62.

Turner, P. (2003). Telling the story of birth. In R. Clair (Ed.), *Expressions of ethnography: Novel approaches to qualitative methods* (pp. 55–64). Albany, NY: SUNY Press.

Turner, P. K., & Norwood, K. (2013). Unbounded motherhood: Embodying a good working mother identity. *Management Communication Quarterly, 27*(3), 396–424. doi:10.1177/0893318913491461

Turnage, A. (2013). Technological resistance: A metaphor analysis of Enron e-mail messages. *Communication Quarterly, 61*(5), 519–538. doi:10.1080/01463373.2013.803995

Tye-Williams, S., & Krone, K. J. (2014). Chaos, Reports, and Quests: Narrative agency and co-workers in stories of workplace bullying. *Management Communication Quarterly, 29*(1), 3–27.

U.S. Department of State. (2011). Trafficking in persons. Retrieved from state.gov/j/tip/rls/tiprpt/2011/index.htm

U.S. Equal Employment Opportunity Commission. (2012). Sexual harassment charges, EEOC & FEPAs combined: FY 1997–FY 2011. Retrieved from eeoc.gov/eeoc/statistics/enforcement/sexual_harassment.cfm

Van Maanen, J. (1979). *Qualitative methodology*. Beverly Hills, CA: Sage.

Van Maanen, J. (1988). *Tales of the field: On writing ethnography*. Chicago, IL: University of Chicago Press.

Van Maanen, J. (1991). The smile factory: Work at Disneyland. In P. Frost, L. Moore, & M. Louis (Eds.), *Reframing organizational culture* (pp. 58–76). Newbury Park, CA: Sage.

Van Tien, D., Moseley, J., & Dessinger, J. (2012). *Fundamentals of performance improvement* (3rd ed.). San Francisco, CA. Pfeiffer.

Varner, I., & Beamer, L. (1995). *Intercultural communication in the global workplace*. Chicago, IL: Irwin.

von Bertalanffy, L. (1968). *General system theory*. New York, NY: George Braziller.

Wagner, R., & Harter, J. (2006). *12: The elements of great managing*. New York, NY: Gallup Press.

Waldeck, J. H., Siebold, D. R., & Flanagin, A. J. (2004). Organizational assimilation and communication technology use. *Communication Monographs, 71*, 161–83.

Walker, G. (2004). *Modern competitive strategy*. Boston: McGraw-Hill.

Warren, E., & Tyagi, A. (2003). *The two-income trap: Why middle-class parents are going broke*. New York, NY: Basic Books.

Watzlawick, P., Beavin, J., & Jackson, D. (1967). *The pragmatics of human communication: A study of interactional patterns, pathologies, and paradoxes*. New York, NY: Norton.

Wayne, S., Shore, L., & Liden, R. (1997). Perceived organizational support and leader-member exchange. *Academy of Management Journal, 40*, 82–111.

Weedon, C. (1997). *Feminist practice and poststructuralist theory* (2nd ed.). Oxford, England: Basil Blackwell.

Weick, K. (1976). Educational organizations as loosely coupled systems. *Administrative Science Quarterly, 21*, 1–19.

Weick, K. (1979). *The social psychology of organizing* (2nd ed.). Reading, MA: Addison-Wesley.

Weick, K. (1990). The collapse of sensemaking in organizations: The Mann Gulch disaster. *Administrative Science Quarterly, 38*, 628–652.

Weick, K. (1995). *Sensemaking in organizations*. Newbury Park, CA: Sage.

Weick, K., & Sutcliffe, K. (2001). *Managing the unexpected: Assuring high performance in an age of complexity*. San Francisco, CA: Jossey-Bass.

Wellins, R., Byham, W., & Wilson, J. (1991). *Empowered teams*. San Francisco, CA: Jossey-Bass.

Wenberg, J., & Wilmot, W. (1973). *The personal communication process*. New York, NY: Wiley.

Wheatley, E. (2005). Discipline and resistance: Order and disorder in a cardiac rehabilitation clinic. *Qualitative Health Research, 15*(4), 438–459.

Wheatley, M. (1992). *Leadership and the new science*. San Francisco, CA: Berrett-Koehler.

White, R., & Lippitt, R. (1960). *Autocracy and democracy: An experimental inquiry*. New York, NY: Harper and Brothers.

Whitelegg, D. (2005). Places and spaces I've been: Geographies of female flight attendants in the United States. *Gender, Place and Culture: A Journal of Feminist Geography, 12*(2), 251–266.

Whyte, W. (1969). *Organizational behavior: Theory and application*. Homewood, IL: Irwin.

Whyte, W. H., Jr. (1956). *The organization man*. New York, NY: Simon and Schuster.

Wilkins, A. (1984). The creation of company cultures: The role of stories and human resource systems. *Human Resource Management, 23*, 41–60.

Wolfe, L. (2014). Facebook vs. Twitter: Privacy issues. *About Money*. Retrieved from http://womeninbusiness.about.com

Wood, J. (1992). Telling our stories: Narratives as a basis for theorizing sexual harassment. *Journal of Applied Communication Research, 20*, 349–362.

Working Mother. (2012). 2012 Working Mother 100 best companies. Retrieved from working mother.com/best-companies/2012-working-mother-100-best-companies

Yedidia, M., Gillespie, C., Kachur, E., Schwartz, M., Ockene, J., Chepaitis, A., . . . Lipkin, M., Jr. (2003). Effect of communications training on medical student performance. *Journal of the American Medical Association, 290*, 1157–1165.

Zander, R. S., & Zander, B. (2002). *The art of possibility: Transforming professional and personal life.* NY: Penguin Books Ltd.

Zellers, K. L., Tepper, B. J., & Duffy, M. K. (2002). Abusive supervision and subordinates' organizational citizenship behavior. *Journal of Applied Psychology, 87,* 1068–1076.

Zoller, H. (2003). Health on the line: Identity and disciplinary control in employees' occupational health and safety discourse. *Journal of Applied Communication Research, 33,* 118–139.

Zoller, H. M. (2010). What are health organizations? Public health and organizational communication. *Management Communication Quarterly, 24,* 482–490.

Zoller, H. M. (2012). Communicating health: Political risk narratives in an environmental health campaign. *Journal of Applied Communication Research, 40,* 20–43.

Acknowledgments

Chapter 1
Excerpt from Sabina Tavernise, "The Story," Public Broadcasting Service, October 2003, PBS.com. Reprinted by permission.

Chapter 2
Excerpt from James A. Anderson, *Communication Research: Issues and Methods*, Hampton Press, 1987. Copyright © Hampton Press. Reprinted by permission.

Excerpt from R. Evered and B. Tannenbaum, "A Dialog on Dialog: A Conversation between Roger Evered and Bob Tannenbaum," *Journal of Management Inquiry 1*(1992): 43–48. Copyright © 1992 Sage Publications. Reprinted by permission of Sage Publications.

Excerpt from NCA Credo for Ethical Communication, 1999. Reprinted by permission of the National Communication Association.

Chapter 3
Morgan, G., *Images of Organization*, Sage Publications, Newbury Park, CA, 1986.

"Maslow's Hierarchy of Needs," from *A Theory of Human Motivation*. Copyright © Pearson Education. Reprinted by permission.

Excerpt from Charles Perrow, *Complex Organizations: A Critical Essay*, Random House Group, 2014. Reprinted by permission.

Excerpt from Douglas MacGregor, *The Human Side of Enterprise*, McGraw-Hill (reprinted 2006). Reprinted by permission of the McGraw-Hill Companies.

Chapter 4
"Weick's Model of Organizing," from Karl Weick, *The Social Psychology of Organizing*, 2e, McGraw-Hill, 1979. Copyright © 1979 by Karl Weick. Reprinted by permission of the McGraw-Hill Companies.

Excerpt from Stephen A. Hawking, *A Brief History of Time*, Random House, 1998. Copyright © The Random House Group.

Thomas, Lewis, *The Lives of a Cell*, Viking Press, 1975.

Bertalanffy, Ludwig von, "General System Theory," George Braziller Inc., 1969.

Weick, Karl, "Sensemaking in Organizations," Sage Publications, Inc., May 31, 1995.

Chapter 5
Meyer, Erin, "When Culture Doesn't Translate," *Harvard Business Review*, October 2015.

Chapter 6
Mumby, Dennis K., "The Political Function of Narratives in Organizations," *Communication Monographs*, 54, 113–127, 1982.

Southwest Airlines mission statement.

Berkelaar, Brenda L. and Buzzanell, Patrice M., "Online Employment Screening and Digital Career Capital Exploring Employers' Use of Online Information for Personnel Selection," *Management Communication Quarterly*, Sage Publications Inc., 29(1), 84–113.

Trethewey, A. and Corman, S., "Ethical Dimensions of Knowledge Management Applications, Anticipating K-Commerce: E-Commerce, Knowledge Management and Organizational Communication," *Management Communication Quarterly*, Sage Publications, 14, 619–628, 2001.

Scott, C. W. and Trethewey, A. C., "Organizational Discourse and the Appraisal of Occupational Hazards," *Journal of Applied Communication Res.*, 23, 297–317, 2008.

Redden, S. M., "Case Study 2: How Lines Organize Compulsory Integration, Emotion Management and 'Emotional Taxes'," *Management Communication Quarterly*, Sage Publications, 27, 121–149, 2013.

Chapter 7

Alvesson, Mats and Wilimott, Hugh, "Identity Regulation as Organizational Control: Producing the Appropriate Individual," *Journal of Management Studies*, John Wiley & Sons, 39, 619–644.

Alvesson, M., "Self-Doubters, Strugglers, Storytellers, Surfers and Others: Images of Self-Identities in Organization Studies," *Human Relations*, Sage Publications, Inc., 63, 193–217, p. 199, 2010.

The College Transition on Minnesota State University at Mankato website.

Martin, J. N., Moore, S., Hecht, M. L., and Larkey, L., "An African American Perspective on Conversational Improvement Strategies," *Howard Journal of Communications*, Taylor & Francis Group, LLC, 12, 1–27, 2001.

Allen, Brenda J., *Difference Matters: Communicating Social Identity*, Waveland Press Inc.

Chapter 8

Wellins, Richard, Byham, William and Wilson, Jeanne, *Empowered Teams*, John Wiley & Sons, Inc., San Francisco: Jossey-Bass, p. 26, 1991.

Senge, Peter et al., *The Fifth Discipline Fieldbook*, Currency Doubleday, The Random House Group Ltd, New York, p. 254, 1994.

Senge, Peter M., Roberts, Charlotte, et al., *The Fifth Discipline Fieldbook*, The Random House Group Ltd.

Senge, Peter M., Roberts, Charlotte, et al., *The Fifth Discipline Fieldbook*, The Random House Group Ltd.

Scott, W. R., *Organizations: Rational, Natural, and Open Systems*, Prentice-Hall, Pearson Education, Englewood Cliffs, NJ, 1981.

Deetz, Stanley, *Transforming Communication, Transforming Business*, Hampton Press, p. 50, 1995.

Wagner, R. and Harter, J., *The Elements of Great Managing*, Gallup Press, New York, NY, pp. xi–xii, 2006.

Goodbody, J., "Critical Success Factors for Global Virtual Teams," *Strategic Communication Management*, Melcrum Publishing, 9:20, Feb/March 2005.

Gibson, Jane Whitney and Hodgetts, Richard M., *Organizational Communication: A Managerial Perspective*, Houghton Mifflin Harcourt Publishing, 1986.

Chapter 9

Blake, R. R. and Mouton, J. S., *The Managerial Grid III: The Key to Leadership Excellence*, Gulf Publishing Company, Houston, TX, 1985.

Hersey, P. and Blanchard, K., *Management of Organizational Behavior: Utilizing Human Resources*, 3e, Prentice Hall, Englewood Cliffs, NJ, 1977.

Adapted from Conger, Jay and Kanungo, Rabindra, "The Empowerment Process: Integrating Theory and Practice," *Academy of Management Review* 13, 411–482, 1988.

Collinson, D. and Grint, K., *Leadership*, 1–10, Sage Publications, Inc., 2005.

Quinn, Robert E., "Moments of Greatness: Entering the Fundamental State of Leadership," *Harvard Business Review*, 74–83, July–August 2005.

Redding, W. Charles, "Communication within the Organization: An Interpretive Review of Theory and Research," Industrial Communication Council, 1972.

Freeh Sporkin and Sullivan, LLP, "Report of the special investigative counsel regarding the actions of the Pennsylvania State University related to the child sexual abuse committed by Gerald A. Sandusky."

Chapter 10

Robert, Michel, *Strategy, Pure & Simple: How Winning CEOs Outthink Their Competition*, McGraw Hill Education.

D'Aveni, R., "Coping with Hypercompetition: Utilizing the New 7-S Model," *Academy of Management Executive* 9:3, 1995.

Mouritsen, Jan and Bjorn-Andersen, Niels, "Understanding Third-Wave Information Systems, Contemporary and Controversy: Value Conflicts and Social Choices," pp. 308–320, Elsevier.

"U.S. Labor Secretary's Commission on Achieving Necessary Skills," June 1991. Retrieved May 15, 2006, wdr.doleta.gov.

Author Index

Subject Index

Metaphor: Balance

Assumptions

1. The duality of structure: Individuals are molded, controlled, ordered, and shaped by society and social institutions; individuals also create society and social institutions.

2. Communication is the moment-to-moment working out of the tensions between the need to maintain order (constraint) and the need to promote change (creativity). As such, communication is the material manifestation of

   a. institutional constraints
   b. creative potential
   c. contexts of interpretation

Representative Model

Creativity ◁══════════════════════▷ Constraint

△

Communication

Description

Creativity	Communication	Constraints
Interpretation of meanings; all forms of initiative; new ways of organizing tasks and understanding relationships; resistance to institutional forms of dominance; uses of storytelling and dialogue to alter perceptions; uses of social constructions of reality to forge new agreements and to shape coordinated actions at work	Reveals interpretations of contexts; asks questions about resources for creativity and the presence of constraints; suggests the possibility of dialogue	Social and institutional forms, laws, rules, procedures, slogans, and management styles designed to gain compliance and limit dialogue at all costs; top-down decision making and problem solving